Bernard Waites

# A Class Society at War
# England 1914–1918

## BERG

*Leamington Spa / Hamburg / New York*

**Distributed exclusively in the US and Canada by
St. Martin's Press, New York**

First published in 1987 by
**Berg Publishers Limited**
24 Binswood Avenue, Leamington Spa, CV32 5SQ, UK
Schenefelder Landstr. 14K, 2000 Hamburg 55, W.-Germany
175 Fifth Avenue/Room 400, New York, NY 10010, USA

© Bernard Waites 1987

**British Library Cataloguing in Publication Data**

Waites, Bernard.
  A class society at war, England, 1914–18.
  1. Social classes — Great Britain —
  History — 20th century   2. World War,
  1914–1918 — Great Britain
  I. Title
  305.5'0941          HN400.S6

  ISBN 0–907582–65–6

**Library of Congress Cataloging-in-Publication Data**

Waites, Bernard.
  A class society at war, England, 1914–18.

  Bibliography: p.
  Includes index.
  1. World War, 1914–1918—Great Britain.
  2. Social classes—Great Britain—History—20th century.
  3. Social classes—Europe—History—20th century.
  I. Title.
  D546.W28  1987     940.3'1      87–6564
  ISBN 0–907582–65–6

Printed in Great Britain by Billings of Worcester

# A Class Society at War
## England 1914–1918

# Contents

# Tables

### Figure

# ─── Acknowledgements ───

For permission to use the tables on pages 102 and 132 I must thank, respectively, Oxford University Press and Routledge and Kegan Paul. The figure on page 267 is reproduced by courtesy of the London School of Economics. I would also like to thank the editors of the *Journal of Contemporary History*, *Literature and History* and the *Journal of the Scottish Labour History Society* for permission to use material which first appeared in their publications. Parts of Chapters 2 and 5 first appeared as a paper which I gave to a conference at Sunderland Polytechnic marking the seventieth anniversary of the outbreak of the First World War. This has since been published by Brasseys in *Home Fires and Foreign Fields* (1985) and I would like to thank both the conference organiser and editor, Peter Liddle, and the publishers for permission to reuse that paper here.

# Preface

This book was written in an attempt to answer the question: what results did the First World War have for the class structure of English society? I cannot claim to have answered that question completely; indeed, I find it difficult to envisage what a complete answer would look like. What I hope I have done is to tackle some problems subsumed by it. The question is, of course, deceptively simple. Anyone with a nodding acquaintance with social history and social science will appreciate its theoretical complexity and the methodological difficulties involved in trying to answer it.

Class is a fundamentally contested concept. Unlike, say, the age structure of the population, the class structure is not constituted by an array of brute demographic facts. Disagreement exists, not only on how we should define class position and formation, but also on the import of class division and conflict for modern history. The disputes are not merely academic; 'class' is a keyword in our social vocabulary and scholarly contention refracts discordant notions and experiences in everyday life. Within our academy, the discord is evident in the differences between Weberian and Marxist approaches to class analysis: in the former, classes are aggregates of social groups with a common set of life chances and circumstances; in the latter, they are determined by the properties of the social system, independently of the styles of life of constituent groups.[1] Even within the Marxist tradition, however, there are distinct variants of class theory which determine for their proponents what data are, and are not, relevant to class analysis. For Nicos Poulantzas, for example, social mobility is a 'bourgeois problematic', since even in the event of a total interchange of classes nothing fundamental about capitalism would have changed if the places of 'bourgeois' and 'proletarian' remained. For other Marxists, however, social mobility (and immobility) is of great interest because of its implications for class consciousness and class action.[2]

I suspect that, as with many other disputes, controversy over the nature and import of class division could not take place without a certain background consensus. Most would agree that the class structure of modern English society was formed on the social division of

---

1. F. Parkin, *Marxism and Class Theory: A Bourgeois Critique*, London, 1979, p. 3.
2. See also N. Poulantzas, *Classes in Contemporary Capitalism*, London, 1978, p. 33; J. Westergaard and H. Resler, *Class in a Capitalist Society*, Harmondsworth, 1976, p. 285.

labour under industrial capitalism and the generalisation of market relations. No one seriously contests that class divisions have had a profound influence on party alignment and allegiance in the twentieth century. It is as much a commonplace of non-Marxist electoral sociology as it is of Marxism, although with its emphasis on the manual–non-manual divide (rather than dependent and independent labour) the former utilises a different concept of class division than the latter.[3] This background consensus should make my original question intelligible to all, even those who reject the class theory which I put forward in Chapter 1 and use throughout the study to advance a particular interpretation of the effects of the First World War on the class structure.

Industrialised warfare is as much the subject of this study as is class structure, but it is less deeply contentious. After 1914 the advanced states of Europe revealed an unforeseen capacity to sustain collective violence. Who can doubt that this capacity has wrought epochal changes in human society? The two world wars have been the dominating events of global history in the twentieth century. We still live with their international consequences; our literary and popular culture constantly represents images and memories of them. Though it is now the Second World War that preoccupies the literary imagination and popular memory, our cultural responses to it are shaped by an ironic sensibility formed and conventionalised during the Great War of 1914–18.[4] So far-reaching have the immediate and long-term consequences of the mobilisation of societies for industrialised warfare been, that it is pertinent to ask how, and to what extent, this has affected the social structures of combatant states, even those which escaped the revolutionary consequences of defeat.

In Chapter 1 I draw upon social theory to identify the processes by which industrialised warfare has redounded on social structures; what little originality this study has in British historiography lies in its attempt to tie the study of war and social change more closely to class theory.[5]

The ordering and purpose of the rest of the study require some brief comment. It seems to me that social historians have a dual duty: to recapture the frames of mind and common meanings of social actors and to define the objective circumstances in which they arose. These

3. See D. Butler and D. Stokes, *Political Change in Britain*, 2nd ed., London, 1974, chap. 4.

4. P. Fussell, *The Great War and Modern Memory*, London, 1975.

5. In this respect, the only comparable study known to me is J. Kocka's *Facing Total War: German Society 1914–1918*, Leamington Spa, 1984.

circumstances set limits to common mentalities and shape their articulation. My tastes have always run to the first part of this duty and I fear that the overall balance of this study may be unduly weighted towards the analysis of 'consciousness' rather than 'structure'. Chapter 2 attempts to map what we have learned to call the 'discourses' of class and the imagery with which class structure has been represented in the social consciousness. This type of cartography is indispensable to recapturing common meanings; familiarising oneself with past usage is, I think, a preliminary part of historical enquiry. Hence my reasons for the place of this chapter in the text. Chapter 3 explores some of the objective circumstances for changes in consciousness, particularly among middle-class people, by examining the changes in income and wealth distribution effected during the First World War and its immediate aftermath. Chapters 4 and 5 examine the consequences of the war for the economic and social structure of the working class, particularly with respect to wage relativities and the stratification of workers by industrial skills. The brunt of these chapters will be news to no one: the war had the effects of homogenising working-class life experiences and culture, not absolutely but relatively to the prewar past. Chapter 6 analyses the social consciousness (not simply the class consciousness) of industrial workers. Although I think that the war sensitised workers to class inequality, there were patriotic and nationalist sentiments in popular culture which set definite limits to the political consequences of this new sensitivity. Chapter 7 is concerned with the social consciousness of salaried employees and other workers who felt themselves to be 'apart' from men who worked with their hands. I take the view that a middle class of employees who sell symbolic skills on the market is as integral to the social structure of modern capitalism as the social classes of capital and labour. The phenomenon of 'middle-class consciousness' was not a collective mental aberration but expressed — among other things — a rational appreciation of the market advantages of symbolic skills. Nor was it linked necessarily to reactionary political attitudes. This chapter attempts to come closer to an empathetic understanding of middle-class consciousness, or at least some facets of it, through an analysis of white-collar unionism. I have included in the study a note on secondary education and social class in order to add some substance to the claim that the chief way that the war affected chances of social mobility was by increasing the opportunities for secondary education.

Industrialised warfare added a new dimension to international conflict by opening up 'inner fronts' where the struggle was for increased production and to sustain civilian morale. This book is about that dimension, and thus will disappoint those readers who, understandably, expect a study of the most mortal war in our history to say something of the men who actually fought the bloody conflict. Even as a study of the Home Front it is radically incomplete, since at an early stage of research I took a decision (in the company of Marxist and non-Marxist sociologists alike) to 'bracket off' women from the class structure. Women suffer systematic injustice because of their sex; I fear that my decision adds an iota of insult to their many injuries. The rationale for this neglect is lamely defended in Chapter 1.

This book is a shortened version of a doctoral thesis undertaken for the Open University while I was a member of its research staff. I am greatly indebted to my supervisor, Arthur Marwick, for his knowledge of the period, his patience with a reluctant writer and his tolerance of theoretical perspectives which he does not share. He has done as much as anyone — probably more — to promote the scholarly study of war and society, both in his independent publications and in an undergraduate course produced collaboratively for the OU.[6] Though he will not agree with everything in this book, there is much for which he is wittingly and unwittingly responsible. My thanks are due, too, to Asa Briggs and Anthony Giddens who examined it in thesis form and commented on it most penetratively. Mrs Wendy Clarke typed and re-typed the manuscript with exemplary good humour. My wife helped to edit a rambling text; without her assistance it would never have been knocked into publishable shape.

---

6. A. Marwick, *The Deluge: British Society and the First World War*, Harmondsworth, 1967; idem, *Britain in the Century of Total War*, Harmondsworth, 1970; idem, *War and Social Change in the Twentieth Century*, London, 1974; see also the course units for the third-level course on War and Society (A301), Milton Keynes, 1976.

# 1

# Warfare and Social Structure in Social Theory and Social History: the Case of the First World War

Before 1914, warfare between industrialised nations was generally expected to be brief. The economies of the great powers were so entangled in an international network of commerce and finance, and their social relations so delicately poised between national integration and class conflict, that these states were assumed to be extremely vulnerable to prolonged war.[1] In the event, the degree of industrialisation achieved by the combatant states brought them an unexpected military and social resilience. Advanced industrial technique proved highly adaptable to the mobilisation of societies for war. The combatants put huge armies into the field but, despite chronic labour shortages, constantly expanded the output of *matériel*, including the volume production of such novel and complex items as tanks and aircraft. Their populations absorbed vast losses and their soldiers endured the terrors peculiar to industrialised trench warfare. The soldiers' stoicism and the material resources of industrialised economies gave rise to a war of hitherto unprecedented intensity and unexpected duration. In the circumstances of this type of warfare, the home fronts acquired a signal importance. On their labour forces rested the burden of producing the armaments needed to prosecute the war, while their social divisions and conflicts came to be seen as scarcely less threatening to the integrity of the state than military defeat.

This threat from the inner fronts was not a simple confirmation of prewar forebodings. Industrialised warfare initially stilled the conflicts and narrowed the divisions of prewar society. The combatant states — including Russia, whose civil accord was the most fragile — were able to secure the requisite degree of national and social cohesion for the great armament drives of 1915 and 1916. The inner fronts cracked only after civil populations had suffered material shortages and psychological pressures; when divisions reappeared they were not

---

1. See G. Hardach, *The First World War 1914–1918*, London, 1977, p. 55. Hardach quotes the opinion of Count von Schlieffen, German Chief of Staff from 1892 to 1906, that 'a strategy based on attrition is unworkable when the livelihood of millions demands the expenditure of thousands of millions . . .'.

identical to those of the pre-1914 era. The stresses of war induced new lines of fault in society (between, for example, demobilised soldiers and non-combatants) and they also compacted patriotism and xenophobia into a new national identity. Unquestionably, the prewar divisions between the propertied and the propertyless, and the endemic conflicts that arose from them, powerfully determined the civil discord and struggles that arose later in the war and with the outbreak of peace; but so too did the pressures of modern warfare.

This is a study of the English — not the British — home front. It began with a question: by what processes and to what extent did the war affect the class structure of Britain? Scotland and Wales became excluded both by a need to limit the empirical dimensions of my study and a respect for national differences in culture and institutions (such as education and housing). It is a moot point whether 'society' co-incides with the British state or its historic constituent nations; since it can be argued that the construction of national identity is integral to the making of modern societies, then the exclusion of Wales and Scotland has a certain theoretical (as well as practical) plausibility.

Perhaps a more serious limitation was the decision to set aside any special consideration of women in the class structure and the war's impact on their condition and experiences. When I began this study some years ago, it was a sociological orthodoxy that the horizontal divisions of class cut across the vertical divisions of sex and the class position of most women is determined by that of the male head of the family to which they belong. If the orthodoxy is sexist, this — it is claimed — is only because it accurately reflects the sexist subordi-nation of women in our society.[2] This orthodoxy can lead to a 'gender-blindness' in the analysis of the empirical forms of class structure and relations in any specific period. Factors such as the rate of female participation in paid employment certainly affect these forms. The chief changes in the occupational structure during, and as a result of the First World War, were in the field of women's employment. Women's labour provided an industrial reserve army that was drawn on by the wartime economy and had a great significance for its 'abnormal' social relations of production.[3] Furthermore, as housewives women bore the brunt of rising food prices and of queueing for

2. For a recent restatement of the orthodoxy, see J. Goldthorpe et al., *Social Mobility and Class Structure in Modern Britain*, Oxford, 1980, p. 288; see also F. Parkin, *Class Inequality and the Political Order*, St Albans, 1972, p. 14; and — for two Marxist writers who shared the orthodoxy — Westergaard and Resler, *Class*, p. 352.

3. For a study of women's labour during the war which uses the Marxian concept of the industrial 'reserve army', see M. Kozak, 'Women munitions workers during the First World War with special reference to engineering', University of Hull, unpubl. PhD., 1977; see also G. Braybon, *Women Workers in the First World War*, London, 1981.

commodities in short supply; when these became class grievances, it was chiefly women's experience that was being articulated. However, to be sensitive to the matter of gender in class relations does not mean completely disavowing the orthodoxy which still seems to me to correspond to the brute facts of women's dependence as wives and daughters. The First World War did far less to liberate women from this dependency than is popularly believed. The great influx of women into wartime industry, transport, commerce and administration was a temporary one. Although the war clearly accelerated the growth of 'white-blouse' clerical occupations — usually of a low-paid and routine kind — it did not affect the overall female participation ratio in the postwar labour force, nor did it appreciably improve married women's opportunities for work outside the home.[4] There is no excuse for gender blindness in social-historical analysis, but there remain theoretical and substantive grounds for believing that the lack of special consideration of women in the class structure does not vitiate the main conclusions of this study.

An enquiry into the effects of war on social class structure necessarily straddles two intellectual debates. One concerns the nature of class: what determines class formation? How are the boundaries to be drawn between one class and another? What is class consciousness? Is class conflict *the* dynamic of historical change or, perhaps, only one among a number which includes war and the control of politico-military power? These are questions on which there is a theoretical literature of bewildering scope and complexity. The second debate concerns the systematic relationships between the social size of a war and the levelling of the social hierarchy which can be attributed to it. Here, the theoretical literature is much sparser and most participants have been historians, concerned primarily with particular wars and particular societies. This book is orientated primarily to the latter debate but it tries to integrate the study of war and social change more closely with class theory. Until recently, social theory has paid scant attention either to war or military power in explaining the development of capitalist or 'advanced' societies; its dominant model of development is one of the unfolding of endogenous influences within society.[5]

Where social scientists have taken a sustained interest in war and social change, they have generally explored three themes. The first, identified with the German sociologist Werner Sombart, is that war

4. See G. Routh, *Occupation and Pay in Great Britain, 1906–60*, Cambridge, 1965, Table 20, p. 44; A.H. Halsey (ed.), *Trends in British Society since 1900*, London, 1972, Table 4.5, p. 116.

5. See A. Giddens, *The Class Structure of the Advanced Societies*, London, 1973, pp. 265–6; idem, *The Nation State and Violence*, Oxford, 1985, is an attempt to correct this dominant model but was not available at the time that this manuscript was completed.

and the preparation for war have accelerated capitalist economic and technological development. Sombart defended the economically constructive effects of war, arguing, for example, that when handguns and artillery became decisive weapons, then the growth in the number of men under arms and the increasing cost of supplying them made it necessary to assemble capital in large units and led to the development of large-scale enterprise in industry, commerce and finance. The economic experiences of capitalised war, he held, served to raise the level of industrial efficiency and productivity within participating nations.[6]

There is evidence of these constructive effects at work in the British economy during the First World War. The shortage of skilled labour encouraged the introduction of automation or semi-automation in a number of industries, most notably engineering, where there was a great increase in the installation of machine tools, but also in the boot and shoe industry. At the same time, there was a rapid electrification of factory plant. Certain industries showed a tendency to move to a much higher level of productivity than in peacetime.[7] The wartime economy proved a forcing house for the growth in the size of individual firms since large numbers of companies used the opportunity afforded by wartime profits to develop their plant and extend their works. In other cases, highly profitable businesses bought up unprofitable concerns as a way of escaping the wartime Excess Profits Duty. The inflationary spiral, which broke in late 1920, was a root cause of the expansion of individual businesses, for firms sank their profits into bricks and mortar rather than see their money shrivel.[8] The horizontal concentration of capital, due directly to the war, took place in the soap and chemicals, artificial fibres, railway transport and foodstuffs industries, as well as in banking. During the postwar boom of 1919–20 there was a merger wave which, though it certainly had a prewar precedent, seems at least indirectly attributable to the war.[9] The rapid development of business trusts, designed to minimise competition and sustain prices, was certainly due to the novel exigencies of wartime when

6. Sombart put forward the thesis in his *Krieg und Kapitalismus* and *Moderne Kapitalismus*; it is summarised and criticised in J.U. Nef, *War and Human Progress*, London, 1950, pp. 65–6, 375. See also J.M. Winter's introduction to the collection of essays, idem (ed.), *War and Economic Development*, Cambridge, 1976.

7. For a brief discussion of some of the technological changes induced by the war, see A.S. Milward, *The Economic Effects of the Two World Wars on Britain*, London, 1970, pp. 33–5. The Ministry of Munitions gathered extensive evidence of technological innovation and the education of manufacturers along lines of repetition production and specialisation; see, for example, Public Record Office (PRO) MUN 4/176 (Pt II) for comments on developments in the machine-tool industry.

8. See J. Morgan Rees, *Trusts in British Industry 1914–21*, London, 1922, 2; P. Fitzgerald, *Industrial Combination in England*, London, 1927, pp. 1–8.

9. L. Hannah and J.A. Kay, *Concentration in Modern Industry*, London, 1977, p. 71.

government departments had to ration *matériel* and standardise contracts, which could be done only through organisations of capital.[10]

The moot point with Sombart's thesis is whether the economically constructive and technologically innovative effect of armaments production has been more than counterbalanced by the use of such weaponry and the disruption of peaceful industry and commerce. The latter part of this reservation clearly applies with some force to England, whose economy was closely geared to the system of international trade which collapsed in 1914. More fundamentally, the 'constructive' effect of the war lends itself to the method, now thoroughly discredited amongst economic historians, of *ad hoc* itemising; it has yet to be measured in a way consistent with economic theory against a counterfactual model of 'peaceful' development.

The second theme, derived from the work of Max Weber, is that war has promoted social discipline and rationalisation and that the administrative apparatus needed for warfare has been in capitalist societies a source of social power distinct from the power that rests in the control of the capitalist enterprise. This theme arose from Weber's attempt to round out Marx's economic materialism by a political and military materialism and can be exemplified by his sustained interest 'in the economic process through which a public and collective economy was substituted for private capitalism as the basis of military organisation'.[11] The passage from late medieval to modern warfare had, he argued, been marked by the transition from private to public enterprise in the provision of arms and armaments; the material means of warfare had become concentrated and nationalised in the modern state (much as the material means of transport were to be nationalised by the nineteenth-century European state for politico-military reasons). In becoming the arsenal of war, the state acquired many of the rationalistic characteristics of the modern enterprise.[12]

As with Sombart's thesis, it is not difficult to itemise ways in which the First World War induced a greater 'rationalisation' of English society (in Weber's sense of the term). As an example of the greater 'formal rationality' of bureaucracy itself, we might cite the expansion of government actuarialism, especially in connection with such matters as war pensions and shipping.[13] The state assumed, during the war, a new role in the promotion of scientific and industrial research. Admittedly,

10. See Ministry of Reconstruction, *Report of the Committee on Trusts*, Parliamentary Papers (PP) 1919, Cd 9236, esp. p. 20.
11. H.H. Gerth and C. Wright Mills (eds.), *From Max Weber*, London, 1948, p. 260.
12. Ibid., pp. 221–4 for Weber's discussion of the relationship between military organisation and the concentration of the means of administration.
13. See Ministry of Reconstruction, *Report on the Machinery of Government Committee*, PP 1918, Cd 9230, p. 26.

the instruments of wartime state control of the economy were rapidly dismantled after the war (although some reappeared in disguised form during the 1930s). The major permanent legacy of the war, with respect to the economic functions of the state, lay in the quite novel importance of monetary policy in public finance. Owing to the war debt and its management, the government became the controlling operator both in the money market and the bond market.[14]

The wartime relationship between the state and industry left another legacy in the impetus given to scientific management and cost accounting. The labour shortage compelled greater efficiency in the measurement and use of labour and the work of the Health of Munition Workers' Committee and Industrial Fatigue Research Board developed a better understanding of the relationship between the hours of labour, output and fatigue, and of the hidden costs of high labour turnover. We can trace the movement towards industrial psychology and the lack of management opposition to the widespread reduction of hours in 1919 to the educative influence of these bodies.[15] Similarly, the scale of government contracting compelled both state departments and private enterprise to introduce more rigorous accounting procedures; since competition for government contracts virtually disappeared, the whole basis of contract prices shifted from the old method of placing orders on the lowest tender to the new method of fixing prices by the cost of production. This familiarised industrialists and officials with cost-accounting methods which industry had been reluctant to adopt before 1914 and opened up a much greater role for accountants in management.[16]

The value of outlining the themes I have identified with Sombart and Weber lies in their pointing us to significant changes in the capitalist context of class relationships. The war was an important staging-post in the transition from individualistic, competitive capitalism to a neo-capitalism based on larger, less competitive units more closely linked than hitherto with the state. One facet of this closer interdependence lay in industry's share of the National Debt and the greater influence postwar governments enjoyed over levels of investment through their repayment of the Debt's principal and interest.

The third theme bears much more directly on questions of social

14. U. Hicks, *The Finance of British Government 1920–1936*, London, 1938, p. 311.

15. See P. Devinat, *Scientific Management in Europe*, ILO Studies and Reports, Series B, No. 17, 1927, pp. 18ff.; L. Urwick and E.F.L. Brech, *The Making of Scientific Management*, London, 1949, vol. II.

16. See L. Hannah, 'Managerial Innovation and the Rise of the Large-scale Company in Inter-war Britain', *Economic History Review*, 2nd series, vol. XXVII, no. 2, 1974, p. 258; also N.A.H. Stacey, *English Accountancy 1800–1954*, London, 1954 for a general discussion of the development of accountancy during the war.

structure. It was developed by Stanislas Andreski in his *Military Organisation and Society*. For Andreski, the struggle for the good things of life — wealth, power and prestige — is a constant feature of society and pugnacity is innate in human nature. When aggression found external enemies, then organisation for war became a basic cause of the development of hierarchies of command, obedience and discipline within societies and led to their stratification according to inequalities of wealth, power and prestige. The supreme stratum is almost always, he claims, formed by those who wield military power. While economic factors might produce fluctuations in the height of stratification, the long-term trends are determined by shifts in the locus of military power. Andreski regards technical and military circumstances as the key variables in determining the extent of social inequalities. Limited wars fought by privileged military castes are conducive to greater inequality, but the intensification of warfare and mass enlistment tends to level the pyramid. Andreski proposes that whether militancy heightens or flattens the social structure depends mainly on whether the cooperation of the masses is, or is not, essential for the prosecution of the war: that is, on the proportion of militarily utilised individuals in the total population, which he calls the Military Participation Ratio (MPR). Of course, the actual participation ratio prevailing at the beginning of a war may be much less than the optimum allowed for by military technique. Changes in social stratification during or after wars are due, he argues, to the compulsory movement towards the optimum. This movement involves the extension of privileges to newly participant groups, such as women during the two world wars.[17]

There are considerable conceptual problems in applying Andreski's ideas to the analysis of the class structure of a modern society. One arises from their being couched in a Social Darwinian framework which assumes that societies universally divide between elites and masses. I will postpone my own discussion of class, but it is important to stress that far more than verbal differences are at issue here. The distinction between the masses and the elite arose, in the sociology of Mosca and Pareto, in opposition to class theory and the Marxian concept of the class struggle. Elites were assumed to be naturally endowed to lead and they decayed because the laws of heredity inexorably diluted their innate quality.[18] Andreski's ideas can, admit-

17. S. Andreski, *Military Organisation and Society*, London, 1954, 1963 edn., pp. 6–29. Andreski does add that the development of the apparatus of political repression at the disposal of the ruling stratum can modify the influence of changes in the MPR on stratification.

18. For a discussion of Pareto's elite theory, see R. Aron, *Main Currents in Sociological Thought*, New York, 1970, vol. II, pp. 179–83. Andreski's views on warfare and social structure clearly owe much to the Paretan tradition of elite analysis.

tedly, be reformulated as a thesis concerning military organisation and the relationship between rulers and the ruled. This does not greatly clarify their application to the class structure of capitalist societies where the links between political and economic power are, to say the least, problematic.[19]

A second problem arises from the absence in Andreski's work of any means of differentiating between the societal consequences of military organisation for historically different types of societies. A highly schematic contrast will clarify this. Feudal society at its most distinctive was characterised by Bloch as involving a virtual identity of the class of manorial chiefs with the class of professional warriors serving in the only way that then seemed effective, that is, as heavily-armed horsemen. This class held the mass of humble folk in a rigorous economic subjection which was sanctioned by law.[20] In such a society, the economy was local and economic power was inseparable from the politico-military system of rule. Changes in military organisation in feudal society had immediate implications for relations between rulers and ruled *and* for the relations of economic production, for these were conterminous. By contrast, the distinctive character of capitalist society is the economy's transcendence of the locality and the particular ties of the manor and its separation from the formal system of rule. In such a society, the economy depends on a free market in labour and the formal equality of the parties to the labour contract contrasts with the command of rulers over ruled. The economy is self-regulated according to laws of supply and demand and, consequently, is compatible with a wide variety of systems of rule. Capitalist society's class structure is determined primarily by economic relationships which enjoy a certain immunity from political power. At the least, therefore, in an analysis of the relationship between war and social change in capitalist societies, we have to differentiate between the effects of mobilisation on market relationships which are normally immune from political control (and these effects come both from the political suspension of that immunity, with the direction of labour, state regulation of wages and profits *and* the dislocation of the normal market) and the effect on the system of rule which may lead to permanent encroachments on that immunity. The normal immunity of market relationships in capitalist societies both dampens the consequences of mobilisation and means that the

19. Ralph Miliband writes of advanced capitalism providing 'the context' for National Socialist rule, Stanley Baldwin's Conservatism and Roosevelt's New Deal and 'accommodat[ing] itself to many different types of political regime . . .', idem, *The State in Capitalist Society*, London, 1973, p. 21.

20. M. Bloch, *Feudal Society*, 1965, vol. II, pp. 443–6.

impact of war on society is multi-linear. As it stands, the MPR theory cannot accommodate that multi-linearity.

Historians of twentieth-century Britain have responded to Andreski's ideas with interest but some scepticism. In an important lecture, Richard Titmuss sketched out the relationship between war and social policy since the nineteenth century in terms that broadly supported Andreski, though he hesitated over endorsing his Social Darwinian ethos.[21] Philip Abrams commented more critically on the MPR thesis in the context of a discussion of post-First World War social reconstruction policy. He pointed out that, though participation by the less privileged generated a huge public rhetoric of national and social solidarity which sanctified an ambitious political programme of reconstruction, this rhetoric actually disabled those radical politicians entrusted with putting the programme into effect. It led them to believe in the immediate reality of harmony between interests and classes when this harmony was far from achieved, and blinded them to the need to constrain groups to work together. For participation to be politically effective, it had to be 'at the right level' and concordant with the dominant ideology. As examples of effective participants, Abrams cited Beatrice Webb and Christabel Pankhurst and wryly concluded that the beneficiaries of the participation effect were middle-aged, middle-class women.[22]

Arthur Marwick, in a number of publications, has attempted to incorporate a measure of Andreski's notion within a synoptic framework for the study of war and social change.[23] Participation, Marwick suggests, should be divested of exclusively military connotations and thought of as one of four dimensions of the process by which war changes societies. These dimensions are: the destructive and disruptive impact on human and material resources; the dimension arising from the testing of institutions by the strain of the supreme communal enterprise (this dimension is analogous to the much-noted 'inspection effect' of war); the participatory dimension involving complex social bargaining with groups whose lives, labour and skills acquire novel value in wartime; and, finally, the affective dimension arising from the psychologically wounding experience of war, which finds a living residue in consciousness and culture. The impact of these different dimensions will depend both on the technique (in the broadest sense)

21. R. Titmuss, 'War and Social Policy', in idem, *Essays on 'The Welfare State'*, London, 1958, pp. 75–87.

22. P. Abrams, 'The Failure of Social Reform 1918–1920', *Past and Present*, no. 24, April 1963, pp. 57, 62.

23. Esp. Marwick, *Total War*, pp. 11–17; idem, *Social Change*; idem, 'Problems and Consequences of Organizing Society for Total War', in N.F. Dreisziger (ed.), *Mobilisation for Total War: the Canadian, American and British Experience 1914–1918, 1939–1945*, Ontario, 1981.

and duration of the war in question and the characteristics of the prewar society. Marwick regards Abrams's conclusions as vitiated by a narrowly political view of where and how the impact of participation is registered. Change is effected primarily in civil society, not the state.[24] It is as much unguided as planned, and results (for example) from the disruption of normal market relationships.

Marwick's attempt to systematise his approach to the historical study of war and social change was made after he had already written a more conventional social history of the First World War, *The Deluge*, in which he contended (amongst other things) that the war had a dissolving effect on Britain's class structure and thereby important consequences for the representation of the working class in the political system.[25] These contentions have been forcibly rejected by some political historians. In his important study of *The Evolution of the Labour Party 1910–24*, Ross McKibbin broke with traditional Labour historiography by attaching minimal importance to the war when explaining Labour's replacement of the Liberals as the major party of the working class. He doubted whether the war significantly modified working-class life and political attitudes and argued that: 'Everything points to Labour's enduring *ante-bellum* character . . .'.[26] More trenchantly, in a joint article on 'The Franchise factor in the rise of the Labour party' he and two colleagues claimed that

> the 'war' argument, though frequently embraced, has never been properly demonstrated, and in some cases not demonstrated at all. . . . It would have to be shown that the war so significantly altered the structure of the British economy and habits of thought and expectation that the social basis of the pre-war party system no longer existed. . . . The war was not responsible for any major structural changes in the economy and it is hard to show that it altered popular attitudes.[27]

In their view, the overwhelmingly preponderant factor in the political transformation that took place between 1910 and the early 1920s was the massive expansion of the electorate by the 1918 Representation of the People Act. This allowed for the political expression of economic class divisions only inadequately represented in a prewar electorate heavily weighted towards the middle class and greatly under-representing

24. Marwick, *Total War*, p. 15.
25. For his discussion of the war's consequences for the class structure, see *The Deluge*, pp. 324–9; for some remarks on the deeper sociological reasons for political change that took place during the war and its aftermath, see idem, 'The Impact of the First World War on Britain', *Journal of Contemporary History*, vol. 3, no. 1, 1968.
26. R. McKibbin, *The Evolution of the Labour Party 1910–24*, London, 1974, p. 240.
27. H.C.G. Matthew, R. McKibbin, J.A. Kay, 'The Franchise Factor in the Rise of the Labour Party', *English Historical Review*, vol. XCI, no. 361, October 1976, pp. 723–52, esp. p. 736.

the less-skilled urban working class. The Liberal constituency was in an extremely privileged position in this electorate and the Liberals' failure to expand that constituency, in spite of the trebling of voters in 1918, is ample testimony to their dependence on the prewar forms of political life. If the war did precipitate political change, it was by placing intolerable strain on the franchise and electoral registers.[28] Martin Pugh casts doubt even on that, arguing that we have to distinguish between what took place *because* of the war and what took place *during* but *independently* of the war. By this token, the 1918 Act was 'an accident of wartime. . . . The magnitude of the political reform generated during the Great War can be explained in the first instance by the politicians' sense of previously missed opportunities and the lessons they drew from Edwardian politics, rather than by their reaction to mass participation in war'.[29]

Pugh sees an *inverse* relationship between the growing size of the war, marked by the introduction of conscription in 1916 and the increasing state control of the Home Front, and the process of social and political levelling, for — he argues — the growth in the scale of the war resulted from the political ascendancy of reactionary Unionists, allied to David Lloyd George, who were determined to prosecute the war to the full. It was this very coalition which proved the major stumbling block to egalitarian reform.[30] This argument is only persuasive, however, within a narrowly political framework of discussion that excludes the unintended consequences of policies wartime

---

28. D. Tanner has argued that the pre-1914 franchise was less discriminatory against the working class than McKibbin et al. suppose; see 'The Parliamentary Electoral System, the Fourth Reform Act and the Rise of Labour in England and Wales', *Bulletin of the Institute of Historical Research*, 1983, pp. 205–19; see also M. Hart, 'The Liberals, the War and the Franchise', *English Historical Review*, vol. XCVII, no. 385, Oct. 1982, pp. 820–31, for some interesting criticisms of the McKibbin article.

29. Martin Pugh, *Electoral Reform in War and Peace*, London, 1978, pp. 180–1.

30. Ibid., p. 183. Other political historians have given far greater weight to the war than does Pugh in their accounts of the democratic change that took place after 1914; see, in particular, D.H. Close, 'The Collapse of Resistance to Democracy: Conservatives, Adult Suffrage, and Second Chamber Reform, 1911–1928', *Historical Journal*, 20, 4, (1977), pp. 893–918. Close argues that: 'The war quickly made a vast extension of the franchise inevitable, by establishing the claim to vote of new categories of people — especially servicemen and women — and by making intolerable the difficulties of access to the register . . .'. He notes, too, the surprising Conservative support for the abolition of political disfranchisement for outdoor relief recipients (pp. 898, 902). In a Cabinet Discussion Paper of May 1916, Arthur Henderson expressly linked universal primary rights of citizenship to military conscription: 'I should not like it to be thought that I regarded the extension of the suffrage . . . in the light of a bribe. But I am sure that an undertaking by the Coalition Government to consider the whole question of universal suffrage without prejudice from previous controversies would be very cordially welcomed by the working classes, and would go far to reconcile them to the inevitable hardships of universal compulsion', 'Necessary Election Changes', 12 May 1916. There is a copy in the Lloyd George Papers D/24/1/2 (located in the House of Lords Record Office).

governments, irrespective of their political complexion, had to adopt. The fiscal measures of the Unionist Chancellor, Bonar Law, were, for example, indubitably egalitarian and progressive, and an important factor in the levelling that can be shown to have resulted from the war. They were introduced in spite of normal political ideology (and the protests of Tory backwoodsmen) and they originated with the scale and cost of modern warfare.

This study is not intended as a contribution to the political history of the war, but clearly the objections and doubts voiced by McKibbin and others are highly relevant to the issues discussed in it. Some of these objections rest, however, on flawed reasoning. The Labour Party and the trade union movement have played such pivotal roles in the political and industrial mediation of class divisions that there is a strong presumption that continuity in their institutional history is expressive of the continuity in the social bases of politics. Working with this presumption, it is possible to ascribe a particular mental set to the working class (a Labour mentality) and, having demonstrated the long-term continuities in the organisation and ideology of the Labour movement, claim the same continuity for popular consciousness. Consciousness, I feel, needs to be looked at in its own right and not simply in terms of its putative institutional mediations. Once this is attempted, then certain interesting historical questions are raised which McKibbin's resolutely 'head office' approach to Labour's history simply avoids. If it can be shown, for example, that the war did lead to certain changes in working-class self-awareness and in the group references through which popular conceptions of social equity are formed, then how these changes were articulated in the political sphere becomes an open and worthwhile question. Such changes were certainly *perceived* by contemporaries; there are no pressing reasons for doubting that they were real. What gave rise to them? I shall argue that the wartime economy and the public rhetoric of the war effort had the (unexpected) effect of greatly clarifying connections between class position and social privilege and disadvantage. They became more transparent. It is far from my contention that all shifts in popular attitudes were straightforwardly propitious for the Labour movement; none the less, some were and they are a significant absence in McKibbin's account. Furthermore, these subjective changes were accompanied by objective changes in the economic relations between the different working-class strata of sufficient magnitude for historians to talk of a *re*-making of the English working class without debasing that coinage. It will be argued here that the levelling induced by the war took two distinct forms: one was a reduction in the largest personal incomes and a small redistribution of the national income in favour of labour and at the expense of income from rent and fixed securities; the other, a redistribution of the wage bill in favour of the poorer, less-skilled sections of the working class and at the expense of the stratum of skilled artisans, particularly those employed in the staple export industries. The second was an important transformation in the social bases of popular politics. The exclusion of a large stratum of the prewar working class from the electorate was the least of its disadvantages. It was excluded from many of the forms of social life enjoyed by artisans and denied the minimum needed for a healthy family existence. There is incontrovertible evidence that the wartime economy compressed the economic and social distance between the poorest and the artisan strata. The postwar Labour Party was attempting to establish itself within a significantly altered constituency.

I have postponed a discussion of the concept of class until this point and it is now time to turn to this complex problem. Social theorists distinguish between a European tradition of class analysis — concerned with the implications of social divisions for social dynamics — and an American descriptive theory of social ranking.[31] My interest lies with the former. Class theory originated in classical political economy's perception that market forces generated a new type of functional social division. Though he did not use the term 'class', Adam Smith introduced a trichotomous division of agrarian society into landed proprietors, proprietors of stock (farmers) and labourers, three groups differentiated by clearly defined economic functions and by source of income: rent, profit and wages.[32] His heirs extended his analysis to 'the industrial community' which, as J.S. Mill argued, 'may be considered as divided into landowners, capitalists and productive labourers', the classes (Mill's term) who embodied the requisites of production.[33] This functional conception of class became an indispensable part of the Marxian synthesis. Marx reproduced Smith's trichotomy in the incomplete fragment of *Capital* where he broached the question of class structure and there is a real sense in which Marxist class theory is only a critical variant of a more general conception with which Europeans have envisaged the dynamic social structure formed on the capitalist economy. Marx himself gave due credit to the classical political economists and the 'bourgeois historians' for 'discovering the existence of classes in modern society [and] the struggle between them'.[34]

31. Giddens, *Class Structure*, p. 19.

32. A. Smith, *An Enquiry into the Nature and Causes of the Wealth of Nations*, vol. 1, London, 1931 ed., pp. 41–8, 57–60.

33. J.S. Mill, *Principles of Political Economy*, 1848, 1892 ed., p. 168.

34. Marx's fragmentary remarks are reproduced in *Karl Marx: Selected Writings in Sociology and Social Philosophy*, ed. T. Bottomore and M. Rubel, London, 1956, pp. 178–9. Marx gave credit in his letter to Wedemeyer, 11 Sept. 1852; see *Selected Correspondence of Karl Marx and Friedrich Engels*, transl. and ed. by D. Torr, London, 1934, p. 57.

Although Marx accepted the existence of at least three classes in modern society based on the capitalist mode of production, for heuristic purposes he devised an 'abstract model' of a two-fold class structure. In so doing he wished to uncover the development immanent within that society. This model was two-class because it discarded, as no longer contradictory, divisions based on the ownership of land and capital and focused on the conflict between the two groups who were indispensable to a free wage-labour economy and mutually presupposed each other: capitalists and the owners of mere labour power. He made the conflict between the social interests of property in production and its negation the major dynamic of modern society.[35]

In so doing, Marx fused economic theory with philosophical concepts drawn from dialectical thought. In an economic category — mere labour power — he found a social subject, the proletariat, so alienated by its conditions of existence that its self-emancipation implied the abolition of class society and the end of that history of humanity which had culminated in modern capitalism. There seems good reason to suppose that the visionary Marx was heir to older, eschatological traditions; the term is not rejected by those Marxists, such as Herbert Marcuse, who stand closest to the Hegelian philosophical method which (in the opinion of some) Marx never discarded. This method has given rise to a particular conception of a social class as a subject which can 'know' its own interests; when it exists 'for itself' its knowledge of its own interests is infallible. That knowledge is the body of ideas, outlook on the world and so on which is instrumental to its objective historical situation. In Lukács's formulation, '[true] class consciousness consists in fact of the appropriate and rational reactions "imputed" to a particular typical position in the process of production'. Such consciousness is 'neither the sum nor the average of what is thought or felt by the single individuals who make up a class . . .'. It is very distant from 'the psychologically describable and explicable ideas which men form about their situations in life'.[36] This highly idealised conception of class consciousness has to be rejected as of merely historical interest for students of Marxism. No class in history has ever been sufficiently homogeneous to be usefully likened to an individual subject and seldom (if ever) displayed the consciousness we can appropriately impute to it. As E.P. Thompson remarked, the conception fosters a theory of substitution: it is 'the party, the sect, or theorist who disclose class-consciousness, not as it is, but as it ought to be'.[37]

35. For scholarly accounts of Marx's model, see R. Dahrendorf, *Class and Class Conflict in Industrial Society*, London, 1959, pp. 9–35; Giddens, *Class Structure*, pp. 27–33.

36. G. Lukács, *History and Class Consciousness*, London, 1971, p. 51.

37. E.P. Thompson, *The Making of the English Working Class*, Harmondsworth, 1968, p. 10.

Neither Marx's abstract model nor the Hegelian scheme of class consciousness are useful guides to the social structures and popular mentalities of early-twentieth-century capitalist society. The model cannot account for the 'new' middle class which grew so rapidly from the last decade of the nineteenth century; everyday working-class consciousness in the twentieth century fell far short of the ideal type. Social scientists who wish, in the spirit of Marx, to reserve the concept of class for the analysis of conflict usually respond to these defects of model and method by disentangling class from its exclusive association with the possession of property in production and arguing that in several important ways the capitalist system has been modified or even superseded since Marx's death. This is the strategy of Ralf Dahrendorf's famous study, which attempts to define classes by the characteristic of participation in or exclusion from authority and which would substitute 'advanced industrial' for 'capitalist' society. In Dahrendorf's view, critical changes in the economic system — particularly the separation of the ownership and control of industrial capital, the stratification of the working class according to levels of skill, the growth of the salariat and the institutionalisation of class conflict — have accomplished a supersedence of capitalist society. In Dahrendorf's view, industrial society does not tend to classlessness — indeed its potential classes are legion since the proliferation of positions of command leads to endless conflict over authority`— but it does tend to maximise equality of opportunity and personal mobility, since in a rationalistic society positions of command go to the able and ascribed status is eroded by achievement.[38]

The significance and even the empirical content of the critical changes which Dahrendorf mentions are open to debate. The formal separation of ownership and control by 'the managerial revolution', for example, masks the fact that members of families with extensive industrial holdings enjoy privileged access to top management positions and, conversely, top managers are rewarded by share-holding privileges.[39] Equally, the empirical measurement of *relative* social mobility belies the idea that in recent decades there has been any marked tendency towards 'openness'.[40] Without doubt, the set of developments we can describe, summarily, as the 'institutionalisation of class conflict' (the growth of the Labour movement and its associated

38. Dahrendorf, *Class and Class Conflict*, esp. chap. 2.

39. Giddens, *Class Structure*, pp. 170–2.

40. See Goldthorpe et al., *Social Mobility and Class Structure*; esp. p. 252. There has, of course, been a great increase in *absolute* mobility because of changes in the occupational structure but the 'increasing "room at the top" has been shared out more or less *pro rata* among men of different class origins . . . so as to produce no change in their relative chances of access . . .' (ibid., p. 76).

political party, the development of labour law and industrial arbitration, and triangular bargaining between unions, employers, organisations and government) does amount to an exceptionally important change in the mediation of class antagonism, and one to which the industrial relations of the First World War made a signal contribution. However, in this study they are not interpreted in terms of a partial supersedence of capitalist society. The contrary argument of Giddens is, I believe, much more compelling: the customary identification of the heyday of capitalist society with mid-nineteenth-century Britain is misleading.[41] Large areas of industry remained at an artisanal level of economic organisation with ownership of the means of production dispersed among small masters; labour subcontracting delegated the command and management of much of the work-force to working-class chargehands; outwork was commonplace in many trades; in short, capitalist development and the making of an industrial working class were incomplete. Equally incomplete was the bourgeois revolution in politics, for the traditional agrarian ruling class preserved much of its political power (as well as its wealth) throughout the nineteenth century.[42] To take the mid-nineteenth century as capitalist society's heyday is to make the institutionalisation of class conflict in some sense aberrant, but it has been a quite typical concomitant of the development or 'completion' of the capitalist economic system in Western Europe.

The same objection can be made against T.H. Marshall's revision of class theory in the light of the social consequences of democracy. Marshall argued that for most of the nineteenth century, economic, political and civil inequalities overlapped, for political rights were the rights of propertied men and there was no community of citizenship on which to base rights to collectively-provided welfare. Indeed, 'the Poor Law treated the claims of the poor, not as an integral part of the rights of the citizen, but as an alternative to them — as claims which could be met only if the claimants ceased to be citizens in any true sense of the word'.[43] Pauperism was a civil status penalised, until 1918, by political disfranchisement. The association of political rights with property was broken down by piecemeal electoral reform and the curtailment of the status of pauperism while, from the 1900s, the inequalities of economic class were steadily counterposed by the social rights of citizenship: '. . . in the twentieth century, citizenship and the capitalist class system

41. Giddens, *Class Structure*, p. 22.

42. See F.M.L. Thompson, *English Landed Society in the Nineteenth Century*, London, 1963; W.L. Guttsman, *The British Political Elite*, London, 1963; and, for a study which stresses the considerable predominance of landed wealth in the elite of the rich, W.D. Rubinstein, *Men of Property*, London, 1981.

43. T.H. Marshall, *Citizenship and Social Class*, Cambridge, 1950, p. 24.

have been at war'.[44] This war seems rather phoney when we recognise that the creation of welfare states has been a virtually universal feature of industrial growth since the later nineteenth century.[45] Citizens' rights appear to be at war with the capitalist class structure only if we imagine that capitalist development was complete by 1900. Since this was patently not the case, it seems more appropriate to link them to the consolidation of capitalism than to its undermining.

Amongst recent authors, Giddens has provided the most densely-argued post-Marxian attempt to theorise the class structure in the European tradition and I have found his analysis of class structuration invaluable in making sense of the heterogeneous materials looked at for this study. 'Structuration' denotes the processes which reproduce certain social forms and is a useful (though inelegant) corrective to the figurative metaphor of a static structure in which classes are layered. Classes are better envisaged, not as tiers in a pyramid, but as the social clusters effected by the asymmetrical relationships of the market and workplace. Giddens takes the market to be intrinsically a structure of power to which groups of individuals bring differentiated marketable capacities. The Marxian abstract model arrives at a dichotomous class structure by envisaging the essential market capacities as capital and labour power. Giddens argues that the sophistication of industrial and administrative technique has meant that three sorts of market capacity are crucial to structuration: the ownership of property; educational or technical qualifications; and manual skill. Limited social mobility, caused by economic inequality, restricts access to these capacities and each becomes an axis around which 'social closure' takes place. Because of immobility within the individual's life experience and between generations, market divisions take on a social substance through time. These overall sources of class structuration, which give rise to the three-fold form of upper, middle and working class, operate in conjunction with more proximate sources of structuration: the division of labour within the productive enterprise; the divisions arising out of the authority relationships of industry; and the tendency for the social division of labour to give rise to large-scale distributive groupings (notably in the housing market). It is important to stress that classes are not 'closed', as were the feudal estates, have no legal existence and are not determinate social bodies, as is a university.

Giddens suggests that class becomes a subjective phenomenon through, initially, the existence of a common 'style of life' and a common awareness amongst individuals similarly placed in the

44. Ibid., p. 29.
45. See G.V. Rimlinger, *Welfare Policy and Industrialisation in Europe, America and Russia*, Chichester, 1971.

market. 'Awareness' does not imply class consciousness in the accepted sense; it might take the form of an outlook on the social world which denies the significance of class. Class consciousness itself implies acknowledging the separate identity of other classes, but whether consciousness entails the notion of conflict or takes the still-more-developed form of a belief in revolutionary social change through class action is contingent on the visibility of class structuration. Factors such as the concentration of the work-force in large-scale units and cyclical economic instability clarify the class structure for individuals and allow class to become a mode of social action.[46]

This model of class structuration is, of course, scarcely less abstract than the Marxian dichotomy and orientated towards the present. In everyday language we speak of a multiplicity of middle classes (lower-middle, upper-middle, professional middle-class) and these terms obviously correspond to profound differences in reality. Empirical classes are differentiated by (to name but the most salient factors) skill within the working class, professional power and property ownership within the middle class and source of wealth in the upper class. Their boundaries are blurred by both upward and downward social mobility. In early-twentieth-century England two factors were particularly significant in countering the tendencies towards a three-class structure. Firstly, recruitment to the middle class, largely from the children of skilled workers, was often via a buffer zone of low-paid salaried, clerical and other white-collar employment, such as elementary-school teaching. True, empirical research into contemporary mobility patterns has discredited the idea that a buffer zone effect continues to operate, but this does not invalidate the notion that it existed in the past and evidence for it can be seen in Morris Ginsberg's pioneer studies of interchange between social classes.[47]

The second factor was small property ownership which, until at least the interwar period, remained the basis for an extensive 'old' lower-middle class. In both distribution and production the incidence of small property remained greater than classical Marxist economic theory had predicted (although it accurately forecast its long-term decline). In spite of the distributive revolution that began in the late nineteenth century, retailing was, in 1914, overwhelmingly the

---

46. Giddens, *Class Structure*, chap. 6.

47. The term 'buffer zone' is used by Frank Parkin, *Class Inequality and Political Order*, p. 56, and the metaphor describes the area of limited intergenerational mobility between the working and middle classes. Goldthorpe et al. find the metaphor inapt because of the frequency of long-range mobility; see idem, *Social Mobility and Class Structure*, pp. 50–3. However, Ginsberg found a marked difference between working-class mobility into the professional stratum and the salaried lower-middle class; see M. Ginsberg, 'Interchange Between Social Classes', *Economic Journal*, Dec. 1929, pp. 554–65.

business of small-scale property owners. Although multiple-shop firms doubled their share of consumer goods sales between 1900 and 1915, individual small-scale retailing was the most important business form in all retail trades in 1914, and in some trades large-scale retailing had scarcely made a start.[48] The numbers in small-scale distribution fell between 1911 and 1921 (possibly because of the particularly adverse effects of conscription on one-man businesses) but rose again when the interwar depression drove some of the unemployed into shopkeeping.[49] Small-scale property ownership in production was frequent in trades with a low capital threshold and these tended to be geographically confined. In Sheffield's light metal trades (such as cutlery) there persisted a complex system of labour organisation based on large numbers of independent or semi-independent craftsmen, some of whom were small employers ('little mesters').[50] Small-scale producers controlled much of Birmingham's precious-metal and jewellery industries.[51] In Norwich, immediately before the First World War, boot-and-shoe manufacture was in a stage of transition from an artisanal industry largely in the hands of small employers ('garret masters'), to factory-based production, utilising American technology and electric power.[52] In the North Lancashire textile industry, the weaving branch was fragmented amongst large numbers of small-scale employers, many of them operatives who had set up in business by obtaining looms and yarn on credit.[53] Small-scale property ownership provided mobility opportunities atypical of the present class structure and gave rise to a social stratum of urban peasants that has now virtually disappeared.

Gidden's analysis of class structuration is attractive partly because it corresponds to lay perceptions of class while offering a powerful explanation of the processes behind these phenomena.[54] More particularly,

48. See J.B. Jeffreys, *Retail Trading in Britain 1850–1950*, Cambridge, 1954, pp. 14–36.

49. For evidence of the adverse effects of military service on one-man businesses, see PRO CAB 24/19 G.T. 1360, memorandum of 9 Sept. 1917, by W.H.F. [Fisher] on 'Man Power': 'The case of the "one-man business" man who is taken for the Army and whose business consequently collapses seems to call for some special treatment after the war'. The numbers in the distributive trades classified as employers and working on their own account fell from 495,000 to 468,000 between 1911 and 1921; see Routh, *Occupation and Pay*, Table 7, p. 20.

50. See Sidney Pollard, *A History of Labour in Sheffield*, Liverpool, 1959, pp. 61ff. Between the 1890s and 1914 the industrial structure of the light trades underwent considerable changes, including the buying up of small masters, the closing of the 'public wheels' at which independent workers could rent power and the introduction of team-work, but the small firm and 'out-work' system still survived. See chap. 8.

51. Asa Briggs, *A History of Birmingham*, London, 1952, vol. II.

52. C.B. Hawkins, *Norwich: A Social Study*, London, 1910, pp. 23–32.

53. Committee on Industry and Trade, *A Survey of the Textile Industries*, Pt. III of a Survey of Industries, London, 1928, p. 26.

54. In 1950 the great majority of respondents to an enquiry thought in terms of a

this analysis can be referred to in order to steer a path between two different interpretations of the war's effects on the class structure. Although there have been few sociologically systematic studies, the impressions given in the literature of the war's impact suggest either class *polarisation* or class *emancipation*.

For obvious reasons the first is favoured by Marxian writers, and here it is argued or at least implied that the war 'laid bare' Marx's heuristic model with its hostile dichotomy of capital and labour.[55] The proof of this is seen in the industrial and political turbulence of 1919–21, the growing organisational cohesion of capital and labour, evinced in the formation of the Federation of British Industries (FBI) and the General Council of the Trades Union Congress (TUC), and the birth of a revolutionary movement drawing on wartime rank-and-file organisation. This impression or image of the war's impact accurately reflects parts of the historical reality, but takes too short-term a view of the war's social consequences and is defective in one crucial respect: polarisation did not take place amongst the middle class (or, to speak descriptively, classes) as the dichotomous Marxian model would lead us to expect. The economic fortunes of the different segments of the middle class diverged considerably between 1914 and the early 1920s. It is true that during the war itself and the rapid inflation of 1919 and early 1920, the income differential between waged manual labour and salaried employment narrowed, chiefly because manual workers were awarded flat-rate wage increases geared to the cost of living. But wage labour did not sustain its gains during the post-1920 depression when the same mechanism was put into reverse and employers imposed flat-rate cuts proportional to the fall in prices. Salaries followed a different trajectory during the war and postwar period: 'Their rise began later and moved more slowly between 1914 and 1920 [but] when wages tumbled in 1921 and 1922, salaries remained almost unscathed'.[56] By the early 1920s, it was evident that there had occurred a strengthening of the market position of those whose incomes came from salaried employment and a weakening of those with incomes from small property and (with several exceptions) from professional fees. Clerical employees of the 'new' lower-middle class enjoyed economic gains in the postwar years relative to skilled manual labour and the professional and administrative stratum. Econ-

three-class system and used the same set of names: upper, middle and working. See F.M. Martin, 'Some Subjective Aspects of Social Stratification', in D.V. Glass, ed., *Social Mobility in Britain*, London, 1954, p. 58.

55. For early examples of this view, see A. Hutt, *The Postwar History of the British Working Class*, London, 1937, chap. 1; also J.T. Murphy, *Preparing for Power*, London, 1934, esp. pp. 171–2.

56. Routh, *Occupation and Pay*, p. 151.

omic differences within the middle class were compressed by the war (just as they were within the manual working class).

Much more needs to be known about the war's impact on the urban peasantry of small producers, but it seems highly likely that the acceleration of technological change encouraged the shift from small-scale artisanal units to factory production. This certainly occurred in Birmingham, for by 1918 the industrial structure of the city had changed irrevocably from the prewar organisation of production around small workshops: factories had been extended, plants increased in scale and new industrial buildings erected.[57] The jewellery trade had been severely affected by wartime shortages of labour and material. Elsewhere, the boot-and-shoe industry had, as a result of wartime demands, virtually completed the movement to factory production based on semi-automatic machinery.

In the context of this study, the most important changes concerned the salariat, particularly the clerks of industry, transport and government. A plausible case for the image of class polarisation was made from their temporary 'immiseration' and the upsurge of clerical unionism during 1916 to 1921 by Francis Klingender in his study of London's black-coated workers, published in 1935. Klingender asserted that by 1920 the allegiance of the majority of clerical workers to the social order of capitalism had been profoundly shaken and concluded that the 'economic status of the great mass of clerks has . . . finally and irrevocably been identified with that of the manual working class'.[58] That conclusion appears to rest on an erroneous estimate of salary reductions in the later 1920s.[59] The growth of white-collar unionism seems less certain evidence for 'proletarianisation' now that several studies have established the contingent connection between unionisation and class consciousness, let alone alienation from the capitalist social order.[60] A more persuasive explanation of the upsurge of white-collar unionism after 1916, which declined almost as precipitately from 1921, lies in a collective desire to defend certain advantages (of permanency, pensions and promotion prospects) which many clerks enjoyed and a reaction to the erosion of customary market relationships in the clerical sector. The differentials between the hitherto prestigious

57. Briggs, *A History of Birmingham*, vol. II, pp. 213ff. In August 1914 Austin's Longbridge plant employed 2,800 men and by 1918, 20,000. In the postwar period many of the locally expanded firms were overcapitalised but the transformation of the industrial structure (and the social relations of employers and employed) was none the less decisive: see Briggs, chap. IX.

58. F.D. Klingender, *The Condition of Clerical Labour in Britain*, London, 1935, pp. 99–100.

59. See Routh, *Occupation and Pay*, p. 80.

60. See K. Prandy, A. Stewart, R.M. Blackburn, *White-Collar Unionism*, London, 1983, pp. 10–13.

clerical occupations (such as banking) and those in transport and industry narrowed considerably. The break-up of accustomed frames of reference drove clerks to new modes of bargaining. The novel consciousness of the salariat was primarily a market consciousness.

Moreover, though we may agree with Klingender that the economic consequences of the war and its aftermath profoundly disturbed the mentalities or traditional attitudes of white-collar workers, it is by no means the case that all the evidence points to a politicisation of a socialistic or radical kind. There was, for example, an amorphous movement in the aftermath of the war of middle-class protest whose rhetoric was both anti-labour and anti-capitalist. This movement cohered round a revulsion against both labour militancy and profiteering and was directed into anti-waste campaigns (that is, against government spending), opposition to the high level of taxation of 1919/20, and criticism of the out-of-work donation (which supposedly discouraged former munitions girls from returning to domestic service). This movement openly expressed a middle-class consciousness — a feeling, that is, of being in the middle between capital and labour. One of its institutional forms was a Middle Classes Union.[61] Whence, exactly, came the grass-root support for this movement is uncertain, but it certainly made some appeal to the salariat.[62]

The defect of the image of class polarisation is chiefly one of historical perspective. In the longer term the war did not objectively polarise society into two classes by reducing the economic standing of non-manual employees to that of wage labour (on the contrary, it improved their standing). Nor can it be shown convincingly that the war tended to bring about a polarisation in consciousness. In the aftermath of the war, many middle-class people were expressing a heightened awareness of their class and though it remained a very diffuse socio-cultural entity, there are some indications (in housing and children's education, for example) that its different elements were moving towards a common style of life during the 1920s.

In what I have called the 'emancipatory' image, the war is identified with a liberalisation or partial dissolution of the class structure. Writers evoking this image stress the relaxation of barriers between the classes

61. It was sometimes referred to as the Middle Class Union. On postwar middle-class consciousness, see K.O. Morgan, *Consensus and Disunity: the Lloyd George Coalition Government 1918–1922*, London, 1979, pp. 298–300. I return to this neglected topic when discussing the language and imagery of class in chap. 2 and the subjective response to changes in income differentials in chap. 3.

62. Morgan writes that 'lower-middle-class groups such as clerical workers and minor civil servants, even though increasingly organised in white-collar unions, clung all the more passionately to order and free enterprise' (ibid., p. 300). However, he overlooks the increasing support amongst white-collar employees in the public sector for the Labour Party. See chap. 7 of the present study.

and easier social intercourse at all levels of society.[63] The very appearance and social demeanour of workers changed in this period as the traditional garb of corduroy or moleskin fell into disuse and mass-produced ready-to-wear clothing came to be marketed to both the working and lower-middle classes. Certain middle-class fashions, such as tunic shirts, 'percolated through to the working class'.[64] Workers sloughed off some of the servile manner which had often been part of everyday exchanges with professional men or officials enjoying considerable social command. Robert Roberts, recalling the change in popular mentalities during the years of comparative affluence between 1917 and 1920, has written: 'Old deference died: no longer did the lower orders believe *en masse* that "class" came as natural as "knots in wood"'.[65] A.L. Bowley, in his still-invaluable summary of the economic consequences of the war, linked the 'general inter-mixture of classes' to the stimulation of 'the sentiment of democracy' and argued that it 'led to a more serious realisation of possibly avoidable economic inequalities and hardships, thus paving the way for the development of insurance schemes and of more socialistic legislation'.[66]

The emancipatory image can — as Bowley's remarks suggest — be associated with Marshall's theory of citizenship, and it is scarcely surprising that two world wars, with their democratic, fiscal and welfare reforms, should be seen by many as periods of marked 'class abatement' (to use Marshall's phrase). This facet of the emancipatory image certainly deserves respectful attention and could be empirically supported by reference to the legitimising ethos behind wartime educational reform. Other facets of the emancipatory image rather trivialise class by mistaking it for the attribute of a person, displayed in face-to-face relationships, and trivialise class structure by mistaking it for hierarchies in taste, consumption, leisure and so on. The claim that the war liberated the class structure has, if it is not to be an empty figure of speech, to be demonstrated by an objective measure of the 'openness' of society to movement either by workers themselves, or their children, to non-manual occupations. Alternatively, greater openness might be inferred from the greater access of workers' children to a type of education which qualified the school-leaver for white-collar employment.

63. For a particularly explicit expression of the image of class emancipation, see. C. Carrington, *Soldier from the Wars Returning*, London, 1965, pp. 160–1.
64. See A.L. Bowley, *Some Economic Consequences of the Great War*, London, 1930, p. 192; and S.P. Dobbs, *The Clothing Workers of Great Britain*, London, 1928. Though primarily a study of the conditions of labour in the industry, the latter valuably refers to changing patterns of consumption. On tunic shirts, see Board of Trade, *Industrial Survey of the Lancashire Area (excluding Merseyside)*, London, 1932, p. 184.
65. R. Roberts, *The Classic Slum*, Harmondsworth, 1973, p. 220. There are many contemporary references to the decline of deference; I discuss the matter further in chap. 7.
66. Bowley, *Some Economic Consequences*, p. 22.

A notion of social class liberalisation that does not rest upon such measures is shallow. Although Ginsberg did, in 1929, discover some recent increase in upward social mobility, the conclusion that society was becoming, in a statistically significant sense, more fluid was not borne out by the larger and methodologically more sophisticated study of occupational achievement in 1949, supervised by D.V. Glass.[67] The latter study analysed five decennial cohorts of men in England and Wales (the first born before 1890 and four by each decade up to 1929) and found no important changes over time in mobility measured by occupational achievement.

One minor qualification to that conclusion is relevant here. The upper echelons of the occupational hierarchy have had to recruit from the sons of manual workers throughout the twentieth century for both demographic and structural reasons. It would appear that, in terms of movement between the skilled working class and the professional, administrative and managerial strata, the cohort born between 1900 and 1909 entered a perceptibly more fluid society than those born before or after; in 1949 26.4 per cent of the men in the top occupational strata born in this decade had fathers who were skilled working class or routine non-manual. This was markedly higher than the corresponding percentages for the two earlier and two later cohorts. Of the boys born to skilled and routine non-manual fathers during this decade, 5.6 per cent rose to the top occupational strata (as compared with 2.3 per cent of the sons of skilled workers born between 1890 and 1899 and 3.2 per cent born between 1910 and 1919).[68] This fluctuation in an historical picture which is otherwise highly stable over time is probably attributable to the widening of access for skilled-workers' children to secondary education between 1911 and 1920. The Glass study revealed the overwhelming occupational advantages resulting from attendance at secondary schools; the probability that an important (if not the most important) way in which the war could be said to have liberalised the class structure was through its impact on educational chances is one I return to in the note on pages 265–9. This widening — which reached a plateau in the later 1920s — produced (if my inferences are sound) what even those kindly disposed to the emancipatory image must concede was a minor improvement in mobility chances which scarcely touched the sons of unskilled and semi-skilled manual workers.

This study puts forward an alternative image to the two I have discussed in arguing that the war strengthened the class structure by consolidating those immanent tendencies in capitalist society which

67. Ginsberg, 'Interchange between Social Classes', p. 565; D.V. Glass and J.R. Hall, 'Social Mobility in Britain: A Study of Inter-Generation Changes in Status', in Glass, ed., *Social Mobility in Britain*, pp. 177–217.
68. For these figures, see ibid, Tables 6 and 7, pp. 186–7.

give rise to the threefold form. This argument can embrace some features of the other two images: the disappearance of the middle class does not necessarily follow from the polarisation of capital and labour, for social conflict can be three-cornered; the liberalisation of social demeanour and the status-hierarchy does not necessarily imply the attenuation of social class, for it may lead to greater solidarity within classes. The argument, as a whole, can scarcely surprise twentieth-century social and economic historians already familiar with the inter-war solidity of the working class, the development of middle-class suburbia and the blending of wealthy elites into a single upper class. Our growing knowledge of the historical distribution of wealth and income, of social mobility and of the 'political arithmetic' of edu-cational chances is familiarising us with those long-term continuities which keep the class structure in being.

Class is a societal phenomenon which calls for societal history, a type of history which tries to account for both the duration and change in time of that coherent relationship of social forces and institutions which gives society its shape. Although political events are not a primary focus of this study, the links between the class structure and the political system can scarcely be excluded from societal analysis. Politi-cal factors are not simply an outcome of class divisions: they condition the empirical forms taken by classes, levels of consciousness within them, and go far towards explaining the differences in class structura-tion in, for example, Britain and the United States. To the image of the war consolidating the threefold class form it is necessary to add an interpretation of the way the war altered the ties between class div-isions and the political system.

It is incontestable that the wartime demand for labour compelled a political accommodation of the working-class movement. Trade unions were recognised as the accredited agents of the working class, their officials were recruited to government advisory committees to ensure that labour, an increasingly scarce commodity, was used fully and effectively for the purpose of prosecuting the war and they were drawn into decision-making processes from which they had traditionally been excluded.[69] How this is interpreted will depend partly on one's theor-etical perspectives, and partly on an assessment of its longer-term results for the political system, for in the postwar years the trade union

---

69. For a discussion of the entry of trade unions into Whitehall, see V.L. Allen, *Trade Unions and the Government*, London, 1960, pp. 28–31. A full list of the official wartime committees on which trade unions were represented can be compiled from N.B. Dearle, *A Dictionary of Official War-time Organizations*, London, 1928; see also H.A. Clegg, *A History of British Trade Unions since 1889*, vol. 2, Oxford, 1985, p. 225.

presence in the corridors of power greatly diminished. From a Leninist point of view, it was the incorporation of a 'labour aristocracy' of trade-union bureaucrats within the apparatus of the state.[70] In a recent and scarcely less controversial interpretation, Keith Middlemas has argued that a major political readjustment took place during the war, when the state was compelled to adopt a new corporate political role in industrial capitalist society and to begin effecting that continuous series of compromises between organised labour and capital which is the stuff of modern domestic politics.[71] In doing so, it elevated trade unions and employers' associations to a new sort of status: from being interest groups they became 'governing institutions'. With this adjustment, the basis was laid for 'a new form of harmony in the political system'.[72] The Leninist interpretation errs in seeing trade union officials as more quiescent agents of class rule than was the case and ascribing to them powers to contain a revolutionary threat that can scarcely be shown to have existed. Middlemas exaggerates the degree of consensus between employers, the state and the trade unions that was, in fact, achieved, and his description of trade unions as 'governing institutions' is, to say the least, question-begging.[73]

My interpretation — doubtless no less open to criticism — is that wartime industrial bargaining gave a specific impetus to the emergence of the institutionalised forms of class conflict that are now taken for granted (witness, for example, the encouragement of industry-wide bargaining, the use of national wage awards on a cost-of-living basis, the coalescence of unions and employers into single units for bargaining purposes).[74] Furthermore, government departments during the war acquired a working commitment to 'constitutional' trade unionism (as opposed to 'unofficial' organisations) whose legacy was a political

70. For an interesting interpretation of the period that uses Leninist political concepts, see J. Foster, 'British Imperialism and the Labour aristocracy', in J. Skelley, ed., *The General Strike 1926*, London 1976, pp. 3–57, esp. p. 31. In Foster's hands the concept of the labour aristocracy is, unfortunately, devoid of sociological content and explanatory value.

71. K. Middlemas, *Politics in Industrial Society*, London, 1979. Middlemas dates the beginnings of this readjustment to the industrial crisis of 1911–14, but it is clear that he considers that the industrial politics of the war led to the critical break with the past; see, e.g., pp. 20–1.

72. Ibid., p. 18.

73. For the breakdown of the wartime industrial consensus see R. Lowe, 'The Failure of Consensus in Britain: the National Industrial Conference, 1919–1921', *Historical Journal*, vol. 21, no. 3 (1978); and idem, 'The Ministry of Labour: Fact and Fiction', *The Bulletin of the Society for the Study of Labour History*, no. 41, Autumn 1980, which levels many damaging criticisms at Middlemas's thesis.

74. For an early but still invaluable analysis of wartime industrial relations and the changes in bargaining practices, see H. Clay, *The Problem of Industrial Relations*, London, 1929; see also Clegg, *History of British Trade Unions*, chap. 5. I return to some of the implications of these developments for working-class mentalities in my chap. 5.

context which would help foster these institutionalised forms. In time of war, and in the postwar period, they certainly expected that industrial order was the *quid pro quo* of this commitment. The protestations of Christopher Addison, then Minister of Munitions, made at a conference with the Amalgamated Society of Engineers (ASE) during the most serious industrial crisis of the war in May 1917 expressed unequivocally the government's commitment:

> . . . we have gone out of our way to take great risks to maintain the authority of the Trade Unions. . . . We have been besought by all kinds of deputations from works and so on, but we have said, No, we cannot deal with you in that way: we must deal with the orthodox Trade Union which represents the trade collectively. . . . This Ministry has consulted Trade Unions in season and out of season more than any other Government Department has ever done. . . . We are entitled to ask your Union [i.e. the ASE] . . . to keep your Members in hand as much as you can . . . the whole principle of Trade Union discipline and order is at issue. There has been a determined and concerted attempt in different parts of the country to upset the authority of the established unions, and we have stood in the breach and helped for all we were worth.[75]

The residue of this commitment, evident in the postwar coalition's handling of the industrial crisis of 1919–21, was the government's preference for allowing industry to settle its own problems in properly constituted ways in the first instance, and to keep open the channel of negotiation between government and the Labour movement where disputes proved intractable. The Minister of Labour stressed, in January 1919, the importance of giving

> organisations representing employers and workpeople in the different trades . . . every possible opportunity of themselves dealing with the various troubles. This is particularly the case so far as regards the Trade Unions. The extremist and 'unofficial' sections of the Unions . . . are making renewed efforts to capture the machine, and the executives of the Unions would view with disfavour any intervention on the part of the Government before they have themselves tried to put their own house in order.[76]

In spite of the scale of industrial conflict in the next two years and the sometimes inflammatory tone of its own rhetoric, the government made real efforts to retain the atmosphere of wartime conciliation and constantly asserted the need to govern through consent.[77]

This political accommodation of the working-class movement was,

75. PRO MUN 5/63/322/22, verbatim record of a conference with the ASE on the trade card, 5 May 1917.
76. Lloyd George Papers F/27/6/2. Memorandum, 'Industrialist Unrest', from the Minister of Labour (Robert Horne) to Lloyd George, 27 January 1919.
77. See Morgan, *Consensus and Disunity*, chap. 3, esp. pp. 59, 76.

primarily, a concession forced by the power of labour at the point of production, but it also took place in other areas of civil society where working-class people were organised as consumers or recipients of welfare. The rationing and distribution of basic foodstuffs adapted to the pressures of working-class Food Vigilance Committees and Trades and Labour Councils. The administration of dependants' allowances and pensions was modified to restrict the influence of middle- and upper-class voluntary organisations and amplify that of the organised working class. The official circular letter advising on the setting-up of local committees to help administer war pensions gives the flavour of accommodation in these spheres:

> As regards labour, it is unnecessary to point out that what is sought for in connection with its representatives . . . is not merely the presence on the Committee of persons who are cognizant of working-class conditions or who themselves belong to the manual working-class, but the representation on the Committee of working-class opinion and the cordial and continued co-operation of working-class organizations in the work of the Committee.

The claim of local working-class organisations to the direct nomination of the representatives of labour was, as the Parliamentary Committee of the TUC acknowledged, specifically recognised.[78]

The rise in the political status of the 'constitutional' working-class movement was a logical, even predictable outcome of its accommodation in these different spheres. It led to the belief that the balance of class power had shifted; as J.R. Clynes expressed it:

> If the war does not change fundamentally the relations between Capital and Labour, it will at least tend greatly to modify in favour of Labour the basis of these relations. Before the war, Labour was in a very subordinate position, and Capital was regarded as conferring a favour upon workmen in providing them with employment. . . . Labour has been curiously elevated by the demands of the war. . . .[79]

In my interpretation, this 'elevation' in political status greatly facilitated the emergence of a social-democratic version of the class structure, that is to say one in which the Labour Party, more explicitly socialist than hitherto, became the vehicle for the systematic political

---

78. The circular is quoted in the appendix to the *Report of the War Pensions Statutory Committee for 1916*, PP 1917, Cd 8750; see also the letter from C.W. Bowerman, of the Parliamentary Committee of the TUC, to the committee acknowledging the more effective representation of Labour organisations on the Local War Pensions Committees, in ibid., p. 29.

79. J.R. Clynes in S.J. Chapman, ed., *Labour and Capital after the War*, London, 1918, pp. 17–18.

inclusion of the working class within capitalist society. It was the party, rather than the Parliamentary Committee of the TUC, which acted as the national representative of organised working-class interests.[80] It was a party body — the War Emergency Workers' National Committee — which provided the crucial forum for maintaining the unity of the Labour movement in the face of the deep political antagonisms amongst trade unionists and socialists aroused by support for and hostility to the war.[81] The party was strengthened by the particularly rapid growth of its affiliated unions in 1917 and 1918 and the easy conversion of trade unionists to socialism once they had witnessed the successes of war collectivism and planning.[82]

In this version of the class structure, its divisions became more important in determining political consciousness, but their revolutionary implications were (further) marginalised.

80. See R.M. Martin, *TUC: the Growth of a Pressure Group, 1868–1976*, Oxford, 1980, pp. 132–63.

81. See R. Harrison, 'The War Emergency Workers' National Committee, 1914–20', in A. Briggs, J. Saville, eds., *Essays in Labour History*, vol. 2, London, 1971, pp. 211–59.

82. See Clegg, *History of British Trade Unions*, pp. 196, 232.

# 2

## The Language and Imagery of 'Class'

During the early nineteenth century, the language of 'class' came to designate the social divisions of an increasingly industrial, capitalist society, not entirely to the exclusion of older terms appropriate to the pre-industrial hierarchy, but in such a way as to be the dominant convention.[1] This language became enmeshed in social practices and relations, and helped constitute the sense people made of their society. Since its adoption, there have been several important shifts in 'class' usage and reference. For example, in the early twentieth century, under the influence of eugenic thought, class formation was widely interpreted in sociobiological terms and mobility between classes taken to be the result of individual superiority in innate ability.[2] Similarly, class mentalities were interpreted in terms of a 'herd' instinct — a notion made fashionable by the new social psychology of the 1900s which was self-consciously aligned with evolutionary biology.[3] Even where social commentators did not share the eugenic preoccupation with differential fertility, the superfluity of 'stocks' of lesser worth and consequent 'racial degeneration', their discussion of class differences was often interlaced with the vocabulary of the new, sociobiological sciences.

This chapter is concerned with a different kind of shift in the language and reference of 'class' which took place between 1910 and the early 1920s, a shift indicated by the assertion of Carr-Saunders and Caradog-Jones in their pioneer social survey that: 'We hear less than formerly of the "upper", "middle", and "lower" social classes. We do, however, hear much more about "class consciousness" and "class warfare"'.[4] This remark did not simply echo the circumstances of the

1. See A. Briggs, 'The Language of Class in Early Nineteenth-century England', in A. Briggs, J. Saville, eds., *Essays in Labour History*, London, 1960, pp. 43–73; see also G. Himmelfarb, *The Idea of Poverty*, London, 1985.

2. For some contemporary instances of this, see W.C.D. and Mrs Whetham, *Heredity and Society*, London, 1912, pp. 25–6; G.G. Butler, *The Tory Tradition*, London, 1914, pp. 97, 100; J.M. Winter, D.M. Joslin, eds., *R.H. Tawney's Commonplace Book*, Cambridge, 1972, which records the belief of William Beveridge that: 'The well-to-do represent on the whole a higher level of character and ability than the working classes, because in the course of time the better stocks have tended to come to the top. A good stock is not permanently kept down: it forces its way up in the course of generations of social change, and so the upper classes are on the whole the better classes', ibid., pp. 26–7.

3. See W. McDougall, *An Introduction to Social Psychology*, London, 1908, p. 73; W. Trotter, *Instincts of the Herd in Peace and War*, London, 1916, 1953.

4. A. Carr-Saunders, D. Caradog-Jones, *A Survey of the Social Structure of England and*

immediate context in which it was published, the aftermath of the General Strike. Historians have been struck by the violent imagery of class discourse throughout the early 1920s; as Alan Bullock wrote, we find in the speeches and newspaper comments of the period 'the frank recognition by both sides that industrial relations had become a running class war and the concession or rejection of wage demands symbols of victory or defeat for one side or the other'.[5] There can be no doubt that much of this violent imagery was drawn from the experience of war and I will try to show in this chapter how the shift in the primary reference of the language of class from stratification to conflict was intimately connected with the changes in social consciousness wrought by the conflict which engulfed Europe.

The language of class cannot be precisely distinguished from the conceptions used in different social milieux to visualise the way society is shaped, which I will term the imagery of class society. This imagery usually comes to us in the medium of language; pictorial representations are only an incidental source. Conversely, the language of class is connotative and allusive; it evokes mental pictures. The term 'middle class', for example, implies the existence of at least two other classes and conjures up different historical associations from 'bourgeoisie'.[6] A distinction does arise, however, because the imagery of class need not be expressed in the language of 'class' (the Edwardian class structure was commonly represented by such metaphors as the 'social ladder' and the 'social scale'). Furthermore, class imagery is a more complex matter than linguistic convention. It expresses the social actor's lived relationship with the everyday world of work and neighbourhood and is, in consequence, socially variable between and within social classes. A seminar paper by David Lockwood suggested a typology of working-class imagery and the sources of its variation but testing it demands ethnographic research denied to the historian, for only this can give us the systematic insights into working-class habits of mind to judge the usefulness of his categories.[7] The materials looked at here come overwhelmingly from the public sphere, where issues of concern to the national community (such as industrial relations or the causes of poverty) were debated. Much of the evidence is drawn from trade union and Labour sources, but the public idiom and frames of refer-

*Wales*, London, 1927, p. 70.

5. A. Bullock, *The Life and Times of Ernest Bevin*: vol. I, *Trade Union Leader*, London, 1960, p. 150.

6. See, on this point, G.D.H. Cole, 'The conception of the Middle Classes', in *Studies in Class Structure*, London 1955, esp. pp. 90–1.

7. D. Lockwood, 'Sources of Variations in Working-class Images of Society', in M. Bulmer, ed., *Working-Class Images of Society*, London, 1975, pp. 16–31. This volume contains a number of studies critical of Lockwood's thesis.

ence of the Labour movement were very different from colloquial working-class speech and habits of mind. Labour spokesmen were using a form of abstraction out of character with everyday speech when they adopted the language of 'class'.

Edwardian England produced an interesting amateur sociology, based on participant observation and a keen ear for the demotic, which saw its task as interpreting the language, and social and domestic habits of wage earners, for a predominantly middle-class reading public.[8] From this sociology we learn of those concrete empirical colloquialisms (which spoke, for example, of a funeral as 'putting so-and-so under the dirt' or 'a slow walk and a cup of tea') now taken to be characteristic of working-class culture.[9] Where 'class' figured prominently in popular idiom it appears to have referred to personal and family status within the local community, rather than the social divisions of wider society. Working-class people referred to themselves as 'the likes of us', 'working people', 'labouring sort' and outside this circle were 'the likes of they', 'the higher ups', 'the gentry' or simply 'the rich'. True, there were conventions for differentiating between classes which were not 'the likes of us' (the lower-middle class of clerical workers were, for example, 'collar-and-tie men') and it would be misleading to infer from the idiom that working-class people only perceived two classes in society. Unfortunately, this amateur sociology does not span the war period and there is little comparable until the social criticism of Orwell and the Mass Observation of the 1930s. It is impossible to say whether the imagery of class society expressed in popular idiom changed during and because of the war.

Even though the analysis is confined to the public sphere, the materials are so profuse and diverse that they cannot be approached without categories (which are at least incipiently theoretical) of class imagery and some notion of their determination and function. Stanislaw Ossowski categorised class imagery into three basic types: dichotomous images where society is perceived as divided into rulers and ruled, or rich and poor, or the workers and the idle; schemes of gradation where more than two classes are ranked either by one objective criterion (in which case we can speak of a simple scheme) or by a number of criteria which include socio-psychological factors (a synthetic scheme); and, finally, functional conceptions of the class

8. Amongst the best-known works of this sociology were Lady F. Bell, *At the Works*, London, 1907; Mrs M. Loane, *The Next Street But One*, London, 1907; idem, *From Their Point of View*, London, 1908; idem, *Neighbours and Friends*, London, 1910; S. Reynolds, *A Poor Man's House*, London, 1908; idem, *Seems So! A Working-Class View of Politics*, London, 1908; George Bourne, *Change in the Village*, London, 1912.

9. The classic delineation of this culture remains R. Hoggart, *The Uses of Literacy*, London, 1957.

structure as a network of reciprocal relationships (such as classical political economy's trichotomous division into classes deriving their income from rent, profit and labour, where these classes can only exist interdependently). Ossowski argued that the most socially significant view of stratification is the dichotomous one because it is an *idée force* in its function in social movements.[10] Many of the historical materials confirm this: George Askwith, for long the leading official industrial conciliator, wrote that 'the well-known phrase 'Capital and Labour' emphasises the view that there are in this country two rival camps or armies, acting sometimes in veiled and sometimes in open opposition to each other, and, according to some prophets, preparing with speed for an open and bitter fight'.[11] Given Askwith's strictures it is somewhat surprising that the phrase should have been used in the government information posters of 1919 advertising the services of the employment exchanges.[12] In fact, this dichotomy could be taken as the functional harmony of interests, not only by ministers and officials who were coming to see the main business of government as the harmonisation of those interests, but by trade union leaders and the workers they represented. A central theme in the language of 'class' in the public sphere between 1910 and 1920 was the 'play' or contention between 'conflict' and 'harmony' interpretations of that dichotomy.

### The Three-Class Scheme

Edwardians used the language of 'class' promiscuously. 'The word "class"', complained two members of the Marxist Social Democratic Party, 'is used in many ways. For instance, we speak of the professional class, the clerical class, the military class, the leisured class, the artisan class, the labouring class, etc., as well as of the upper and lower classes.'[13] This did not, in their view, alter the fact that society was separated into two main divisions or classes: one section which, for all practical purposes, possessed the material means of production and the other which had no effective ownership in, or control over, these things. They conceded that, in their own terms, the great majority of people were not class conscious. Though the word was often used, it was rarely

10. S. Ossowski, *Class Structure in the Social Consciousness*, London, 1963, p. 20.
11. G. Askwith, *Industrial Problems and Disputes*, London, 1920, p. 67. Askwith was appointed Chief Industrial Commissioner in 1911, but he was already the Board of Trade's leading authority on labour disputes. He chaired the wartime Committee on Production and became a leading official in the Ministry of Labour when that was set up in 1916.
12. A government information poster placed in *John Bull* in January 1919 read: '"Where Capital and Labour Meet" — at the Employment Exchange'.
13. E. Belfort Bax, H. Quelch, *A New Catechism of Socialism*, London, 1909, pp. 7–8.

defined: A.L. Bowley, in one of the few attempts at a definition in liberal thought, suggested that 'a social class . . . consists of a group of persons and their dependants . . . who have intercourse on equal terms so far as sex and age will allow'. By this definition, he argued, it was more accurate to speak of 'working classes' than 'the working class'. The manual working class was 'minutely graded' and its divisions could be marked off by types:

> . . . taking the foreman, or the highly skilled artisan, perhaps owning or acquiring house property, as one; the ordinary skilled journeyman as a second; the machine-tending, partly skilled operative as a third; the un-trained man in steady employment as a fourth; and the man irregularly employed in muscular labour living from hand to mouth as a fifth. The streets in which these typical persons live and the people they associate with might be found to give fairly distinct classes in many towns.[14]

This promiscuous use of the word 'class' and the notion of many working classes coexisted with a number of concepts or schemes of the social structure in which the many specific classes were aggregated into a few social classes. Of Ossowski's categories, the image of class society favoured in early-twentieth-century literate circles, and, as far as one can judge, at least widely current amongst the working class, was a synthetic scheme of gradation which envisaged three classes ranked by function, wealth and culture. Purely functional accounts of a class trichotomy, derived from classical economics, which were a feature of Victorian treatises on political economy, survived in the writings of economists.[15] There was a literary connection in Edwardian social class analysis with the class trichotomy of political economy; a major inspiration for the synthetic scheme of gradation was Matthew Arnold's *Culture and Anarchy*, which delineated 'our aristocratic, our middle and our working class . . . the three great English classes' and in a brilliant chapter lit upon the names Barbarians, Philistines and the Populace to denote and dissect their respective mentalities.[16] Arnold took the class of trichotomy of Land, Capital and Labour and subjected it to a 'culturalist' analysis.

This mode of analysis was consciously adopted by Charles Master-man in his *The Condition of England* (1909), where the three main classes appear as the Conquerors, the Suburbans and the Multitude, and to

14. A.L. Bowley, *The Nature and Purpose of the Measurement of Social Phenomena*, London, 1915, pp. 85, 91–92.

15. See, for example, E. Cannan, *The Economic Outlook*, London, 1912: 'What determines the proportions in which the total produce is divided between the class of labourers, the class of capitalists, and the class of landlords, or as it is put metaphorically, between Labour, Capital and Land?'

16. M. Arnold, *Culture and Anarchy*, London, 1869, chap. 3.

which there was added a fourth sub-class of Prisoners, chiefly the sweated, often female labour of the domestic or 'putting-out' trades, although he included in this sub-class the half-million or so genteel shop assistants who 'lived-in' or were affected by the living-in system.[17] To compare Masterman's classes with Arnold's gives us indications of both the objective historical changes which separated the mid-Victorian and Edwardian class structures and of the new intellectual or discursive categories (including those drawn from eugenics and social psychology) through which these changes were interpeted. Masterman's Conquerors are not a landed aristocracy. They are a plutocracy who, during the Unionist political ascendancy from 1885 to 1905, had failed to take the 'opportunities offered to the children of wealthy families for the elaboration of a new aristocratic Government of a new England . . .'. Rich landed proprietors figured in this plutocracy but, in Masterman's view (and it was typical of his radical Liberal circle) they had forfeited an aristocracy's functions and honour by their neglect of the countryside and their inability to provide a governing class: 'It maintains large country houses . . . but it sees rural England crumbling into ruin just outside their boundaries, and has either no power or no inclination to arrest so tragic a decay'. To 'the governance of Empire . . . [it] contributes but little . . .'. From its imperial achievements, and the insular hauteur it displayed in Continental watering places, the class derived the title 'Conquerors', but Masterman discerned 'the weakening or vanishing of the qualities by which . . . conquest was attained: in an aristocratic caste which is merging itself in a wealthy class, and undergoing weakening in the process. It is not from the "Conquerors" but from a rather harassed and limited Middle Class that the "Empire builders" are now drawn . . .'.[18] The plutocracy was 'continually being recruited from below', particularly by the infusion of new wealth drawn from South Africa and America. The dominant motifs in Masterman's description of this wealthy class are parasitism and the gathering pace of conspicuous consumption; in his enumeration of the typical members of the class, captains of the staple industries are remarkable for their absence.

Masterman's Suburbans 'are practically the product of the past half-century, and have so greatly increased, even within the last decade. They are the creations not of the industrial, but of the commercial and business activities of London'. This was the 'new' middle class of office employees (in striking contrast to Arnold's middle class of industrial capitalists). Men in this class were 'sucked into the City at daybreak' and scattered to suburban villas as darkness fell. They are

---

17. C.F.G. Masterman, *The Condition of England*, London, 1909, 1911, chap. 5.
18. Quotations from ibid., pp. 32, 33, 43, 59–60.

seen as devoted to the private pleasures of families they strove — with
increasing success — to limit by late marriage and restraint or con-
traception (evidence of 'the considerable undermining process which
suburban religion has undergone'). The Suburbans, in Masterman's
caricature, are haunted by organised Labour and 'harassed by the
indifference or insolence of the domestic servant'. From a blend of these
two anxieties they had 'constructed in imagination the image of
Democracy — a loud-voiced, independent, arrogant figure, with a
thirst for drink, and imperfect standards of decency, and a determination to be supported at someone else's expense'. The Suburban
mentality envisaged — as ample independent evidence testifies —
society as a scale and its 'ideals are all towards the top . . .'. Suburbans
identified with the symbolic pinnacle of that scale: 'In the literature
and journalism specially constructed for the suburban mind you will
often find endless chatter about the King, the Court and the doings of a
designated "Society"'. Hence, in part, the political deference of Suburbans to Conservativism which 'is supposed to be the party favoured
by Court, society, and the wealthy and fashionable classes'. In spite of
the Suburban class's many unattractive features, Masterman saw in it
the new leading cadres of civil society. For example, elementary school
teachers, of a type 'practically unknown forty years ago . . . appear as
the mainstay of the political machine in suburban districts, serving
upon the municipal bodies . . . the leaders in the churches and chapels,
and their various social organisations'. Masterman envisaged the
possibility of the Suburbans creating their own class ideal and 'no
longer turning to a wealthy and leisured company above it for effective
imitation of a life to which it is unsuited'.[19] What the ideal was to be is
unclear (doubtless Masterman had in mind his own 'Progressivism' or
advanced Liberalism). In any event, though the Suburbans remained
the mainstay of organised religion, this had ceased to generate that
inward solidarity of a class which Hebraic Dissent had brought Arnold's Philistines.

Masterman's conception of the class structure reflected the ascendancy of London as an imperial and administrative capital and the
cultural dominance which London Society had achieved over the
provinces.[20] It was a conception pervaded by a liberal's fear of a mass
society, and the intimations of the future were made sharper by
frequent reference to the United States and borrowings from sociobiological and socio-psychological thought. These themes are particularly evident in his discussion of the Multitude. London had bred 'a

19. Ibid., pp. 65, 67, 73, 74, 76, 77.
20. See A. Briggs, *Victorian Cities*, Harmondsworth, 1968, for the cultural ascendancy
of London during the age of 'High' Imperialism, pp. 48, 360.

special race of men . . . also produced, and that in less intensive cultivation, in the few other larger cities — Glasgow, Manchester, Liverpool — where the conditions of coagulation offer some parallel to this monster clot of humanity'. For Masterman, this race had given birth to a new form of social life: the Crowd, menacing, capricious, eager only for laughter, with 'panic and wild fury . . . concealed in its recesses'. It was 'a kind of life grotesque and meaningless'.[21] For Arnold, the threat to culture had come from the integral, moral individual 'doing as he likes'. For Masterman, the threat to civilisation lay in the individual losing his volition in the collective will of the Crowd. Masterman's portrait of the working class was by no means entirely repellent — he drew on the growing number of studies which attempted the sympathetic appraisal of working-class culture, but its most distinctive feature was a distrust of the malleability and irrationality of the common man in the aggregate.

The scheme of synthetic gradation which took three classes to be basic units of the class structure was used by Stephen Reynolds in an article on 'Class', published in 1914. As had Masterman, he cited Chiozza Money's investigation of the distribution of wealth and income to argue that: 'Roughly corresponding with the above-mentioned gradations of wealth and income, we have still three main classes — the upper, the middle, and the lower; the wealthy controlling class, the class of the intermediaries and middlemen, controlled and in turn controlling, and the wholly controlled wage-earning class — capital, organization and labour — owners, the artful, and the tools . . .'. He added that 'within each class are many sub-divisions, notably the upper and lower sections of the middle class'.[22] Some years earlier, Reynolds, a talented amateur sociologist who specialised in reporting the common man's speech (with what faithfulness we cannot tell), had claimed that this structure had its specific acknowledgement in demotic usage. West Country working men, familiar with most social types through the spread of holiday-making, would refer to a member of the upper class as a 'gentleman' while a workman or tramp was a 'man' but the inhabitants of a neutral zone between the gentry and themselves were 'persons'. Tradesmen belonged to the class of 'not real gentlemen'. Even if the usage was fancifully recorded, it indicates how the scheme of gradation became a hierarchical conception amongst 'traditional deferentials', a fact emphasised by the embarrassing insist-

---

21. Masterman, *The Condition of England*, pp. 88, 105.
22. S. Reynolds in a series 'Wealth and Life. No. 9, Class (i)', *The Nation*, 28 Feb. 1914. L. Chiozza Money's *Riches and Poverty* was first published in London in 1905 and revised in 1910 and 1913. It was a highly influential study which, through its successive editions, showed an increasing maldistribution of wealth.

ence of Reynolds' working-class friends on addressing him as 'sir'.[23]
But Reynolds did not record his friends using the language of 'class'.

There are sufficient examples of the three-class hierarchy being
acknowledged in common speech and modes of address to allow us to
take that imagery for a widespread historical social fact. Domestic
service was clearly one important means by which it was reproduced
(as well as being a source of knowledge of the non-local character of the
class structure, for it drew single girls from the countryside and small
towns into middle-class suburbs). An enquiry by the Women's Industrial Council (WIC), which set down in their own words the numerous
complaints by servants of the sheer lack of manners on the part of their
employers, recorded sentiments such as: 'The better bred people, the
*real* gentlefolk do treat their employees as flesh and blood, the "jumped
up rich middle classes" as cattle'.[24]

## The 'Social Ladder'

While a three-tier scheme provided the basic paradigm of the class
structure, it coexisted with much more complex spatial metaphors
likening society to a multi-tiered building or a many-runged ladder.
This way of visualising society presumed that it was a structure the
individual could ascend and descend. In popular thought it was most
firmly entrenched in (to adopt Masterman's usage) the Suburban
mentality for which there were socially visible bench-marks by which
individual and family position on the social scale could be identified. In
a sociologically interesting novel, *Robert Thorne: London Clerk*, on which
Masterman drew for his delineation of the Suburban mentality, Shan
Bullock recorded some of these bench-marks or 'standards'. It is the
story of 'a twopenny clerk' who, with his wife (an ex-office girl) slowly
makes his way up the scale. When newly married: 'We were not likely
for many a year, to rise to the slavey line in the social stage. . . .' (i.e.
the standard represented by a single domestic servant, usually a young
girl). The residential zoning of their neighbourhood inspired upward
aspirations: there was 'the brass-knocker zone' to look up to, where
'£200–£300 a year and a lodger could, with care, make both ends
meet . . .'. There was the goal of the villa with 'the Study [which] gives
evidence that already we had in view the great suburban ideal of being
superior to the people next door'. Pretensions to a truly 'middle' class
status were justified 'when a man attains to the privileges of a voter and

23. Reynolds, *A Poor Man's House*, pp. 81–2.
24. C.V. Butler, ed., *Domestic Service: An Enquiry by the Women's Industrial Council*,
London, 1916, p. 35.

ratepayer, when his wife reaches the servant standard, when it comes to living in a dining room, and receiving in a drawing-room [then] pretensions are excusable . . .'. In due course, Thorne's wife 'reached the card-case standard and had her Day'.[25]

In the Suburban mentality, the 'social scale' metaphor was combined with an extremely sharp sense of the dichotomy between manual and white-collar labour and an almost grotesque aversion to social intercourse with manual workers, or to allowing their children to mix with workers' children. The London County Council (LCC) adopted the practice, through scholarships, of sending large numbers of working-class children to the middle-class secondary schools somewhat in advance of the Board of Education's Free Place regulations; this excited an extraordinary declaration of that aversion, penned jointly by Shan Bullock, a solicitor, an employer, an insurance agent, a broker, a journalist and a tradesman. Amongst them, the authors had thirteen school-age children and estimated their total yearly education bill at £195, exclusive of the education rate. The large public schools were 'of course entirely beyond our means. We have, for our boys, to be content with what may be called second-class public schools — Foundation Schools, Grammar Schools, High Schools . . .'. They might have had their children educated at the County Council Schools (or Board Schools, 'to give them their old reproachful name') where girls learnt domestic science and boys 'carpentering, plumbing and other necessary trades . . .'. But they were

> possessed of the most ridiculous aspirations in regard to our children's futures . . . . We confess to sharing the feeling, widely, if not universally, entertained by the middle classes of London, that the Board Schools were never intended to provide education for the children of people like ourselves . . . at the bottom we are too timorous, too superior-minded, too snobbish, ever to think of allowing our children to mix with the children of the lower orders . . . [and] the lower orders are too independent, careful of their rights, imbued with the spirit of class prejudice and hatred, ever to welcome the idea of having their children consort peaceably with the children of clerks and tradesmen. The experiment now being tried of sending large numbers of scholarship boys from the Board schools to the large Secondary Schools is, we fear, none too successful.

They claimed that the Secondary Schools were 'divided against themselves' and that between the scholarship lads and ordinary lads there was 'much antagonism, and hatred'. They heard of scholars taught in separate classrooms and ostracised in play-grounds and concluded 'it would have been better to leave the middle class its Secondary Schools . . . we desire to have our children kept as much to themselves

25. S.F. Bullock, *Robert Thorne: London Clerk*, London, 1907.

as are the children of the classes above us . . .'.[26]

There are many parallels between popular thought and the systematic social sciences and the Suburban conception of the 'social ladder' had its replica in liberal economic theory, as had the Suburban dichotomy between the world of white-collar respectability and the social abyss of manual labour. Admittedly, economists seized on another dichotomy — that of capital and labour — and treated it as, theoretically, a benign, functional relationship. This was particularly true of those who had absorbed 'marginalist' theory. Walter Layton, in a popularisation of that theory, argued that: 'Capital and Labour constitute a mutual demand for one another to co-operate in production, and wages and interest are fixed by their marginal respective net products, which will be great or small according to the relative abundance of Labour and Capital respectively'. Layton, however, envisaged the social structure in which that dichotomy operated as a pyramid of grades between which there was no general 'right of way':

> In this respect the nation is divided up like a many-storied building, of which the lowest floor is thronged with people. . . . The first floor is not quite so over-crowded as the ground floor and the number of occupants in the upper stories dwindles as one nears the top. It is true that there is an educational ladder by which certain fortunate persons are able at the outset of their career to mount from the bottom to one of the upper stories; but the number who are able to do so is still lamentably small. . . . [Consequently] the numbers on any floor of the social edifice are recruited in the main from their own descendants.[27]

In the many-runged ladder paradigm of the class structure the ladder was often envisaged as extending downwards to the lowest stratum of unskilled labour or, more usually, the working class was thought of as having its own narrow ladder which permitted only a restricted upwards movement and led to quasi-hereditary classes within the class. This immobility of labour was authoritatively regarded as a structural cause of unemployment since the social divisions amongst workers were taken to lead to surpluses of unskilled and shortfalls of skilled labour. H.S. Jevons, the labour economist, argued that, to a great extent 'the young labour recruited to any skilled occupation consists of the children of parents who are themselves

---

26. Idem et al., 'The Burden of the Middle Classes', *Fortnightly Review*, Sept. 1906. The authors greatly exaggerated the difficulties within the schools; see the replies from headmasters circulated with an LCC questionnaire in Greater London Council Record Office, Higher Education scholarships sub-committee: 'Reports on county scholars', 16 Feb. 1906, EO/PS/3–3. Nevertheless, Bullock et al. were voicing a widely-held set of prejudices; see, for example, 'Some Danger Ahead', *The Times Educational Supplement*, 6 Oct. 1910.

27. W.T. Layton, *The Relations of Capital and Labour*, London, 1914, pp. 15, 73.

engaged in this or kindred employment'. Because of powerful 'class distinctions' within working-class communities there was 'much difficulty in the passage of sons of an unskilled or partly skilled status to work of a higher wages and status than their fathers . . .'.[28]

The empirical content of this view of working-class social structure and inter-generational immobility is, in fact, questionable (and it is an issue I return to in Chapter 4). None the less, many parallels to it can be found in workers' own social imagery. In a popular study, which has done much to create a new academic orthodoxy as to the consciousness and culture of the prewar working class, Robert Roberts drew attention to the highly stratified form of prewar working-class society and the very parochial notion of 'class' within it.[29] With rather heavy irony, he described the neighbourhood 'class struggle' that would break out into drunken brawling and shrieked abuse that some party and its kindred were 'low class' or no class at all: 'Then one saw demonstrated how deeply many manual workers and their wives were possessed with ideas about class, with some, involvement almost reached obsession'. In this account, the class struggle, 'as manual workers in general knew it, was apolitical and had place entirely within their own society. They looked upon it not in any way as a war against the employers but as a perpetual series of engagements in the battle of life itself'.[30] In many ways, Roberts's view of working-class society harks back to that of contemporary social conservatives, such as Helen Bosanquet, of the Charity Organisation Society, who were wont to explain the localisation of extreme poverty and the social standing of streets by reference to habit of mind: if the lowest class of labour congregated in certain localities it was because common temperament and culture brought them there.[31] In spite of the authenticity and frequent shrewdness of Roberts's observations, they similarly mislead by reducing the well-known economic differentiation within manual labour, derived from market relations of a wider society, to its cultural effect in the neighbourhood. The working-class sense of its own social ladder or social

28. H.S. Jevons, 'The Causes of Unemployment; Pt.ii', *Contemporary Review*, July 1909.
29. R. Roberts, *The Classic Slum*, Harmondsworth, 1973. The American historian, Standish Meacham, acknowledges how heavily he drew upon Roberts for his own study *A Life Apart: the English Working Class 1890–1914*, London, 1977, p. 9.
30. Roberts, *The Classic Slum*, pp. 24, 28.
31. See, for example, H. Bosanquet, 'The local distribution of poverty', *Contemporary Review*, Sept. 1909. She suggested: 'Much is explained by the proverb, "Birds of a feather flock together". . . . A district "goes down" or "goes up", as a whole, because the rich are uneasy in the proximity of working-class neighbours . . . [the same phenomenon] applies again to the streets or "models" where the degraded poor of the lowest type pay exhorbitant rents for the privilege of herding together. They also do not feel at ease in too close proximity to the worker'. C.S. Loch managed to inflate this banality into a 'social philosophy' and a 'social science': see idem, *Charity and Social life*, London, 1910, esp. pp. 386ff.

scale is not in doubt, but to limit working-class social imagery and awareness to this perception is rather one-sided, since it excludes the well-attested solidarism of manual workers and working-class communities and the perceptions they had of non-manual classes.[32] Of course, we have evidence that where working-class people had a highly-graded notion of their own class, then this was clearly displayed to the community in the furnishings of their homes and the greater respectability of certain streets over others. A French sociologist, Paul Descamps, in his well-observed field study of the West Riding, found workers who greatly approved of the style of artisan's dwelling where the front parlour gave directly on to the street, for this revealed the domestic standard of life to the public. The parlour furnishings of sofa, armchairs, large square table, piano and half-glazed dresser were on occasional public view and this gave neighbours the sense of belonging to the same social category and excluded others from this category.[33] The fundamental source of this differentiation lay elsewhere; in the relatively good wages and regular employment of the labour elite of spinners and croppers of the local textile industry.

The notion of the minute gradation of the working class was a commonplace of empirical social observation, but it will already have been apparent from much of the material cited that the 'artisan class' was a crucial category in Edwardian social classification (it was far more commonly employed than the 'labour aristocracy', which may not be irrelevant to the scholarly debate over that concept). Its usage often implied a distinct social cleavage in manual labour which was of a different order than a gradation in a social pyramid. Thus we read in the enquiry into domestic service that 'the town girl who goes into service . . . had been brought up in one of two very clearly marked social classes; the labouring class, for whom the alternative to service is rough factory work . . . [or] the artisan class'.[34] Occasionally, Edwardian social categories carry the implication that the skilled artisans were part of the 'old' lower-middle class of small shopkeepers, innkeepers and so on (as in the remark that voluntary organisations, such

32. On the social solidarism of the urban poor in York, see B.S. Rowntree, *Poverty: A Study of Town Life*, London, 1902 ed., p. 43: 'In cases of illness neighbours will almost always come in and render assistance, by cleaning the house, nursing, and often bringing some little delicacy which they think the patient would fancy'. On the social solidarism of the self-respecting poor in Lambeth, see Mrs P. Reeves, *Round About a Pound a Week*, London, 1914 ed., p. 39: 'A family who have lived for years in one street are recognised up and down the length of that street as people to be helped in time of trouble. These respectable but very poor people live over a morass of such intolerable poverty that they unite instinctively to save those known to them from falling into it. . . . It was not mere personal liking which united them; it was a kind of mutual respect in the face of trouble'. See also Bourne, *Change in the Village*, p. 17.

33. P. Descamps, *La Formation sociale de l'Anglais moderne*, Paris, 1914, pp. 60–1.

34. Butler, ed., *Domestic Service*, p. 74.

as the Women's Co-operative Guild (WCG), 'affect the woman of the shopkeeping and the upper artisan class, rather than the wife and daughter of the labourer').[35] Generally, however, usage underlined that artisans and the artisan class were definitely part of the working class. Descamps, attempting to pin down English usage (and class consciousness) for a French audience, wrote:

> Les *artizans* sont encore des ouvriers, mais ils ont bien le sentiment d'être une élite dans leur classe. Ils sont un peu une classe dirigeante dans la classe ouvrière et ils sentent toutes les responsabilités de cette situation. . . . La petite bourgeoisie, au contraire, ne veut plus être confondue avec la classe ouvrière, et elle préfère être la dernière des classes qui sont au-dessus de celle-ci.[36]

The idea of a directing or commanding elite within the working class rested on the fact that many artisans would have been found in such industries as iron-and-steel, shipbuilding, and textiles where systems of sub-employment and labour contracting gave artisans industrial authority over unskilled labourers and assistants. More important, however, in sustaining the idea of an artisan class was the artisan dwelling, which connoted furnishings and amenities rarely afforded by semi-skilled and unskilled labour. 'Artisan' remained the commonest term for a skilled worker in the postwar period, but one way the homogenisation of the working class was registered was by much less frequent reference to an 'artisan class'. This was one facet of a complex meshing of language with the social processes (described more fully elsewhere) which undermined the privileged position of artisans in the housing market and the authority structure of industry.

## Between Capital and Labour: the Middle Class

A fundamental change in English social consciousness between 1914 and 1920 was the displacement of three-fold class imagery, the social ladder paradigm and notions of the working class as finely graded, by dichotomous conceptions which, whether they were conflict or consensual models, took the social axis to run through the wage-labour market. 'Displacement' should not be taken to imply that they ceased to be used to envisage the social structure; rather, dichotomous images of society became preponderant. They monopolised public discussion,

---

35. C.V. Butler, *Social Conditions in Oxford*, London, 1912, p. 64. E.J. Hobsbawm argues that, in the late Victorian period, the term 'lower-middle class' covered the labour aristocracy of skilled workers and small proprietors: idem, *Industry and Empire*, Harmondsworth, 1969, pp. 155–6.

36. Descamps, *La Formation sociale*, p. 277.

penetrated popular imagery and ideology, and they were an unmistakable sign of the growing public consciousness of the conflict immanent in the social relations of production. Even the idea of civic integration was closely associated with the dichotomous usage — 'the employers and the employed' — adopted by the Whitley Report. This displacement was partly a recognition of the objective changes in the capitalist economy and union organisation for, as Askwith stressed:

> The War . . . tended towards big organisations in both Capital and Labour. In the one case, big organisations had been effected by Government action, in the railways, mines, etc., and by control of shipping, engineering, national factories, etc. They had also been effected by voluntary action, with a view to economy of production and greater efficiency. . . . In the other case [Labour], the equality of wage demands had brought unions together, insurance through approved societies and other agencies already acting before the War had increased their strength . . .'.[37]

Within the Labour movement it was argued that employers as a class had gained enormous political power by the concentration of capital; not only was the identity of their interests expressing itself, by the end of the war, more openly by federation and amalgamation, but the organisation of capital was giving them 'an increasing, if not a determining voice in the policy of the State, and an ever firmer grasp on the machinery of government'.[38]

Paradoxically, one way this change in social consciousness was registered was by attempts to define and reassert the separate identity of the 'middle classes', for the very preponderance of dichotomous images was one reason for the middle class to believe that it was becoming economically and politically marginal. The terrible accident that befell the Liberal party (run over, if we are to believe Trevor Wilson, by the rampant omnibus of the war)[39] was both part of, and reason for, this belief. The Liberal Party of 1914, though electorally sustained by the urban working class, was the political vehicle of the liberal and intellectual professions or, more broadly, the professional middle class. Many Liberals faced the postwar world in peculiar distress of mind. Like Masterman, they saw 'Liberalism . . . dumb and crushed between truculent Labour and equally truculent Capital'.[40] They also believed that the war had had a devastating economic impact on the social stratum most active in Liberalism. Masterman

37. Askwith, *Industrial Problems and Disputes*, p. 470.
38. From the monthly circular of the Labour Research Department, January 1919, quoted in the 'Report on the General Labour Situation of the Demobilisation and Resettlement Branch of the Ministry of Munitions', 25 Jan. 1919. PRO MUN 4/3541.
39. T. Wilson, *The Downfall of the Liberal Party 1914–1935*, London, 1968, pp. 20–21.
40. See Lucy Masterman, *C.F.G. Masterman*, London, 1939, p. 317.

devoted much space to the collapse of the professional middle class's way of life in *England After the War* (1922) and that belief (and its objective content) is examined more closely in the next chapter. Suffice to note here that the eclipse of the political party and the economic decline of the social group were, for him, inextricably linked.

Up to a quite late point in the nineteenth century, 'the middle class' was unambiguously identified with industrial and commercial capital[41] and the image of the class (not uncommon by 1914 and commonplace by 1920) as crushed between labour and capital would have been incomprehensible. Before the image of the middle class as 'crushed' could become part of class discourse, there had to be both immense material change and shifts in the social definitions of the class which tied it to capital. One shift, which corresponded to the reemergence of liberal professionals as the social leaders of civil society, identified the top echelon of the class with the traditional professions. Another, formed partly in response to the Marxian immiseration thesis, identified 'the middle class' with small property, usually in distribution. From the perspective of 1914 it can be seen that contemporary definitions of the middle class had shifted since as recently as the turn of the century. In an article of 1901 on the Labour movement in which he was at pains to refute those predictive elements in Marxism which had forecast the proletarianisation of petty capitalists, J.H. Harley made it clear that he considered them to be the central part of the middle class: 'Statistics show us', he wrote, 'that, to a very large extent the middle class is still holding its own . . . there is, even in your working-class district, a large number of small capitalists who are keenly interested in keeping their little all together'.[42] The growth of 'the clerical class' made consciousness and culture (rather than property) the hall-mark of the middle class. Nowhere is this more evident than in the constant complaint that organisation of clerical and black-coated distributive workers was inhibited by their middle-class 'gentility', 'respectability' and 'snobbery'. The journals of the clerical and distributive unions and their conference records contain a litany reproaching the clerk and shop-assistant for their 'middle-class' consciousness:

'The clerk is perhaps the most typical instance of what may be described as the 'middle-class" worker.'
'The clerk is a kind of social amphibian — middle class in speech and clothes but often lower than the dustman in pay.'

41. Thus Arnold took as 'the happy mean of the middle class . . . [the man who] sums up the middle class, its spirit and its works', Thomas Bazley, the Manchester cotton-spinner and for a time chairman of the Manchester Chamber of Commerce, see *Culture and Anarchy*, p. 90. I am unable to say *when* 'the middle class' ceased to be identified with industrial capitalists.
42. J.H. Harley, 'The New Social Democracy', *Contemporary Review*, November 1901.

'Clerks are, undoubtedly, a most difficult class to organise; they do not, even where they work together in comparatively large numbers, display that spirit of comradeship that is in evidence among other workers.'

'There is no class in existence that is obsessed with this particular fallacy ['respectability'] more than shop assistants and clerks, and it is mainly owing to this particular thing that these two sections of the community are where they are on the social ladder.'[43]

Though this litany corresponded to the many ways in which clerical and service skills were losing their objective market advantages over manual labour, it discounted others that remained: regularity of work and salary increments; the career structure of clerical employment; holidays with pay and payment during sickness; promotion on personal merit. The individualism of clerical workers was, in principle, a rational response to their market situation rather than just a habit of mind that took combination to be *infra dig*. However, since the habit of mind persisted in spite of the many discrepancies with objective economic condition, it provided a minimal social definition of the class:

The middle class are not easy to define, on the one hand it may be a man with an income of several thousands per annum, and on the other a poor clerk with the miserable pittance of one hundred. If one may judge by the pitiable plaints in the columns of the press, all who are not mechanics or artisans hold the view that they come under the category of the middle class . . . a very large proportion of the people who claim to come under the category of middle class are simply salaried workers who ape the well-to-do and have not the wherewithall [sic] to maintain the station they fain would have their neighbours believe they occupy. . . .[44]

We find, in the public discussion of the middle class which took place on the eve of the war, many expressions of a kind of class insecurity which often echo themes in Masterman's analysis of the Suburbans. For example, in a magazine popular amongst lower-middle-class households, a series entitled 'The Searchlight on the Middle Classes' condemned 'middle-class amusements [as] a slavish and cheaper copy of the amusements of the upper ten', berated the middle class for its failure of natality and dismissed middle-class literature as 'fiction dealing almost exclusively with the aristocracy'.[45] A writer in the same

43. These quotations are from the president's Address to the National Union of Clerks' Annual Conference, June 1908 (in *The Clerk*, July 1908); *The Clerk*, May 1910; the President's Address to the 1911 NUC Annual Conference (in *The Clerk*, July 1911); *The Shop Assistant*, 20 Dec. 1913 (an article on 'Respectability'). These are but a tiny sample (though wholly representative) of the clerical union organiser's complaint. See also D. Lockwood, *The Blackcoated Worker*, London, 1958, p. 14 and elsewhere.

44. Editorial in *The Shop Assistant*, 15 Mar. 1919.

45. 'The Searchlight on the Middle Classes — Middle-class Recreations';'. . . Middle-class Parents';'. . . Middle-class Literature', *Cassells' Saturday Journal*, 6 April, 27

journal warned in August 1914 that:

> Society today tends ever to divide itself into two main sections — those of
> Capital and Labour, with a smaller but important section, that of the
> hard-working Middle-Classes between, which runs the risk of being ground
> to powder in the coming impact of the upper and nether millstones of the two
> big sections.[46]

The war heightened this class insecurity in two ways. Firstly, by the
autumn of 1915 the war economy was having a differentiated impact on
the social classes; though manual workers' wage rates lagged behind
the rise in prices, working-class family earnings did not and the
unskilled in particular benefited from regular employment in the
better-paid sectors of industry. Many professional incomes and salaries
fell substantially behind inflation and there were fewer ways middle-
class families could compensate. The emergence of two non-official
charitable agencies — the Professional Classes War Relief Council and
the Professional Classes Special Aid Society — is evidence of the
relative deprivation of families who (as a spokesman for the Council
put it) '. . . have got to live the "simple life" with a vengeance. It
involves among other things a smaller house, less food and clothing,
fewer servants and a cheaper education for our children'.[47] The Council enjoyed a close relationship with the Eugenics Society, for eugenists
looked on professional families as those genetically endowed with the
greatest 'civic worth'. Major Leonard Darwin, a leading figure in both
the Society and the Council, specified in May 1917 what had been done
on behalf of the families of musicians, artists, architects, journalists,
owners of private venture schools, as well as stockbrokers, lawyers and
clergymen 'to prevent a harmful descent from a fairly high standard of
well-being'.[48] Up to Christmas 1916, over £10,000 was disbursed to
help pay the school fees of 617 children and numerous schools had been
persuaded to waive or reduce the fees of children from professional
families.[49] The Professional Classes War Relief Council was, clearly,
but one symptom of the fall in a stratum's living standards which
continued until the peak of the inflationary spiral. With the outbreak of
peace, the class resentment incipient in this was openly expressed as a
hostility towards manual workers and profiteers in a journalistic sub-

April, 4 May 1912.

46. 'Labour's coming Struggle', *Cassells' Saturday Journal*, 1 Aug. 1914.

47. P. Saundeman, 'Problems of Living in War-time', *Charity Organisation Review*,
February 1916.

48. See the *Charity Organisation Review*, May 1917. Darwin was for many years President
of the Eugenics Society. The occupations given are in the order in which professional
people were assisted by the Professional Classes War Relief Council.

49. Ibid.

genre lamenting 'The New Poor', 'The Black-coated Poor' and 'The Despair of the Middle Class'. The language was quite blunt; to give one example from a London suburban: 'Mechanics and labouring folk are looking after themselves. It is as well they are, for our suburb hates them'.[50]

During the postwar period, this resentment focused on the large national pay claims lodged by certain workers who had been greatly strengthened in organisation and bargaining power by the war. During the Shaw Court of Inquiry into the transport workers' wage claim, Ernest Bevin acknowledged that: 'We are accused of demanding these wages at the expense of our fellow workmen, and particularly of the lower middle class'. During the inquiry Bevin engaged in a notable exchange with A.L. Bowley, which testifies to the fluidity and imprecision of contemporary definitions of the middle class, yet articulates the idea of its professional stratum being crushed and suggests the new, relative deprivation of salaried workers' families. Bevin rested his case on the demand for a new standard of life for the transport worker. The employers' strategy was to attempt to hold dock wages to a percentage increase on the minimum needed for a healthy family existence; the latter was arrived at by taking Bowley's prewar estimate and allowing for inflation. Bevin protested that this minimum assumed a scandalously impoverished notion of family life; to make his point he produced a plate of unattractive bacon bits, without vegetables, which had to be part of the working-class family diet if it was to live within the minimum. Bowley commented:

> . . . the recorded observations of working-class life show that this is the kind of food which, in fact, they have, and on which they can be, in fact, adequately fed . . . I do not think it is any serious hardship that there should not be two vegetables every day of the week. It is quite a common thing in middle-class families.
>
> *Bevin*: But they have all sorts of food that the workers do not get?
>
> *Bowley*: Not the middle class.
>
> *Bevin*: What do you describe as 'middle class'?
>
> *Bowley*: For example, the budget that was put in on your side by clerks and shop assistants.
>
> *Bevin*: They are not middle class, are they? They are known as sweated workers, because they are putting a Trade Board down for those trades. Take the shop assistant, whose budget was put in, living in three rooms at a rent of 6/- . . . You would not call him middle class, would you? I should class him the bottom dog.
>
> *Bowley*: The middle class families I should have in mind would be the small

50. The quotation is from 'The Despair of the Middle Class', *The Nation*, 24 Jul. 1920. See also Holford Knight 'The Black-coated Poor', *Contemporary Review*, May 1920; and C.F.G. Masterman, *England After the War*, London, 1922, which drew on extensive journalistic coverage of the 'The New Poor', p. 59 and elsewhere.

professional or clerical families — civil servants, if you like, who have from £400 to £500 a year, and considerable expenses . . . I should very much doubt whether you find that two vegetables for every day in the week is all that common.

*Bevin*: Is not there very great complaint of the tremendous economic pressure from the war profiteers on that class of people at the moment?

*Bowley*: There is.

*Bevin*: Do you suggest because the profiteers have succeeded in crushing the professional classes, that therefore a budget would be provided which admits the crushing of us as well?[51]

The second cause for middle-class insecurity arose from the ostentatious use in wartime of representatives of both capital and labour as government advisers and temporary civil servants. This led to a sense of middle-class political and social interests being ignored, which became acute during the industrial crises of 1919 when the government was engaged in publicly effecting a series of industrial compromises seen as damaging to the interests of the middle-class consumer and traveller. The feeling was crystallised in the Middle Classes Union whose founder complained, at a meeting in Manchester in May 1919, that: 'When Capital and Labour went to Downing Street they were invited into the parlour at once, and soon had the government kow-towing and touching its cap to them . . . [he] was anxious to see a movement which would bring to bear upon the Government the just and due influence which ought to belong to the middle classes'.[52]

The constitution of this body deployed the now customary image of the middle class squeezed between upper and lower classes: 'We are being taxed out of existence. We are being exploited for the benefit of the lower classes or for the benefit of the financial groups and profiteers of the upper classes'.[53] The very existence of a Middle Classes Union led to an extensive, but inconclusive, discussion of whom the middle class were. A maverick Tory MP, Major Pretyman Newman, who was active in the Union, used the sense of being crushed between social antagonists as the defining quality of the class: ' . . . any person [was middle class], whether peer or peasant, who is of opinion that his interest and his liberty are not safe-guarded by organised labour on one side and federated capital on the other'.[54] Pretyman Newman called for a new middle-class solidarity and consciousness to replace the party loyalties which had divided the class before the war. The organisation

51. *Report (and Minutes) of a Court of Inquiry Concerning Transport Workers — Wages and Conditions of Employment of Dock Labour*, PP 1920. Cmd. 936, p. 32, pp. 186–7.

52. The speaker was Kennedy Jones, a Tory back-bencher, one-time Director of Food Economy and a former advertising executive for the Northcliffe Press. See 'The Middle Class. The New Union and its Policy', *Manchester Guardian*, 21 May 1919.

53. Lorthrop Stoddard, *Social Classes in Post-war Europe*, New York, 1925, p. 96.

54. See 'Meeting of the Middle Classes Union in the City', *The Times*, 4 April 1919.

of labour and the federation of capital 'make it clear to the middle-class man that the party rosette, put away in a drawer against the next election, must now be left to the moth'. In the prewar conditions of the 6d income tax, and with the triple alliance of railway worker, miner and transport worker undreamt of, 'the middle interest could afford to split its votes as its fancy led it'. Now, the middle class had to acknowledge its class interest and organise itself as a class.[55]

This rhetoric was an important part of the postwar political ferment and was used by a minority of reactionary but individualist Tories to attack the social, labour and fiscal policies of the Coalition.[56] Something more will be said of it in the context of the changes in income distribution and taxation brought about by the war, for these clearly ensured that there was a large, disgruntled public receptive to such appeals. The language and imagery of the spokesmen for the MCU conformed closely to the social ideology which political scientists identify with the 'extremism of the centre' and fascism.[57] We can suggest a number of reasons why a mass movement never cohered round this ideology: firstly, contrary to popular stereotypes, clerical and salaried employees were not impoverished *en masse* and their numbers were necessary if middle-class populism was to be a serious political force; secondly, the government's financial retrenchment, and the established Conservative party, assuaged and contained middle-class extremism; thirdly, the economic grievances of white-collar and professional workers such as draughtsmen, technical engineers and central and local government officials, were more effectively channelled through white-collar unions and professional associations (some of which affiliated to the Labour movement) than through a purely reactive protest movement such as the MCU. Despite the comparative ease with which the 'extremism of the centre' was contained in England, the war's effects on middle-class ideology were, by contemporary account, considerable. Lorthrop Stoddard, in an American study, stressed 'the growth of middle class group consciousness [in Britain]. . . . Before the war the middle classes showed almost no sense of group solidarity. Their misfortunes during and since the war, however, have roused them to a sense of their numbers and potential strength'.[58]

55. Letter to the Editor of *The Times*, 14 Nov. 1919.

56. See K.O. Morgan, *Consensus and Disunity*, London, 1979, pp. 240ff. Curiously, in an otherwise impeccable discussion, Morgan misses Kennedy Jones's and Pretyman Newman's connections with the Middle Classes Union (as well as Kennedy Jones's association with the Northcliffe press).

57. See S.M. Lipset, *Political Man*, London, 1960, pp. 132–40.

58. L. Stoddard, *Social Classes in Post-war Europe*, p. 94. The author was a prominent American eugenist and 'Nordic' racist, and sympathetic to the European radical right. His book is not without interest however.

## The Capital–Labour Dichotomy

When we turn to the effects of the war on perceptions of the capital–labour dichotomy within the Labour movement and working-class circles, and the relationship of these perceptions to working-class consciousness, then these can only be assessed in the light of the use of that phrase in preceding years. Our knowledge of the way it was perceived by the great mass of the unorganised working class is, predictably, thin. Reynolds argued that before the politicisation of economic and fiscal issues by the Tariff Reform campaign:

> Capital and labour were vague terms, much used in trade-union speeches, but not brought home to each man as things that make a difference to his Sunday's dinner. The working man's view of finance went very little further than the coin that could be handled and changed, and his main idea was, that money must be circulated somehow. . . . The rich were supposed to have done their whole duty if they spent their money freely, no matter how they acquired it, no matter what sources of profit to the community they keep locked up for their own sport and pleasure.[59]

Working men were wont to say that 'the master's got the capital and we haven't and that there wouldn't be no work for us without his capital . . .'.

George Bourne recorded very similar attitudes amongst Surrey villagers and they were fictionalised by Robert Tressell in *The Ragged Trousered Philanthropists* (completed by 1910, published in 1914) in which the philanthropists' gratitude to the capitalist class for providing work and their mockery of Frank Owen's socialist economics are key themes.[60] Reynolds believed that the Tariff Reform campaign had awakened working men, and working-class Tories in particular, to the political importance of economics and led them to look favourably on collectivist, even socialistic solutions to the problems of unemployment and trade depression (albeit: 'The word *Socialist* is still a lump of political mud; handy to throw at any opponent . . .').[61] In Tressell's satire, however, the Tariff Reform agitation had merely confirmed working men in their deluded perception of wealth as a source of work.

Trade unionists of the later nineteenth century — particularly the leaders of the more exclusive craft societies — had seen the capital–labour dichotomy in a way that did not differ radically from the common man's perception of wealth as a source of work. The coming of the Great Depression in the 1870s, and the need to meet keener foreign

59. Reynolds, *Seems So!*, p. 173.
60. G. Bourne, *Change in the Village*, pp. 69–71; R. Tressell, *The Ragged-Trousered Philanthropists*, St. Albans, 1965.
61. Reynolds, *Seems So!*, p. 169.

competition, evoked many avowals of the mutual interests of capital and labour.[62] The Ironfounder's general secretary declared, for example, in 1880: 'We are desirous to be at peace with capital; the two interests capital and labour should work harmoniously together, for they cannot otherwise succeed. . . . We should realise that we have the world to compete with . . .'.[63] This harmonious interpretation of the dichotomy had stout defenders on the eve of the war. In 1913, James Cox, general secretary of the Associated Iron and Steel Workers, rejected the idea that trade unions were fighting organisations and argued: 'Capital and labour, employers and workmen, combined were essential to industrial development, and that both were benefiting by the maintenance of industrial peace and goodwill . . . on the one side capital, organisation, and brains; on the other skill, industry and muscle; both cooperators for the mutual benefit of each'.[64]

The occasion for these remarks is scarcely less revealing than their content, for he was speaking at the annual works dinner of John Lysaght Ltd., when the firm's managing director presided, flanked by officials of the union. The men Cox represented were contractors, or sub-employers paid on a tonnage basis with a reputation for treating their day labourers as 'chattel' and, clearly, disposed to see capital and labour as a functional harmony. The philosophy of John Hodge, leader of the rival and more democratic Steel Smelters' Association (SSA) was very little different. He believed in collaboration with the employers and in accepting technical change, 'provided we got a fair share of the plunder'. Stoppages he condemned because they reduced profits, 'consequently, there must be less to divide between capital and labour'.[65] Hodge was to be a leading public figure in the National Alliance of Employers and Employed, an organisation set up during the war in order to give the harmonious image of the capital–labour dichotomy institutional form (see below, p. 63). Amongst the leaders of the mining unions, there was an equally powerful consensus that the capital–labour relationship was a functional harmony, and acceptance that wages were governed by laws of the market which could not be contravened, and these beliefs were often conjoined with a religious and political solidarity with employers.[66] Robert Moore has shown that

62. See, E.J. Hobsbawm, 'Trends in the British Labour Movement', in idem, *Labouring Men*, London, 1964, p. 320.

63. H.J. Fyrth, H. Collins, *The Foundry Workers: A Trade Union History*, Manchester, 1959, p. 40.

64. See *The Ironworkers' Journal*, November 1913.

65. J. Hodge, *From Workman's Cottage to Windsor Castle*, London, 1931, pp. 91, 69; also H.A. Clegg, A. Fox, A.F. Thompson, *A History of British Trade Unions since 1889*, vol. I, *1889–1910*, Oxford, 1964, p. 206.

66. For a useful summary, see R.S. Moore's contribution in Bulmer, ed., *Working-Class Images*, pp. 36–7.

in the north-eastern coalfield, at least, this consensus was shared by the miners themselves. Class consciousness and socialism were forms of deviance in the pit villages and notions of class and class politics did not begin to gain real currency until the economic crisis of the mining industry during the 1920s.[67] The tardy and reluctant affiliation of the mining unions to the Labour Party, rather than injecting into it the conflict consciousness of 'traditional proletarians', weakened the position of the minority of socialists and brought a cadre on MPs whose political and social imagery owed most to the Bible.[68]

Unquestionably, the industrial consensus expressed in the harmonious image of capital–labour was foundering before the war. About 1910, there was a generational change in British trade union leadership when it appeared that there were no successors to the older generation of moderate leaders, men such as Burt, Fenwick and Mawdsley, and that Victorian theories as to the relations of capital and labour were becoming obsolete within the Labour movement.[69] This change was by no means complete by 1914.

Trade unionists who saw the capital–labour dichotomy as a harmony of interests did not, in their own terms, lack class consciousness, but 'class' connoted for them the forces of privilege and legal conservatism which prevented labour from securing a fair place in the civilisation of industry. The devil in their social thought was not the capitalist class but the judiciary. In this was one source of solidarity of organised and unorganised labour, for hostility to the law, the bench and the police were common to all working-class social milieux.[70] Amongst ordinary working people, the police were seen as servile agents of the 'gentry' or 'the higher ups', charged with 'the enforcement of a whole mass of petty enactments, which are little more than social regulations bearing almost entirely on working-class life. At the bidding of one class, they attempt to impose a certain social discipline on another'.[71] Trade unionists engaged in trade disputes encountered the police and the magistracy as consistent opponents of picketing, even utilising archaic legislation to undermine legal rights to picket. The 1913 Annual Report of the General Federation of Trade Unions (GFTU, a body representative of the most moderate trade union opinion) complained: 'During the year the judiciary has kept before the public eye

67. R.S. Moore, *Pitmen, Preachers and Politics*, Cambridge, 1974, esp. p. 17.

68. Almost fifty of the 142 Labour MPs in the 1922 Parliament had preached on Sundays in churches or at Evangelical meetings and a high proportion of them sat for mining constituencies: see A. Siegfried, *Post-War Britain*, London, 1924, p. 225.

69. This was noted by Askwith in his memorandum to the Cabinet, 'The Present Unrest in the Labour World', 25 July 1911, PRO CAB.37/107 (70).

70. See H. Pelling's chapter on 'Trade Unions, Workers and the Law', in idem, *Popular Politics and Society in late Victorian Britain*, London, 1968, pp. 62–81.

71. Reynolds, *Seems So!*, p. 86.

its apparently irremovable antipathy to trade unionism'.[72]

The prewar industrial unrest reintroduced into the discourse of industrial relations the language and imagery of violent class war. In September 1910 Ben Tillett, the dockers' leader, addressed the members of his union in chiliastic style: '. . . the future is with you, brothers and comrades, in a great battle that must only end with the workers being masters of their destinies and that of their respective countries. We must not rest until the cause of poverty is removed and the abolition of the capitalist system is complete . . .'.[73] At a mass meeting of striking dockers on Tower Hill in July 1912, he virtually parodied the chiliastic style when he called on the assembly to pray to the Almighty to strike Lord Devonport (the leading London port employer) dead[74] (a piece of demagoguery which craft society leaders found deeply embarrassing).[75] The real and rhetorical violence of the period led to a 'power' and 'conflict' interpretation of the capital–labour dichotomy reaching a wider public. Visual representations of Capital as an oppressive force, familiar to socialist readers of the *Daily Herald* and *Plebs*, began to enjoy a wide currency. *Cassells' Saturday Journal*, which was slanted to a lower-middle-class readership of clerks, 'respectable' shop assistants and minor professionals, used as its frontispiece cartoon in August 1912 the picture of a vast, bloated capitalist, whip in hand and cigar in mouth, being hauled to the top of a hill by Lilliputian workmen. At its pinnacle is a dazzling coronet.[76] The image signifies both the compenetration of the capitalist class and the aristocracy and the public notoriety of individual noble employers such as Lord Devonport and Lord Claud Hamilton. The repressive role of the police during the industrial conflicts of the prewar years led, within the workers' press, to visual and literary imagery which linked the traditional hostility to the law with the conflict image of the capital–labour dichotomy. 'The police', wrote a regular columnist in the *Cotton Factory Times*,

> so far from being the servants of the community at large, only serve ordinary people, like ourselves, when our interests do not conflict with the dominant class; but . . . once a struggle between the common people (the poor) and the uncommon people (the rich) is entered upon the police force is the tool of the latter. In other words, the capitalist class and all the machinery of the law

72. Quoted in *Cotton Factory Times*, 27 June 1913.
73. Cited in E. Halévy, *A History of the English People in the Nineteenth Century: the Rule of Democracy 1905–1914*, London, 1934, vol. 2, p. 455.
74. See Bob Holton, *British Syndicalism 1900–1914*, London, 1976, p. 124, for this incident and other examples of Tillett's rhetoric.
75. See the comments of Robert Young, President of the ASE, in *ASE Monthly Journal and Report*, Nov. 1912.
76. 'The Progress of Capital'. *Cassells' Saturday Journal*, 10 Aug. 1912.

summed up as Law and Order are comrades in arms.[77]

However, rather than the class conflict dichotomy of capital–labour replacing the class harmony dichotomy, the two images persisted as alternatives and, with the development of formalised industrial bargaining amongst large sectors of the labour force and the greater organisation of both capital and labour, these alternatives became more clearly delineated. A leader-writer in the *Railway Review* of August 1913 commented that, amongst NUR militants,

> there were two quite obviously conflicting ideals prevalent. . . . These may be conveniently summed up in the two words 'business' or 'war'. . . . the choice of word denotes a whole world of difference in method and mental outlook. . . . Whether we look upon the new programme as a business proposition, to be won by determined effort as the result of methods in which bargaining is to play an important part or as a demand to be held at the heads of the railway companies, like the pistol at the head of a foe and failure to comply with which will be immediately interpreted as a declaration of war to be fought out to the bitter end . . . will colour all our thought and decide all our actions. . . . The evidence that these two conflicting ideals are present in the minds of the rank and file is overwhelming.[78]

The article was almost certainly written by George Wardle, MP, who served on the executive committee of the Labour Party between 1913 and 1919 and edited the *Railway Review* until appointed Parliamentary Secretary to the Board of Trade in August 1917. He made it clear that the image he favoured was 'business' rather than 'war'. In a later passage he explicitly acknowledged the legitimacy of the existing property relations and his willingness to see them altered only through legal process. In this, Wardle was representative of the dominant ideology of the Labour movement. An historian's judgement on the *Daily Citizen* (the newspaper of official trade unionism between 1912 and 1915) has characterised its editorial policy as 'geared to the incorporation of labour unrest into conciliatory forms of protest and pressure, harmonising relations between labour and capital and redirecting energy towards the Parliamentary arena'.[79]

The First World War brought into the open a clash of social

---

77. 'Bruce', in *Cotton Factory Times*, 16 Jan. 1914. The behaviour of the police during the Dublin transport strike elicited considerable working-class indignation. See, *inter alia*, the cartoon in the *Railway Review*, 12 Sept. 1913, depicting a giant constable, his truncheon dripping with blood, captioned 'The capitalists' tool in the attempt to crush Trade Unionism'.

78. 'Business or War', *Railway Review*, 22 Aug. 1913.

79. R.J. Holton, 'Daily Herald versus Daily Citizen, 1912–1915: the struggle for a Labour daily in relation to the Labour unrest', *International Review of Social History*, vol. xix, 1974, pt. 3.

consciousness in the Labour movement which divided the leaders of
'business' trade unionism from socialists. It did not arise because
socialists (or at least the majority of them) differed from trade unionists
over their attitude to the class struggle. The functional interpretation of
the capital–labour dichotomy and organismic views of society of union
leaders were complemented, rather than contradicted, by a form of
socialism indebted to evolutionary social theory and echoing Liberalism in the rejection of class as a dynamic of political action. As Ramsay
MacDonald protested in the course of a public controversy with a
Liberal intellectual: '. . . the explanation of historical change by the
operation of class conflicts has been more emphatically and categori-
cally denied by the British Labour Party than by similar parties in any
other country. It has not entered into the political programme of the
party; it has no part in its manifestoes. The party has never made a
class appeal'.[80] Socialists of his persuasion saw the Labour Party, its
policy and programme as standing for a higher ideal of humanity to
which social class divisions were inimical. The uneasiness between
trade unionists and socialists resulted, at least partly, from a cultural
antipathy between trade unionists whose normative framework was
*ouvrièrisme*, or a social solidarism of manual labour and socialists who
were distrusted as 'intellectuals', abstract theorisers and 'faddists'. As
the socialist societies became refugees for radicalised bourgeois politicians, so this antipathy became more acute.[81]

*Ouvrièrisme* was a form of class pride with which most working-class
families could identify for it was linked to the solidarism with which the
respectable poor met the precariousness of their daily lives and it was a
defence against the blatant aversion of the non-manual classes to social
intercourse with workers. This class pride was strengthened by the
war. A sectional patriotism of the workers was not antagonistic to a
larger patriotism and, with the greater prestige of manual labour in
popular stereotypes, the demands for productivity and a public rhetoric proclaiming the war a war of industrial producers, the two patri-
otisms could feed on each other. We find the most explicit expression of
this class pride amongst men (and their representatives) who were at
the centre of working-class chauvinism, opposed moves towards a
negotiated peace and who also broke with the Labour Party over the
1918 Constitution 'on the ground that it gives the so-called intellectuals
a chance of getting inside the . . . Party and moulding its policy and
dominating its activities. They allege that it does this to the detriment

80. J.R. MacDonald, 'The "Corruption" of the Citizenship of the Working Man: A
Reply [to Prof. Henry Jones]', *Hibbert Journal*, vol. 10, 1912.
81. See R. McKibbin, *The Evolution of the Labour Party 1910–1924*, London, 1974, p. 90;
see also M. Cole, ed., *Beatrice Webb's Diaries 1912–1924*, London, 1952, p. 132, on 'the
undercurrent of mutual antipathy between leading trade unionists and leading ILPers'.

of the "real worker", the worker who takes off his jacket and performs what is commonly known as manual labour'.[82]

At a conference called in August 1918 to discuss the formation of a purely trade union Labour Party, George Milligan of the Dockers' Union argued that

> with the opening of the gates of the Labour party to all and sundry the *bona-fide* workers did not know where they were. They did not want middle-class or higher-class ladies to come and tell them what to do, or theorists like Mr H.G. Wells or Mr Bernard Shaw. The time had come when they ought to start a pure trade unionist Labour Party.

At the same occasion, Havelock Wilson (whose seamen's union had prevented Labour delegates sailing for Russia in May 1917) averred that he 'never knew a trade union which was a success where the working man had to depend on the intellectual'.[83] This minority break-away movement from the Labour Party was based on a comba-tive class-awareness which was at the same time content with the subordinate position trade unionism had secured in industry and the state. Identical sentiments could certainly be found amongst the majority who remained within the Labour Party; at a special conference convened in West London in February 1918 to consider contesting the Hammersmith constituency, the Party's National Organiser referred to the 'tendency on the part of prominent men in the Labour party to think [it] was big enough . . .'. From the floor, a trade union delegate said 'they felt very distinctly that it was about time that they were represented in Parliament by a real Labour man . . . one who had gone through the hoop, knew what it was to go short, and to have a bath in a wash-tub . . .'.[84]

Class pride, such as this, provided a moral reserve on which workers drew both in their daily lives and in industrial conflicts, such as the General Strike, where the working class was on the defensive. It was a mentality constantly reproduced within the working-class way of life until the dissolution of that culture in a period outside my purview. The war did far more, however, than merely encourage a sectional patriotism which was already deeply engrained in working-class life and organisations, for it linked this moral strength to a popular contempt for those who did well out of the war. Hostility to profiteer-ing, and the demand for equality for sacrifice, helped fuse working-class solidarity to a 'conflict' interpretation of the capital–labour

82. From the editorial in *Cotton Factory Times*, 2 Aug. 1918, on responses to the new Labour Party constitution in the Labour movement.
83. For a record of the conference, at which fifty trade unions with branches in Lancashire and Cheshire were represented, see *Cotton Factory Times*, 9 Aug. 1918.
84. For a report of the conference, see the *West London Observer*, 15 Feb. 1918.

dichotomy.

We can best begin tracing this shift in the language and imagery of class through the public debate on the reform of industrial relations that arose from the specific labour problems of the wartime economy and the wish to utilise wartime experience in the reconstruction of postwar society. From mid-1916, there began to appear what became a huge wartime literature on reconstruction, the largest part of which was written by those whom P.B. Johnson has termed the 'reconstructionists', a group of predominantly radical liberal persuasion convinced that a great era of reform was imminent.[85] They provided much of the intellectual force for the large programme of reconstruction planned by Addison and his colleagues in the Ministry of Reconstruction after that was set up in July 1917. The primary emphasis of their thought was, as Johnson remarks, 'postwar industrial cooperation — as a good in itself, as a cherished hope, and as a simple functional necessity — which precluded equally a reconstruction based on industrial autocracy or on class triumph'.[86] By 1918 they pinned their hopes for the reform of class society on the devolution of functions, authority and status to new voluntary organisations, the Whitley Councils, which were seen as the key to industrial peace. Although proposals for the institutional reform of industrial bargaining predated 1914, the war brought a major rhetorical change because it was said to have instilled a much greater willingness to sacrifice; above all it was held to have created a new unity, transcending class differences, and a 'new vision of fellowship' that might 'transform class antagonism into class alliance'.[87]

The idea of the wartime industrial truce being made the basis for a new and permanent 'alliance between employers and employed' was first publicly enunciated by Neville Chamberlain, then Lord Mayor of Birmingham, to the September 1916 Trades Union Congress. Chamberlain warned the TUC that the postwar peace would be a period of exceptional difficulty, with unemployment resulting from demobilisation and the revival of intense international economic competition. To meet these difficulties he suggested that employers and workmen should come together to see whether they could not make arrangements to enable them to take place, both in the international competition and in the industrial order, to which they believed they were entitled.[88] The implication of Chamberlain's speech was that workmen should exchange, *en permanence*, their trade practices for higher pro-

85. P.B. Johnson, *Land Fit for Heroes*, Chicago, 1968, Chap. 12.
86. Ibid., p. 220.
87. W.C.D. Whetham, *The War and the Nation*, London, 1917, p. 114, quoted in Johnson, *Land Fit for Heroes*, p. 229. See Johnson for a lengthy catalogue of such sentiments.
88. See *The Times*, 5 and 6 Sept. 1916 for reports of his speech.

ductivity, a greater share in the distribution of wealth, regular and highly-paid employment and reasonable subsistence in the event of unemployment. The atmosphere of hostility and suspicion in which industrial negotiation was conducted could, he believed, be cleared 'if trade union leaders were occasionally admitted to the councils of employers and allowed to see a little bit more of the game from the inside'. The response by Harry Gosling, the TUC president, was not unfavourable. 'We are tired', he said 'of war in the industrial field', and asked whether it would not be possible, after the war, 'for the employers of this country . . . to agree to put their businesses on a new footing by admitting the workmen to some participation, not in profits but in control?' He certainly did not conceive the encroachment on control in any revolutionary sense for he added: 'We workmen do not ask that we should be admitted to any share in what is essentially the employer's business'.[89]

Chamberlain's initiative led to the founding in December 1916 of the National Alliance of Employers and Employed, the first of the wartime organisations which attempted to give the spirit of comradeship institutional form in industry. It was formed initially to deal with the problems of demobilisation and, on the employers' side, the newly-founded Federation of British Industries claimed credit for its organisation while the conservative and patriotic trade unionist W.A. Appleton, secretary of the General Federation of Trade Unions, was most active in promoting it amongst organised labour. Within a year nine trade unions were officially represented and local committees of the Alliance had been established in about a dozen provincial industrial centres.[90] Affiliated labour organisations included the Iron and Steel Trades Confederation (whose leadership was, as we have seen, closely identified with the spirit of capital–labour harmony) and the Sailors' and Firemen's Union, led by the extreme jingoist Havelock Wilson. Amongst Labour adherents, there was a considerable cross-membership with the British Workers' League and both organisations attracted those industrial Labour leaders whose political attitudes combined a distrust of middle-class intellectuals, pacifists and socialists with class collaboration in industry.

Coincidentally with the September 1916 TUC, a Committee of the British Association under A.W. Kirkaldy, presented the first of its reports on capital–labour relations and its proposals, which included

89. *The Times*, 5 Sept. 1916.
90. See 'Report on Labour in Great Britain, November 1917', dated 15 Nov. 1917, PRO MUN 5/56 300/108, for an account of the work and programme of the Alliance; also 'Memorandum on the Foundation of Industrial Peace', by A.M. Paterson, read at a meeting of the National Alliance of Employers and Employed,? April 1918 and the report of the ensuing discussion, MUN 5/51 300/45.

the setting up of permanent boards or committees to consider all matters of common interest to employers and employed, as well as joint national boards to which local boards could refer unsettled disputes, foreshadowed those of the Whitley Committee on the Relations of Employers and Employed.[91] The class-conciliatory overtures of Chamberlain and Kirkaldy's Committee were coolly received in the industrial press. The ASE's *Monthly Journal* remarked that

> generalisations about the essential unity of interest between capital and Labour are not new, are not helpful, and, at present, are not even true. If the proposals which will eventually crystallise out are in the direction of real responsibility and real control a little courage may take us a long way; on the other hand, we are better as rank outsiders than as poor relatives occasionally admitted to the drawing room.[92]

Successive issues of the *Railway Review* gave considerable space to Chamberlain's speech and the BA report; the first asked 'Can the Leopard change his spots?' and though it conceded that there was 'genuine desire amongst the best of the employing class for a truce in the industrial field after the war' added that 'we cannot accept the supposition that the class struggle had ended . . .'. The second was more receptive to the already considerable public debate on the reform of industrial institutions which had begun with Chamberlain's speech; it sensed that: 'The balance of forces [in industry] is changing. There is growing an inversion of the parts which Capital and Labour have hitherto played in their own and the country's development'.[93]

The BA Committee had warned that:

> An insidious element of friction threatening to develop into class war has been sapping our energies. . . . The separation of employers and workmen in ordinary life has led to a wide divergence in their ideals and points of view. Class consciousness exists amongst both, and the effect of this can only be mitigated by greater contact with each other and by free discussion of matters affecting both.[94]

There was a similar warning in the first of the memoranda on the industrial situation published by the Garton Foundation in October 1916. It referred to the 'prevalent belief that "the brotherhood of the trenches" and workshops . . . will remain a permanent factor in our national life', and warned that this fraternisation was but a 'temporary alliance between different parties and different classes similar to that

---

91. A.W. Kirkaldy, ed., *Labour, Finance and the War*, London, 1916.
92. *ASE Monthly Journal and Report*, October 1916.
93. *Railway Review*, 6, 13 Oct. 1916.
94. Kirkaldy, *Labour, Finance and the War*, pp. 3, 40.

frequently effected between states . . .'. The idea that the united front shown to the external enemy 'implies of itself the burial of class hatred and suspicion and that the suspension of controversy during the war foreshadows the cessation of industrial disputes after the war, is dangerous just because it is so attractive'. The memorandum argued that class consciousness and conflict were being injected into the capital–labour relationship by wartime industrial changes and were manifested on both sides of the dichotomy: they took the form of labour discontent which was no longer exclusively a matter of wages and hours, but 'is based to a very large extent on *status* and social conditions' [original emphasis]; and, on the opposite side, the desire of reactionary employers to use the Military Service Acts, the state control of war industries and the temporary abandonment of trade union restrictions 'to establish once and for all the ascendancy of Capital over Labour'.[95] Amongst the memorandum's catalogue of working-class grievances, the resentment of restrictions on industrial mobility and the operation of the disciplinary munitions tribunals were of first importance. As another commentator expressed it at the time, workers felt that they were experiencing the 'advance draft of a possible servile state'.[96] The terms 'servility', 'serfdom', 'helot class', even 'slavery' were frequently used to record workers' reactions to the Leaving Certificate regulations and the disciplinary powers embodied in the Munitions of War Act.

The fear that the war was, in spite of the infusion of the rhetoric of 'comradeship', actively promoting class polarisation led the government to expedite the proceedings of the Whitley committee and to circulate its first report amongst the witnesses to the Commission of Enquiry into Industrial Unrest. The causes and the course of the strikes which led to the setting up of this Commission are discussed in a later chapter; here I wish to dwell on the terms and social imagery of the working-class response to the attempt to establish a new consensus in industry. J.T. Murphy, the Marxist theorist of the Shop Stewards' Movement, condemned both the Whitley Report and 'the vested interest' of trade union officialdom which had divorced industrial negotiation from the interests of the rank and file and sought class collaboration in industry. Murphy thought it was 'nothing short of hypocrisy and cant to assert that there has been "co-operation of all classes"', for capitalists had not renounced the rights of property to profit or of management to coerce; nor were human relations in industry those of social equals: 'Why do men dodge behind machines and in lavatories to smoke whilst the employers can and do stroll through the shop smoking cigars, etc.?' The talk of the 'mutuality of

---

95. Garton Foundation, *Memorandum on the Industrial Situation after the War*, 1916, pp. 8–10, 28–9.

96. J.H. Harley, 'The Conscription of Industry', *Contemporary Review*, May 1916.

interest' of employers and employees became most clamorous, he claimed, when there was a shortage of labour. 'The war period brought accidentally to the organised workers an accession of power not known before in its [sic] history, and it has been accompanied by the loudest song about 'mutuality' we have ever heard.'[97] By contrast, none of the trade union bureaucracies who where circulated with the details of the Report were opposed to it in principle (although half of the mining unions were lukewarm) and in the building and printing trades and the pottery industry employers and employed were already at work establishing Joint Standing Industrial Councils when the Whitley Report was published.[98] Many trade union leaders, including extremely cautious men such as J.R. Clynes, put a far more radical interpretation on the industrial change that would flow from the Whitley proposals than the Committee intended or employers would tolerate. Clynes intimated that 'the manner in which [the workman] is to be treated, hours, wages, conditions of employment, relations between section and section, and working division, all those things which were regarded previously as the private monopoly of the foreman or manager' would, with the implementation of the Whitley proposals, 'become the common concern of the workmen collectively, and they must have some voice in how these things are to be settled'.[99]

In spite of the widespread endorsement in principle of joint consultation, and the optimism of men such as Clynes, there was an entrenched scepticism within the Labour movement as to the reality of an industrial consensus which the reconstructionists took for an achieved fact.[100] Ernest Bevin, for one, questioned whether 'the utter disregard of the workman as a human unit in society' had been much altered by the wartime truce. As trade union leader of workers' deputations to employers during the war, he had often been struck by the different treatment meted out by the employer to the workmen on the deputation and to the union representative:

97. J.T. Murphy, *Compromise or Independence: An Examination of the Whitley Report*, Sheffield, 1917.

98. See the Report by the Minister of Labour on the attitude of employers and employed to the Whitley Report, 26 Sept. 1917, PRO CAB 24/27, GT 2176.

99. See J.R. Clynes's contribution in D.H.S. Cranage, ed., *The War and Unity*, Cambridge, n.d., pp. 126–7.

100. There was, too, a difference between endorsing the principle of joint consultation and actively promoting the formation of Consultative Committees. In February 1919 it was noted: 'The Whitley Councils have been well advertised, but they have failed to win the support even of old-fashioned conservative trade union leaders', in General Labour Situation Report (provided by the Intelligence Department of the Ministry of Munitions, 3 Feb. 1919) PRO MUN 4/3541. The most penetrating analysis of Whitleyism remains Elie Halévy's 'La Politique de Paix Sociale en Angleterre', 1919, repr. in *L'Ere des Tyrannies*, Paris, 1938, pp. 95–137.

[the] workman often enters in a state of fear that his action in representing his fellows, although appointed by them, will lead to his dismissal. . . . How can there be a truce while one side practices an attitude of dominance to enforce servility by the other?. . . . The servility of the working class must be relegated to the limbo of the past.[101]

Before there could be any peace in industry, he argued, certain fundamental principles had to be admitted — such as the right of labour to control its conditions of employment, the adjustment of payment on the basis of relative instead of subsistence wages and the regulation of industry to prevent unemployment — which went quite beyond the modest proposals for joint consultation put forward by the Whitley Committee. Bevin's most outspoken attack on the meretricious (as he saw it) character of the industrial consensus was made at the February 1919 National Industrial Conference. He opposed a resolution moved by Lloyd George to set up a Joint Committee of industrialists and union leaders, arguing that the Conference had been called 'to sidetrack the efforts of the men and women who are struggling for better conditions at this moment . . .'. His experience, 'with all this good feeling, whether on Trade Boards or in Whitley Councils, [was] that the leopard had not changed his spots. It [was] as big an effort now to get a bob or two for your workpeople as ever it was, and no Labour leader . . . [could] deny it'. He then turned to attack Seebohm Rowntree, a leading figure amongst reconstructionists, who had recently published *The Human Needs of Labour*, which set out a new poverty line:

I met that gentleman in conference this week. He told us that it took something over 30/- to keep a woman and yet he refuses to pay his workpeople more than 28/- . . . I have never yet convinced an employer. I will tell you what has convinced him — the economic power of the Unions we represent and no other weapon. . . .[102]

Although Bevin failed to dissuade his fellow union leaders from supporting Lloyd George's resolution, he articulated (as was officially recognised) a suspicion of joint consultation which was shared by at least a large minority.[103] (There were recalcitrant sceptics amongst the rank and file as well. Rowntree suffered another rebuff in 1919 when a worker at one of his own factories told him: 'If you want me to speak straight, I'll speak straight. All these councils, where we workers sit around a table with you, we know it's nothing but the last dodge for

101. E. Bevin, 'The Reconstruction of Industry', *The Athenaeum*, May 1917.
102. See the Minutes of the Proceedings of the National Industrial Conference, 27 Feb. 1919; copy in PRO MUN 5/52 300/78.
103. See the Report on the Labour Situation, 5 Mar. 1919, PRO CAB 24/76 GT 6948.

picking our brains, and getting a bit more money out of us!')[104]
Moreover, though in a minority on this specific issue, the mode and
style of Bevin's address, the way he articulated the material claims of a
class and the separate indentity of that class, make him highly representative of the consciousness and diction of the Labour movement.

In a later chapter, I discuss the complex effects of the war on
working-class consciousness and here I merely wish to emphasise how
consciousness was both manifested and changed by the growing stock
of imagery after 1915 which depicted Capital as immoral and predat-
ory. The first revelation of excess profit-making in the spring of 1915
reintroduced into everyday speech the term 'profiteer' and induced in
working-class circles a feeling that the capitalist class had betrayed the
social truce of August 1914. The rapid rise in the cost of basic foodstuffs, partly attributable during the early months of the war to panic-
buying and hoarding by middle-class consumers, added to the indignation. For a particularly clear expression of it, we can turn the debate on
a resolution protesting the rising cost of living at the Railway Clerks'
Association 1915 Annual Conference. Mr Ridley, for the executive,
declared that the revelations of profiteering 'can only be regarded as a
grave indictment of our commercial classes for their breach of faith and
their general class selfishness'. He concluded that if the war had served
no other good purpose, it had 'at least revealed and emphasised the
selfishness and immorality of modern capitalism'.[105] In the Labour
press, the profiteer was vividly depicted as 'The Vampire on the Back
of Tommy' and the 'Brit-Hun', and the 'contrast [between] the conduct of the workers who had toiled in the industries so necessary for the
successful prosecution of the war [and] the conduct of shipowners, food
exploiters, war contractors, and other profiteers who had scrupled at
nothing so long as it secured their enrichment' became a basic theme of
Labour rhetoric.[106] It is true that 'the profiteer' was excoriated in the
middle-class press quite as vehemently as he was by working-class
representatives and, furthermore, the detestation of 'the profiteer' by
Labour arose as much from an affront to its patriotism, as it did from
latent class consciousness, and the victim of capital was seen as the
patriotic community no less than the working class. But the effect of the
'profiteering' scandal amongst organised workers was to realert them
to the antagonistic character of capital–labour relationships. Askwith
wrote that there was no greater cause for the waning of working-class
patriotism than

104. B.S. Rowntree, 'Labour Unrest and the Need for a National Ideal', *Contemporary Review*, November 1919.
105. See the Conference Record in the *Railway Clerk*, July 1915.
106. See, *inter alia*, the *Railway Review*, 16 June 1916. The quotation is from Gosling's Presidential Address to the 1916 TUC; see *The Times*, 5 Sept. 1916.

the fact that some people were making money out of the War without any restraint upon their methods. . . . A shipowner who stated that he had made profits, was going to make profits, and had a right to make profits, did more harm than a great naval defeat would have done. To name 'defeat' would rouse the nation to set their teeth and fight against an alien foe. The profiteer's statement would rouse class against class, and only tend to disruption within the nation itself.[107]

When the USA entered the war in April 1917, its officials were warned of the growing 'tendency [in Britain] to revert to the pre-war method of industrial warfare' and the most important of the factors producing this was 'the gradual awakening of the workmen to the fact that their employer is profiting from the war . . . of all the factors that have been contributing to the difficulty in handling the labour problem in this country, the most formidable has been what has been called "Profiteering by Contractors"'.[108] The government's Commissioners of Enquiry who reported on London and the south-east Area recorded that: 'Statements of prices ands profits in the newspapers, admissions made in Parliament, [the workmen's] own source of information and their personal and family experience make them feel, to use their own language, they are "being bled white"'.[109] Their colleagues for the Yorkshire and Midlands Area reported a general 'conviction that insufficient steps had been taken by the Government departments to prevent profiteering, exploiting and plundering, such as make the poor contribute heavily to the abnormal advantage of those traders and others, who by their selfishness secured immense gains from the sacrifices and sufferings of the poor'.[110]

The Commissioners for the south-west Area argued that the techniques of war finance had undermined the moral consensus of the early period of the war:

> We have committed a serious mistake in making excess profits duty the corner-stone of our war taxation. This tax does not take money out of the rich man's pocket in the same way that direct tax on his income would have done, and it has consequently failed in its moral effect on the working classes as a symbol of equality of sacrifice.

Witnesses in the south-west had insisted on the contrast between the common soldier, compelled to serve at a shilling a day , and the *rentier* who voluntarily lent his capital to the government at an inflated rate of

107. Askwith, *Industrial Problems and Disputes*, p. 372.
108. See 'Notes on Labour Problems in Wartime' (being a copy of a Memorandum which Mr Garrod took with him to the USA . . .), PRO MUN 4/3335, 21 Apr. 1917.
109. PP 1917, Cd. 8666, p. 2.
110. PP 1917, Cd. 8664, p. 2.

interest.[111] Even where, as in the north-east, the Commissioners reported that wartime labour relations had on the whole been cordial, and employers evinced considerable sympathy for the social aspirations of labour, this cordiality was disturbed by 'the widespread belief that persons other than the working classes are making undue profits out of the war'.[112]

Earlier, I cited evidence to the effect that in prewar working-class social imagery, wealth was looked on as a source of work and the working man's view of finance was governed chiefly by the idea that money must somehow circulate. Certainly, these notions were profoundly shaken by the popular resentment of ostentatious wealth which was a significant feature of the prewar labour unrest, but the war completely disrupted such conceptions. Six out of the seven reports on industrial unrest in England and Wales speak of 'bitter resentment amongst workers at the thought that someone is making an excessive profit out of them'[113] (or adopt very similar terms). A scarcely less consistent theme is resentment of the contrasting experiences of the rich and poor: 'Better-off people can buy anything they require while the working classes must want'; 'the belief among the working people is that the rich people receive [sugar] and the poor do not'; a Canon Peter Green from an industrial parish in the north-west of England asked: 'Can we wonder that with growing education and intelligence, the workers of England are beginning to contrast their lot with that of the rich and to ask whether so great inequalities are necessary?'[114] Contemporary comment recognised the links between the ability to draw strong contrasts in life experience and the language of class. The *Manchester Guardian* warned in August 1917 that the contrast between such 'substitutes' as war-bread and sterilised tuberculous flesh for the poor 'with luxury foods still available for the rich cannot but encourage "class consciousness" and plays into the hands of those who preach "class war"'.[115] It must be emphasised that these were not the direct causes of wartime strikes and the effects of the war on working-class consciousness were much more complex than a change in the social imagery of wealth and profit. However, references to the resentment of war profiteering in social comment (and claims that it was 'poisoning the mind of the working classes')[116] are too frequent not to take that feeling for a social fact and this fact represents a striking change in

111. PP 1917, Cd. 8667, pp. 5–6.
112. PP 1917, Cd. 8662, p. 11.
113. These words used by the Commissioners for the West Midlands Area, PP 1917, Cd. 8665, p. 9.
114. See Cd. 8662, p. 3; Cd. 8663, pp. 11, 15.
115. *Manchester Guardian*, 4 Aug. 1917.
116. See, *inter alia*, 'The War Profiteers', *The Nation*, 9 Feb. 1918.

working-class social imagery. Furthermore, by the later stages of the war, when the dominating influences on everyday life-experience were universal conscription, the concentration of men's employment in productive industry, food shortages and inequalities of distribution, the interpretation of society in terms of sharp dichotomies was a characteristic feature of social comment. The *Co-operative News*, representing a hitherto apolitical organisation that drew much closer to the Labour movement because of the war, wrote of: 'Conscription at a shilling a day for the private soldier; excess profits for the manufacturer and dealer. Suppression for the workers' papers; license for the Harmsworth press; tall prices for producers; queues for consumers. Imprisonment for strikers; autocracy for a War Cabinet of Three'.[117] In the working-class movement, the 'conflict' or 'power' image of the capital–labour relationship subsumed many of these dichotomies.

## Class Imagery and the Language of War

That 'conflict' image, which Wardle had before 1914 summed up in the word 'war', became more powerful by being suffused with metaphors and allusions drawn from the bloody struggle in which Britain found herself. Obviously, the whole area of labour relations was particularly prone to dicussion in military terms and these had, for example, coloured the writing of G.D.H. Cole before the war.[118] But as the war progressed commentators of all shades of opinion learnt the vocabulary of modern warfare and borrowed it for the analysis and description of social conflict. They found parallels between the division of the international order and the capital–labour dichotomy. The *Railway Review* commented on the conclusion of the Triple Industrial Alliance in December 1915:

> The position of the Labour movement is gradually reaching the stage which was occupied by the European nations just before the war. Both Capital and Labour are becoming highly organised and face each other with their forces raised as far as possible to the highest perfection of pitch and power. . . . Theoretically the new alliance is based on the same assumption as the balance of power in Europe.[119]

Lloyd George used the arms race analogy when he addressed the first of the postwar conferences of representatives of employers' associations

117. *Co-operative News*, 26 May 1917, quoted in S. Pollard, 'The Foundation of the Co-operative Party', in A. Briggs and J. Saville, eds., *Essays in Labour History*, vol. II, London, 1971, pp. 185–210.
118. G.D.H. Cole, *The World of Labour*, London, 1913, p. 285.
119. 'The Pursuit of Power', *Railway Review*, 17 Dec. 1915.

and federations and trade unions. On the same occasion a leader of the building trade unions suggested that the prime minister was 'asking for an armistice from the organised workers of this country'.[120] During the industrially troubled postwar years, some of the key terms of the real war of attrition became the commonplaces of industrial relations: a minimum wage movement was 'the bid push', contending parties in industrial disputes were advised to 'stand down', 'unconditional surrender' was demanded of strikers, and so on. The 'conflict' image was made sharper by being juxtaposed with reconstructionists' belief that from the common enterprise of the war could be derived the moral precepts for a new social solidarity: Rowntree argued that the war had encouraged men to see the possibility of 'a new kind of class distinction, founded upon the value of an individual's life to the community' but this was obscured by the fact that 'at present, employers and workers often resemble two regiments, which are not quite clear as to whether they mean to fight each other or a common enemy! Group prejudice and misunderstanding were never perhaps more rife . . . .'.[121]

The event which did most to bring the 'conflict' imagery of industrial relations before a huge public was the 1919 railway strike. A *Times* leader demanded that 'this like the war with Germany, must be fought to the finish' and it was recalled by an emerging Labour politician as: 'The first occasion when the Government took the field against a body of workers with all the paraphernalia of Press propaganda and military preparations'.[122] The conduct of the strike testified to the 'discovery' of 'public opinion' during the war, the refinement of techniques of public persuasion by press, poster and film propaganda, and government's new role as a creator of opinion.

However, the war had led to such novel techniques of destruction and persuasion that their example continued to inspire metaphors and analogies in industrial relations long after their return to 'normality'. In April 1921, for example, the Amalgamated Engineering Union (AEU) likened a pamphlet circulated by the Engineering and National Employers' Federation to 'the most dangerous of the poison gases used in the late war'.[123] By contrast, Philip Kerr, Lloyd George's secretary, when in correspondence with the Prime Minister during mid-1921, drew upon the memory of wartime class harmony and the success of

120. See the Minutes of a conference with representatives of the Employers' Association and Federation and trade unions, 13 Nov. 1918, PRO MUN 5/31, 300/93.

121. 'Labour Unrest and the Need for a National Ideal', *Contemporary Review*, November 1919.

122. See A. Hutt, *The Post-war History of the British Working Class*, London, 1937, p. 26; A. Greenwood, 'The Labour Crisis: A Labour View', *Contemporary Review*, July 1922.

123. AEU Pamphlet, 'Some Comments on "The Economic Position of the Engineering and Allied Industries"', April 1921. The AEU was attacking a press circular put out by the Engineering and National Employers' Federations.

wartime productivity drives when suggesting solutions for a situation
in which 'capital and labour are fighting like blazes to-day for the
distribution of a bone which does not exist'. What was needed was 'a
manifestation of the trench spirit in that most difficult of all matters,
where £.s.d. comes in'[124] (what he had in mind was the working class
accepting large-scale wage reductions and, at the same time, increasing
its productivity). But as the memory of wartime social solidarity
retreated, and the failure of the attempt to establish the machinery for
harmonising class relations in industry became patent, the reconstructionists' vision of the harmonisation of class interests was recalled
in come circles with sardonic disillusionment: Arthur Shadwell, the
economist, told Stoddard:

> The war was generally expected to lead straight into a sort of Utopia, in
> which the lion would lie down with the lamb. . . . There was no substance in
> this sanguine vision; it was simply a nebulous hope, born of war-excitement
> and fed by politicians' phrases . . . such as the blessed word 'reconstruction'.
> I can remember no such prolific begetter of nonsense as this idea of
> 'reconstruction'.[125]

The reconstructionists were themselves forced to admit that the dominant image of the capital–labour dichotomy in the postwar years was
itself evidence of their failure to bring about the industrial cooperation
on which their hopes had rested. Rowntree complained:

> So long as we accustom ourselves to the idea that industry is merely a
> scramble, and that everyone is trying to see what he can get out of it for
> himself, so long shall we continue to use such phrases as 'Capital is on top',
> or 'Labour is on top', phrases which imply a perpetual conflict. It is this
> conception of industry that we must change if the Labour Problem is to be
> solved. . . .[126]

That conception was greatly reinforced by a rhetoric of industrial
warfare, which, in its acerbity, could only be likened to the orches-
trated hate between warring nations. Henry Clay, one of the most
knowledgeable students of industrial relations during the 1920s, lamented the fact that:

> The strike, which should be the type of pacific passive resistance, takes on

---

124. Kerr to Lloyd George, 18 May 1921, House of Lords Record Office, Lloyd
George Papers, F.334/2/1. The Kerr–Lloyd George correspondence during the summer
and autumn of 1921 testifies very vividly to the preoccupation of the ruling elite with the
capital–labour dichotomy and the great influence of the wartime experience in shaping
responses to industrial conflict.

125. Quoted in Stoddard, *Social Classes in Post-war Europe*, p. 61.

126. B.S. Rowntree 'The Labour Problem', *Contemporary Review*, April 1923.

the temper of war and invokes the methods of war propaganda. . . . The opponents in the recent dispute in the mining industry spoke of each other in terms reminiscent of the war propaganda that in England was directed against Germany and in Germany against England; they did not think of each other as fellow-countrymen in a difficulty for which in the last resort neither was responsible.[127]

## Conclusions

It would be false to give the impression that the simple class dichotomy of capital and labour entirely replaced the discussion of class in terms of working (or lower), middle and upper classes. Indeed, because of the tendency to 'read off' political parties as the representations of social classes, some commentators took the three-party system of the early 1920s as a clear expression of the three-class structure:

> . . . if [before the war] the division of Church and Chapel or of upper and middle class was the chief factor giving reality to the two-party system, then the division of upper, middle and lower class should, it might be thought, provide sufficiently strong and enduring support for the newly emerging tripartite system . . . [for] there is no weakening in the social and economic differentiation upon which the three-class division rests.[128]

Furthermore, much contemporary discussion of class in the immediate postwar years focused on the disappearance of the traditional agrarian elite, the decline of established notions of social honour and the domination of 'Society' by an *arriviste* plutocracy which had made its money by munitions contracting and smart investment in the war loans. Some of these themes will intrude on the discussion of the war's impact on the distribution of wealth and income. However, the capital–labour dichotomy came to serve, between 1911 and 1920, as a first point of reference in class discourse. It was a change in social consciousness that began before the war but was palpably quickened by the war. One feature of that change was an altered conception of the 'social problem' and the working class (it is particularly evident in Rowntree's journalism). Before 1914 the social problem was still dominated by the problem of poverty, and though poverty was itself recognised as a detailed social hierarchy, 'the poor' and 'the working classes' were interrelated terms. When writing on the industrial unrest of 1911, Rowntree argued that the first and principal reason for it was low wages. By 1919, 'organised labour' and 'the working class' were

127. H. Clay, *The Problem of Industrial Relations*, London, 1929, p. 210.
128. P.J. Hughesden, 'The Future of the Party System', *Sociological Review*, vol. 18 1926.

interrelated terms and, though low wages continued to be a central concern of Rowntree's journalism, the social problem was seen as capital–labour conflict.[129]

With these changes in class imagery there occurred a change in the use to which the word 'class' was put. As we have seen, it was often used before the war to refer to exclusive ranks within manual labour and this usage was frequently linked to elaborate spatial metaphors likening society to a many-runged ladder. This usage and these metaphors were far less frequent in the social comment of the postwar world. To this degree, therefore, there took place something of a convergence of popular usage and ideology with radical value systems. It was, after all, a complaint of Marxists in 1909 that popular usage diverged deplorably from Marxist concepts (see p. 37) and this complaint could not have been made so forcibly by the end of the war.

We may conclude that the contending ideas of class polarisation and civic integration (with its language of 'community', 'citizenship' and 'a new status for labour') were mutually clarifying. The war certainly revealed the possibility of social harmony and a classless society but, in the disenchantment of peacetime, this itself was conducive to an image of a more deeply divided society. This editorial on 'the Class War' from the Transport and General Workers' Union (TGWU) journal, written during the depths of the postwar depression, illustrates how the tangible steps towards industrial conciliation and workers' representation, which had been inspired by wartime unity, could themselves sharpen the image of a conflict dichotomy:

> The war of today is not a war between armies, equipped upon a basis of equality, but a war between an impoverished multitude, physically weakened and mentally distressed, against a handful of well-fed financiers and captains of industry. . . . Goodwill, cooperation, were to become the order of the day, Whitley Councils, Joint Industrial Councils, Courts of Inquiry and Arbitration — all were to be the instruments by which lock-outs, strikes and industrial disputes might be avoided. The class war was to be completely eradicated from our social system. . . . What a sardonic mockery. . . . [now] demands for reductions, for increased hours, are always in the form of an ultimatum.[130]

129. See B.S. Rowntree, 'The Industrial Unrest', *Contemporary Review*, October 1911, and compare with 'Labour Unrest and the Need for National Ideal' and 'The Labour Problem', *Contemporary Review*, November 1919 and April 1923.

130. Editorial on 'The Class War', TGWU's *The Record*, July 1922.

# 3

## Income, Wealth and Social Class in England 1914–24

### Introduction

The precise relationship between the distribution of income and wealth and social class is not easy to specify, but it seems entirely reasonable to claim that the proportions into which the national income is divided and the distribution of wealth play an important function in binding the class structure over time. Social classes are not income groups; as I argued in the introductory chapter, they arise in the first instance from the different relationships different individuals enjoy *vis-à-vis* the capitalist market. None the less, income and its disposal are clearly very significant in making classes identifiable socio-cultural entities which persist because of a marked measure of intergenerational immobility. The differentials between the major types of incomes (from wages, salaries, property, professional fees) reflect the inequalities of class but also reproduce them through time, for they establish a pattern of 'unequal life chances' which is, in effect, quasi-hereditary.

Furthermore, income distribution has an important bearing on the relationship between consumption and the mentalities of class. Comparable income levels within the different classes allow for those common styles of life whose social acknowledgement is a basic component of class awareness. They translate economic roles into social positions recognisable by such items of consumption as housing and (for the early-twentieth-century middle class) domestic service and independent education for one's children. The disruption of the socially basic differential between wages and middle-class incomes (a common feature of periods of inflation) tends to threaten common styles of life and heighten class consciousness, particularly for the middle class. Sometimes the inflation which erodes standards is directly attributed to allegedly excessive wage demands ('greedy workers'); sometimes the greater resistance of wages to inflation is attributed to collective organisation ('the might of labour'). Both these — crudely delineated — responses testify to the greater salience of class division and antagonism in the social consciousness.

Clearly, these relationships between income, consumption and mentalities have been painted with a broad brush. They need to be qualified by the recognition of hierarchies of distinctive styles of life within both the middle and the working class and the fact that inflationary pressures create antagonisms between competing groups of manual workers (a matter discussed in a later chapter). The plurality of middle-class styles of life can be illustrated in historical detail by reference to D'Aeth's paper on 'Present Tendencies of Class Differentiation', published in 1910, which we have no reason to believe anything but an accurate assessment of the pattern of income and consumption in prewar England.[1] D'Aeth argued that 'the present class structure is based upon different standards of life. There may be said to be in theory two standards of life — the standard of simple necessities, and the standard of refined and educated necessities. The former can be secured for an average family on about 25/- a week; the latter on about £600 a year'.

This huge divide roughly corresponded with working-class and middle-class styles of life. Within this division D'Aeth put forward a sevenfold classification. The first three classes (A,B,C) were the broad strata of manual labour; casual workers; the semi-skilled; artisans and foreman. I will not repeat the details of his analysis of their income and styles of life here. Above these (class D) he identified what could appropriately be termed a social 'buffer zone' between the working class and middle class. This was an occupationally-varied social group on incomes of about £3 a week which included clerks, shopkeepers, tradesmen, commercial travellers, printers and elementary school teachers. If they were shopkeepers, they usually lived above the shop. Otherwise they were paying rent of £25 to £30 a year. Customarily, they furnished their houses and entertained visitors. Some had a young servant. They were usually educated at elementary school, though were occasionally technically qualified.

There is strong inferential evidence that this class D was disproportionately recruited from the working-class strata and that intergenerational movement from classes B and C to D was, in aggregate, the most important form of mobility in pre-1914 England. The evidence comes chiefly from the estimate made by the British Association for the Advancement of Science of the rapid growth in numbers, between 1880 and 1910, of those with incomes not assessed to income tax and not generally classed as wage earners.[2] In 1910, there were 4.053 millions so classified. In 1880, the comparable group of 'intermediate incomes' was between *ca* 1.5m and 2.2m. During the thirty years up to 1910, the

1. F.G. D'Aeth, 'Present Tendencies of Class Differentiation, *Sociological Review*, Oct. 1910. For a more extended discussion of the prewar class hierarchy which drew on D'Aeth's paper, see P. Descamps, *La Formation sociale de l'Anglais moderne*, Paris, 1914.

2. BAAS, *Report of the Cannan Committee on the Amount and Distribution of Income (other than Wages) below the income tax exemption limit in the United Kingdom*, London, 1910.

occupied population increased by 39 per cent and if the group on 'intermediate incomes' had grown at the same rate, it would only have reached a total between 2.1m and 3.0m. Bowley concluded that 'a population has been drawn from the manual working class into the ranks of independent workers, shop assistants, clerks, teachers and other occupations where many of the salaries are small . . .'.[3] A truer comparison, which compensated for price inflation between 1880 and 1910, was with the group on incomes up to £225 per year in 1910, and this comparison was even more suggestive of a rapidly expanding 'buffer zone'. As Bowley stressed, 'if it is presumed that the income-tax paying class has as a group of families contributed less than the average to the growth of population, there would appear to be a greater flow out of the manual working class than [the figures] suggested . . .'.[4]

Above the 'buffer zone', D'Aeth identified three classes (E,F,G) which represented 'the fluctuation round the second theoretic standard' (i.e., that requiring £600 a year). Class E had a style of life which demanded an annual income of £300. House rents on this standard were about £48 a year. The occupation of its members included various forms of business, small manufacturing and the professions. Social customs ran to formal visiting and the leaving of visiting cards, and dining late. The class was educated at grammar-school and showed such refinements of manner as avoiding provincialisms in speech. Its sons were typically selected as clerks in 'good-class buildings' such as banking and insurance. Class F — which D'Aeth termed 'Professional and Administrative' — had a style of life which demanded an annual income of £500. Houses, if rented, would be between £60 to £80 rental. The occupations of its members included heads of business firms, the professions and administrative posts. They had generally been educated at secondary or public schools and universities. D'Aeth's final class, G, he called simply 'the Rich' and it had a standard which demanded an annual income of £2,000 and upwards. Before 1914, very few incomes of that magnitude were derived from employment in any socially meaningful sense; the great majority arose from the ownership of wealth in such forms as real estate, domestic and foreign investments, government securities and privately controlled enterprises.

The purpose of this chapter is to assess the impact of the war on the distribution of income and wealth and to interpret the influence of such changes as there were on social class structure and mentalities. Socio-economic change within the working class is dealt with separately elsewhere. My interest here lies, firstly, with the changing differentials between income from manual labour, salaried employment, rent and

3. A.L. Bowley, *The Change in the Distribution of the National Income*, Oxford, 1920, p. 12.
4. Ibid.

profits and, secondly, with the extent to which the economic and fiscal consequences of the war brought about a more equitable distribution of wealth and made its accumulation more difficult. One preliminary methodological necessity is to determine the prewar trends in income and wealth distribution so that the specific consequences of the war can be isolated from long-term historical tendencies. Three trends are particularly noteworthy: the first, already mentioned, was the disproportionate growth of 'intermediate' incomes; the second was the checking, after about 1900, of the rise in real wages as a result of inflation and the sharp fall, after 1909, of wages' share in the national income; the third was the steady accumulation of wealth which indicates that economic inequality was increasing before 1914.

From 1880, real wages rose rapidly in Britain, advancing by some 40 per cent in fifteen years, and reached a temporary maximum in 1895–6. For the next twenty years, they oscillated about that maximum, with (it must be stressed) considerable differences in the degree of fluctuation in different industries.[5] Between 1902 and 1909, the cost of living rose fairly gently, by about 4 to 5 per cent, and between 1909 and 1913, much more rapidly, by nearly 9 per cent.[6] Though wages did increase, they generally lagged a few points behind inflation. Between 1904 and 1913, the upward movement in wages was about 9 per cent and in retail food prices about 12 per cent.[7] Were wage earners as a class becoming absolutely poorer? Bowley argued that they were not since, he claimed, changes in the occupational structure were increasing the numbers in better-paid jobs. The occupational immobility of mature workers meant that this structural change principally benefited the new recruits to industry:

> The vast majority of men below the military age at the beginning of the war began adult working life after 1896, the date of lowest prices, and throughout their experience as householders have found prices rising against them, and having chosen their occupation have not benefited by that part of the increase in average wages which is due to the shifting of the rising generation to better-paid work.[8]

Here, surely, was the underlying cause of the prewar wave of industrial unrest. The optimistic gloss Bowley placed on the consequences of changes in the occupational structure should be treated with some

5. Idem, *Wages and Income in the United Kingdom since 1860*, Cambridge, 1937, pp. xiii–xiv; idem, *The Change in the Distribution of the National Income*. For the fluctuations between different industries see J.W.F. Rowe, *Wages in Practice and Theory*, London, 1928, p. 8 and elsewhere.

6. Bowley, *The Change in the Distribution*, p. 19.

7. Idem, *Prices and Wages in the United Kingdom 1914–1920*, Oxford, 1921, p. 97.

8. Idem, *The Change in the Distribution*, p. 20.

scepticism. The proportion of the GNP accruing to wage-earners fell
from 38 per cent in 1900–9 to 34.5 per cent in 1910–14, one of the
sharpest downward movements in the national income accounting
series between the later nineteenth century and the Second World
War.[9] The optimistic gloss would be justified only if there was an
equivalent contraction in the proportion of manual wage-labour in the
total occupied population. Though some did occur (more in women's
than in men's employment) it was insufficient to compensate for
manual wage-labour's declining share of the national income. Falling
prices between 1913 and the outbreak of war,[10] combined with advances in major trades, did something to relieve the day-to-day economic
struggle which, for some years, working-class families knew they had
been losing. None the less, in August 1914, the majority of adult
workers were securing a standard of living for themselves and their
families significantly below that prevailing at the turn of the century.

The impact of economic adversity on social consciousness and class
conflict was magnified because the present position was judged not
only relative to better times past but to other, more fortunate, groups.
Capital was accumulating rapidly in the prewar economy and income
from its profits was being consumed in increasingly visible ways. One
measure of the growth of wealth is the tax statistics which can be
earmarked to income from investment. In 1890/1, the gross income
assessed under Schedule D in the income tax returns upon public
companies was £123.68m. It rose to £219.797m in 1900/1 and
£302.835m in 1910/11.[11] That this increase was not due simply to the
conversion of private businesses into public companies but largely
represented a genuine growth of capital can be shown by the fact that
there was no decrease in the gross income from private returns. Other
forms of investment were proving no less profitable: after 1897 there
took place a rapid rise in the return to be secured by the purchase of
high-class fixed interest securities.[12] Not all new capital was owned
directly by individuals, for much was accumulating in the hands of
municipal corporations, insurance companies and other institutions.
Personal wealth was, however, being flaunted and advertised in new

9. C.H. Feinstein, 'Changes in the Distribution of the National Income in the United
Kingdom since 1860', in J. Marchal and B. Ducros, eds., *The Distribution of National
Income*, London, 1968, p. 119.

10. A.L. Bowley, *Prices and Earnings in Time of War*, London, 1915, p. 1, notes a steady
fall in prices after March 1913.

11. These figures are given in the memorandum drawn up by the Inland Revenue for
the Chancellor of the Exchequer, 'The Growth of National Wealth', 17 Sept. 1912, PRO
IR64/20. The Inland Revenue found other indications of the steady growth of wealth in
the capital subscriptions in London and other markets.

12. This was noted by G.R. Askwith in his memorandum to the Cabinet, 'The Present
Unrest in the Labour World', 15 July 1911, PRO CAB37/101 (70).

ways. In the twenty years before 1914 there was a great expansion in the size and number of very large fortunes, much of the new wealth being derived from overseas investment, particularly in South Africa.[13] At the same time, there was a quickening of the process by which a plutocracy of finance capitalists, shipowners and industrialists displaced the landed gentry and aristocracy as the dominant element in the upper class. This shift was associated with a novel degree of conspicuous consumption which altered the whole tone of 'Society', undermining the moral authority the wealthy needed to secure the acquiescence of the masses in a regime of extreme inequality. G.R. Askwith, the Liberal Government's Chief Industrial Commissioner, drew attention in his analysis of the industrial unrest to the fact that the 'more extravagant of the doings of the wealthy classes secure a publicity of ever wider extent through the agency of the cheap newspaper . . . this publicity of private luxury may not be without importance [in generating workers' discontent]'.[14] Most evident of the forms of 'visibly greater expenditure on luxury' (to use Bowley's words) was the motor car; in a week it testified to 'wasteful and arrogant expenditure over several counties, while an equal sum spent on carriages and horses would have a much more limited effect'. Bowley doubted whether the wealthy, as a class, were getting richer (recent scholarship indicates they were) but concurred that wealth appeared to be 'passing into the possession of persons who enjoyed ostentatious expenditure'.[15]

## The Contemporary Sense of Change

The most illuminating point from which to begin an analysis of the impact of the war on the distribution of income and wealth is with some of the highly-coloured descriptive evidence which, though of little value as an objective measure of material change, graphically illustrates the heightening of class consciousness by the disruption of the pattern of income distribution and customary styles of life. In the aftermath of the war, many sensed that its financial burden and the inflationary impact of the wartime economy had borne disproportionately on the intermediate social strata (particularly the professions) and landed pro-

13. W.D. Rubinstein, *Men of Property*, London 1981, p. 41: he also notes the reaching of a plateau among all fortunes above £100,000.

14. Askwith, 'The Present Unrest in the Labour World'.

15. Bowley, *The Change in the Distribution*, pp. 20–1. For a different contemporary view to Bowley's, see L. Chiozza Money, *Riches and Poverty; 1910*, London, 1913 ed., esp. p. ix. Rubinstein notes that Money's calculations have stood the test of time: see *Men of Property*, p. 56.

prietors, groups who, together, were often taken to be the patriotic, socially disinterested backbone of the nation. They, it was felt, had paid an unequal toll in both blood and money during the war and their plight was contrasted with the immoral gains of war profiteers and the high wages of truculent labour. Charles Masterman voiced these sentiments in his melancholic survey of *England After the War* (1922). The system of land-holding was, he claimed, being transformed by enormous taxation:

> . . . smaller squires went first . . . passing from the homes of their ancestors to the suburbs or dingy flats of London or the villas of the salubrious watering-places. Then came the outraged cry of the owners of large historic estates, proclaiming that with the burden of income-tax and super-tax, and the fall in the value of securities, and the rise in the price of all estate necessities, they also would be compelled to relinquish the gigantic castles and houses which have been the pride of the countryside for hundreds of years. Their property perished in battle, no less than their children.[16]

Alongside the vanishing aristocracy '. . . the Middle Class is engaged in a struggle, and seemingly a losing one for the bare maintenance of any semblance of its acquired standard of life'.[17] There followed a highly-coloured depiction of 'the influence of the war and of the rise in prices in the slow disintegration and decay of [the] whole standard of civilisation of Middle-Class England . . .'. The value of savings had been halved in the inflationary spiral, domestic servants dispensed with and private education foregone. Taking his evidence from the correspondence columns of 'a great London newspaper', Masterman instanced as typical of the new middle-class poor, the man who had supported a wife and three children on a salary of £250 in 1914 and now earned £300 and supported his wife and five children. Other correspondents told of 'the maid long since gone' and domestic help reduced to the weekly charwoman. 'This Middle Class' — Masterman concluded — '. . . from the clergyman or Civil Servant or medical man at the top to the small shopkeeper or the clerk . . . at the other end of the scale, is being harassed out of existence by the financial after consequences of the war.'[18]

Mrs C.S. Peel, in one of the early social histories of the war, was equally convinced that 'the English middle class, who form such a satisfactory core to our Society, are passing through a very bad time',[19] although her tone was less doom-laden. The most striking changes in the middle-class way of life in her account were the reduction in

16. C.F.G. Masterman, *England after the War*, London, 1922, p. 34.
17. Ibid., p. 24.
18. Ibid., pp. 57, 58–9, 67.
19. Mrs C.S. Peel, *How We Lived Then*, London, 1929, p. 192.

domestic service and the lowering of housing standards. 'Prior to 1914', she claimed,

> it was almost unheard of for people of some position and possessed of incomes which ran into hundreds to inhabit part of some one else's house, a custom which has now become general, [or] to live in mews in the quarters formerly occupied by coachmen and chauffeurs. . . . Commodious houses were then inhabited by families who could afford to employ a staff sufficient to keep them in order. The large houses in superior residential districts of London or of other cities appeared what they were, well-kept private residences, for but few of them had been converted into hotels, boarding-houses, flats and 'open-flats'. . . .[20]

Houses, which before the war were rented for £30 per annum, were now unobtainable to young middle-class married couples (although the legal rent on such property would not have risen above £42) and couples were forced to buy modest housing at the cost of annual repayments of some £70. For other commentators, such as the eugenic propagandist Dean Inge, the most insidious consequence of the socio-economic changes was racial deterioration for they were an added inducement to middle-class family limitation.[21]

Bowley's summary account of the economic consequences of the war contains a sober echo of these strident voices. Wartime and postwar inflation, he argued, had had a particularly adverse affect on 'elderly members of the middle-class whose investments were completed before 1913, usually at a fixed rate of interest [and] there [had] been a visible fall in the standard of living of the professional classes'.[22] The more senior civil servants, for example, on salaries of £500 in 1914, experienced a drastic decline in real income since salary increases of only 42 per cent by 1922 were inadequate to meet a cost of living that had doubled.[23] Purchasing power had been transferred from certain types of stockholders, notably prewar railway investors, to sections of the labour force, such as railway workers. Similarly, purchasing power had been transferred from landlords to their working-class tenants, as a result of wartime rent control. The disparate impact of inflation, the much higher levels of taxation and the deteriorating market situation of the great landlords of prewar society had, in combination, reduced 'the number of the rich, defined as those who had £10,000 to spend . . . in 1914 and the equivalent amount in 1925 . . . from 4,000 to 1,300'.[24]

20. Ibid., p. 5.
21. W.R. Inge, 'The Future of the English Race', Galton Lecture of 1919, publ. in *Outspoken Essays*, London, 1921, pp. 98–9.
22. A.L. Bowley, *Some Economic Consequences of the War*, London, 1930, p. 77.
23. Ibid., p. 155; Bowley stressed the narrowing of income differentials in the Civil Service. For further remarks on this point see p. 91.
24. Ibid., p. 138.

These impersonal forces had, Bowley argued, brought about a considerable redistribution of the ownership of capital.

These opinions and judgements date from the 1920s when the
contrasting of pre- and postwar styles of life was a reflex action in the
public consciousness of the mature population. It brought a novel
dimension in time to class consciousness by establishing a universally
acknowledged historical bench-mark against which relative changes in
condition could be measured. There was, in this reflex action, a civilian
equivalence, doubtless less intense but more diffuse, to the cleavage in
experience and historical consciousness that resulted from trench com-
bat. The divisions of society were seen, not just in terms of the present,
but by contrast with those prevailing before the war, as — for ex-
combatants — life would be remembered before and after the trenches.

When we focus more closely on the outbreak of peace then the
resentment of the economic advances made by labour and of the
disruption of social norms is still more evident. It induced a new sense
of middle-class solidarity which expressed itself in a determination to
pursue class interests with the same ruthlessness perceived in capital
and labour. Resentment of the working class was hardened by the
beliefs that working men were evading taxation and that the new
industrial and political strength of labour as a class made the government reluctant to increase the tax level on manual earnings. Some part
of this complex of feelings was expressed negatively in, for example, the
financial crisis experienced by voluntary organisations closely identified with the ethic of social disinterestedness of the prewar professional
middle classes. The 50th Annual Report of the Charity Organisation
Society's Council implored its readers in revealing terms in March
1919: 'DO NOT HOLD BACK your generous support of former years
because of strikes and rumours of strikes. . . . You who are hard hit by
taxation and high prices, think of those who are knocked over all
together'.[25] Some part was manifested positively in the formation in
March 1919 of the MCU by Kennedy Jones, a skilled publicist who
had worked on Harmsworth's *Daily Mail* and been employed as wartime Director-General of Food Economy (a post whose sole duty was
the promotion of the middle-class virtue of thrift). Jones argued that, if
they combined, 'the middle-classes . . . had co-operative powers for
their protection not less potent than . . . organised workers', although
his suggested boycotts of taxis and gas services by middle-class con-

25. *Annual Report of the Council of the Charity Organisation Society for 1917–18* (publ. 1919),
p. 4 (original capitals). The COS underwent a severe financial crisis in the latter part of
the war and the postwar years and experienced a crippling shortage of voluntary
workers. These difficulties are attributable partly to the economic consequences of the
war for the social stratum of 'professional urban gentry' from which volunteers were
drawn.

sumers now seem comic witness to consumer powerlessness.[26] One specific object of the Union was to see that the government extracted income tax from manual workers, another to restrict the out-of-work donation. It also voiced opposition to nationalisation and demanded cuts in public expenditure and taxation. The Union became part of the reserve army of social order on which the government counted in preparing emergency transport arrangements; though its numbers were not known with certainty 'there is no doubt that its members belong to the classes who would be only too anxious to help the Government in the event of industrial unrest'.[27]

The complex of sentiments which lay behind the Union's formation was evident at the highest levels of state and was a perceptible influence on the government's intervention in industrial conflict. In February 1919, William Sutherland wrote to the Board of Inland Revenue from 10 Downing Street asking for a statement showing the increase in the Income and Super Taxes during the war years. The information was to be deployed by Lloyd George in a speech on the 'labour question' in the House of Commons: 'One of the points I should like to be shown', wrote Sutherland, 'if as we believe it is borne out by the facts, is the very large proportionate increase in burden thrown on the middle and richer classes. It may be an argument in relation to the continual demand from Miners, Railwaymen, etc for increases on their pay'.[28] A few days earlier, a Colonel Douglas Dawson of the Lord Chamberlain's Office complained to Austen Chamberlain (who had just returned to the Exchequer): 'So much has been done recently for the so-called working classes, that the majority of them not being subject to direct taxation have profited by the war, while the small percentage of the Community directly taxed pays for it. . . . the condition of the salaried official, especially if he owns property however small, is rapidly becoming desperate'. The unprecedented levels of taxation seemed, to the Colonel, 'the first step in legalising Bolshevism'.[29]

## The Redistribution of Personal Income

How closely did these perceptions accord with the objectively measur-

26. See *The Times*, 4 Mar. 1919, reporting a speech by Kennedy Jones calling for the setting up of the MCU; for a report on the progress of the Union, see *The Times*, 26 Apr. 1919.
27. See 'Industrial Unrest Committee: Reorganisation of Emergency Transport Arrangements', memorandum to the Home Secretary by Maj. Baird, 17 Jul. 1919, in PRO CAB27/59.
28. Sutherland to Hamilton, 3 Feb. 1919, PRO IR64/34. Sutherland was head of Lloyd George's secretariat.
29. Dawson to Chamberlain, 22 Jan. 1919, PRO T172/970.

able redistribution of income and the real changes in the economic differences between social classes? There are considerable methodological pitfalls in the way of answering questions of that kind, as was shown in Titmuss's admirable study of income distribution and social change in another historical context.[30] Our knowledge of the distribution of incomes comes to us in terms of individual incomes, although the more socially meaningful units are family or kin group incomes. A true assessment of the altering differentials between social classes cannot be made without considering demographic change and the changing ratio of adult workers to dependants. The contraction of the wealthy upper class, which struck Bowley and others, may have been in reality the wider dispersion of wealth amongst rich families by more frequent gifts *inter vivos*, other family settlements and trusts, and such tax-avoiding measures as the creation of 'one-man companies'. There is certainly evidence, referred to later, of the increasing use of these devices. Moreover, while the measurement of the effects of new levels of taxation on net incomes is straightforward, assessing the long-term consequences of wartime government borrowing from its own wealthy citizens (the chief instrument of war finance) is not. War finance created an increasingly profitable field of new investment which compensated some *rentiers* for the loss of overseas investment income and the decline of domestic stock.

A start can be made in unravelling these complex issues by comparing estimates of the overall distribution of the national income between persons both before and immediately after the war. The distribution of national income in the United Kingdom in 1910 was calculated by Bowley, whose table is reproduced below (Table 3.1). This excludes undistributed income (such as company profits held in reserve) and makes no allowance for evasion but is a highly authoritative estimate. Is it possible to estimate and compare the distribution for the immediate post-war period? The Board of Inland Revenue's 64th Annual Report does show the approximate distribution of income above £130 (the post-1916 tax exception limit) during 1919/20 and, taking account of the rise in the cost of living, we can estimate the share of comparable income groups (Table 3.2). No reliable data on incomes below £130 per year in 1919/20 exists and I have used J.C. Stamp's estimate that there were thirteen million of these incomes, averaging £100.[31] On 1 June 1920 the official cost of living index stood at 250 per cent in relation to July 1914 and this figure has been used in calculating comparable income levels.[32] No allowance has been made for inflation between

30. R.M. Titmuss, *Income Distribution and Social Change*, London, 1962.
31. Given in J. Wedgwood, *The Economics of Inheritance*, London, 1929, p. 40.
32. N.B. Dearle, *An Economic Chronicle of the Great War for Great Britain and Northern Ireland*, London, 1929, p. 316.

**Table 3.1.** The distribution of personal incomes in the UK, 1910

| | Size of income £ | No. of incomes | % of no. of incomes | Aggregate value of incomes (£m) | % of total value of incomes |
|---|---|---|---|---|---|
| **A.** | under 160 | 18,850,000 | 94.52 | 1,055.0 | 56.357 |
| **B.** | 160–700 | 880,000 | 4.41 | 250.0 | 13.355 |
| **C.** | 700–5,000 | 200,000 | 1.00 | 415.0 | 22.167 |
| **D.** | 5,000–10,000 | 8,143 | 0.04 | 55.05 | 2.941 |
| **E.** | 10,000–20,000 | 2,903 | 0.0146 ⎫ | 39.1 | 2.089 ⎛ |
| **F.** | 20,000–45,000 | 1,026 | 0.005 ⎬ 0.012 | 29.0 5.181 | 1.549 ⎨ |
| **G.** | 45,000 and over | 327 | 0.0016 ⎭ | 28.9 | 1.543 ⎝ |

*Source*: A.L. Bowley, *The Change in the Distribution of the National Income 1880–1913*, 1920

**Table 3.2.** The distribution of personal incomes in the UK, 1919–20

| | Size of income £ | No. of incomes | % of no. of incomes | Aggregate value of incomes (£m) | % of total value of incomes |
|---|---|---|---|---|---|
| **a.** | under 400 | 20,057,000 | 96.43 | 2,546,044 | 70.98 |
| **b.** | 400–1,750 | 642,270 | 3.08 | 479,279 | 13.36 |
| **c.** | 1,750–12,500 | 94,098 | 0.45 | 361,684 | 10.08 |
| **d.** | 12,500–25,000 | 4,247 | 0.02 | 74,749 | 2.08 |
| **e.** | ⎫ | | | | |
| **f.** | 25,000+ ⎬ | 2,385 | 0.01 | 125,423 | 3.50 |
| **g.** | ⎭ | | | | |

*Source*: Board of Inland Revenue's *64th Annual Report*

1910 and 1914, in the belief (voiced by Bowley and others) that the official index exaggerated somewhat the effective rise in prices by neglecting substitutions. The neglect of prewar inflation should be accounted for by the bias in the official index. It must be stressed that the second table is a far less authoritative estimate, because of the uncertainty about the number and amount of low incomes and the probably greater level of tax evasion.

What does comparing the two tables show us? The increase in the share of the lowest incomes is striking, as is the sharp decline in the numbers above the equivalent of the prewar tax level; they fell from 5.48 per cent to 3.57 per cent of total numbers. The changes at income level B–b are surprising: fewer people were securing the postwar equivalent but their share of total incomes remained constant; individuals within this income range were presumably better off. The fall in the numbers of those receiving incomes which, before the war, afforded the social style of the upper-middle and upper class (D'Aeth's classes F and G) is very marked. The calculation, however, conceals the doubling in the number of incomes between £5,000 and £10,000 (from 8,143 to 16,720) which can be taken as a measure of those who profited from the war.[33] Broadly, the comparison confirms the impression given by descriptive sources. It must be stressed that Table 3.2 represents a brief point in time when the redistributive effects of inflation were most favourable to wage earners and the lower-paid amongst the salariat; real wages rose until June 1921 when they turned rapidly downwards.

A number of sources confirm that the pyramid of income distribution was still significantly flattened, as compared with pre-1914, during the mid-1920s, in spite of the reversals in manual earnings during the 1921–3 depression. That which demonstrates it most clearly is the Board of Inland Revenue's 'Report on National Income', printed in 1929 but not published.[34] The Board established the declining share of the biggest incomes by this method: it estimated that in 1913/14, there were about 1.175m income tax payers, of whom 16,000 (A) enjoyed incomes of £5,000 and above, 45,000 (B) individuals had incomes between £2,000 and £5,000 and 1.114m (C) had incomes between £160 and £2,000. Allowing for population growth, the corresponding layers of individuals in the year 1925/6 would have been 17,000 (A), 47,000 (B), 1.181m (C). In 1925/6, these three 'wealthy' layers were receiving a substantially reduced share of total income (from 39 per cent to 33 per cent).

Increases in taxation and death duties since 1914 emphasised the relative decline in the well-being of the better off; the net income, including death duties, of the wealthiest (A) was actually less in 1925/6 than it had been immediately before the war, irrespective of the decline in the value of money. When allowance was made for inflation, it was found that net real income in 1925/6 of groups A and B combined was 64 per cent of the prewar equivalent, excluding death duties (or 60 per cent including them). The net real income of C was 90 per cent of prewar equivalent. By contrast, the aggregate net real income of those not included in these three wealthier groups had increased by 10 per cent.

Bowley and Stamp, in their study of *The National Income 1924* (1927), where its distribution was compared with 1911 also stressed the declining shares of the very wealthy. In 1911, they suggested, the pro-

33. This is noted in Rubinstein, *Men of Property*, pp. 47–8.
34. 'The Inland Revenue Report on National Income', dated 21 Feb. 1929, PRO IR/74/238. This very important document has been published by the Cambridge Department of Applied Economics since the research for this study was undertaken.

**Table 3.3.** Income distribution in 1913/14 and 1925/6

|  | 1913/14 | | | 1925/6 | | |
|---|---|---|---|---|---|---|
|  | No. | Total income | Average | No. | Total income | Average |
| A. | 16,000 | £205m | £12,812 | 17,000 | £320m | £18,324 |
| B. | 45,000 | 145m | 3,222 | 47,700 | 220m | 4,612 |
| C. | 1.114m | 485m | 435 | 1.181m | 850m | 720 |

|  | % of total | | % increase of |
|---|---|---|---|
|  | 1913/14 | 1925/6 | 1925/6 over 1913/14 |
| A. | 10 | 8 | 56 |
| B. | 7 | 5 | 52 |
| C. | 22 | 20 | 75 |
| Balance | 61 | 67 | 108 |
|  | 100 | 100 | 92 |

*Source*: PRO IR 74/238, Board of Inland Revenue's 'Report on National Income'

**Table 3.4.** The distribution of net income, 1913/14 and 1925/6

| | Net income (including death duties)(£) | | % increase |
|---|---|---|---|
| | 1913/14 | 1925/6 | of net income |
| A. | 169m | 156 | − 8 |
| B. | 126m | 151 | + 20 |
| C. | 435m | 674 | + 55 |
| Balance | 1,220m | 2,409 | + 97 |
| | 1,950m | 3,390m | + 74 |

| | Net income (excluding death duties)(£) | | % increase |
|---|---|---|---|
| | 1913/14 | 1925/6 | of net income |
| A. | 184m | 191m | + 4 |
| B. | 130m | 162m | + 25 |
| C. | 440m | 687m | + 56 |
| Balance | 1,223m | 2,412m | + 97 |
| | 1,977m | 3,452m | + 75 |

*Source*: Board of Inland Revenue, 'Report on National Income'

portion of the national income which belonged to individuals with incomes over £5,000 was about 8 per cent of the total; in 1922, the proportion going to individuals with equivalent income (£9,500) was about 5.5 per cent of the total. They concluded that: 'If deduction is made for the greater progression in the present direct taxation, the percentage of net income going to this richer section is considerably less than it was in 1911. When the full effects of taxation are taken into account, the real income for saving or expenditure in the hands of the rich is definitely less than before the war'.[35]

## The Redistribution of Factor Incomes

When we turn to the analysis of the redistribution of income between different economic functions (and the groups who fulfilled them) then the most fundamental change was the greater proportion accruing to income from employment as opposed to property. C.H. Feinstein has noted that, in the history of income distribution in the UK since 1860, the rise in the proportion of income from employment was achieved almost entirely in two abrupt shifts, occurring during or immediately after each of the two world wars.[36] This is chiefly attributable to the growth of the salariat's share; during 1910–14, salaries took 10 per cent of GNP and in 1921–4 they took 16.2 per cent. Over the same period, wage-earners' share of GNP rose to 38 per cent (a recovery to their proportion in the early years of the century). The rise in the share of salaries reflected, in some small part, the changing structure of women's occupations. The proportion of manual workers in the male labour force scarcely altered between 1911 and 1921, falling only from 78.2 per cent to 77.3 per cent. The proportions in the male salariat rose only slightly, from 12.6 per cent to 13.16 per cent between 1911 and 1921, some of this change being due to the displacement of independent employers and men working on their own account.[37] Over the same period, the proportion of manual workers in the female labour force fell from 83.25 per cent to 75.68 per cent, most of the change being accounted for by the rise in the number of salaried women clerical workers (from 3.3 per cent to 9.9 per cent of the female labour force).

It would be pleasant to see in the salariat's greater share a measure of the material gains made by women during the war and postwar period on which Marwick and others have placed great stress. Doubt-

35. A.L. Bowley, J.C. Stamp, *The National Income 1924*, Oxford, 1927, pp. 57, 58–59.

36. C.H. Feinstein, 'Changes in the Distribution of the National Income', in Marchal, Ducros, eds., *Distribution of National Income*, p. 118.

37. For the changing occupational structure of Great Britain, see G. Routh, *Occupation and Pay in Great Britain 1906–1960*, Cambridge, 1965, Table 1, p. 4. I have arrived at a figure for the male salariat by aggregating lower professional employees, employed managers and administrators, clerical workers and foremen, inspectors and supervisors. By 1931, the male salariat — reckoned as such — was still only 13.7 per cent of the male labour force.

less there was some, but many of the gains of the salariat went to the low-paid male sector which had been economically depressed before the war. The pay of male civil service clerical officers was, in 1924, 245 per cent of its level in 1911–13. Since the cost of living index was then about 180 per cent of 1914, their real income had risen by more than half. Male railway clerks made still greater gains; their pay in 1924 was 291 per cent of prewar levels. Bank clerks — the elite of the prewar clerical labour force — did not fare so well (there was a remarkable compression of the differential between railway and bank clerks) but their incomes in 1924 were still about 10 per cent, in real terms, above prewar levels.[38] A further part of the gains of the salariat went to men who would have been accorded lower professional (and modestly paid) status in prewar society. Civil service executive officers who, in 1913, earned £195 or just over half an assistant principal's pay, received £383 in 1924, an increase of 96 per cent which brought them just over two-thirds of a postwar assistant principal's income.[39] These figures indicate forcibly that salaried clerical and lower professional workers were not, objectively speaking, amongst the 'new poor' of postwar society. Before the war, only 1.9 per cent of the occupied population were in receipt of salaries above £160 a year. By 1931, 5.6 per cent received the postwar equivalent; much of this difference occurred by the early 1920s.[40]

Within the professions proper (whether salaried or independent) there was a strong trend for income levels to be less dispersed after the war. The estimates produced by the Colwyn Committe on National Debt and Taxation of the percentage increases in 1922/3 over 1913/14 indicate, for example, that the real incomes of the richest doctors and dentists of prewar society had fallen quite considerably. (The Colwyn figures agree closely with Guy Routh's except in the case of solicitors and these should be treated with reserve.) The relative improvement in the 'new' profession of accountancy was, as the Committee noted, 'not unexpected [given] the heavy and increasing demands which had been made upon [the] profession with the great development in taxation and finance since 1914'.[41] These figures tempt us to amend Bowley's judgement on the postwar standard of living of the professional classes (see page 83) and to suggest that it had not so much fallen as homogenised. Poorly-paid doctors and dentists were in real terms better-off than before the war, and their position relative to the elite within their professions had much improved. According to the Colwyn

38. For these figures, see Routh, *Occupation and Pay*, Table 37, p. 79.
39. Ibid., Table 34, p. 70.
40. Colin Clark, *National Income and Outlay*, London, 1937, Table 41, p. 101.
41. *Committee on National Debt and Taxation*, Appendix XI to the *Minutes of Evidence*, London, 1927.

**Table 3.5.** Professional earnings: estimated percentage increase of earnings in 1922/3 over those in 1913/14

| Representative point in 1913/14 | % increase 1922/3 on 1913/14 |
|---|---|
| **Accountants** | |
| Average of 200 highest | 98 |
| £1,560 | 96 |
| 796 | 131 |
| 414 | 158 |
| 248 | 169 |
| **Solicitors** | |
| Average of 300 highest | 57 |
| £1,617 | 58 |
| 885 | 69 |
| 492 | 75 |
| 297 | 76 |
| **Doctors** | |
| Average of 200 highest | 36 |
| £1,218 | 45 |
| 800 | 64 |
| 484 | 78 |
| 314 | 94 |
| **Dentists** | |
| Average of 50 highest | 45 |
| £1,294 | 50 |
| 611 | 73 |
| 322 | 78 |
| 215 | 101 |

*Source: Committee on National Debt and Taxation, Appendix XI, Table 21*

figures the standard of living of all accountants rose, at the lower- and middle-income levels very considerably.

The incomes which, in real terms, fell most markedly were those derived from rent. According to the schedules which identify by source the aggregate income brought under review for tax purposes, income from property (excluding income from property rented for business purposes) rose by only 9.9 per cent between 1912/13 and 1922/3.[42] We must allow for some exaggeration, in this figure, of the true decline because of the growth of owner-occupation (which the fall in the value of rents would have encouraged) immediately after the war. That is to say income from rent was coming from a smaller volume of property in

42. Ibid., Appendix XI, Table 18, which shows distribution by sources of the aggregate income of the UK brought under review for income tax purposes.

the postwar years. Incomes from rent are, normally, more stable than almost all other types of income, but the specific factor inhibiting their rise was the introduction of rent control under the Rent and Mortgage Interest (Rent Restriction) Act of 1915, a measure intended to mollify working-class unrest and the clearest instance of the redistributive consequences of wartime government's intervention in the market. Under it and subsequent Acts, rent increases on existing dwellings were restricted to 40 per cent above 1914 levels. New houses were not subject to the Acts, but the legislation depressed the market for rented accommodation and nearly all houses built solely by private enterprise in the postwar years were for sale. The Board of Inland Revenue calculated that income from real property amounted to 10 per cent of the national income in 1913/14 and only 7 per cent in 1923/4.[43] Though this share increased slightly from the mid-1920s it remained below the pre-1914 level. Behind these anonymous figures lies a significant change in the social composition of the *petite bourgeoisie* (the term is very apposite in this context). Most urban working-class houses in the early twentieth century were rented from small-scale capitalists owning two or three properties (in industrial Lancashire some were known to be prosperous working men).[44] The changes brought by the war — rent restriction, the intervention of the government into the housing market, new fields for small-scale investment — 'signalled the beginning of the end of this particular variety of small-scale capitalism'.[45]

The agrarian estate owners were hard hit by the decline in the real value of rent, especially if they had no other appreciable source of income, such as mineral rights or the profits of farming. They were faced, particularly in the last year of the war and the first years of peace, with increased tax demands, the rising cost of estate mainten- ance and, in the event of estates passing hands, higher death duties which were (in effect) discriminatory compared with other forms of wealth. Landlords who farmed on a large scale could compensate by the great increase in agricultural profits. Most, however, lived primar- ily on their rent rolls and the war brought considerable changes in their relationships with their tenants, to the advantage of the latter. Refer- ence has already been made to the long-term shift in the social balance of the upper class and it is worth dwelling on the ways the war palpably accelerated that process by encouraging the sale and breakup of estates and the transfer of wealth from land to finance. Doubtless, this process, which had been in train since the agricultural depression of the late 1870s, was inevitable in an industrial and commercial economy. Further-

43. 'The Inland Revenue Report on the National Income', PRO IR74/238.
44. Paul de Rousiers refers to this in his *The Labour Question in Britain*, London, 1896.
45. See S. Glynn and J. Oxburrow, *Inter-war Britain: a Social and Economic History*, London, 1976, p. 220.

more, the dispersal of estate had already been hastened immediately before the war by the uneconomic rents at which farms were let, the pressing need of many landlords to pay off mortgages and — following Lloyd George's land campaign — a feeling of apprehension among landowners as to the probable tendency of legislation and taxation in regard to land.[46] Nevertheless, the scale of land transfers between 1917 and 1921 — when one-quarter of England changed hands — had no precedent in modern times.[47] There was a quantitative leap in the changing social structure of agriculture that calls for particular explanation, namely the rise in the number of occupying owners (from 49,000 to 70,000 in England and Wales) in spite of the fall in the total number of agricultural holdings.[48] Land sales and the spurt in owner-farming heralded 'a startling social revolution in the countryside'.[49]

As an illustration of the difficulties landowners were facing towards the later phase of the war, we can cite the letter of Lord Knaresborough to Bonar Law of January 1917. Knaresborough had been pressed by

> some of my friends who are landowners . . . to put . . . their points of view to [Law] as leader of the Unionist Party and Chancellor. . . . The general public believes that, on account of the high prices of agricultural produce, land-owners are benefiting by the war. The exact contrary is the case. They are not getting, and cannot possibly get, a penny more in rent, and the absolutely necessary expenses of the estate are immensely higher on account of the cost of labour and materials. Far from being prosperous, the great majority of them are extremely hard hit by the present taxation following on the great fall of rent of late years, which amounted on average to about 33 per cent in this district. . . .

Knaresborough's own estate at Kirby Hall, in Yorkshire, yielded £5,191 in rents — a relatively modest sum compared with the greatest landed magnates — out of which his unavoidable expenses were, he claimed, £1,592. The law, none the less, now obliged him to pay super-tax 'on a large amount of purely imaginary income'. He concluded that: 'Radical finance, cunningly adapted to the purpose, is bleeding landowners to death'.[50] Subsequent correspondence by officials shows that Knaresborough had no legitimate grounds for com-

46. See the *Report of the Departmental Committee on Tenant Farmers and Sales of Estates*, PP 1912–13, extract given in W.L. Guttsman, ed., *The English Ruling Class*, London, 1969, pp. 120–1.

47. See F.M.L. Thompson, *English Landed Society in the Nineteenth Century*, London, 1963, pp. 322–3; Masterman, *England After the War*, pp. 31–2.

48. The figure is given in Henry Clay, 'The Distribution of Capital in England Wales', *Transactions of the Manchester Statistical Society 1924–1925*, p. 70.

49. Thompson, *English Landed Society*, p. 323.

50. Knaresborough to Bonar Law, 26 Jan. 1917, PRO T172/970.

plaint, but there is no reason to doubt that his economic difficulties were real.

Farmers, on the other hand, were identified as early as 1915 as amongst the war profiteers.[51] Long before the war, the Schedule B basis of taxing farm profits (under which they were assumed to be one-third of rental value) was widely thought to be highly favourable to farmers. At a conservative estimate, farm profits were averaging two-thirds of rental value in 1915 and 1916.[52] Under the 1917 Finance Act, the tax basis was raised to the equivalent of the annual rental value, but farmers were still taxed relatively lightly compared with other business-men since they escaped the Excess Profits Duty. Lucrative military contracts for horse fodder and the greater productivity of agriculture enabled farmers to make a great deal of money.[53] The boom in agricultural prices raised the value of farm land and encouraged many landowners to put their estates on the market, especially in the years 1919–21 when gilt-edged securities offered a greater return than rents. There is some evidence that farms were sold at slightly less than their market value. The occupying tenants were usually the only prospective buyers and J.E. Allen instanced the sale of Lord Beauchamp's estates near Malvern where 'the tenants intimidated owner, auctioneer, and outside purchasers alike, and secured the land for themselves, presum-ably at less than the market value'.[54] Even allowing for factors such as this, there was still a major discrepancy between the market value of estates and their owner's income, and here lay the temptation to sell. This discrepancy was revealed when estates became liable for the more steeply graduated scale of estate duty introduced under the 1919 Finance Act. The Central Landowners' Association argued before the Committee on National Debt and Taxation that for an average of ten large estates in England and Wales, with a size of 16,800 acres and an income of £10,000, the estimated capital value for death duties was £352,000, and the duty payable £81,000. An estate producing the same

51. See 'Note on "profiteering"' by the Board of Inland Revenue in PRO T170/105 (undated); see also 'War and the Farmer', *Nineteenth Century and After*, April 1915; William Diak, 'British Farmers and the War', *Contemporary Review*, April 1915. For a recent discussion, see P.E. Dewey, 'British Farming Profits and Government Policy during the First World War', *Economic History Review*, 2nd. ser., vol. XXXVIX, no. 3, Aug. 1984.

52. See 'Farmers Profits and the Income Tax', memorandum by G.R. Hopkins in PRO T172/971 (undated).

53. For an example of a farmer who prospered during the war, see J.W. Robertson Scott, *England's Green and Pleasant Land*, first published 1925, 2nd ed. Harmondsworth, 1947, pp. 48–9. On increasing agricultural productivity, see J. Sheail, 'Land improve-ment and reclamation: the experiences of the First World War in England and Wales', *Agricultural History Review*, vol. 24, 1976, pp. 110–26.

54. J.E. Allen, 'Some Changes in the Distribution of the National Income during the War', *Journal of the Royal Statistical Society*, vol. LXXXIII, January 1920, p. 90.

income from Consols would pay only £48,862 in duty.[55]

It would be mistaken to see the transfer of landownership wholly in terms of individual fortunes since corporate landowners — such as the Cambridge colleges — also showed a strong tendency to sell land and invest in gilt-edged securities.[56] Nor — despite Masterman's gloomy diagnosis — should this transfer be interpreted as the wholesale impoverishment of a social stratum for, in general, the economic position of the traditional elite improved as land sales wrote off indebtedness and new investments of their proceeds brought larger incomes.[57] A more accurate assessment would, I believe, emphasise the consolidation of elites, based hitherto on different sources of wealth. In a stimulating paper, Rubinstein has drawn attention to the distinctiveness of three elites among mid- and late-nineteenth-century wealth holders (an agrarian elite, a financial and commercial elite and an industrial, manufacturing elite), demonstrated the huge economic preponderance of the first two over the third and argued for a persistent social and political distance between them.[58] Indications of a convergence of wealthy elites antedate the First World War (well-known symptoms being business and industrial peerages and the gravitation of industrial wealth to Conservatism) but the merging of elites was not complete until the 1920s with the tardy development of finance capitalism, in the British economy, the rationalisation of industry through trusts and amalgamations and the decline of landholding as a source of elite wealth. There are a number of ways (apart from the stimulus to land transfer) in which the First World War was important in the timing and speed of the convergence of wealthy elites, probably the most significant being the opportunity for secure investment afforded by the wartime finance policy (its consequences are discussed in more detail below).

Before turning to that issue, specific reference should be made to the types of investment incomes which contracted because of the war. There was a marked depreciation of both the capital value and real income of investments in public utility companies (gas, water, electricity), railway, tramway and other concerns representing social overhead capital. Before the war, stock invested in them had been considered 'safe'; at the end of 1919, it was reckoned that the nominal value of a representative portfolio had declined by slightly more than a quarter and the real income depreciated by half.[59] In the case of the railways,

55. See the evidence and Appendix submitted by the Hon. Lord Clinton (for the Central Landowners' Association and the Land Agents' Society) to the Committee on National Debt and Taxation, *Minutes of Evidence*, pp. 24–7.

56. Ibid., evidence of J.M. Keynes, p. 285.

57. Thompson, *English Landed Society*, p. 337.

58. W.D. Rubinstein, 'Wealth, Elites and the Class Structure of Modern Britain', *Past and Present*, no. 76, 1977, pp. 99–126.

59. Allen, 'Some Changes in the Distribution of National Income', p. 96. For further

the investor's loss was the employee's gain, for the decline of dividends was coupled with a great increase in the share of the product of the railway industry going to wages and salaries. In 1911, wages and salaries took 47.8 per cent and dividends 52.2 per cent of the product of the railway industry; after the period of wartime control when large wage awards were secured, the workers and salaried staff were taking nearly two- and-a-half times the proprietors' share of the product of the industry. This was, moreover, a permanent change.[60] It is doubtful whether changes in product distribution took place on a similar scale in other industries, with the possible exception of shipping, docks and harbours, where comparison of 1923/4 profits with 1913/14 shows a considerable fall.[61] From rises in wages, we can infer that the postwar wage bill was a bigger proportion of the product, in spite of higher unemployment amongst dockers. In this case, however, the comparison is between a boom year in world trade and the postwar slump; the influence of wartime changes is more difficult to pin-point with confidence.

Two general reasons for the decline of *rentier* income in the early and mid-1920s are both worth remarking. The first was a greater tendency, noted by Keynes and others, for companies to finance their growth internally by retaining profits.[62] Shareholders were satisfied with a small dividend and the rest held in reserve as the cheapest way by which companies could expand their business. Though financing from profits was an historical feature of British capitalism, this tendency was certainly encouraged by the war. The self-financing of industry was particularly evident amongst its progressive sectors. The second was the squeeze on profits that occurred with the collapse of the postwar boom and the great deflation of 1921/2. Though wages were cut in this period, the pressure on profit margins was still more considerable. When economic recovery came, and profit margins were restored, it was to substantially less than their prewar level.[63]

In the absence of extensive counter-factual data there is no satisfactory way of positively attributing such developments to wartime economic change and dislocation. However, one important claim that we can confidently make is that during the decade dominated by the war and its after-effects (1914–24) there was a shift in distribution without

---

reference to rates of dividend on different types of public companies, see p. 100.

60. See Allen, 'Some Changes in the Distribution of the National Income'; Clark, *National Income and Outlay*, Table 55, p. 125.

61. The profits of different trade groups in 1913/14 and 1923/4 are given 'in 'The Inland Revenue Report on the National Income', PRO IR/74/238.

62. See Keynes's evidence to the Committee on National Debt and Taxation, *Minutes of Evidence*, p. 276.

63. Glynn and Oxburrow, *Interwar Britain*, p. 39; the authors draw on the work of E.H. Phelps-Brown and M.H. Browne, *A Century of Pay*, London, 1968.

parallel in either the preceding or succeeding decade. By the early 1920s, it was clear to economists concerned with national income accounting that the gains made by labour and salaried employment had come from redistribution rather than overall economic growth, the chief losers being the more conservative (or simply more lazy) amongst the prewar investors. Bowley informed the Committee on National Debt and Taxation that 'the only source of increase to the working class [*sc.* in its share of the product of industry] has been the *rentier* who has depended on fixed interest or fixed rents; I see no other source from which it can have come, and that seems to me a sufficient source'.[64] We now know that labour made greater absolute economic gains during the remainder of the interwar period, but without any further change in distribution; they were gains, that is, which accrued from a static share of an increasing whole. It seems reasonable to attribute this redistributive peculiarity of the war-dominated decade to the war itself.

The point is of fundamental relevance to the interpretation of social consciousness: there is a considerable body of evidence (some of which I quote and discuss elsewhere)[65] that the workers' sense of relative deprivation increased during the war and reached a peak in 1919/20, about the time that economic differences between labour and other social groups were at their narrowest. As a movement was made towards greater economic equality, the working class showed itself less acquiescent in inequalities of condition and social status. One key to the interpretation of this paradoxical phenomenon is the theory of social reference groups which I return to in a later chapter. The point to emphasise here is that the relative material losses and gains of different social groups led to a heightened consciousness of class (in the sense of an acknowledgement that social conflict was endemic to fundamental economic divisions) at all levels of society. This was partly a question of the greater publicity in which economic competition between groups went on. 'The struggle between Capital and Labour has become more fierce and uncompromising . . .' wrote Masterman. 'The newspapers are filled with the record of the [new economic] struggle of one class against another class. . . .'[66] But there was also a solidarism among groups normally identified with an individualist ethos. Collective action undertaken to win or defend economic gains was by no means confined to manual workers: shop assistants, clerks, bank officials, technical engineers, local government officers — all demonstrated a hitherto unusual degree of militancy

64. Bowley, in his evidence to the Committee on National Debt and Taxation, *Minutes of Evidence*, p. 276.
65. Chapter 6 of the present study.
66. Masterman, *England After the War*, p. 13.

directed towards economic ends during the immediate postwar period.[67]
As we have seen, there was even an attempt to unionise the Middle
Class itself. The preconditions for this generalisation of heightened
awareness of economic struggle — an 'economistic' consciousness of
class — lay in the dislocation of normal frames of reference that was
specific to a redistribution of national income.


## The Profits of War

Nothing has been said up to this point on the increases in the income
and wealth of those favourably placed to profit from the extraordinary
circumstances of a wartime economy and the postwar boom. The war
was notorious for its profiteering and historians have tended to accept
the contemporary judgement that the munitions levy and excess profits
duty did nothing to halt the parade of profiteers without specifying by
how much they profited. Evidence from departmental papers and *The
Economist*'s survey of industrial profits and dividends between 1914 and
1919 enables us to establish the broad outlines of capital's profitability
and the effects of the war on investors' income.[68] Overall, it would
appear that the first year of the war was a golden opportunity for
businessmen to make money in the commodity markets, but net
industrial profits declined in this period. Industrial profits rose rapidly
from the second half of 1915 and, until mid-1917, excess profits duty
had no visible effect on net profits. There was a heavy drop in net
profits in 1917/18 when the duty at last began to bite. The postwar
boom — when the fiscal climate was more benevolent — was a period
of remarkable profitability. Dividends did not exactly follow the course
of profits, for during the war, as has already been noted, companies
became accustomed to putting a larger proportion of their profits to
reserve to cover capital wear and tear and finance expansion (there were
fiscal changes which encouraged them to do this). The shareholders' proportion of the profits declined correspondingly. Dividends were, in general,
higher in the last quarter of 1918 and during 1919 as directors relaxed their
caution with the signature of the Armistice. Table 3.6., giving the average
annual rate of dividend on ordinary capital between 1909 and 1919, shows
that the investor's return increased very rapidly during the prewar years
but stabilised during the war. When we take as our measure the ratio of

67. The growth of trade unionism amongst salaried workers is discussed in the 'Report
on the Labour Situation' for week ending 28 Jan. 1920, PRO CAB24/97, CP521, and
ibid. of 11 Feb. 1920, CAB24/98, CP613. I return to the interpretation of this development in Chapter 7 below.

68. *The Economist* published a survey of six years of industrial profits, based on
company reports forwarded to it, on 26 July 1919, pp. 124–6.

**Table 3.6.** Dividend, capital, profits, 1908–1919

|  | Average rate of dividend on ordinary capital (%) | Ratio of profits to total capital (%) |
|---|---|---|
| July–June |  |  |
| 1908/9 | 6.3 | — |
| 1909/10 | 6.8 | — |
| 1910/11 | 8.0 | — |
| 1911/12 | 8.7 | — |
| 1912/13 | 9.7 | — |
| 1913/14 | 10.4 | 9.4 |
| 1914/15 | 9.1 | 8.6 |
| 1915/16 | 10.4 | 10.1 |
| 1916/17 | 10.2 | 10.5 |
| 1917/18 | 10.5 | 10.7 |
| 1918/19 | 11.0 | 11.2 |

*Source*: *The Economist*, 12 July 1919

profits to total capital, we can see that, with the exception of 1914/15, capital was significantly more profitable because of the war (though perhaps less than was popularly believed).

The average figures conceal — as we would expect — considerable variations in both profitability and dividends. In March 1915, Stamp made the first of a series of reports on 'Exceptional Profits Due to the War' and found numerous cases of enormously increased profits: '. . . if businesses [had] done well *at all*, they [had] done *very well*'.[69] Shipowners, corn merchants, millers and sugar merchants were amongst those who effortlessly profited from the increased value of their services and stocks. The whole trading profits for the United Kingdom in prewar years were normally between £500m and £600m and in 1915 profits exceeded that figure by about £80m to £90m exclusive of shipping and £120m to £130m inclusive.[70] In the shipping business, profits were greater for the smaller, independent owners whose ships were not requisitioned by the government. Enormous shipping profits continued to be made until the extension of government control in early 1917 imposed 'blue-book rates' on all shipowners; except for 1915, investors' dividends were good.[71] The opportunities for windfall profits in

69. 'Exceptional Profits due to the War', 16 Mar. 1915, PRO IR74/70 (original emphases).

70. 'Note on "Profiteering"' by the Board of Inland Revenue (undated), PRO T170/105.

71. On shipping profits, see D. Lloyd George, *War Memoirs*, London, 2 vol. ed., vol. I, pp. 730–3. The rate of dividend in shipping fell from 11.6 per cent in 1914 to 7.9 per cent in 1915, but rose to 13.1 per cent in 1916 and remained near that for the rest of the war and the postwar boom. Shipping firms put large sums to reserves, so dividends did not totally reflect wartime profitability.

commodity markets were obviously far fewer during the later years of the war and by 1916 profits from engineering and the metal industries were showing handsome advances on prewar averages. The mid-year declarations of public companies in 1916 showed that for a large sample of coal, iron, shipbuilding and engineering firms average pre-tax profits were 32 per cent above the prewar level. Individual firms did exceptionally well; Cammell Laird, the shipbuilders, showed a 74 per cent increase over 1914. The chemical giant Brunner-Mond was as profitable as the average in coal, iron and engineering; rubber companies more so.[72] The average rates of dividend on ordinary capital in different sectors of industry varied considerably from the aggregate given in Table 3.7. Dividend rates in gas, tramway and other utility companies fell during the war. Oil companies paid out bonanza dividends in 1914 and 1915, but these declined until 1919, when they rose again to surpass the rate of the early part of the war. Rubber, nitrate and motor-engineering firms were the most consistently profitable.

The first attempts to recoup extraordinary profits for the state were half-hearted; the munitions levy on controlled establishments guaranteed manufacturers a 20 per cent increase on average prewar profits and made special allowances for increased output, exceptional wear and tear and capital expenditure. The excess profits duty, brought in under the 1915 Finance Act, recouped half the increased profitability of other manufacturers; the rate was raised to 60 per cent in 1916 and 80 per cent in 1917. The duty became almost as valuable to wartime chancellors as the income tax but business malpractices undermined its effectiveness with inflationary consequences. Up to 1917, at least, there is a strong possibility that excess profits duty was taken into account by businessmen in determining prices.[73] The decision to continue with the duty, at a reduced rate, during the postwar boom (in the attempt to assuage popular contempt for the profiteer) had the unlooked-for effect of cushioning firms against the enormous business losses that followed the breaking of the price spiral. Firms making a loss could reclaim up to 60 per cent of the excess profits duties paid in previous years.[74]

What was the outcome of wartime profitability and the increases in dividends in terms of personal wealth holding? There are clues but the evidence is, frankly, weak and circumstantial. We have already noted in the discussion of income distribution the sudden swelling of numbers in the income bracket of £5,000 and more, and this is probably an index of the new wealth being made by shipowners and munitions contractors. *The Economist* summarised its data with the claim that

72. See 'Companies' great wartime profits. The record of typical enterprises', *Manchester Guardian*, 19 June 1916.
73. J.C. Stamp, *Taxation during the War*, London, 1932, p. 214.
74. Ibid., p. 215.

**Table 3.7.** The distribution of property in private hands in England and Wales, 1911–13, 1926–8, 1936 (figures relate to persons aged 25 and over)

| | Number of persons | | Amount of property | |
| --- | --- | --- | --- | --- |
| | Cumulative number (000s) | Cumulative percentage | Cumulative amount (£m) | Cumulative percentage |
| **1911–13** | | | | |
| total | 18,745 | 100.0 | 6,008–7,005 | 100.0 |
| More than £100 | 2,196–2,529 | 11.6–13.4 | 5,608–6,305 | 89.7–93.4 |
| £1,000 | 558–635 | 2.9–3.3 | 4,987–5,584 | 79.7–83.0 |
| £5,000 | 161–180 | 0.8–0.9 | 4,021–4,485 | 64.0–67.0 |
| £10,000 | 84–94 | 0.4 | 3,423–3,808 | 54.3–57.0 |
| £25,000 | 30–34 | 0.1 | 2,548–2,824 | 40.3–42.4 |
| £100,000 | 5–6 | 0.03 | 1,378–1,516 | 21.6–22.9 |
| **1926–8** | | | | |
| total | 22,266 | 100.0 | 13,996–15,453 | 100.0 |
| More than £100 | 4,802–5,311 | 21.6–23.9 | 13,466–14,553 | 94.2–96.4 |
| £1,000 | 1,334–1,450 | 6.0–6.5 | 11,984–12,933 | 83.5–85.8 |
| £5,000 | 369–397 | 1.7–1.8 | 9,498–10,211 | 66.0–68.0 |
| £10,000 | 187–201 | 0.8–0.9 | 8,076–8,664 | 56.1–57.8 |
| £25,000 | 68–72 | 0.3 | 5,990–6,416 | 41.5–42.9 |
| £100,000 | 10–11 | 0.05 | 3,257–3,493 | 22.6–23.3 |
| **1936** | | | | |
| total | 25,201 | 100.0 | 15,853–17,548 | 100.0 |
| More than £100 | 5,915–6,522 | 23.5–25.9 | 15,403–16,598 | 94.5–97.2 |
| £1,000 | 1,727–1,874 | 6.8–7.4 | 13,604–14,613 | 83.3–85.8 |
| £5,000 | 465–500 | 1.8–2.0 | 10,695–11,458 | 65.3–67.5 |
| £10,000 | 243–261 | 1.0 | 8,983–9,615 | 54.8–56.7 |
| £25,000 | 87–93 | 0.4 | 6,427–6,859 | 39.1–40.5 |
| £100,000 | 12–13 | 0.05 | 2,975–3,155 | 18.0–18.8 |

*Source*: H. Campion, *Public and Private Property in Great Britain*, London, 1939

the record shows that the industrial shareholder cannot, on the average, be convicted of war profiteering. His dividend has risen from 10.4 per cent in 1913–14 to 11 per cent in 1918–19, and the rate of profit on capital has risen from 9.4 per cent to 11.2 per cent. During the same period his income tax has risen from 1/2 to 6/-, so that his actual cash receipt has fallen from £9.16s. to £7.14s., and the buying power of cash reduced by 50 per cent or more.[75]

This was clearly the highly partial gloss of a capitalist journal placed on the defensive by the great moral outrage of those who saw no reason why anyone should profit from the war. A more even-handed summary would stress the selective effects of the war on the owners of capital and

75. *The Economist*, 26 July 1919, p. 126.

the gains made by those shrewd or lucky enough to have property in the mode of destruction. The most striking feature of wartime profits was the increasing discrepancy between the highly profitable and the least profitable sectors of industry. Throughout the war, the suspension of share trading somewhat depressed the capital value of share holdings, but in the postwar speculative boom share values increased rapidly, temporarily swelling the numbers who, on paper, could count themselves substantial property owners. Given the giddy rise in prices, which reached a peak in May 1920, 'any fool could make profits'. Businesses and shares were sold under absurdly advantageous conditions and, according to Cole and Postgate: 'Many capitalists . . . retired with huge fortunes on the proceeds'.[76] Other businessmen, apparently, were caught up in the manic speculation and reinvested foolishly. The sudden rise in share values is reflected in the probate returns (which are accepted as a fair guide to the distribution of wealth amongst the living). These show a remarkable increase in 1919/20 of the number of estates valued at £10,000 or more, and strongly indicate that the gains of the speculative boom were widely diffused.[77] Rubinstein identifies, as an immediate effect of the First World War, a significant increase in the number of top fortunes, but it was one which failed to keep pace with inflation and took place not amongst the very wealthiest contractors and armaments manufacturers, but at a lower level of wealth.[78]

In spite of the opportunities for the few to profit, the overall effect of the war appears to have been a slight redistribution of wealth. An estimate prepared by the Inland Revenue for the purpose of a Capital Levy (much discussed but not introduced) reckoned that, of the total nominal increase in wealth during the war, 69 per cent went to the 340,000 individuals owning £5,000 or more. According to this estimate, the share of the rest of the community (those owning less than £5,000) rose very slightly, from 28.8 per cent of the prewar total to 30.2 per cent of the postwar total.[79] Analyses of the distribution of capital made in the 1920s and 1930s concur in tracing a redistributive effect to the war period and in stressing that this was felt in the highest ranges of wealth.

76. G.D.H. Cole, R. Postgate, *The Common People*, London, 1938, 1961 pb., p. 555.

77. The number of estates liable for duty and exceeding £10,000 in value was: 1912/13 — 4,002; 1913/14 — 4,421; 1914/15 — 4,400; 1915/16 — 4,868; 1917/18 — 4,604; 1918/19 — 4,900; 1919/20 — 5,914; 1920/21 — 5,409. The most convincing explanation for the leap in 1919/20 would appear to be that large numbers of modest property holdings suddenly increased their value. Source: *64th Annual Report of the Inland Revenue*, Table 23.

78. Rubinstein, *Men of Property*, pp. 41–2.

79. 'Suggested taxation of wartime increases of wealth': memorandum submitted by the Board of Inland Revenue to the Select Committee of the House of Commons on the taxation of wartime increases of wealth, PP 1920, Cmd 594.

Clay, for example, compared the distribution of wealth in England and Wales in 1912 and 1920/1 and estimated that the share of the wealthiest (those with capital of £25,000 or more) had declined from 43.4 per cent of the prewar total to 38.5 per cent of the postwar total.[80] There were greater numbers of small property owners, due partly to the introduction of War Savings Certificates which resulted for the first time in an extensive holding of securities by wage-earners. The most significant change, however, was in the numbers and the share of those in the middle ranges of wealth. It scarcely needs stressing that capital remained grotesquely unevenly distributed, particularly in comparison with societies with a large peasant class (such as France and the Irish Free State.) Clay, none the less, concluded that:

> Making all allowances . . . the change is striking, and, so far as it cannot be explained away, suggests that high progressive taxation is having an effect on the distribution of capital; large fortunes do not accumulate so rapidly as they did, and even decumulate while small savings accumulate untouched . . . it would seem as if war and post-war profiteers made their exceptional gains at the expense, not of the poor, but of other members of the same economic class. . . .[81]

In the late 1930s, Campion calculated property distribution in England and Wales on a different basis (by multiplying the number and value of estates passing each year classified according to age- and gender-groups by the reciprocals of the appropriate general and social class morality rates for each group).[82] There are discrepancies with Clay's estimates but the trends are the same: a considerable rise in the number of owners of small capital in the mid and late 1920s as compared with before the war and a significant shift in property distribution from the more to the less wealthy. According to this estimate, 1 per cent of persons owned 70 per cent of the total property in private hands in 1911–13, and 60 per cent in 1926–8. Campion's table[83] allows us to see that the trends in property redistribution continued through the 1930s (by which time 1 per cent of persons owned 55 per cent of the property in private hands) but change appears to have been more rapid between 1914 and the mid-1920s.[84] Given the fluctuations in money values during this period, this is scarcely sur-

80. Clay, 'The Distribution of Capital in England and Wales'.

81. Ibid., p. 76.

82. H. Campion, *Public and Private Property in Great Britain*, London, 1939.

83. Ibid., p. 107, repr. here as Table 3.7.

84. A.S. Milward accepts that 'there is considerable evidence in favour of a redistribution of capital accelerated by the two world wars, but little evidence that this touched the poorest groups. Looking outside the boundaries of Britain . . . it is impossible not to be more impressed by the stability of capital holding in Britain when compared, for example, to Germany . . . ', *The Economic Effects of the Two World Wars on Britain*, London,

prising; the great increase in small property ownership (as shown by the numbers owning more than £100 and less than a £1,000) would have come from the declining value of money, the existence of 'new' savers (such as wage-earners who had invested a surplus for the first time), and would have included some (such as elderly investors) who were in some sense *déclassé*.

## The Social Consequences of War Finance

The redistributive tendency associated with the war stemmed in the first instance from the relative advantage enjoyed by labour over other factors of production in the war economy, but it was strongly reinforced by the fiscal measures adopted by wartime governments. These involved a considerable shift from indirect to direct taxation, so that a smaller proportion of total tax revenue was raised from the working class after the war. This exacerbated the sense of economic grievance felt by direct tax payers (broadly the middle and upper classes), but provided the fiscal means for what T.H. Marshall called 'class abatement' through the social policies of the state. Nevertheless, the global and long-term effects of war finance were complex and may even have stabilised economic differences within society to the advantage of the wealthy. British governments paid for the war by a higher level of direct taxation (with much smaller increases in indirect taxation), borrowing from their own citizens and inflating the money supply. The social consequences of finance policy stemmed from the mix of these policies and the different time-lags associated with them. Inflation acted — as we have seen — as a covert tax on certain forms of capital. Taxation, by 1919, was seriously reducing the tiny minority of very large incomes and by the mid-1920s had some retarding effect on the accumulation of great fortunes with the result that wealth was more evenly distributed amongst the wealthy. But after 1921, with the fall in prices, servicing the legacy of war debt became an increasing proportion of public expenditure and an increasingly valuable source of income to war-loan investors. It also stringently limited the amount of government spending available for 'class abatement'.

Taxation played a larger part in financing Britain's war effort than in any other belligerent power — a tribute to the patriotism and (comparative) probity of her wealthy citizens who 'begged earnestly to be taxed heavily',[85] as well as the highly-developed nature of her tax

---

1970, p. 30. I entirely concur with the proviso that, in a comparative perspective, it is the stability of Britain's wealth and class structure which needs explaining.

85. Stamp, *Taxation during the War*, p. 133.

system. It was still a small part. In 1922, the Treasury estimated that taxation had met only 10.7 per cent of current wartime expenditure (the total cost of the war was then put at £8,215m).[86] When account is taken of deferred payment through taxation, then the proportion of the war costs met through taxes rose to 30 per cent.[87]

In purely quantitative terms, the fiscal consequences of the war are striking evidence of its precipitate impact on state and society, but with respect to the techniques and social objectives of taxation, the war greatly enhanced existing influences, rather than creating novel ones. The years between the Dilke Commission of 1906 and the last prewar budget saw the beginnings of the fiscal adjustment to the social consequences of democracy.[88] Direct taxation became both more progressive and more selective, partly in order to finance the Liberal welfare reforms. The 1907 Finance Act introduced the first measures of graduation by means of the system of abatements and the charging of super-tax on large incomes; it also introduced differentiation between earned and unearned incomes. The 1910 Finance Act extended graduation on larger incomes, revived allowances for children and extended allowances for repairs and maintenance of property. The last peacetime budget carried the principle of graduation much further, so that the rate of tax on earned incomes rose by five steps until it reached its maximum charged at £2,500; on unearned incomes, it rose by three steps to a maximum charged on incomes over £500. The super-tax limit was reduced to £3,000 and charged at seven rates rising from 5d to 1/4d.

Many of the characteristics of modern fiscal policy are broadly discernible in the prewar tax system, with some important exceptions. No allowance, for example, was made to a married man in respect of his wife (an intriguing omission given the climate of opinion created by eugenics). Still more striking was the fact that only a small minority of the employed population was liable to direct taxation (if we exclude, that is, the unprogressive poll tax levied under the National Insurance Act). Of approximately 1.2m tax-payers in 1914, only about fifty thousand were manual workers. This small number cannot be entirely explained by the relatively high threshold (£160 per annum) and we must assume that earnings in some well-paid trades (such as iron and steel puddling and ship-plating) escaped the scrutiny of the Inland Revenue. The tax exemption limit drew a critical dividing line through society:[89] below it stood the vast mass of manual workers and most of

86. 'Memorandum on the cost of the war', dated 31 March 1922, PRO T172/1310.

87. Stamp, *Taxation during the War*, p. 154.

88. On the prewar changes in the tax systems, see Appendix 1 submitted by R. Hopkins, for the Board of Inland Revenue to the Royal Commission on the Income Tax, PP 1919, Cmd 288–1; Stamp, *Taxation during the War*, pp. 134ff.; B. Mallet, C. Oswald George, *British Budgets; Second Series 1913/14–1920/21*, London, 1929.

89. On the social significance of the prewar income-tax line, see A. Marwick, *The*

what I have called the buffer zone. (Even in clerical occupations enjoying high social esteem, such as banking and insurance, only a minority of clerks — about 40 per cent — were paid above the income tax limit.)

During the early part of the war, up to April 1916, budget statements were characterised by heroic claptrap on the need for sacrifice and an extreme reluctance to increase direct taxation to a level anywhere near commensurate with need. The rule of thumb of wartime chancellors was to raise taxes sufficient to meet the interest on the National Debt. The cumulative effect of later wartime budgets was to greatly increase the proportion of direct taxes in total government revenue (from 44.4 per cent in 1913/14 to 75.3 per cent in 1918/19), to make them still more progressive, and to introduce further differentiations (including one between civilians and servicemen). Taxation was tailored to personal status. Successive Finance Acts raised the limit under which the children's allowance could be claimed (from £500 to £800) and in 1918 the married man's allowance (on £25 of income) was introduced.[90] The lowering of the tax threshold to £130 in 1916, combined with the inflation of money earnings, brought for the first time very large numbers of manual wage-earners within the income-tax bracket and so blurred that distinct line of social demarcation of prewar society. A 'softer' demarcation now arose within the fiscal system for there was introduced a series of allowances (for tools, overalls, the extra cost of living away from home) which were more or less peculiar to manual labour. The number of tax *payers* classified as weekly wage-earners (in effect manual workers) rose from 630,000 in 1916/17 to 1.43m in 1918/19.[91] Many more were assessed for tax but because of the generosity of the new allowances paid none. In 1918/19, a married wage earner with three children paid no tax on a £250 income, though this was nearly double the exemption limit. (The majority of weekly wage-earners actually paying tax in the last year of the war and postwar years were bachelors.) In spite of the increasing numbers falling within the tax net, the contribution of weekly wage-earners to the total income tax raised under all schedules never rose above the 3 per cent of 1917/18.[92] This at least makes comprehensible the complaint of the propertied and wealthy that the working class did little to pay for the war.

*Deluge*, Harmondsworth, 1967, pp. 19–20.

90. On changes in the tax system during the war, see Appendix 1 to the Royal Commission on the Income Tax; and Stamp, *Taxation during the War*.

91. The figures are given in a memorandum in the bound volumes of papers submitted to the Royal Commission on the Income Tax, PRO IR75/185, p. 348.

92. See Table 66 (showing the percentage of the income tax raised under different schedules) in the *64th Report of the Commissioners of the Inland Revenue for year ending 31 March 1921*, PP 1922, Cmd 1436.

Arthur Marwick, the most vigorous exponent of the relationship between war and twentieth-century social change, has placed some weight on the great extension of the income tax during the First World War and the question is worth a moment's analysis.[93] It is true that the war made more universal and more pressing the formal, fiscal obligations of citizenship. Furthermore, as the state drew manual workers within the tax net, it was obliged to enter into new forms of social negotiation with them and their representatives. Before July 1916, for example, when the first quarterly payments of tax from weekly wage-earners fell due, Inspectors and Surveyors of Taxes were instructed to attend lodge meetings throughout the South Wales coalfield to explain the tax and the manner in which the forms should be filled in. To help collect the tax, 180 working men (recommended by the South Wales Miners' Federation) were appointed sub-collectors in the pits. Because most of the popular opposition to taxing weekly wage-earners came from the coalfield, it was thought advisable to have William Brace, president of the SWMF, appointed to the postwar Royal Commission on the Income Tax.[94] For weekly wage-earners, the obligations of taxation were, in the short term, exacting their time-honoured rights of political representation. The further construction placed on the extension of taxation is that it more or less permanently removed one of the ostensive class insignia of prewar years. This is much more debatable. For a start the number of new taxpayers created by wartime changes in the fiscal system has been greatly exaggerated by confusing payment with assessment. The maximum number chargeable with tax was 3.9m in 1919/20; an equal number fell within the tax bracket but were entirely relieved of charges.[95] In 1920, there was introduced a new graduation in the income tax and a reduction in its rate which, when combined with the fall in wages in the next year, relieved nearly all weekly wage-earners of tax obligations; by 1924 only 300,000 were being charged to tax, of whom 250,000 were bachelors.[96] Workers were tax-payers in large numbers only for a brief historical moment and for a brief period in their individual lives. The expansion in the 'tax-paying

93. Marwick, *The Deluge*, p. 327; and idem, *Britain in the Century of Total War*, Harmondsworth, 1970, pp. 170–1.

94. See the memorandum by the Superintending Inspector of Taxes on the assessment of manual wage-earners in South Wales, in the papers of the Royal Commission on the Income Tax, PRO IR75/182, p. 167; and Warren Fisher to the Chancellor of the Exchequer, 6 Feb. 1919, on the constitution of the Commission, T172/985.

95. Mallet and George, *British Budgets*, p. 398, give the Inland Revenue's estimates of the number of individuals chargeable to tax. Marwick, *The Deluge*, p. 327, states erroneously that there were 7.75m. tax-paying citizens.

96. Memorandum to the Chancellor of the Exchequer on the quarterly assessment of wage earners, dated July 1924, PRO IR64/45.

**Table 3.8.** Total tax yield on the highest incomes (£)

|  | 1903/4 | 1913/14 | 1918/19 |
|---|---|---|---|
| 5,000 | 229 | 292 | 1,788 |
| 10,000 | 458 | 758 | 4,188 |
| 20,000 | 917 | 1,592 | 9,438 |
| 50,000 | 2,292 | 4,091 | 25,188 |

*Source*: Committee on National Debt and Taxation.
Note that incomes of this magnitude were unaffected by family or earned-income reliefs.

class' came disproportionately from the salariat and the lower-paid professions, as we would expect from their gains in earnings. During the 1920s, the tax-paying line arguably conformed more closely with social class divisions that it had before the war since above it now stood many salaried and professional workers who would have escaped income tax before 1914 and below it stood the vast majority of weekly wage-earners.

The standard rate of income tax imposed in 1918 and 1919 was 6s. in the £, but this oft-quoted figure is not very revealing of the tax burden that was actually borne by incomes of different sizes nor (as I have indicated) should it be considered in isolation from the increasing adjustment of tax assessment to allow for individual ability to pay. The standard rate was borne as the ultimate rate by only a small number of tax payers: with the new graduations and allowances many affluent middle-class incomes were liable to a tax burden far below the standard rate, while with increases in super-tax the effective rate for the highest incomes was much in excess of the 'standard'. In 1913/14, the income- and super-tax burden on a £1,000 income was 3.7 per cent and, by 1918–19 (assuming the income was earned and supported a wife and three children), the tax burden had risen to 14.6 per cent.[97] The increased burden on the wealthiest incomes was proportionally far greater and the figures suggest that wartime changes were such as to seriously impede, for the first time, the amassing of great fortunes.

Much the same could be said of the increases in death duties which were introduced in 1919, although they were not yet as steeply graduated as the income tax. Before August 1914, the maximum duty payable on estates of £500,000 or more was 12 per cent; after that date it rose to 17 per cent and after July 1919 to 26 per cent. The total yield of death duties approximately doubled from £27.2m in 1913/14 to

97. See the table giving the tax yields on various levels of income in the *Report of Committee on National Debt and Taxation*, p. 96.

£52.5m in 1921/2.[98] The death duty rates were, however, only such as to affect extreme concentrations of wealth: the majority report of the Committee on National Debt and Taxation, which was set up because of the fear that wartime increases in taxation had seriously undermined the capacity for saving and investment, conceded that 'the burden becomes severe only on estates greater than £50,000'.[99] One's confidence in the decumulative consequences of income and property taxes would be greater were it not for the indications that the use of tax-avoiding devices, account manipulation and gifts *inter vivos* kept pace with tax increases. Officials of both the Ministry of Munitions and the Inland Revenue were aware of the growing scale of super-tax avoidance as private businessmen set up one-man companies to which profits could be loaned fictitiously, and later reclaimed, thus avoiding super-tax.[100] The postwar Cabinet Committee on tax evasion reported that the device was by no means confined to manufacturers, but also used by landowners and *rentiers* (including war bond holders) and to avoid death duties. The committee considered that 'the incentive to legal avoidance is to be found in the high rates of taxation imposed during the war ... and its practice under the existing law is extremely easy'.[101]

Domestic borrowing was the principal measure of war finance and it can be convincingly (although not conclusively) argued that its longer-term consequences ran counter to the tendencies to income and wealth redistribution. War finance was conducted as if the state was simply one amongst a number of customers in the community. Instead of commanding the goods and services needed to wage the war, governments hired them at what was deemed to be the market rate. The initial financial measure of wartime governments was to borrow on the Ways and Means account and to put huge amounts of Treasury bills on the market. The first war loan, issued in November 1914, took the form of a $3\frac{1}{2}$ per cent loan at 95, redeemable in 1928 or, at the government's option, after 1925. This was popular and subscribed above expectation. The second war loan — issued by McKenna in June 1915 — bore a higher interest yield of $4\frac{1}{2}$ per cent. The rise in interest rates was justified by the need to attract new investors. The loan was under-subscribed not simply because investors were 'unpatri-

98. On death duty rates and the yield of the duty, see Appendix VIII to the *Minutes of Evidence* of the Committee on National Debt and Taxation.

99. (Majority) *Report of the Committee on National Debt and Taxation*, PP 1927, Cmd 2800.

100. See the letter from F. Kellaway, Ministry of Munitions, to McKenna, Chancellor of the Exchequer, on 'one-man companies', 17 Nov. 1915, PRO T172/970.

101. Memorandum by the Board of Inland Revenue appended to the Report of the Cabinet Committee on tax evasion, dated March 1927, PRO CAB27/338 CP 88 (27). Unfortunately, the papers of the Royal Commission on the Income Tax which relate to tax evasion are not available to researchers.

otically' scrupulous, but also because capital was difficult to liquidate during the war. In fact the government found itself in the remarkable position of creating credit to finance its own borrowing; it arranged for the banks to afford their customers special facilities for the raising of money to purchase war bonds. Here was a major impetus to inflation. As later critics of wartime finance policy were to remark, a sizeable fraction of the capitalist class enriched itself by the rise of prices, and emerged from the war better off by the amount of increase in the National Debt to which they were enabled by the inflation to subscribe.[102] Individual subscribers to later war loans were a minority; the greater portion was taken up by the banks and other financial institutions through the use of the additional credit which the government's own operations were making it possible for them to create.

Lloyd George was later to question whether the June 1915 loan needed to have been at a commercial rate of interest, arguing that with the increase in nominal capital reserves due to war inflation and with the restriction on overseas markets for investment, 'the government could have continued to obtain as much money as it required by voluntary investment without raising its interest rates'. Had investors been unwilling to subscribe, 'there would have been a clear and popular ground for the conscription of capital for war purposes . . . '.[103] Nevertheless, under his premiership Bonar Law's loan of January 1917 was issued at 95, bore interest at 5 per cent and over £2,000m was raised at this 'penal' figure (the description is Lloyd George's). Furthermore, it had been felt necessary to offer extensive privileges in the form of conversion rights and tax concessions to make the war loans attractive to investors. Concessions varied from total exemption or exemption from deduction at source ( a cause of postwar evasion) to the right of tendering stock in payment of duties at a premium above the current price. Loans issued at a substantial discount were taxed on their nominal interest, not on the real yield to the investor. Doubtless these concessions were made in the belief that tax rates would soon fall sharply. In the event, the government gratuitously threw away considerable sums in tax receipts. The revenue loss on the January 1917 loan because of the absence of deduction at source was undoubtedly very heavy, though it cannot be quantified.[104]

By March 1920, war debt amounted to £6,226.7m, nearly half (£2,900m)

102. There were two powerful critiques of war finance from different theoretical perspectives: F. Fairer Smith, *War Finance and its Consequences*, London, 1936; and J.M. Keynes, *How to Pay for the War*, London, 1940. They concur in stressing its benevolent consequences for the *rentiers*.

103. Lloyd George, *War Memoirs*, vol. I, p. 74.

104. Ursula Hicks, *The Finance of British Government 1920–1936*, Oxford, 1938, 1969 ed., p. 312.

in relatively long loans of between eight and ten years, about £2,000m in short-term debt and the balance in floating debt. Only about a third of the total was held by private persons.[105] A large part was held by banks and the growing body of institutional *rentiers* (insurance companies, trade unions and building societies) and another large part by joint-stock companies. The private bond-holders were generally considered cautious investors who favoured gilt-edged securities; repayment of their interest and capital had the effect, Keynes argued, of encouraging colonial investment as against all types of English industrials.[106] Repayment to the institutional and joint-stock *rentiers* must have considerably strengthened British finance and industrial capitalism. The attempt to democratise the debt through War Savings Certificates and National War Bonds was not entirely successful since their freedom from income tax made them attractive to richer investors. Nearly 20 per cent of this portion of the debt came from certificates for the maximum permitted holding of £500.[107] Small investors contributed only about 8 per cent to the total debt.

In postwar years, servicing the war debt became a dead weight on public expenditure whose burden increased as prices fell and deferred payments to bond holders grew more expensive in real terms. Debt interest accounted for 12.4 per cent of prewar government revenue, 29.8 per cent of the vastly increased revenue in 1919 and 38.7 per cent in 1925. Total income from British government securities was £13.5m in 1912/13; in 1922/3 it was £161m. As a percentage of taxed income it rose from 1.5 per cent to 6.8 per cent.[108] Expenditure on the debt ran directly counter to providing the fiscal means for 'class abatement' since it diverted public funds from social services. Clark calculated that whereas, in the years 1914–25, annual government expenditure which could be regarded as beneficial to the less-well-off (taken to be those below the income tax limit) rose from £75.5m to £310m, spending beneficial to the well-to-do rose from £36m to £336m (£288m of the latter figure was accounted for by debt interest).[109]

Its critics were certain that the war loans policy accentuated the

105. *Report of the Committee on National Debt and Taxation*, p. 99.

106. Keynes, evidence to the Committee on National Debt and Taxation, *Minutes of Evidence*, p. 282.

107. Mallet and George, *British Budgets*; this is not to deny that savings certificates strengthened lower-middle-class and even working-class property ownership; see Hicks, *The Finance of British Government*, p. 323.

108. Ibid., p. 311; for the figures for the income from government securities see Appendix XI, Table 18, in the *Minutes* and Appendices to the Committee on National Debt and Taxation.

109. Clark, *National Income and Outlay*, Table 62, p. 147. This point qualifies, rather than destroys, the argument that the war accelerated the finding of the fiscal means for 'class abatement' for, because of the shift from indirect to direct taxation, a similar proportion of total tax revenue was raised from the working class after the war.

maldistribution of wealth, although the more benign view was that servicing the debt was a self-financing cycle since bond-holders paid their own interest through high postwar levels of taxation.[110] It is a question on which it is, at the moment, impossible to reach a definitive judgement since the principal historical source, the reports of the committee on National Debt and Taxation, diverged markedly on this issue. The majority report pointed out that higher postwar indirect taxation, borne principally by the less-well-off, contributed to debt interest and added that, in so far as debt holdings of income tax payers increased according to their wealth on a more progressive scale than that of their total liability to taxes, the payment of debt interest involved a transfer from poorer to richer within the income-tax-paying class. Somewhat oddly, however, it concluded that it did not appear that the disparity of wealth had been increased by loan finance. The minority report, on the other hand, thought it 'beyond question that the internal debt involves, on a balance, transfer of wealth such as aggravates the existing inequality in distribution of income, and tends to increase the proportion of the national income which finds its way into the hands on non-producers'. It stressed the huge unearned increment that accrued to the state's creditors with the fall in the general price level in the early 1920s; between March 1920 and March 1925 the value of every pound paid in interest upon the debt increased by about 87 per cent.[111] Given the growing scale of tax evasion and the malpractices known to be associated with war bonds sales, it seems highly likely that the view of the minority report (and other critics) was the correct one, and debt repayments represented a significant counter-tendency to the levelling of wealth.

## Conclusions

Interpretation of the relationship between war and social change continues to be dominated by the notion of participation, and it is to that concept that I will turn first in relating the changes discussed in this chapter to class structure. To a certain extent, we find empirical confirmation of the participation effect: the pyramid of economic inequality was perceptibly flattened by the war. In several respects, however, the participation notion and its attendant metaphor of the pyramid are inadequate to account for, or even visualise, the multi-directional change that took place. Not all the movement of social rewards can be conveniently seen as going upwards or downwards on a

110. For the benign view, see Hicks, *The Finance of British Government*, p. xiii.
111. (Minority) *Report of the Committee on National Debt and Taxation*, PP 1927, Cmd 2800, pp. 364–366.

scale. There was 'lateral' movement from land to finance, within the professions and so on. Income and wealth were not just, or even primarily, redistributed in favour of working-class participants; certain capitalists, professional workers, bond-holders and agriculturalists also benefited. The long-term fortunes of some manual workers whose labour was crucial to the war effort were sometimes pathetically disproportionate to their service to the community; thus, agricultural labourers, who made modest and short-lived gains under the wartime Corn Production Act, had their wages reduced in the early 1920s to a level slightly less, in real terms, than the penurious rate prevailing in 1914.[112] The consequences of participation were greatly qualified by the market power the groups in question already exercised and the specific demands generated by the wartime organisation of production. As has been noted — for example — the fiscal and actuarial revolution ushered in by the war entailed a greater market value for the services of the accounting professions. Historians who have dwelt on the participation effect have linked it to a loosening of the class structure, implicitly assuming that there is a simple relationship between a narrowing of economic differentials and a tendency to 'classlessness'.[113] In this argument, class structure is, in a rather facile way, elided with social stratification or hierarchical ranking. In my view, the empirical evidence will support another interpretation: society was certainly less steeply stratified, but the narrowing of economic differentials took place primarily within the three basic social classes and encouraged the consolidation of each. Rather than loosening the class structure, the war simplified the status hierarchy. In so doing, it strengthened those immanent properties of society which gave rise to the three classes. This interpretation, it must be admitted, goes against the grain of some of the social survey literature of the 1920s which cannot be lightly dismissed. Carr-Saunders and Caradog Jones, for example, accepted that the 'homogeneity of the wage-earning class [had] increased of late years' but declared: 'There is no longer any recognizable "upper" class, and as to the "middle" class, it was never anything more that a heterogeneous assemblage of very diverse and non-cohesive elements'.[114]

112. See *The Land and the Nation: the Rural Report of the Liberal Land Committee 1923–25*, London, 1925, pp. 14–15. For the official returns of wage rates in August 1914 and December 1924, see the *Ministry of Labour Gazette*, February 1925, p. 38. Further reference to agricultural labour is made in Chapter 4 of the present study.

113. Thus Marwick, *The Deluge*, p. 234, speaks of 'the war [having] a dissolving effect on the class structure', and in *Britain in the Century of Total War*, p. 170, of the 'weakening of the barriers between the classes'. Bowley, in *Some Economic Consequences of the War*, anticipated some of these conclusions, for example, p. 22.

114. A.M. Carr-Saunders, D. Caradog Jones, *A Survey of the Social Structure of England and Wales*, London, 1927, pp. 63, 71.

The apparent demise of a recognisable upper class was, I believe, more a question of the changes in its social style and the consolidation within it of historically distinct elites. It was the visible eclipse of an agrarian elite, which had so long been publicly identified as 'the governing class', that gave the impression of the disappearance of the upper class. By the criterion of large-scale capital ownership, the upper class remained in existence, with its wealth slightly more evenly distributed amongst a somewhat wider circle. Thus, in 1929, people with incomes of £7,000 a year — which almost invariably came from the ownership of great wealth — took 7.3 per cent of the national income. In 1911 people with the equivalent real income took 7.7 per cent of the national income but the size of that income group was only two-thirds of the postwar group.[115] Certain changes within the political elite — such as the growing preponderance of industrialists and business-men within the Conservative Party, which the war accelerated — reflected the shifting social composition of the upper class.[116] There is evidence, too, of the greater willingness of upper-class sons to enter business, rather than take up a career in higher administration and this was not unconnected with the eclipse of the landowning elite. According to the Association of First Division Civil Servants:

> The gradual decline of aristocratic traditions, a process accelerated by the economic changes resulting from the War, and the great development of the importance and prestige of business undertakings have . . . transformed [recruitment to the administrative class of the Civil Service]. The old prejudice against business employment has disappeared and . . . University graduates who have been educated at the leading Public Schools now show a marked preference for such employment.[117]

There is no evidence, however, of any significant decline in the influence of the formative institutions (the public schools and ancient universities) which did so much to make the upper class a recognisable socio-cultural entity. On the contrary, contemporary investigations of the educational backgrounds of elite occupations stressed the prepon-derance of ex-pupils of Headmaster's Conference schools. Tawney, who skilfully deployed this evidence in his *Equality*, diagnosed, as a peculiarity of the English class structure, its blending of preindustrial social forms with the dominance of industrial and commercial capital-ism. 'It is the combination of both — ', he believed, 'the blend of a

---

115. See Clark, *National Income and Outlay*, Table 51, p. 115.

116. A number of political historians have discussed this phenomenon; see, for example, John Stubbs, 'The Impact of the Great War on the Conservative Party', in Gillian Peele and Chris Cook, eds., *The Politics of Reappraisal*, London, 1975, esp. p. 24.

117. Statement to the Royal Commission on the Civil Service, 1930, cited in Gutts-man, ed., *The English Ruling Class*, p. 262.

crude plutocratic reality with the sentimental aroma of an aristocratic legend — which gives the English class structure its peculiar toughness and cohesion.'[118] The war made plutocratic reality somewhat more visible but it remained a peculiarity of the English to defer to government by Old Etonians.

Carr-Saunders and Caradog Jones were no doubt correct to stress the heterogeneity of the middle class, which is typically the least compact of the classes for both objective and socio-cultural reasons. The economic differences and social distance between those in the 'buffer zone' who were self-identified as middle-class and higher professionals were huge, comparatively far greater than those in the hierarchy of manual labour which separated skilled from unskilled, the 'respectable' from the 'rough'. There was, none the less, a *tendency* for them to contract. Undoubtedly the purely objective differences were lessened by the war, for the narrowing of income differentials is beyond dispute. Overall, the principal gainers of income redistribution were those earning between £200 and £1,000 a year and, as we have seen, the gains went disproportionately to men on salaries at the lower levels of that range. This is scarcely a novel conclusion, but in some sources it is expressed in ways open to serious misconstruction. Clark, for example, drew attention to the 'most striking growth in the "salariat". The numbers of well-paid salary earners [which were reckoned as those receiving £160 or more in 1911 and £250 or more in 1929] have increased nearly threefold since 1911, and their share of the national income has risen from 7 per cent to 13–15 per cent'.[119]

In fact, little of this difference can be explained by an expansion in the numbers of salaried occupations, which occurred principally in women's employment (and few women, in the 1920s, were on salaries of £250); necessarily most of it came about because of an improvement in the market advantages of male lower-middle- and middle-class employees who had been in work throughout the period and of the postwar recruits to a clerical and salaried labour force whose proportions were only marginally greater (see p. 90 and note 37). For Clark, who for his own purposes identified class with income, the middle class had greatly expanded: 'Since 1911 we have doubled the relative size of

118. R.H. Tawney, *Equality*, London, 1931, 1964 pbk ed., p. 64. He drew on the work of R.T. Nightingale, 'The Personnel of the British Foreign Office', London 1930, repr. in part in Guttsman, ed., *The English Ruling Class*, pp. 250–5; and of M. Ginsberg, 'Interchange between Social Classes', *Economic Journal*, Nov. 1929, repr. in *Studies in Sociology*, London, 1932. It is, of course, the case that the full effect (if there was any at all) on the pattern of recruitment to elite occupations traceable to the war would have been evident at a later date.

119. Clark, *National Income and Outlay*, p. 100. This scarcely detracts from the extraordinary value to historians of Clark's work, which was an entirely private investigation of a mass of data.

our middle-class . . . '.[120] In an important sense, this was illusory. What had doubled were the numbers (chiefly clerical and salaried men) who could achieve an income which brought a middle-class 'style of life'. We have seen that generally, in the same period, the best-paid higher professionals and administrators experienced a reduction in real incomes. The inescapable conclusion is that the admittedly still diffuse middle class, which began with the 'buffer zone' and reached to the higher professions, had been economically compressed. This compression took place by the early 1920s, for after 1924 there was no further tendency to income equality. Another conclusion is that movement through the 'buffer zone' to a position commanding a truly middle-class income (i.e. about 30 per cent higher than skilled manual earnings) must have become more frequent. There was not much more mobility between manual and non-manual occupations, but the chances of well-rewarded mobility were twice as great.

While we can be virtually certain of the greater equality of market rewards for those in middle-class positions, it is more difficult to be confident about any convergence in styles of life and the narrowing of social distance. This is partly a matter of the absence for the early 1920s of the type of descriptive sociology in the Le Play tradition, with its careful scrutiny of common 'standards', such as we find in D'Aeth and Descamps. The official sources are no less reticent: the Ministry of Labour deliberately excluded the salariat for its family budget inquiry of 1927 (for fear the results would be used in determining Civil Service salaries)[121] and this reluctance to scrutinise the middle class with the same thoroughness to which the working class was subject is typical of social survey procedure. Historians have neglected such topics as middle-class housing and the one essay collection on that theme stops short at 1914 with only a few hints as to the changing pattern of consumption in housing after that date. Though these indicate the drift from private single-family accommodation to commercialised accommodation and the wholesale conversion, in middle-class suburbs, of older Victorian houses into flats, bed-sitting rooms, private venture schools, and so on, they add little to testimony such as Mrs Peel's.[122] Her scarcely impeccable evidence suggested (as we have seen) a lowering of standards in D'Aeth's classes E and F in such key areas of consumption as housing, domestic service and private education; she compared, for example, the uses made of a £500 family income in 1914

120. Ibid., p. 144.
121. See 'Note of a discussion on the Family Budget Enquiry', 2 Dec. 1926, PRO LAB 17/2.
122. See the chapter by F.M.L. Thompson, 'Hampstead, 1830–1914', in M.A. Simpson and T.H. Lloyd, eds., *Middle-Class Housing in Britain*, Newton Abbot, 1977, esp. p. 113.

and the same money income in 1928 and it would appear that a typical status sacrifice for the once comfortably off members of the middle class whose incomes had not kept pace with inflation was preparatory education and second-class public schooling.[123] This would accord with the known influx of middle-class children into the scholarship system that led to local authority and state-supported grammar schools. As culturally formative institutions, they were coming to have an analogous role for the middle class as did the public schools for the upper. The reasons for this were complex, but one would appear to be the real fall in incomes of certain middle-class groups.

While this does imply a tendency towards the convergence of styles of life, by no means all the indicators point the same way. The war brought about one considerable divergence between standards at the top of the buffer zone and the more affluent groups since the decline in servant-keeping was (in London, at least), attributable to the great falling-off amongst those employed in single-servant lower-middle-class households. This falling-off began sooner and was proportionally much greater in the less wealthy London areas by comparison with the prosperous suburbs.[124] The implications are that the greater cost of domestic service and extra expenditure on mortgage repayments (combined with the greater reluctance to serve in that type of household) outstripped the gains of lower-middle-class employees. If so, then there was an important change in the set of social expectations typical of the clerical career. A characteristic aspiration of the prewar clerk in 'a good berth' (revealingly caught in Shan Bullock's *Robert Thorne: London Clerk*; see pp. 42–3) was that his wife should reach 'the servant standard' and receive in the drawing-room. The social changes brought by the war lessened the likelihood of achieving that ambition; though the numbers of women in domestic service rose again from 1921 (having fallen during the war) many returned as non-residential maids and 'chars'. Furthermore if, as so many believed, the middle class went through a hard, but consolidating, time during the inflation of 1914–20, it went through a good, but differentiating time during the long deflation of the interwar period. With the cheapening of money, mortgages and domestic labour, stratification according to patterns of consumption within the class reappeared so that for retailers in the late 1920s and 1930s: 'A realistic assessment of middle-class demand involved reference to both a lower-middle-class and an upper-middle-class and sometime even to a middle-middle class. The groups with

123. Mrs C.S. Peel, *How We Lived Then*, App. II: a comparison of the expenditure of a middle-class family of four with an earned income of £500 in 1914 and in 1928. The family was known to Mrs Peel.

124. See H. Llewellyn Smith, ed., *The New Survey of London Life and Labour*, 9 vols., London, 1930–35, vol. 8, p. 34.

different income levels and slightly different patterns of social behaviour . . . required of the distributive trades increasing flexibility of approach'.[125]

It would, however, be mistaken to see this as simply a return to the old prewar pattern of stratification which D'Aeth described, for a fundamental improvement in the relative position of the 'new' lower-middle class had taken place. If, as I suggested at the beginning of this chapter, class structure is both reflected and reproduced by the distribution of income and wealth, then its conclusion must be that the 'moving' picture of income and wealth distribution does not reveal any weakening of the socio-economic differentiation upon which the three class division rests. On the contrary, it suggests a strengthening of that differentiation.

125. J.B. Jeffreys, *Retail Trading in Britain 1850–1950*, Cambridge, 1954, p. 43.

# 4

## The Effects of the First World War on the Economic and Social Structure of the Working Class: Wages and Skills

### Introduction

Few can doubt that between the 1910s and the mid-1920s, there were certain striking changes in the condition of the English working class. The relative economic position of manual labour, judged by its share of the national income, improved slightly and real weekly wages advanced considerably on their 1914 level, up to 1921.[1] Since the 48-hour week was widely adopted in 1919, without a commensurate reduction in weekly rates, the advance in hourly wages was still greater. However, the most striking changes in working-class conditions came about primarily with the alteration of economic relationships *within* the class, with a radical improvement between 1906 and 1924 in the pay of the unskilled and a consequent narrowing of the differentials between craftsmen's and labourers' wages. There was a parallel improvement in the wages of the sheltered domestic trades as compared with the staple export industries. Furthermore, the prewar district variations in pay rates largely disappeared, with the standardisation of rates which levelled low-paid districts up to the high-paid.[2] Relationships within the working class were also affected by technological innovation and

1. Bowley and Stamp estimated that wage-earners obtained 43 per cent of the national income in 1911 and 44 per cent in 1924; see A.L. Bowley and J.C. Stamp, *The National Income 1924*, Oxford, 1927, p. 50. Feinstein calculated that the wage earners' share of GNP increased by 2.1 per cent between the 1910s and early 1920s; see C.H. Feinstein, 'Changes in the Distribution of the National Income in the United Kingdom since 1860', in J. Marchal and B. Ducros, eds., *The Distribution of National Income*, London, 1968 pp. 115–38. For wages, see G. Routh, *Occupation and Pay in Great Britain 1906–1960*, Cambridge, 1965, Table 49, p. 110. His table gives us these indices of real weekly wage rates (1914 = 100); 1920 = 104/118; 1921 = 128; 1922 = 117; 1923 = 113; 1924 = 115; 1925 = 114. See also Tables 4.10 and 4.11 in A.H. Halsey, ed., *Trends in British Society since 1900*, London, 1972, pp. 121–2.
2. In 1914, the standard district rates for fitters and turners in the engineering industry ranged from 30s. to 40s. 6d., although the large majority worked at rates within a smaller range between 35s. to 38s. See J.W.F. Rowe, *Wages in Theory and Practice*, London, 1928, p. 84. Variations in wage rates in other large industries, such as building, were also considerable.

the increasing number of occupations demanding only one or a small number of specialised skills, and not requiring lengthy training. Within the working-class community, these changes were manifested in two major ways: by the fall in the numbers in unavoidable primary poverty and the decline in the standard of life of the skilled artisan. For many of the latter this was a decline only relative to the unskilled and other tradesmen; for some, an absolute decline in earning power.

The lifting of large numbers out of primary poverty can be linked with what I have called the emancipatory image of the war's social consequences. The decline in the artisan standard of life has been referred to by Eric Hobsbawm, in a seminal essay, as the collapse of the English 'labour aristocracy'.[3] The phrase is often rather loosely used to refer to the elite of skilled workers, but in Marxist historiography it has been a concept which explains the trajectory of class relations in capitalist society. If such a collapse did take place, this would be consistent with the polarisation of class relations.

Working-class life had also undergone moral and cultural change in the same period, with the decline in family size, the decrease in drinking and the more 'gentle' tone of the local community. Furthermore, by the late 1920s, an entirely new type of working-class residential zone with a distinctive cultural pattern was arising on the outer suburbs of London, Birmingham, Liverpool and in such overspill developments as Becontree and Dagenham. A movement from the 'classic slum' to the working-class estate was in train. It would be an elementary historical error to casually assume that because a war intervened between the 1910s and the late 1920s, then the war caused these changes in working-class conditions. It often gave, however, a demonstrable impetus to long-term cultural and demographic trends. For example, the rapid fall between 1914 and the early 1920s in the number of children under five in the working-class family is principally attributable to an estimated 600,000 birth losses due to the separation of married couples.[4] This demographic loss intermeshed with the secular trend towards smaller family size and was a subsidiary cause of the decline in poverty. Again, wartime liquor regulations palpably accelerated a longer-term process, and much of the evidence for the improvements in workers' homes, the 'gentling' of their manners during the war and a new pattern of consumption, comes from the official body set up to enforce liquor control. It had, of course, a vested interest in gathering it, but the evidence for a new sobriety has been regularly echoed in working-class autobiography and Edwardian memory, and is confirmed by the gross statistics. Weekly prosecutions for

3. E.J. Hobsbawm, 'The Labour Aristocracy in Nineteenth-Century Britain', in idem, *Labouring Men*, London, 1964, pp. 272–315; this essay was first published in 1954.
4. See P.R. Cox, *Demography*, Cambridge, 1970 ed., p. 319.

drunkenness were five times higher in prewar London than they were at the end of the war.[5]

That the war had been a great divide in the history of everyday working-class life is strongly evident in the canon of empirical sociology. When Hubert Llewellyn Smith and his colleagues published the first of their volumes in the New London Survey they had no hesitation in singling out the war as the watershed dividing Booth's London from the interwar present:

> The reader . . . will again and again be confronted with the fact that the most fruitful comparison is not so much between now and forty years ago as between the post-war and pre-war conditions — so much greater and more striking have been the sudden changes wrought in the conditions of London life and Labour by the great catastrophe, than by the slight and more gradual movement of the whole preceding generation.[6]

The principal changes they recorded were a disproportionate rise in the hourly money wages of the unskilled (an entirely post-1914 phenomenon), the emergence and growing importance of semi-skilled workers in the mechanical industries, the expansion of factory employment at the expense of workshop trades, and the substitution of the dynamic poverty of unemployment for the static poverty of low wages.[7] Doubtless, London was a favoured industrial region during the 1920s; after the recovery from the 1921–3 depression an imaginary line, running from the mouth of the Severn to the High Peak and thence to Scarborough, divided the country into two parts of almost equal economic importance, but greatly contrasting fortune. To its left (in the north and west) unemployment was almost exactly double what it was on the right. The line divided areas of economic stagnation from dynamic centres such as the capital city, Bristol, Coventry and Doncaster, where the stimulus the war had given to industrial development could be seen in the growth of the electrical apparatus, vehicles, aircraft and light engineering industries.[8]

Though London was a favoured industrial region, many of the changes recorded by Smith and his colleagues had occurred elsewhere, and other social scientists were equally convinced that the war had

5. See P. Thompson, *The Edwardians*, London, 1975, p. 198. For descriptions of drunken brawling in the Edwardian working-class community, see M. Phillips, *The Young Industrial Worker*, Oxford, 1922, p. 23; H.M. Burton, *There was a Young Man*, London, 1958, pp. 18–19; A.S. Jasper, *A. Hoxton Childhood*, London, 1969.

6. H. Llewellyn Smith, ed., *The New Survey of London Life and Labour* (9 vols., London, 1930–5), vol. 1, *Forty Years of Change*, p. 5.

7. See ibid., vol. 1, pp. 115–17; vol. 2, *London Industries*, pp. 5ff.; vol. 3, *Survey of Social Conditions, I The Eastern Area*, pp. 9–10.

8. See H.D. Henderson, 'The New Industrial Revolution', first published 1926, repr. in idem, *The Inter-war Years and Other Papers*, Oxford, 1955, p. 29.

profoundly modified the pattern of working-class life. In 1913, Bowley had concluded from a random sample survey of Northampton, Warrington, Stanley, Reading and York that 'to raise the wages of the worst-paid workers is the most pressing social task with which the country is confronted today'.[9] In 1923–4, he surveyed the first four towns and added new data from Bolton. He found that, despite higher unemployment, the proportion in poverty in 1924 was little more than half that in 1913. The two chief factors in causing this fall were the approximate doubling of money wages for unskilled labour during the period and the reduction in the number of dependent children in the working-class family. Bowley calculated that the effect of the first in reducing poverty was perhaps twice as great as the second. He recalled the most pressing task that prewar society had to undertake and concluded 'it had needed a war to do it'.[10]

## The Structuration of the Working Class

Since Marx's death, what may be called the 'structuration' of the working class — the variable process by which manual labour is both homogenised and differentiated — has had a central place in the analysis of class society as a whole and the debate over the salience (or otherwise) of class in social development. Marx believed that the subordination of wage labour to capital would entail labour becoming an increasingly homogeneous commodity. Though he ceased to believe at some point in the 1850s that the working class would become absolutely impoverished by the inexorable pressures of capitalist competition and the falling rate of profit, he remained convinced that the accumulation of misery was 'a necessary condition, corresponding to the accumulation of wealth'.[11] In this dual process of homogenisation and social polarisation lay the revolutionary dynamic of capitalist society.

Marx's critics have happily seized on these prognoses to refute him. In the 1890s, one of them argued that where industrial capitalism was longest established — in the Lancashire cotton industry — then the evidence of the operatives' family budgets, of their thrift and local share-holding, of their domestic culture, all contradicted Marx's vision of the proletariat in mature industrial capitalism.[12] More recently, Dahrendorf has asserted that technological innovation and investment,

9. A.L. Bowley, A.R. Burnett-Hurst, *Livelihood and Poverty*, London, 1915, p. 42.

10. A.L. Bowley, M.H. Hogg, *Has Poverty Diminished?*, London, 1925, chap. 1.

11. K. Marx, *Capital*, vol. 1, Harmondsworth, 1976, p. 799.

12. G. von Schulze-Gaevernitz, *The Cotton Trade in England and on the Continent*, London, 1895, pp. 178–91.

far from creating 'a homogeneous group of equally unskilled and
impoverished people' had led to 'a stratum differentiated by numerous
subtle and not-so-subtle distinctions'.[13] Differentiation, he suggested,
has come about with the emergence of new categories of industrial
worker: by the 1900s, the semi-skilled who had not been apprenticed
but trained directly on the job were a well-recognised category, particularly in engineering; by the interwar period, there was a group of
highly skilled technicians not trained through trade apprenticeships
but through engineering studentships. Dahrendorf concluded that in
place of the proletariat, 'we find a plurality of status and skill groups
whose interests often diverge'.[14]

The question of the structuration of the working class has been just
as important for Marxist historians as it has for Marx's critics. But
rather than seizing on skill- and status-differentiation into many
groups, it is to the theory of the labour aristocracy that they have
turned for *the* explanation of why 'in the world's first capitalist society,
the pattern of class formation, of class consciousness, and class conflict
did not take the form predicted by Marx'.[15] Between 1850 to about
1880, the labour aristocracy appears to have been a distinct social
stratum of craft workers, with a high rate of inter-marriage between
'aristocratic' families and a strong tendency to reproduce itself through
the handing down of trades from father to son.[16] It was marked off, as a
socio-cultural entity, both from the middle class and the rest of the
working class, by its leisure pursuits and by a common set of beliefs
about 'respectability', the legitimacy of trade unionism and voluntary
collectivism. There are good reasons — to which I will return — for
doubting whether such a socio-cultural stratum still existed in Edwardian England.

The chief proponent of its existence up to 1914 is Eric Hobsbawm,
who has suggested that as a stratum of the working class the labour
aristocracy was probably at its peak in the late-nineteenth and early-
twentieth centuries.[17] Hobsbawm wishes to retain most of the explanatory value given to the notion of the labour aristocracy by Lenin: that is
to say, the stratum was the basis of the 'economism' of the Labour
movement for it established a pattern of craft and trade militancy

13. R. Dahrendorf, *Class and Class Conflict in an Industrial Society*, London, 1959, p. 48.
14. Ibid., p. 51.
15. H.F. Moorhouse, 'The Marxist Theory of the Labour Aristocracy', *Social History*,
vol. 3, 1978, p. 61: an incisive critique of the theory.
16. See, in particular, R.Q. Gray, *The Labour Aristocracy in Victorian Edinburgh*, London,
1976; G. Crossick, *An Artisan Elite in Victorian Society: Kentish London, 1840–1880*, London,
1978. For a survey of work utilising the concept see R.Q. Gray, *The Aristocracy of Labour in
Nineteenth-Century Britain c. 1850–1914*, London, 1981.
17. E.J. Hobsbawm, 'Lenin and the "Aristocracy of Labour"', in idem, *Revolutionaries*,
London, 1981.

which disrupted the unity and consciousness of the proletariat. It infected the workers with bourgeois ideas and led to 'opportunist' forms of working-class politics.[18] When attempting to define empirically the stratum Hobsbawm puts forward six criteria for membership of a labour aristocracy: high and regular earnings; prospects of social security; conditions of work, including the way the aristocrat was treated by foremen and masters; relations with social strata above and below him; general conditions of living; the prospects of future advancement and those of his children. Of these, earnings were 'incomparably the most important ... '.[19] Hobsbawm stresses the social merging, up to the 1890s, of the labour aristocracy with the lower-middle class, through the entry of aristocrats' children into white-collar work such as elementary-school teaching, and other factors. This social merging 'helps to explain political attitudes. Thus the persistent liberal-radicalism [of the labour aristocracy] in the nineteenth century is easily understood, as also its failure to form an independent working-class party'.[20] Imperialism, he suggests, began to cut off the aristocracy of labour from the managerial and small-master groups with whom it had merged, and from the vastly expanded white-collar classes, and only then was the aristocracy of labour attracted to a Labour Party.

We must note immediately that the one part of this claim is not consistent with the empirical data if it is taken to mean that, from the 1890s, the intergenerational flow between the artisan stratum and white-collar employment slackened off. The white-collared classes expanded so rapidly precisely because the flow became much greater. As Bowley stressed in 1915, his 'five town' survey and other data showed that 'the children of artisans become clerks and teachers with increasing frequency ... '.[21] If liberal-radicalism can be so mechanically linked to social position and mobility prospects (and the links between social structure and political consciousness are decidedly mechanical in Hobsbawm's analysis) then it should have been greatly strengthened by mobility patterns in the early twentieth century.

Hobsbawm argues that, though the relationship between the aristocracy and the strata above it was fluid, the boundary between it and those below was precise. This boundary was marked by the large differential between skilled and unskilled, 'aristocratic' and 'plebeian' occupations, a differential maintained by the restriction of entry into

18. Idem, 'The Labour Aristocracy in Nineteenth-Century Britain' and 'Lenin and the "Aristocracy of Labour"'.

19. Idem, 'The Labour Aristocracy in Nineteenth-Century Britain', p. 273.

20. Ibid., p. 274.

21. See A.L. Bowley, *The Nature and Purpose of the Measurement of Social Phenomena*, London, 1915, 1923 ed., p. 88.

the trade, and the force of customary ideas of a 'fair' wage for a skilled man in comparison to other skilled men and to labourers. As a general rule, he suggests that the differential approached 100 per cent, the stronger, the more exclusive and 'aristocratic' the craft. As he recognises, this rule of thumb excludes a sizeable proportion of men, recognised as skilled and paid substantially above the rate for unskilled labour, from the prewar labour aristocracy. Hobsbawm limits the aristocracy to the best-paid elites within the skilled ranks of certain occupations in certain industries and assumes that 'as a rough guide [it] included not more than 15 per cent of the working class . . .'.[22] By the late nineteenth century, the centre of gravity of the labour aristocracy had shifted from traditional crafts, carried on in small workshops, to the sectors of the metal trades organised in large units of production: iron and steel manufacture, heavy engineering and shipbuilding. The Board of Trade Enquiry into Earnings and Hours, carried out in 1906, has enabled Hobsbawm to identify the 'aristocratic' industries (and the 'aristocratic' occupations within industries) with confidence. The industries with the highest proportion of aristocratic workers were the metal trades already mentioned, followed by cotton, building and printing. As he notes, however, this list does not include the largest aggregate of highly-paid workers: the 600,000 (in 1906) coal-miners averaging 43s. a week. It is extremely difficult to assimilate coal-miners to the labour aristocracy as Hobsbawm defines it, since they were a socially and economically homogenous labour force. Only in the Midlands Counties coalfield where the 'butty' or contract system survived until 1919 can we identify a vestigial aristocracy *within* the mining labour force.[23] The preeminent aristocratic occupations — measured by the percentage in them earning 45s. a week or more — were skilled piece-work in shipbuilding (plating, riveting, etc.) 'fine' cotton spinning, skilled piece-work in engineering, and piece-work in iron and steel manufacture. All were 'export' trades or highly exposed to foreign competition.

As a guide to the best-paid industries and occupations open to prewar workers Hobsbawm's analysis remains invaluable, but many of the assumptions about working-class social structure which lie behind the 'labour aristocracy' thesis are suspect. A preliminary problem is the validity of Hobsbawm's aristocracy as a demographic entity for he tends to lump together the top 15 per cent of wage-earners in different industries without enquiring too closely into such questions as their

22. Hobsbawm, 'The Labour Aristocracy in Nineteenth-Century Britain', p. 285.
23. The butty system in the Nottinghamshire coalfield was ended by a miners' strike in January 1919; see PRO MUN4/3541, Ministry of Munitions Demobilisation and Resettlement Department — Intelligence and Record Section. Report on the General Labour situations, 11 Jan. 1919.

different life-work cycles and the stability — or otherwise — of their employment. Where 'aristocratic' status went with piece-work and output — as, in Hobsbawm's view, it so often did by 1900 — then it must frequently have been a phase in a man's working life that ended with declining physical powers. In the iron and steel trades, heavy specialised labour could bring a man 'aristocratic' earnings as long as his strength held. Lady Bell noted that: 'Over and over again one finds . . . a man doing the work of a labourer . . . in his old age, at 18/- a week, who has been in receipt of twice or even three times that amount when he was younger'.[24] A man such as this was in a quite different occupational life-cycle as compared with the aristocrats amongst train drivers who reached their top rate when they were approaching fifty.

A more fundamental objection is that the notion of a sharp divide between 'the labour aristocracy' and the rest of the working class is borne out neither by the distribution of wages and earnings nor by what is known of personal intergenerational mobility within the class. Amongst an occupationally homogeneous group of 1,197 adult male workers in Middlesbrough (an iron and steel centre of 'aristocratic' occupations), Lady Bell found that 8 per cent were paid less than 20s. a week, 33.2 per cent between 20s. and 30s., 34.3 per cent between 30s. and 40s., 19.5 per cent between 40s. and 60s., and 5 per cent over 60s.[25] This distribution is discrepant with the view of a precise boundary and large differential between aristocrats and other workers. The size of the group earning more than a labourer's and less than an aristocrat's wage is discrepant, too, with the notion of only a tiny elite winning more than the price of subsistence from the 'super-profits' of capitalism. Moreover, the income levels between 20s. and 45s. a week did not represent closed social aggregates but an earnings cycle through which a man could move. There is no reason to believe that this distribution of earnings at either one point in time or in the individual life cycle was particularly exceptional. If we turn to the distribution of wages amongst 8m. weekly wage earners, as shown in Bowley's table (Table 4.1), we find an identical percentage of men on a rate above the unskilled labourer's and below the aristocrat's. We have fairly reliable testimony that, even in the preeminently aristocratic trades in engineering, boilermaking and shipbuilding, the skilled tradesman had little chance of finding a fresh situation at his top rate after the age of about forty-five or fifty. The unreliability of industrial employment meant that a fall in earnings in middle age was still a common experience in the late 1940s.[26]

24. Lady F. Bell, *At the Works*, London, 1907, p. 109.
25. Ibid., p. 48.
26. See the evidence of Sir Benjamin Browne, of the Engineering Employers' Federa-

**Table 4.1.** Weekly wages of 8m men in regular employment in the UK, 1910

| Wage | No. of men (000s) | % of total |
|------|-------------------|------------|
| Under 15s. | 320 | 4 |
| 15s.–20s. | 640 | 8 |
| 20s.–25s. | 1,600 | 20 |
| 25s.–30s. | 1,680 | 21 |
| 30s.–35s. | 1,680 | 21 |
| 35s.–40s. | 1,040 | 13 |
| 40s.–45s. | 560 | 7 |
| Over 45s. | 480 | 6 |

*Source*: Calculated by A.L. Bowley, publ. in B.S. Rowntree, 'The Industrial Unrest', *The Contemporary Review*, October 1911.

When we consider total working-class *household* earnings, then it is even more evident that between the minority of best-paid and the larger minority of wretchedly exploited there lay a majority of the working class who were not aristocrats but were none the less able to participate in an increasingly dense urban culture. In Rowntree's York, average working-class *family* earnings were 32s. 9d. per week and the majority (52.6 per cent) of the wage-earning population belonged to his class D, consisting 'largely of skilled workers'. This class could secure some amenities which indicate a diffusion of (in strictly historical and comparative terms) affluence. There was, for example, the 'growing practice for families of "Class D" to take a few day's summer holiday out of York'.[27] The point would be of limited significance were it not for the probability that a common culture was binding the differentiated grades of labour more decisively than the exclusivity of elite workers was fragmenting them.[28]

For a common culture to persist required a substantial degree of short-range mobility between the different grades of labour. As we have seen (Chapter 2) much contemporary opinion envisaged labour ranked in exclusive social classes, but personal mobility and intergenerational mobility were sufficiently frequent to suggest that this view was mis-

tion, to the 1905–9 Poor Law Commission, cited in J.B. Jefferys, *The Story of the Engineers 1800–1945*, London, 1946, p. 132. Engineering and shipbuilding workers were liable to unemployment because of the susceptibility of their industries to cyclical depressions in trade. Little research has been done on the *demotion* of the middle-aged men, but Ferdynand Zweig observed that it 'affects the vast majority of working men at a certain age', idem, *The British Worker*, Harmondsworth, 1953, p. 23.

27. B.S. Rowntree, *Poverty: A Study of Town Life*, London, 1902 ed., p. 76.

28. See S. Reynold et al, *Seems So! A Working-class View of Politics*, London, 1911, p. xix, for an explicit claim that working people were coming to see themselves as 'more in touch' with each other.

taken. Satisfactory data on mobility within individual life-experience is hard to obtain, but Paul Thompson — drawing on the oral testimony of a large sample of Edwardians — has stressed that the insecure employment of Edwardian men meant that they were constantly on the move, not only geographically, but also between industries and occupational grades. 'There was a constant interchange between unskilled labouring, semi-skilled work in transport, skilled work in building and small-scale trading.'[29] Entry into aristocratic trades where craft societies could enforce apprenticeship regulations was clearly more difficult, but there was a number of craft occupations that could be learnt by 'following-up' and 'improving': a process epigrammatically summed up by a master plumber as 'Bad Mate, Good Mate, Bad Plumber, Good Plumber'. Norman Dearle, the investigator who was told this, recorded several employment histories which fully endorse Thompson's assertion. Dearle also claimed that most London bricklayers (whose average earnings for a full-time week were an 'aristocratic' 44s. 5d. in 1906) were recruited 'from the younger provincial labourers who obtain a knowledge of the simpler processes by observation, and then get hold of a trowel and start to lay bricks'.[30] There were clearly some aristocratic groups of pretty plebeian pedigree.

The data on intergenerational mobility do show that the unskilled working class had a stronger tendency to self-recruitment than other strata; of the sons born to fathers in the unskilled and semi-skilled manual working class before 1890, 57.5 per cent were, according to the Glass survey, in the same occupational status in 1949.[31] This was compatible, however, with a good deal of movement out of the unskilled working class, including upgrading by the traditional method of apprenticeship. Bowley found from his prewar survey that, amongst families where children had taken up occupations, 35 per cent of unskilled households had children in skilled, apprenticed or otherwise higher-grade occupations.[32] It is of some interest to note that when Ginsberg classified Bowley's data from the postwar survey of the same towns he found that amongst the sons of the unskilled who had entered the labour force, 46.7 per cent were in skilled occupations. He pointed out that 'the notion the unskilled form a stable group is not borne out by these figures . . .'.[33] The data do not justify firm conclusions, but they would suggest that the raising of the economic position of the unskilled relative to the other working-class strata between the two

29. Thompson, *The Edwardians*, p. 218.

30. See N.B. Dearle, *Industrial Training*, London, 1914, pp. 117–19, 137.

31. D.V. Glass, ed., *Social Mobility in Britain*, London, 1954, Table 6, p. 186.

32. Bowley, *The Nature and Purpose of the Measurement of Social Phenomena*, p. 89.

33. M. Ginsberg, 'Interchange between Social Classes', *The Economic Journal*, Dec. 1929, p. 564.

surveys increased the short-distance mobility chances of their children. In a preliminary report on his oral history investigation, Thompson emphasised how the frequency of short-range mobility and the extension of family ties to many groups cast grave doubts on the idea of the labour aristocracy as a social stratum:

> [It] has proved very difficult to discover the families of 'labour aristocrats', whose role has been so much emphasised in working-class political history . . . only one family has so far been found which clearly fits this description. It seems possible that the pattern of individual occupational mobility and therefore of social structure was rather more flexible in this period than has been assumed.[34]

## War and the Wage Structure

It would be presumptuous to imagine that the debate over the labour aristocracy can be settled lightly. My own belief is that the upper, artisan stratum of the working class was a larger, more fluid and more permeable formation than the labour aristocracy concept would allow and, furthermore, 'the artisan class' persisted as a stratum because, after about 1890, it was primarily a distributive and status grouping marked off by the notable division in the working-class housing market between accommodation regarded as 'artisan standard' and the abysmal dwellings of labourers, casuals and outworkers.[35] Access to this distributive grouping could be achieved by workers who were in no sense labour aristocrats (the male workers of the Yorkshire woollen industry would be a case in point).[36] Clearly, wage differences were of fundamental importance in bringing about a partial social closure around the artisan style of life, but 'skidding' by skilled artisans and the up-grading of labourers made differentials smaller and less rigid, and led to a two-way penetration of the line between skilled and unskilled.[37] The artisan stratum was not exclusive (as the term 'aristocracy' suggests) but it was more strongly differentiated and entrenched in the export trades by virtue both of earnings differentials within those trades and the generally higher earnings that could be achieved in them as compared with domestic industries.

34. Cited in Moorhouse, 'The Marxist Theory of the Labour Aristocracy', p. 67.
35. A.S. Wohl dated the improvement in artisan housing in London to the 1880s; see idem, 'The Housing of the Working Classes in London 1815–1914', in S.D. Chapman, ed., *The History of Working-class Housing: A Symposium*, Newton Abbot, 1970), pp. 13–54. Before that date, miserable conditions were not confined to labourers.
36. See P. Descamps, *La Formation sociale de l'Anglais moderne*, Paris, 1914.
37. On upgrading in the engineering industry, see the evidence of Sir Benjamin Browne to the Poor Law Commission, quoted in Dearle, *Industrial Training*, p. 147.

Such generalisations could obviously be overthrown by more detailed research into the artisan stratum of the years between *ca* 1900
and 1914, but it is not strictly necessary to take the exact form of the
stratification of the prewar working class as a settled matter in order to
appreciate the historical significance of the war in restructuring the
working class. Whether we believe the upper stratum to have been
narrow and 'closed' or wide and 'open' we are bound to recognise the
importance for working-class structuration of the modification of economic differences between the grades of labour that took place after
1914, and it is to the thorough upheaval of wage relativities which
resulted from the combination of wartime wage policy and the distor-
tion of the labour market that I will now turn. It has long been
recognised that the disruption of the wage structure affected economic
differences within the working class in the short term and had important implications for the way the wage structure was determined thereafter. Up to the end of 1920, both policy and a distorted market led to a
remarkable tendency towards the quality of working-class incomes. To
stop the analysis at that point would clearly be unsatisfactory for it is at
least reasonable to think that the severity of the 1921–3 slump was a
consequence of the war's disruption of world trade. The historical
moment we choose to consider as the date when the wartime dislocation ceased to influence the labour market will be pretty arbitrary;
however, 1925 provides a clean, if rather symbolic end, to more than a
decade's discontinuity in economic history with the return to the Gold
Standard in April of that year.[38]

To proceed as far as that date involves complex issues for it con-
cludes an unprecedently violent economic movement since August
1914, with a price-wage inflation that broke between August 1920 and
January 1921, followed by a savage recession involving a sharp fall in
basic commodity prices and widespread wage reductions. The two
movements of the economic pendulum involved, respectively, unpre-
cedentedly full employment and unprecedented unemployment. The
complexity arises from the quite varied consequences for different
working-class groups of inflation and recession. All authorities agree
that the wage movements in the inflationary period were proportionately more favourable to the unskilled and semi-skilled, but many of
these gains were wiped out during the recession triggered off by the
war. Table 4.2 shows the oscillation of wage differentials in five major
industries. Moreover, there began, during the recessionary period, that

---

38. A.C. Pigou argued that 'the plateau of relative stability . . . reached by [1925],
affords a convenient stopping place', idem, 'An Analytical Account of the General
Economic Movement in the United Kingdom, between the Armistice and the Restoration of the Gold Standard', PRO LAB17/112, p. 1. This invaluable memorandum was
published as *Aspects of British Economic History, 1918–1925*, n.p., 1948.

**Table 4.2.** True weekly wage rates in five major industries (1913 = 100)

|                | Building | Coalmining | Cotton | Engineering | Railways |
|----------------|----------|------------|--------|-------------|----------|
| **1886**       |          |            |        |             |          |
| Skilled        | 80       | 63         | 79     | 77          | 93       |
| Semi-skilled   | 83       | 72         | 72     | 73          | 89       |
| Unskilled      | 75       | 72         | 82     | 82          | 91       |
| **1920** (The cost of living was 265 per cent over 1913) |  |  |  |  |  |
| Skilled        | 250      | 291        | 312    | 256         | 240      |
| Semi-skilled   | 278      | 314        | 325    | 290         | 275      |
| Unskilled      | 328      | 325        | 331    | 319         | 330      |
| **1926** (The cost of living was 175 per cent) |  |  |  |  |  |
| Skilled        | 182      | 170        | 185    | 162         | 205      |
| Semi-skilled   | 205      | 168        | 193    | 171         | 215      |
| Unskilled      | 212      | 174        | 196    | 184         | 222      |

*Source*: J.W.F. Rowe, *Wages in Practice and Theory*, 1928, pp. 44–5

divergence between the economic fortunes of the staple export industries and the domestic industries which was a marked feature of the
interwar years as a whole.

The empirical facts as to the narrowing of differentials between 1914
and 1920 are quite familiar; what is worth emphasising is the change,
during this period, in the popular mentalities which sanctioned economic differences between wage earners. Until at least the 1880s wages
in most sectors of industry were determined by customary notions of
'fairness' which harked back to the idea of a 'just wage' prevalent in
preindustrial society.[39] The equity of wages was judged by comparison
with other men's earnings (rather than by comparison with the cost of
living or profits or in relation to a certain standard of affluence) and
there can be little doubt that this was the test normally employed by
trade union leaders and the bulk of wage-earners. This was seen most
clearly in the relation of skilled to unskilled wages. Skilled and unskilled were accustomed to a certain differential between their wage
rates and provided this was maintained both were satisfied. The test of
comparison was also applied by both skilled and unskilled to the actual
level of their wage rates, for wages were reckoned as fair not only by
comparison with each other's rates but with the wages of similar grades
in other industries. An increase in wages in one industry was a sign for
a wage increase in any industry in the same locality. The standard
trade union district rate did not so much supersede customary reckon-

39. Rowe, *Wages in Practice and Theory*, p. 156. The rest of this paragraph follows
Rowe's argument very closely.

ing as solidify it.

From about 1890, the common test of comparison began to break down for two reasons: the first was the growth in numbers and organisation of semi-skilled workers which, because of technical changes, was particularly marked in engineering. The second was workers' collectivism (sometimes allied to socialism) which stressed the common claims of different grades of labour within an industry and led to a more militant type of trade union policy, motivated by the inequality of income between wage-earner and capitalist and aiming to restrict profits to a minimum. There were definite signs that, in the years immediately preceding the war, the combined results of technical change and collectivism were becoming very marked. The customary wage differentials between skilled and unskilled were no longer regarded as sacrosanct (though few had been greatly disturbed by 1914) and wage movements in individual industries became much more autonomous. With the development of trade unionism, the labour force of each industry tended to become a compact group with a corporate individuality. By 1913, however, these developments had not proceeded very far: there was still a tolerable symmetry in the wages of the same grade of labour in different industries.

The war period greatly accelerated these changes. There was a further, very marked, shift from a wage basis determined by custom to a basis of bargaining strength. 'The last lingering traces of the old idea of "just", meaning customary and therefore fair and proper, wages was completely swept away.'[40] During the inflationary and recessionary movements of the economic pendulum there were powerful tendencies towards wage homogenisation within industries and wage differentiation between them. One profoundly important change was the enormous disrepute into which capitalist profit-making fell, for this sanctioned large claims (such as the miners' in 1919 and the transport workers' in 1920) based on the demand for a more equitable share in the profits of industry. Another was the growth in the collective bargaining power of the less skilled between 1914 and 1920. A further factor was the extraordinary labour mobility of a time of war: the official *History of the Ministry of Munitions* noted that 'the immense transfer of workers from one occupation to another and from one district to another accustomed individuals to wages they would never have commanded in their original occupations, and gave them new conceptions of their economic value'.[41]

Wartime wage control played a very important part in bringing about this shift from customary (often local) comparison to nation-

---

40. Ibid., p. 159.
41. *The History of the Ministry of Munitions*, London, 1920–4, vol. 5, pt. 1, p. 232.

wide bargaining. Controls were unnecessary between August 1914 and February 1915, for patriotic restraint led unions to rapidly settle outstanding disputes with employers and they lodged no new demands in spite of the rise in food prices which occurred on the outbreak of war. The industrial truce was broken in February 1915 when unprecedented advances in money wages were secured by groups of workmen whose labour was critical for war purposes, although even these were not sufficient to compensate for the rise in the cost of living.[42] The first public revelations of profiteering were one reason for the men's throwing over the truce. In general, advances were secured where the need for labour was greatest and labour was backed by organisation. At this date, advances were not uniform as between districts; munitions centres showed advances long before other centres, and retained their advances when general advances were made. The adoption of first voluntary and later compulsory arbitration brought a new element into the wage structure. The body controlling wage advances became the Committee on Production, set up in February 1915 to facilitate the provision of engineering and shipbuilding labour for war work. The Munitions of War Act of July 1915 made the Committee the supreme compulsory arbitration authority. Under the conditions of wartime inflation the idea that wages ought to increase systematically with the cost of living gained many adherents and it became the principal ground on which union leaders lodged claims.[43] From February 1917, the Committee itself instituted the practice of automatic three-month wage reviews to protect workers from inflation. Equally powerful was the idea that the less-well-paid were more in need of protection from inflation than the better-paid workers and the Committee adopted a policy of making flat-rate percentage awards, often linked to special concessions adjusting local rates up to the rates of the best-paid districts. Preferential treatment for the unskilled was made a pressing necessity by the fact that their weekly expenditure rose proportionally more than that of other working-class groups. Price inflation most affected food, an item which accounted for a larger segment of the unskilled worker's family budget than the skilled, and increase, by 1918, in the cost of living for the unskilled was reckoned 14 per cent greater (see Table 4.3). J.W.F. Rowe regarded this preferential treatment as having 'entirely obliterated the old ideas as to the fair and proper differential between skilled and unskilled'.[44] This oversimplifies and foreshortens the three and a half years of industrial relations between June 1915 and November 1918; the strength of those 'old

42. Ibid., p. 16; see also A.L. Bowley, *Prices and Wages in the United Kingdom 1914–20*, Oxford, 1921, pp. 89ff.

43. Bowley, *Prices and Wages in the U.K.*, p. 96.

44. Rowe, *Wages in Theory and Practice*, p. 158.

**Table 4.3.** Approximate average weekly expenditure of a standard urban working-class family in July 1914 and June 1918, UK

|  | Skilled | | Semi-skilled | | Unskilled | |
|---|---|---|---|---|---|---|
|  | 1914 | 1918 | 1914 | 1918 | 1914 | 1918 |
| Food | 27s. 0d. | 49s. 10d. | 23s. 5d. | 46s. 3d. | 20s. 7d. | 42s. 9d. |
| Sundries | 1s. 2d. | 3s. 6d. | 1s. 2d. | 2s. 6d. | 1s. 2d. | 3s. 6d. |
| Fuel and light | 2s. 4d. | 4s. 2d. | 2s. 4d. | 4s. 2d. | 2s. 4d. | 4s. 2d. |
| Rent | 7s. 3d. | 7s. 5d. | 6s. 3d. | 6s. 5d. | 5s. 7d. | 5s. 9d. |
| Fares | 1s. 0d. | 1s. 2d. | 9d. | 11d. | 8d. | 10d. |
| Insurance | 3s. 6d. | 3s. 6d. | 2s. 6d. | 2s. 6d. | 2s. 0d. | 2s. 0d. |
| Clothing | 7s. 0d. | 13s. 9d. | 3s. 3d. | 10s. 3d. | 4s. 0d. | 7s. 10d. |
| Total | 49s. 3d. | 82s. 4d. | 41s. 2d. | 73s. 0d. | 36s. 4d. | 65s. 10d. |
| Increase (%) | 67 | | 75 | | 81 | |

*Source*: *Report of the Working Classes Cost of Living Committee*, Cd 8980, PP 1918, p. 7. The *Report* noted that: 'The averages shown for the families in 1914, especially the unskilled families, will appear high to those who are familiar with the pre-war estimates of the cost of family living', which implies an even greater relative increase in living costs for the unskilled.

ideas' can be seen in the immense resentment skilled time-workers felt when their earnings were outstripped by dilutee machine minders on piece-work.

The first cycle of wartime wage awards was completed under the aegis of the Committee on Production by about September 1915. Wage increases averaged between 3s. 6d. and 4s. 0d. *per capita*, engineers obtaining that amount by the end of June. Many large groups of workers were left out of this wage cycle who would customarily have expected an increment to maintain district comparability; no awards were made to builders, printers and dock labourers till after the end of 1915. Labourers and semi-skilled workers who did not transfer to repetition work (and a large number of assistant workers could not be transferred because their services were indispensable in the foundries, forges and metal-making shops) fell behind during 1915. During the autumn of that year and in 1916, they were organised and their claims advanced by the Workers' Union, the general labourers' organisation whose wartime growth was phenomenally rapid and which was, by 1919, the largest trade union in the country.[45] Two groups found that the labour shortage did not mean that increases were to be effortlessly wrested from employers: in March 1915 Lord Devonport on behalf of the Port of London Authority refused to submit the dockers' demand for an increased war bonus to arbitration and in early June a

45. See R. Hyman, *The Workers' Union*, Oxford, 1971.

strike by London tramwaymen for a further war bonus was settled on the employers' terms, with no reinstatement of strikers of military age during the war.[46] In November 1915, a Cabinet minute to the Committee on Production instructed it, on the grounds of economy, to limit wage advances to those arising from existing sliding-scale agreements and to others strictly necessary for the adjustment of local conditions.[47] Meanwhile, a further instrument of great importance in fixing the wages of dilutees had appeared in October 1915 in the form of the Ministry of Munitions' Circulars L2 and L3, with their recommended rates of pay for non-skilled men on skilled work. Summing up the results of wage policy by late 1915, the official historians of the Ministry wrote: 'The normal relationship between wages of different classes and grades of workers in the same industry, between different industries and between different districts had been altered and the new relations had neither authority nor stability'.[48]

In late June 1916, after a trade union deputation to the President of the Board of Trade had demanded either a reduction in prices or a lifting of the wage embargo, the Committee on Production began a new cycle of advances which brought an average *per capita* rise of about 4s.[49] At this date, the working-class cost of living was officially estimated as 50 per cent above the 1914 level and the indices of 'true' weekly wage rates in building, coal-mining and the railways (which are genuinely comparable with the cost of living index) show average earnings in those industries to have been substantially behind inflation (see Table 4.4 and the note explaining the term 'true'). Railwaymen boosted their earnings with overtime and Sunday working. Since their normal working week was sixty hours, this was at considerable cost to their health. In engineering the influence of piece-work was, by 1916, of overwhelming importance in determining earnings and the index figure is not comparable either with other industries or with the cost of living. Here, too, overtime boosted wage packets: a seventy-seven-hour week, with one Sunday off a month, was normal practice in national fuse factories during 1915 and 1916.[50] Certain types of piece-work in metal-making and castings were the preserve of 'gang' labour and the virtually unlimited demand for production did nothing to disturb relativities, for the earnings of all gang members rose proportionally. A

46. See N.B. Dearle, *An Economic Chronicle of the Great War for Great Britain and Northern Ireland 1914–1919*, London, 1929, pp. 33, 39.

47. *The History of the Ministry of Munitions*, vol. 5, pt. 1, p. 70.

48. Ibid., p. 26.

49. Ibid., p. 76; see also Bowley, *Prices and Wages in the United Kingdom*, p. 96.

50. See H.M. Vernon, *Industrial Fatigue and Efficiency*, London, 1929, pp. 20ff.: Vernon was responsible for the inquiries into hours, turnover and labour efficiency made by the Industrial Fatigue Research Board.

**Table 4.4.** Changes in weekly wage rates, 1914–20

| | Building[1] | Coalmining[1] | Railways[1] | Cost of living | Cotton[2] | Engineering[2] skilled | unskilled |
|---|---|---|---|---|---|---|---|
| 1914[3] | 100 | 100 | 100 | 100 | 100 | 100 | 100 |
| 1915 | 102 | 115 | 110 | 125 | 100 | 110 | — |
| 1916 | 111 | 129 | 120 | 145–50 | 105 | 111 | — |
| 1917 | 128 | 136 | 155 | 180 | 110 | 134 | 154 |
| 1918 | 171 | 195 | 195 | 210 | 157 | 173 | 213 |
| 1919 | 204 | 224 | 225 | 215 | 205 | 199 | 255 |
| 1920 | 269 | 260 | 280 | 255 | 271 | 231 | 309 |

*Source*: J.W.F. Rowe, *Wages in Practice and Theory;* A.L. Bowley, *Wages and Prices in the United Kingdom 1914–1920*
1. 'True' wage rates, indicating the current average of earnings. See Rowe, *Wages in Practice and Theory*, p.3.
2. 'Nominal' wage rates, referring to rates set by price lists, etc., giving a very imperfect indication of the movement of earnings.
3. In July of each year.

sub-contractor from the Brass Workers and Metal Mechanics' Association told the Committee on Production in August 1917: 'I have two men and a boy at work for me. The boy gets £1–13–6 a week. The two men pay income tax, so they must earn £4 or £5. I pocket the rest — a great deal . . . but I worked on average eight and a half days per week for two years'.[51]

Repetition piece-work undertaken by dilutee machine-minders had entirely different results, for their earnings outstripped those of the skilled men on time rates who set up the machines, made the job foolproof and maintained factory plant. It was a signal cause of working-class unrest. In March 1916, a deputation from skilled time-workers at Sheffield to the Ministry of Munitions claimed that whereas their own earnings were £3 per week, semi-skilled workers (till lately 'gardeners and coachmen') were earning at least £6.[52] The Government's Commission of Enquiry into industrial unrest that followed the May strikes of 1917 found in every district in Yorkshire and the East Midlands 'typical instances . . . in which unskilled workers, labourers, women and girls were earning more than double that of skilled men . . .'. Earnings as high as £10 to £18 per week were reported for unskilled workers, although we should treat sums of that magnitude with some scepticism.[53] In the West Midlands, the Commissioners found the inequality of earnings between semi-skilled machine minders

51. Quoted in *The History of the Ministry of Munitions*, vol. 5, pt. 1, p. 122.
52. Ibid., p. 167.
53. *Report of the Commission of Enquiry into Industrial Unrest: No. 3 Divisions: Yorkshire and*

and the skilled 'as great a revolution in industry as any similar period has witnessed . . .'.[54] Though the anomaly was reported in other industrial areas, this problem was most acute in the engineering heartland of the Midlands where mass manufacturing and the interchangeability of parts were transforming production before the war and where, from 1915, these principles were applied on a huge scale to machine-gun, aero-engine and vehicle manufacture.

Wage awards in 1917 and 1918 were designed to correct this anomaly and at the same time protect all workers from the rising cost of living. Their cumulative effect was to complete the undermining of the wage structure. During 1917, increases were still wider in scope than they had been in previous years and averaged 9s. *per capita*. There was even greater uniformity in wage bargaining, with government departments generally preferring to give flat weekly war-wage awards to adult male time-workers and piece-workers alike.[55] In October, a special 12.5 per cent bonus on weekly earnings was given to all skilled time-workers on munitions work in engineering and iron-founding. This increase had very far-reaching effects; intended to equalise increases in earnings, it in fact destroyed what balance still remained between payment for different kinds of work.[56] In November there were strikes in Salford, Manchester, Burnley and other places to extend the award to categories of workers excluded from its original terms. After industrial action was threatened, a subsequent award gave the same percentage increase to time-wage labourers. The difficulties with the award were particularly acute in the shipyard engineering trades where skilled workers' earnings were made up from a basic time-wage and bonus and piece payments. In Newcastle, during December, three mass meetings of skilled workers denied the 12.5 per cent were held to discuss the whole question:

> The singularity of the matter of these meetings was the unanimity of disapproval of all forms of payment by results. Bonuses and piece rates are based, or supposed to be based, on time wages. The difference in money earned at the week-end by the piece-worker over and above his colleague's time wage is the pieceworker's profit. If, however, time wages increase in amount equal to the earnings of pieceworkers the latter's profits vanish. In many cases, this is what is happening, hence a cry is raised that bonus and

---

*East Midlands Area*, PP 1917–18, Cd 8664, p. 4. For an interesting study of the Commission, see W. Craig Heron, 'The Commission of Enquiry into Industrial Unrest of 1917', University of Warwick MA dissertation, 1976. This would suggest that the Commissioners' investigative methods were rather amateurish and we should not place too much reliance on the earnings figures given.

54. *No. 4 Division: West Midlands Area*, Cd 8665, p. 7.
55. Bowley, *Prices and Wages in the United Kingdom*, p. 98.
56. Ibid., p. 99.

piece-workers should have been included in the twelve and a half per cent. The whole thing bristles with difficulties not seen or provided for [by the Committee on Production].[57]

In response to such protests, the Committee was forced, in January 1918, to concede an increase of 7.5 per cent to piece-workers on munitions work in engineering, iron-founding and shipbuilding. The skilled time worker's complaint remained unremedied and was a constant source of labour friction until the end of the war.[58]

Full employment, war-wage awards, payment by results, the transfer of workers from low-paid sectors of the economy to better-paid occupations, all produced the appearance, at any rate, of great prosperity among the working class. Whether, on average, real incomes kept pace with inflation up to the end of 1917, seems rather unlikely although there is extensive evidence that those groups most prone to distress before the war (casual workers, low-paid labourers with large families) enjoyed a considerable rise in living standards from 1915. By November 1917, the average rise in wage rates was between 35 and 40 per cent whereas the increase in the cost of living over July 1914 was 80 per cent. Actual earnings were, of course, greater because of the factors already mentioned and family incomes were boosted by opportunities for women and children to work at rates that had increased more rapidly than men's. The Cabinet was given a breakdown of wartime wage increases up to October 1917 and informed:

It is not possible, from any available statistics, to estimate the amount of the increase in family incomes resulting from the combined operation of all these factors . . . [but] It is . . . extremely improbable that the increase in total earnings is more than double the increase in rates of wages, as it would need to be if it were to be made commensurate with the increase in the cost of living . . . for the majority of workpeople the increase in earnings has not kept pace with the rise in the cost of living, and real wages, on the average, are still appreciably lower than in the first half of 1914.[59]

The success with which different groups achieved advances approaching the level of price inflation was largely 'proportional to the extent to which the claimants' labour was essential to the state'.[60] By late 1917, the largest increases had gone to coalminers, the less skilled in the

57. *ASE Monthly Journal and Record*, December 1917.
58. See the memorandum by Gordon Campbell on 'The Administration of Wages in the Munitions Industries', 3 Oct. 1918, PRO MUN5/51/300/61.
59. 'Wages and Prices', memorandum by G.H. Roberts, Minister of Labour, 29 Oct. 1917, with accompanying memorandum by Professor Chapman, from the Department of Labour Statistics, 2 Oct. 1917, PRO CAB24/30 G.T. 2465.
60. 'State Regulation of Wages', memorandum by G.N. Barnes, 5 Oct. 1917, CAB24/28 G.T. 2203.

engineering industry and such key workers as the iron-ore miners of Cumberland, blast-furnacemen and iron and steel millmen. Relatively non-essential groups, such as the cotton workers who had only received a 20 per cent advance on list prices, were lagging far behind the cost of living.[61] The considerable awards made in 1918 probably mean that, on average, the earnings of the worker who did some overtime caught up with inflation. One reason for thinking this lies in the defects of the official cost of living index which, since it was calculated according to a prewar pattern of working-class expenditure, made no allowance for the increasing purchase of substitutes which were cheaper and not necessarily inferior. Another lies in the evidence for increased working-class spending power to which I will return in the next chapter.

The influence of flat-rate increases on narrowing differentials within an industry's workforce can be most clearly seen in the case of the railways. In prewar years the low pay of many of the grades was justified by the channel of promotion. More importantly, the penurious wages paid in agriculture kept the cost of railway labour down; many of the outside grades were drawn from the countryside and since agricultural wages scarcely increased between the 1880s and 1913, the railway companies did not find it necessary to raise their unskilled rates in order to obtain an adequate supply of recruits.[62] This rural source of cheap labour dried up during the war and railwaymen developed a more acute sense of what the traffic could bear.[63] The first bonus to railway workers in February 1915 granted 3s. to men earning under 30s. a week and 2s. to those earning more, a compromise accepted by the National Union of Railwaymen rather than 2s. 6d. all round, in order to protect the lowest-paid men.[64] This was the first time that complete recognition had been conceded to the union by the companies — an interesting reflection on the influence of the war on collective bargaining. By August 1917 additions to the bonus brought it up to 15s. a week and at that point it was converted to a war wage and therefore entered into the calculation of overtime payments. By the spring of 1918 this had advanced to a 25s. war wage for all.[65] For a fireman who in 1914 had been earning 24s. to 27s. a week, wartime increases amounted to from 92.5 per cent to 104 per cent; on the other hand wartime increases represented only 49 per cent to 69.5 per cent advance on a driver's wage, considerably less than the officially esti-

61. Ibid.

62. See Rowe, *Wages in Practice and Theory*, p. 169.

63. Ibid., p. 170.

64. See *The Railway Review*, 19 Feb. 1915, for J.H. Thomas's account of the negotiations for the first war bonus.

65. 'Railwaymen's Wages', memorandum by the President of the Board of Trade, 29 Aug. 1918, CAB24/62 G.T. 5550.

mated rise in the working-class cost of living at 110 per cent between July 1914 and August 1918. Before 1914 all drivers earned at least twice as much as porters, by February 1919 drivers' wages were not more that 60 per cent above those of porters.[66] The same movement towards the narrowing of differentials saw the labourer's wage in engineering increase from 59 per cent of the fitter's in August 1914 to 76 per cent in April 1919 and nearly 80 per cent in June 1920. In the building industry, the bricklayer who had had 10d. an hour in 1914, had 22d. at the beginning of 1920; his labourer had $6\frac{1}{2}$d. and $18\frac{1}{2}$d. at the same dates. For centuries, labourers in the building industry had received two-thirds of a craftsman's rate. Under the National Building Agreement of 1919, concluded at a time of acute labour shortage, the labourer's rate was henceforth to be not less than three-quarters of the craftsman's.[67]

However, the principle of national flat-rate increases related to the cost of living introduced into the railway service, the engineering industry and other trades during the war was a double-edged weapon for the lower grades since, following the fall in prices in 1921, uniform flat-rate reductions proportional to the fall in the cost of living were forced on employees and these reopened differentials. In the railway service, weekly wages of good porters were 70 per cent of engine drivers' wages in 1920, but only 56 per cent by 1926; their relative position was still very modestly improved on that which had prevailed before the war and some of the lower grades in certain districts benefited from the standardisation agreement negotiated by the railway unions and the companies in 1919.[68] In engineering, the labourer's weekly wage rate was only 65 per cent of the craftsman's by 1926 and the discrepancy in earnings was possibly greater because of the amount of piece-work undertaken by skilled men.[69] It is doubtful whether, by the later 1920s, the relative position of labouring grades in engineering was much different from what it had been in 1914. The disadvantages of the less skilled and lower-paid during the slump of 1921–3 were compounded by their greater susceptibility to unemployment and the fragility of their trade union organisations. Membership of the Workers' Union collapsed as spectacularly in 1921 to 1923 as it had grown during the war and postwar boom.[70] Indeed, if our attention were focused solely on differentials within particular industries, then the conclusion would be that the combined results of proportionally grea-

---

66. P.S. Bagwell, *The Railwaymen*, London, 1963, p. 349.
67. Bowley, *Prices and Wages in the United Kingdom*, p. 129.
68. On the standardisation of wages in the railway service, see Rowe, *Wages in Practice and Theory*, pp. 74–82.
69. Ibid., p. 38.
70. Hyman, *The Workers' Union*, pp. 128ff.

ter wage reductions, higher unemployment and the contraction of general labouring unions during the postwar slump wiped out the earlier gains. A somewhat different picture emerges if we compare the percentage improvements in the rates paid to unskilled labour in different industries between 1914 and late 1924, for these show that the advances made in protected employment (such as building and local authority) were much greater than in the exposed trades (shipbuilding, agriculture). Where, as in London, there was a large market for unskilled labour in protected employment then the improved position of the unskilled relative to the skilled remained apparent in the indices of hourly wage-rates throughout the 1920s, as is shown in Table 4.5.

**Table 4.5.**   Improvement in hourly wage-rates, 1894–1928

|            | 1894  | 1906  | 1910  | 1914  | 1920  | 1924  | 1928  |
|------------|-------|-------|-------|-------|-------|-------|-------|
| Skilled    | 100.0 | 108.0 | 109.0 | 114.0 | 292.0 | 222.0 | 226.0 |
| Unskilled  | 100.0 | 102.5 | 109.0 | 115.0 | 369.0 | 260.0 | 272.0 |

*Source*: *New Survey of London Life and Labour*, vol. I, p. 115

The striking fall in agricultural wages indicated by Table 4.6 calls for brief comment. Agricultural labourers were the lowest-paid male occupational group in 1913: despite this their relative position by 1924 had deteriorated still further and it seems scarcely credible that this occurred without grave effects on the nutritional standards of the farm worker's family. There are reliable reports from the early 1920s of undernourishment and ill-health amongst rural schoolchildren which affirm that improvements in living standards that had come with the war were wiped out by the collapse of agricultural prices in 1921 and the remorseless pressure on agricultural wages.[71] Farm workers experienced something like the two movements of the economic pendulum through which the industrial economy had moved, but the gains made during the inflationary swing (when wages had risen and a statutory minimum was imposed by the Corn Production Act of 1917) had been smaller in comparison with industrial workers and the losses endured during the slump were greater. After 1921, wages were scaled down for agricultural labourers more drastically than in any other industry and the discrepancy between agricultural and urban wages had never been larger. Average agricultural wages in 1924 were about 32s. and cash payments were now almost invariably the total wage for, with the

---

71. See F.D. Acland, 'Agriculture — The Election, and After', *Contemporary Review*, February 1924. For a personal memoir which recalls the rural distress of the early 1920s, see Spike Mays, *Reuben's Corner*, London, 1969.

**Table 4.6.** Average increase over August 1914 of rates of various types of unskilled labour at 31 December 1924 (%)

|  | Hourly increase | Weekly increase |
|---|---|---|
| Builders' labourers | 128 | 105 |
| Engineering | 98 | 76 |
| Shipbuilding | 90 | 68 |
| Local authority employees | 120 | 99 |
| Gas works | 124 | 98 |
| Electricity supply industry | 132 | 103 |
| Agriculture | N/A | 56 |

Ministry of Labour cost of living index: 175 (1914 = 100)

*Source*: Ministry of Labour *Gazette*, February 1925: survey of relative levels of rates of wages at August 1914 and December 1924

operation of the agricultural Wage Boards, farmers tended to reckon up the cash value of allowances.[72] The low wages of agriculture were reliably reckoned to have had, before 1914, a retarding effect upon unskilled wages in industries which drew upon the rural population (notably the railways, but also building, road and water transport) and it is a reasonable presumption that this effect was exacerbated by the widening discrepancy between rural and urban wages in the early 1920s.

The marked differences in the percentage increases of unskilled labour rates which are shown in Table 4.6 reflected the varied impact of the war as between the exporting, usually older, industries exposed to foreign competition and the sheltered industries, particularly those based on more modern technology whose development had been stimulated by the war.[73] Broadly speaking the labour forces of the exporting trades gained least, and in many cases lost, from the disruptive influence of war, partly because the war increased the difficulties implicit in technological backwardness and industrial retardation evident well before 1914, above all because these workers were the chief victims of the slump in world trade which the war triggered off. Even in these trades, however, the basic tendency remained for wage movements to be more favourable to the unskilled. In the sheltered trades, on the other hand, the rate of increase in money wages was distinctly greater than the rise in the cost of living. The Balfour Committee

72. See *The Land and the Nation: the Rural Report of the Liberal Land Committee 1923–1925*, London, 1925, p. 15 and elsewhere.
73. Balfour Committee on Industry and Trade, *Survey of Industrial Relations*, London, 1926, pp. 7ff.; D.S. Landes, *The Unbound Prometheus*, Cambridge, 1969, pp. 421ff.

estimated that prevailing rates of increase in money wages for the trades most exposed to competition in the decade 1914 to 1924 ranged from 45 to 75 per cent with an average of about 60 per cent; while for sheltered trades the range was 80 to 120 per cent with an average of about 100 per cent. They suggested that a rough average of weekly rates of time-wages in June 1925 for the industries most directly exposed to competition was about 58s. for skilled men and 45s. for labourers, but in more sheltered trades average rates exceeded 73s. and 50s. respectively.[74] Workers in a domestic industry such as boot and shoe manufacture experienced increases in minimum time rates between 1914 and 1925 of the range of 100 to 111 per cent while some of the largest percentage increases went to the lowest-paid adult workers in the trades with rates fixed by the prewar Trade Boards: women workers in the ready-made-tailoring trade had increases of 115 per cent between these dates, in paper box manufacture of 154 per cent, in chain-making 170 per cent, in lace finishing 127 per cent. Male day labourers in the heavy chemicals industry were receiving an average rate of 23s. for a 53- to 54-hour week in August 1914 — a sum insufficient to sustain health and efficiency for a man, his wife and three children: in June 1925, they were receiving 49s. 6d. for a 47-hour week[75] — no princely sum but substantially above the minimum standard Seebohm Rowntree used in his second survey of York in 1935 when prices had fallen below their mid-1920s level. These workers had been amongst the most exploited members of the Edwardian working class.

It is quite possible that the Balfour Committee somewhat exaggerated the divergence between the sheltered and unsheltered industries because it neglected the influence of piece-work on real earnings in engineering and other export industries. Rowe, who made this criticism of the Committee, went so far as to claim that any rigid distinction between sheltered and unsheltered was quite illusory.[76] However, I have put the distinction to a test (of sorts) by using the returns from the survey of actual earnings in four weeks of 1924 made by the Ministry of Labour and I am satisfied it was founded on fact. Over three million male workers from eleven industry groups were covered by the inquiry and their average earnings in four weeks of 1924 were 56s. 3d. The inquiry did not cover certain large groups, such as coal-miners, and had it done so the average would have been considerably depressed. The preponderance of better-than-average earnings in the sheltered industry groups and of below-average earnings in the exposed groups

74. *Survey of Industrial Relations.* p. 7.
75. Ibid., pp. 19, 93.
76. Rowe, *Wages in Practice and Theory*, p. 19.

broadly confirms the distinction (see Table 4.7). Indeed, the distinction is apparent in the much higher earnings of workers in large firms in the motor-vehicle and cycle sector of engineering (which was heavily reliant on the home market) as compared with shipbuilding and textile engineering which had exported a large proportion of their output before the war. (What is also remarkable is that the latter employed a higher proportion of skilled workers.) Although the metal-making trades retained their position near the top of the earnings league, the best-paid workers in them had experienced a considerable decline in real earnings as compared with 1914; in 1925, the rates for tinplate and iron and steel workers showed increases of only 20 to 35 per cent on prewar weekly wages.[77] One of the striking facts revealed by the inquiry is the generally high earnings for men such as motor-coach and bus drivers and electricity supply workers; groups which had scarcely figured amongst the prewar working class but were already displacing the skilled craftsmen in the export trades as its economic elite. The figure given for average earnings in the building industry is curiously low. Bricklayer's weekly rates in 1924 were 73s. 4d. and labourers' 55s. 5d.; from the composition of the labour force (and making due allowances for loss of earnings through bad weather) we might have expected a higher average figure for building workers' actual earnings.

The adverse position of the export trades during the postwar slump and slow recovery up to 1925 was greatly exacerbated by the problem of labour surplus which derived from the extraordinary labour mobility of wartime. During the war, workers were drawn out of service industries, building, agriculture and non-essential occupations and into industrial production. At the same time, the war was sufficiently long to attract permanently new entrants to the labour force to high-paid employment in the metals and engineering industries who would not otherwise have entered these trades. The Board of Trade Z8 returns show that the number employed in industrial occupations in April 1919 was only 2.9 per cent less (or roughly 250,000) than in July 1914. This was far fewer than might be accounted for by the casualties of war. The official interpretation of the figures was that about 1 million males (not including men returned from the forces) and 800,000 females were drawn into these occupations during the war. Possibly 100,000 of the men may have been engaged previously in industry as employees or workers upon their own account but the great majority undoubtedly represented a net gain to the industrial labour force.[78] The women

---

77. See 'Relative Levels of Rates of Wages at August, 1914, and September, 1925', *Ministry of Labour Gazette*, October 1925, p. 343.

78. *Confidential Report on the State of Employment in All Occupations in the United Kingdom at the end of April 1919 as compared with July 1914 and November 1918*, prepared by the Industrial (War Inquiries) Branch of the Board of Trade, p. 14 (copy in the LSE Library).

**Table 4.7.** Average weekly male earnings in selected industries in 1924: average of *all* wages = 56s. 3d.

| Sheltered | Nos. employed | Amount | Exposed | Nos. employed | Amount |
|---|---|---|---|---|---|
| Tramway & omnibus service (private) | 40,922 | 74s. 5d. | Tinplate | 12,883 | 73s. 7d. |
| Canal, dock & harbour authority services | 25,204 | 73s. 11d. | | | |
| Paper and printing | 20,963 | 69s. 11d. | | | |
| Government industrial establishments | 41,538 | 65s. 7d. | | | |
| Electricity supplies | 37,166 | 64s. 10d. | | | |
| Tramway & omnibus services (local authority) | 50,430 | 64s. 7d. | | | |
| Motor vehicle & cycle (large firms) | 91,200 | 63s. 0d. | Pig iron | 28,466 | 63s. 2d. |
| Gas supply (local authority & other) | 89,299 | 60s. 9d. | Smelting, rolling, etc. of iron & steel | 151,382 | 62s. 0d. |
| Building & allied industries | 278,728 | 58s. 2d. | | | |
| Food drink & tobacco | 218,223 | 57s. 2d. | Smelting & rolling of non-ferrous metal | 24,441 | 58s. 7d. |
| Pottery, brick, glass | 171,702 | 56s. 6d. | Bleaching, printing, dyeing and finishing | 58,793 | 56s. 9d. |
| Total | 1,165,375 | | Total | 275,965 | |
| Clothing | 113,756 | 54s. 10d. | Woollen and worsted | 60,496 | 53s. 10d. |
| Miscellaneous sheltered trades* | 224,807 | 53s. 11d. | Engineering (not specified elsewhere) | 260,283 | 52s. 9d. |
| Woodworking | 144,060 | 53s. 6d. | Shipbuilding | 125,833 | 51s. 11d. |
| Local authority non-trading services | 181,863 | 50s. 11d. | Cotton | 80,698 | 47s. 0d. |
| Motor vehicle & cycle (smaller firms) | 28,492 | 46s. 11d. | Textile engineering | 39,053 | 44s. 8d. |
| Total | 692,978 | | Total | 566,363 | |

*Source*: 'Earnings and Hours of Labour of workpeople in Great Britain and Northern Ireland', *Ministry of Labour Gazette*, July 1927 (and earlier issues of the *Gazette*)

\* Includes leather goods, indiarubber, pianos and musical instruments etc.

workers were expected to withdraw voluntarily, for as many as 40 to 60 per cent of these exceptionally employed because of wartime circumstances were married. In the short term, about half of these female entrants did not withdraw and it would appear that their experience of gainful occupations in wartime had created a new attitude favourable to such occupations amongst a large number of women. But this attitude did not generally survive the 1921 slump. The 'surplus' male recruits to industrial production represented a more intractable problem. Between 1911 and 1921, the occupied male population of Great Britain increased by an estimated 780,000 and over three-quarters of this increase (575,000) went into the labour force of the engineering, shipbuilding, vehicle, iron and steel and other metal industries.[79] Not all of this increase was abnormal growth, for the labour forces of these industries had expanded more rapidly than the working male population as a whole between 1901 and 1911, but the rate of movement was much accelerated. Male employment in the engineering, shipbuilding and metal trades grew by about 40 per cent between 1911 and 1921 as compared with an increase of approximately 20 per cent between 1901 and 1911. (Exact comparison is made difficult by changes in classification between censuses.)

The onset of structural unemployment in 1921, brought about by the collapse of world trade, proved extraordinarily unfavourable to the war-expanded industries; in 1924 the percentage unemployed in shipbuilding was 29.4, in iron- and steel-making 21.1 and in general engineering and iron-founding 15.2, as compared with a national average of 10.3 per cent. These industries employed less than one-fifth of the insured population and accounted for more than one-third of the unemployed in insured trades.[80] The expulsive powers of unemployment worked very slowly; the number of men and boys insured in the overcrowded engineering trades continued to grow throughout 1922 in spite of the depressed state of the trade. Though the numbers insured in engineering, metal-making and shipbuilding fell between July 1923 and July 1925, the decrease was much less than the continuing high levels of employment would have given us to expect. There were no doubt a number of complex reasons for this immobility of labour, but one lay in the distorted way the labour force was reproduced by new drafts of young workers between 1914 and 1920. This period was long enough — about the duration of a normal apprenticeship — to induct considerable numbers into the war-expanded industries and give rise to the expectation that they had entered a life-time occupation. The plight of many was worsened by the fact that they took up repetition labour for which there was a great demand in the war economy and acquired few of the skills suitable for peacetime production. The Ministry of

79. This calculation was made by Bowley and first published in the *Economic Journal*, vol. XXXIV, p. 5, repr. in J.J. Astor et al., *The Third Winter of Unemployment*, London, 1923, p. 6; see also Pigou,'An Analytic Account of the General Economic Movement in the United Kingdom between the Armistice and the Restoration of the Gold Standard', PRO LAB17/112, pp. 66ff.

80. Astor et al., *The Third Winter of Unemployment*, p. 6.

Labour estimated that amongst unemployed youths in late 1923, about one-fifth of those aged sixteen to seventeen and one-third of those aged eighteen to nineteen were out of work because of the disruption of their industrial careers by the abnormal conditions of the war and its aftermath.[81] During the slow recovery from the postwar slump, money-wage rates were much more markedly depressed in the over-crowded, predominantly export, industries than elsewhere and there seems no reason to doubt that the reverse of surplus labour acquired in 1914 and 1920 helped to make them so.

## Skill and Apprenticeship

Earlier, I referred in a general way to the complex relationship between capitalist organisation, technological change and the range of skills within the working class. Here I will attempt to summarise the ways wartime production modified that relationship. Contemporary comment would certainly lead us to believe that the war had, by inaugurating an era of mass production, brought to a head the tendency towards the degradation of skilled labour. This is evident in liberal economic writing of the early 1920s which, in its conception of labour in capitalist development, was far closer to the classical Marxian prognosis than to later views of labour as highly differentiated by skill. For example, in 1923 D.H. Robertson, the Cambridge economist, described 'the typical modern workman' as 'specialised not merely to a single craft, but to a single tiny process in a single craft. . . . With the invention of complicated and accurate machines . . . the need for purely manual skill has on the whole declined'.[82] This conception of the workman was, without doubt, powerfully influenced by the development of standardisation during the war, the newly-won prestige of Taylorist scientific management bent on so adapting human labour as to ensure the maximum output from expensive machinery, and the recent wave of capital concentration.[83]

How accurately does this conception reflect the real interaction between the wartime industrial experience, the development of the labour process and the structure of skills in the working class? To answer that we must make a preliminary distinction between those short-term effects which were absorbed by the labour force at the time and the longer-term consequences for those institutions through which

---

81. Ministry of Labour, *Report on an Investigation into the personal circumstances and industrial history of 10,000 claimants to unemployment benefit*, London, 1924, p. 20.

82. D.H. Robertson, *The Control Industry*, Cambridge, 1923, pp. 17–18.

83. Ibid., pp. 20–36.

skill in the labour force was reproduced. This is to distinguish between, let us say, the experience of the lads and young men who forewent skilled training to become machine-minders during the war and the more muted and indirect consequences of wartime industrial change for the system of apprenticeship. Furthermore, we have to distinguish between the rhetoric of a technocratic ideology inspired by the productivity of war industrialism and intent on perpetuating the abnormal conditions of production after the war, and its limited achievements. The historians of the Ministry of Munitions provided a still salutary caution against overestimating the applicability of the technological and labour processes used in munitions production to peacetime industry: 'large-scale production, standardisation, scientific management, improved labour conditions, all the gains of these and kindred methods must leave some mark on industry. The experience gained cannot be lost. Yet the effects may be over-estimated, for to an important extent the war-time experience of the national factories is inapplicable to peace-time conditions'.[84] This is much more cautious than the declarations coming out of the Ministry during the war; in May 1918 its *Dilution of Labour Bulletin* proclaimed that the methods of production fostered by the Ministry represented 'lines of thought [which] are not, like most enlistment, "for the period of the War", but must have a far-reaching effect in the change of working conditions for all time'.[85]

It is clear that some industries did experience a gamut of technological and managerial innovation during the war which profoundly influenced their later development. One which appears to have been virtually revolutionised was the optical and scientific instruments industry; a summary of wartime changes stated that they

> have been mainly improvements in method of production, in the use of specialised machinery for manufacture on a repetition basis, and a consequent largely increased use of unskilled labour; the recognition of women as eminently suitable to highly skilled work in the industry; the introduction of a spirit of cooperation; the recognition of the necessity of well-trained and well-paid scientific staff; extension of the number of contractors capable of dealing with manufacture in bulk; elimination of garret work; and finally greatly improved morale in regard to competition after the war.[86]

The industry doubled its labour force in the London region between 1911 and 1921 and doubled the percentage of women employed, and it is highly unlikely that its growth would have been so rapid without the

---

84. *The History of the Ministry of Munitions*, vol. 8, pt. 1, p. 84.
85. *The Dilution of Labour Bulletin*, May 1918.
86. PRO MUN4/5089: A file of papers on 'The Reorganisation of Existing Industry, Establishment of New', n.d.

intervention of the war.[87] The rapidity of its development was directly related, however, to its backwardness before 1914; it was typical of a cluster of industries stemming from the Second Industrial Revolution in which Britain had performed most indifferently up to 1914. During the war, she was forced to manufacture many products of this Revolution which before 1914 had been imported from abroad; magnetos, optical and chemical glass, ignition plugs, ball-bearings, dyestuffs amongst them. This was the launching-pad for the 'new' industrial development of the 1920s.[88] In the industries so initiated or accelerated, labour was typically employed in highly-specialised, machine-minding capacities, unionism was ineffective or non-existent and craft controls negligible. Many of these industries developed in regions (such as outer London) where trade unionism itself was weak.

The one sphere of rapidly-expanding industry in which skilled workers greatly strengthened their position and were able to pursue a policy of craft militancy were the electrical trades. There was a considerable development of industrial electrification during the war. The plant capacity of 557 municipal and company power-stations doubled between 1914 and 1918; in Sheffield and Rotherham electricity was adopted for steel production and plant capacity rose still more rapidly (in Rotherham, from 5,000 to 70,000 kilowatts).[89] Typical of the new uses made of electric power was its introduction into the shipyards to drive compressors. By early 1918, the key position of electricians in munitions production was enabling the once-weak Electrical Trades Union to adopt the objectives, such as the limitation of apprentices, typical of militant craft organisations. By October 1918, the ETU was the centre point of industrial agitation in the munitions industries (and had been 'for a long time past'). It was prominent in resisting the manpower proposals and dilution, in opposing the employment of non-unionists, in raising the apprenticeship question and 'in producing on many other topics an atmosphere of unrest'. There was movement amongst electricians to compel foremen and clerical assistants to enter the union.[90] In the power-stations, the union's 'forward' policy was rebuffed by the separate organisation of the electrical power engineers and supervisory grades and as the stations developed they employed a good deal of unskilled labour under professional supervision. In electrical contracting, by contrast, the ETU won a monopoly position from which it was able to insist on indentured apprenticeship, a limitation

87. See *New Survey of London Life and Labour*, vol. 1, Table C. p. 422.

88. See D.H. Aldcroft, H.W. Richardson, *The British Economy 1870–1939*, London, 1969, pp. 230–4.

89. *The History of the Ministry of Munitions*, vol. 8, pt. 3, p. 105.

90. See 'Report on the Labour Position in the Munitions Industries', 2 Oct. 1918, PRO CAB24/65 G.T. 5887.

on the number of trainees to each journeyman and the other controls which had been customary amongst elite workers thrown up during every phase of industrialisation. It should be added that the employers' federation appears to have endorsed the need for these controls in order to maintain the skill of the labour force and was in favour of a union closed shop.[91]

As I have already indicated, the short-term effect of the war in the already firmly established industries was to dislocate the supply of new, skilled labour and by 1919 it was evident that the shortage of apprentices and other trainee skilled workers was a serious impediment to industrial reconstruction. From Birmingham, it was reported in December 1918 that there was 'an urgent necessity for more skilled men. . . . The situation is rendered worse by the fact that there had been practically no apprenticeship during the war, that is to say there has been a loss of four years' output of properly trained skilled men'.[92] In the locally important coopering trade, there was not a single apprentice. Throughout 1919, the question of apprenticeship was the focus of considerable concern amongst Ministry of Labour officials, who diagnosed the problem as the interruption of apprenticeship by military service, the attraction of high earnings for young workers on repetition work and the unwillingness of boys to serve their time in dirty and disagreeable trades. The range of industries where an apprenticeship problem was specifically mentioned was wide: in printing, the scale of wages in the first years was too low to stop boys drifting into other occupations; in iron-founding there were similar complaints; at Keighley, it was 'stated that the blacksmiths', coppersmiths' and ironmoulders' trades are becoming depleted of skilled labour owing to the unwillingness of boys to be apprenticed in these less pleasant branches of engineering'; in Doncaster, boys of fifteen and sixteen were giving up engineering apprenticeships which brought them less than a pound a week to go into the mines where they could earn two pounds. The furniture trades, farriering, sail-making were also mentioned as being depleted of apprentices.[93] The concern over the future supply of skilled workers led the government to launch the Interrupted Apprenticeship Scheme in February 1919 and by the end of October 16,000 apprentices were in receipt of state aid to complete their training. Nearly 45,000 apprentices were, in total, accepted into the Scheme, the

91. See the chapter on the electrical industry in J. Hilton et al., eds., *Are Trade Unions Obstructive? An Industrial Inquiry*, London, 1935, pp. 128–36.

92. See 'Munitions Council — Daily Report on Industrial Transition', 17 Dec. 1918, PRO MUN4/3412.

93. See the lengthy discussion on the apprenticeship problems in the 'Report on the Labour Situation', 3 Sept. 1919, PRO CAB24/88 G.T. 8107; see also 'Labour Situation Report', 5 Oct. 1919, PRO CAB24/92 C.P. 68.

largest number being in engineering.[94] Unfortunately, it is not possible to tell whether the men assisted were predominantly ex-soldiers or whether they included significant numbers of young men who had worked as dilutees. The Balfour Committee was to give a much larger figure (100,000) as the total directly and indirectly assisted, but it is not clear what indirect assistance involved.[95] Even if we take that larger figure as the total helped by the Scheme, this was but a minority of the generation of skilled workers 'lost' between 1914 and 1920.

The shortfall of young skilled workers was an acute but temporary problem. Of more long-term significance for the economic and social structure of the working class were the effects of the war on systems of industrial training and it is by examining these that we can come a little closer to 'the typical modern workman' of the 1920s. The war undoubtedly quickened existing tendencies towards the disintegration of formal apprenticeship, the devaluation of its educative content and the development of 'up-grading' systems whereby unskilled men could be rapidly trained for semi-skilled tasks. It must be stressed that since the last decades of the nineteenth century there had been complaints that the tradition of apprenticeship was in decay and in many respects the war merely hastened the inevitable. There was, for example, a distinct trend between the 1910s and the 1920s in the direction of substituting an oral agreement for a well-defined instrument of apprenticeship or written agreement; between 1909 and 1925, the proportion of boys apprenticed under oral agreement increased from about one-third to one-half of trainee skilled workers.[96] In engineering this trend was already marked in 1914. Those trades in which a very sharp fall in formal apprenticeship appears specifically attributable to the war include precious metals (where indentured apprenticeship amongst trainee male workers fell from 70.9 per cent in 1909 to 25.5 per cent in 1925) and boot and shoe and clothing. As has already been mentioned, the war completed the mechanisation of the boot and shoe industry and greatly stimulated the mass production of clothing. In 1909, 51 per cent of boy trainees in the boot and shoe industry were still classed as apprentices (half of them indentured): by 1925 only 8 per cent were classed as apprentices of any description and the vast majority (92 per cent) were 'learners'. The trend in the clothing industry was rather less marked: the proportion of 'learners' rose from 42.4 per cent to 78.8 per cent.[97] In boots and shoes, the difference between 'the apprentice' and

94. Ministry of Labour, *Report of an Enquiry into Apprenticeship and Training for the skilled occupations in Great Britain and Northern Ireland: General Report*, London, 1928, p. 13.

95. Committee on Industry and Trade, *Factors in Industrial and Commercial Efficiency: Being Part I of a Survey of Industries*, London, 1927, p. 138.

96. Ministry of Labour, *Report of an Enquiry into Apprenticeship. General Report*, p. 3.

97. Ibid., p. 25.

'the learner' was, broadly, that the latter trained as a machinist to carry out one, or at the most a small number of tasks, in a process of mass-production, while the apprentice trained as an artisan who made the boot throughout. The decline of apprenticeship was, of course, symptomatic of the collapse of the 'bespoke' trade and the rise of wholesale factory production.

The effects of the war on the levels of skill in the rapidly expanding conglomerate of trades lumped under 'metals, machines, implements and conveyances' were more complex and varied. The Balfour Committee gave the following very approximate breakdown of the proportions of skilled, semi-skilled and unskilled labour in engineering:

**Table 4.8.** Proportions of skilled, semi- and unskilled labour in engineering, 1914–26

|  | Skilled (%) | Semi-skilled (%) | Unskilled (%) |
|---|---|---|---|
| 1914 | 60 | 20 | 20 |
| 1921 | 50 | 30 | 20 |
| 1926 | 40 | 45 | 15 |

*Source*: Committee on Industry and Trade, *Survey of Metal Industries*, 1928, p. 152

The proportions of the labour force did not, however, alter uniformly across the multifarious engineering trades and the growth in the numbers of semi-skilled workers took place, to a large extent, because of the disproportionate expansion of industries which drew heavily on 'upgraded' labour. Only 5 per cent of all engineering employees worked in electrical engineering in 1907; by 1924, 15.4 per cent did so. The motor, cycle and aircraft section employed 7.4 per cent of total engineering workers in 1907 and 20.4 per cent in 1924.[98] Large firms in motor engineering did not employ apprentices but relied on systems of upgrading, and the same tended to be true for electrical and light engineering.[99] The latter also employed considerable numbers of women workers (about 35 per cent of the labour force in electrical engineering in the early 1930s, a proportion three times larger than in general engineering). The localised development of these industries led to a distinct regional variation in the number of apprentices taken on by engineering firms, with more firms in southern than in northern districts without apprentices or learners.

On the north-east coast, the proportions of the grades of labour in

98. See Jefferys, *The Story of the Engineers*, p. 198.
99. Ministry of Labour, *Report of an Enquiry into Apprenticeship: Report No. VI Engineering, Ship-building and Ship-repairing and other metal industries*, London, 1928, p. 8.

the heavy and marine engineering and shipbuilding trades remained much more stable (again the figures should be treated as approximate):

**Table 4.9.** Proportions of skilled, semi- and unskilled labour in the NE, 1913–30

|      | Skilled (%) | Semi-skilled (%) | Unskilled (%) | Misc. (%) |
|------|-------------|------------------|---------------|-----------|
| 1913 | 47.0        | 12.58            | 25.16         | 15.22     |
| 1925 | 49.47       | 17.28            | 22.61         | 10.64     |
| 1930 | 47.61       | 15.11            | 32.78         | 4.5       |

*Source*: Board of Trade, *An Industrial Survey of the North-East Coast Area*, 1932, p. 273.

These marine engineering and shipyard trades were not diluted during the war and though they underwent some technological innovation, it was not such as to displace skilled by semi-skilled labour. For the skilled workers in them, the principal changes of the early 1920s were a major loss of earning power compared with craftsmen in sheltered industries, such as building, and a loss of job opportunities as the industry contracted. This may have modified the strong local tradition of sons following their fathers into the trades. According to an East Coast shipbuilder:

> During the industrial slump following the Great War, a number of large employers ceased binding apprentices by indenture and subsequently stood them off when reducing hands. This course lowered the dignity of the trade which existed prior to 1914, and the natural result followed that both parents and apprentices lost interest and lads turned to other occupations. Another great factor is the financial position of skilled workers generally, whose social status has been undermined by the serious advances accorded to unskilled labour. This factor has a deterring effect on the sacrifices made by parents in placing a lad for apprenticeship, as in the past a trade brought with it a financial benefit over the labouring classes.[100]

In general engineering, there was a complex of changes associated with the war which altered the proportions of grades in the labour force and, on the whole, lowered the skill embodied in the craftsman: amongst them were dilution and the inauguration of schemes for rapidly training machinists; the introduction of machinery which did away with the skill of the craftsman; closer managerial control; the greater specialisation of an individual firm's output; the spread of piece-work[101] which cut down the time the craftsman could spend

---

100. Ibid., *General Report*, p. 64.
101. See Committee on Industry and Trade, *Factors in Industrial and Commercial Efficiency. Part I*, pp. 137–48.

instructing the apprentice. None of these was entirely independent of the minor revolution in engineering workshop machinery and organisation which was taking place in the twenty years before the war. The introduction, between about 1885 and 1890, of such products as the safety bicycle had led to changes in the machine technique for milling, grinding and turning operations.[102] These had been combined with a general reorganisation of industrial methods which had slowly spread out from the Midlands. Technological innovation made redundant most of the hand skills of the engineering fitter; when he received an article correctly ground to a thousandth of an inch, it was hardly conceivable that he would aid matters with his file. The redundancy of this form of skill had to some extent been balanced by the emergence of highly-skilled gaugemakers to make the jigs which transformed skilled work on the new machinery into almost foolproof unskilled labour. Specialisation of production and the introduction of capstan and turret lathes had similarly reduced the skills required of the engineering turner while some of the mental labour of his job — such as 'feed and speed' calculations — was taken over by specialist (often supervisory) workers. Though considerable skill was required to set up capstan and turret lathes, once this was done their operation was semi-automatic.

The demands of wartime production greatly accelerated the installation of this technology where it was not already in use and, no less important, these demands educated employers in the principles of capital-intensive, labour-efficient engineering which had already been so thoroughly applied in prewar America.[103] One principle was that on long runs rapidly trained labour should be deployed on the new technology and the craftsman's skill reserved for those tasks where it was indispensable. This required shop facilities for training machinists and the war palpably hastened their development, as this document from the Ministry of Munitions explains:

The development of training has proceeded apace in proportion as the Production Engineer with his gospel of manufacture on specialised repetition lines has gained general acceptance. Prior to the outbreak of war his voice in England was that of one crying in the wilderness. Owing to the development of the motor industry, considerable ground had been gained in the Midlands, notably in Birmingham, Coventry, Rugby, and to some extent, London, but with the exception of these districts little headway had been made. . . . At first the [Training Section of the Ministry of Munitions] fumbled rather blindly preaching a gospel it half believed to a limited

102. See Rowe, *Wages in Practice and Theory*, pp. 89–103, for a description of the technical changes in engineering.

103. See PRO MUN4/176 for a memorandum on the educative work of the Ministry of Munitions Machine Tools Department, 11 June 1917. See also *The History of the Ministry of Munitions*, vol. 8, pt. 3 generally.

number of somewhat sceptical adherents. . . . It owes its technical salvation in the first instance to four men, Mr Purdy and Mr Buscard, representatives of leading American machine tool manufacturers, Mr Alfred Herbert and Mr Oscar Harmer of Coventry. . . . Trade Union prejudices have undoubtedly been a lion in the path. . . . [But] Bad works management in the hands of men to whom the production idea was totally unfamiliar has been another more serious difficulty. Such officials have seen in it a convenient method of tinkering with wages and have been blind to its real possibilities. . . . But the production idea has gained acceptance, and progress has been made and is continuous.[104]

The training methods introduced were most successful where manufacturing operations could be standardised and repetition processes widely introduced and they were not, for example applicable to marine engineering. The document continues: 'Under no circumstances must the epithet skilled be applied to the trained product. It is a total misnomer'.

With the return to peace, engineering production diversified and the opportunities for deploying rapidly-trained labour were fewer. It is, none the less, impossible not to see in the wartime experience the basis for the expansion of forms of training suitable for machine operators. There was, by the mid-1920s, a category of 'operator apprenticeship' designed to enable suitable boys to become machinists. Lads in this category were typically engaged by firms in which extreme specialisation and subdivision of processes occurred and it was explicitly acknowledged that they did not become complete tradesmen. They were not expected to have, and may even have been slightly disadvantaged by, anything but the most rudimentary symbolic qualifications. A spokesman for a Leicester engineering firm who took on operator apprentices told the Ministry of Labour inquiry: 'We obtain boys direct from elementary school as near 14 years as possible. In these days of repetition engineering, we have not, broadly speaking, experienced any great benefit by taking boys at a later age . . . from a secondary school'.[105] During the interwar period, the Engineering Employers' Federation carefully prepared a scheme of up-grading designed to promote young workers with nothing but shop-floor experience to semi-skilled and even skilled work.[106] This practice had its most far-reaching consequences in the Midlands motor-car industry where in the 1920s many semi-skilled workers managed to gain skilled status after only a few months' training; indeed, for a man to be classified as skilled in the industry meant simply that he was being paid the district

104. 'Introductory Note on Training', 7 Dec. 1916, PRO MUN4/1276.
105. Ministry of Labour, *Report . . . into Apprenticeship, General Report*, pp. 88–9.
106. Hilton et al., *Are Trade Unions Obstructive?*, p. 143.

skilled rate.[107] The Amalgamated Engineering Union (as the ASE became in 1920 when combined with nine other societies) took it to be one of several ways in which the status and skill of the apprenticed craftsman had been more or less intentionally eroded since the collapse of the postwar boom and the defeat of the engineering workers in the 1922 lock-out. From the date of that dispute over managerial functions, employers were generally able to assert their long-contested prerogative to man their machines with whatever grade of labour they deemed appropriate. In the early 1930s, a spokesman for the engineering union expressed the steadily-growing complaint that formal training was being deliberately devalued:

> There is evidence to-day that employers are minimising to the fullest possible limit the work which shall be allocated to the skilled man. This can only result in affecting the question of apprenticeship. When it becomes evident to parents that notwithstanding the very low wages paid during the period of apprenticeship, no guarantee is given that the skilled work shall be ratained by the skilled man, then I am afraid the apprenticeship system is doomed.[108]

There is a kernel of truth in that conception of 'the typical modern workman' I quoted earlier and one of its illuminating social symptoms was the lowering of the prestige of apprenticeship in working-class culture. Apprenticeship was, of course, an important source of differentiation within the working class and was associated with the different orientations to work of the skilled and less skilled, orientations which can be illustrated by the observations from a young engineer that E.W. Bakke recorded:

> My father was an artisan working down at the gas works. I just naturally fell into that work. I used to carry his tools around, and I was anxious to put out the right wrench or hammer. That way I got the feel of the tools and I was crazy for the time to come when I could use them myself. But a labourer's boy, now, he don't see all that, does he?[109]

To stress the class-divisive character of apprenticeship would, however, be mistaken since, for several generations, it had represented a form of class pride and dignity. In popular imagery, apprenticeship was often contrasted with symbolic qualification for clerical work to the disadvantage of the latter and there seems little doubt that they in-

107. See A.L. Friedman, *Industry and Labour*, London, 1977, p. 204.
108. Hilton et al., *Are Trade Unions Obstructive?*, p. 155.
109. E.W. Bakke, *The Unemployed Man*, London, 1933, p. 23. Bakke also gathered extensive evidence for the popular conviction that there were decreasing opportunities for skilled men, p. 23.

volved a different kind of psychic passage for the working-class boy. In Walter Greenwood's *Love on the Dole* (1933), for example, an engineering apprenticeship conjures up, for the youthful hero, a vision of mastery over great machines and a social dignity incomparably superior to collar-and-tie clerical work. Structural unemployment in those industries which had traditionally recruited skilled labour through apprenticeship, growing awareness of the threat of technological redundancy and a bitter conviction that employers exploited cheap apprentice labour merely to turn it on the streets when it had served its time brought about a shift in popular attitudes: 'Many a parent has found that his own apprenticeship training has not prevented him from walking the streets. He sees more and more the skilled man's preserve disappearing into the maw of the machine, and he may very well think that the prospects of employment do not justify the expense of a similar training for his son'.[110]

By the end of the interwar period, social surveys were pointing to something of a divergence in working-class generations in attitudes to apprenticeship. Younger working-class parents were coming to regard office work as the highest mark of respectability — principally because of the greater freedom of white-collar workers from unemployment, but also because of slackening trade union control over apprenticeship and the lack of a recognised status for industrial trainees. They were developments which the Pilgrim Trust survey *Men Without Work* regarded as having 'a profoundly unsettling effect on something which used to be the hallmark of working-class respectability, the status of a tradesman who had "served his time"'.[111]

The devaluation of skill and of formal qualifications for industrial posts was part of a wider process of change in the structure of relations between manual workers which took place between 1900 and 1930. It was a change which led to the economic and social homogenisation of the working class for it compressed the earnings differential between skilled and less skilled work and narrowed the social distance between the artisanal and labouring strata. Comparison of Rowntree's first and second survey of York reveals how the social composition of that echelon of the working class which could lead a life of some dignity had altered considerably between 1900 and 1935, principally because of technical and industrial innovation. At the turn of the century, the 52.6 per cent of the working-class population who belonged to class D, and who could take a few day's annual holiday, afford the evening paper and had a way of life so much richer than the 15 per cent of the working

---

110. Hilton et al., *Are Trade Unions Obstructive?*, p. 328 (from Hilton's summing-up chapter).
111. The Pilgrim Trust, *Men Without Work*, p. 198.

class in the destitute classes A and B, were largely the families of skilled workers. In 1935, Rowntree modified his classification and the top echelon (36.1 per cent) of the working-class population was a class E. Half of this class E were the families of unskilled and semi-skilled workers whose relatively high household earnings were due in part 'to the high contributions from subsidiary earners, and the small number of dependents, and in part to the fact that many unskilled and semi-skilled workers, working "on piece" in York factories earn higher wages than those normally paid in York to most skilled workers, who almost invariable work on day rates'.[112]

112. B.S. Rowntree, *Poverty and Progress*, London, 1941, p. 153.

# 5

## The Effects of the First World War on the Economic and Social Structure of the Working Class: Standards of Life

### Patterns of Experience

In the introduction to the preceding chapter, I argued that the war occasioned a profound break in the history of the working-class way of life. Having outlined some of the changes in wage and skill differentiation between 1914 and 1925, I will now indicate how these were registered in the patterns of lived experience.

The initial impact of the war threw into sharp relief the chronic economic insecurity of the urban millions who relied on the low, often irregular, wages of unskilled work. They were not to be confused with the social residuum. Mrs Reeves made this abundantly clear for her readers:

> The poorest people — the river-side casual, the workhouse in-and-out, the bar-room loafer — are anxiously ignored by those respectable persons whose work is permanent, as permanency goes in Lambeth, and whose wages range from 18/- to 30/- a week. They [the respectable persons] generally are somebody's labourer, mate, or handyman. . . . These people are respectable, hard-working, sober and serious. They keep their jobs, and stay in the same rooms.[1]

For such people, the autumn of 1914 was a period of acute domestic hardship because of the unchecked rise in food prices, extensive unemployment and short-time working (particularly in the service and consumer goods industries) and delays in the payment of dependants' allowances to servicemen's families. Wherever a working-class community was particularly dependent on employment in service or consumer goods industries (as was Shoreditch with its many furniture-makers or Hackney and Islington where many worked as piano-builders) then the combination of unemployment and price rises rapidly drove families to the only means they had of raising credit: pawnbroking and withholding rent. In Bethnal Green, the considerable distress of the opening weeks of the war was reported by the

---

1. Mrs Reeves, *Round About a Pound a Week*, London, 1914, p. 2.

160

London Intelligence Committee of the Local Government Board as 'becoming more acute' at the end of August. While 'the chronic casual' was 'much as usual', families who always lived on the margin of destitution were now actually experiencing it because of the prevalence of short-time working. In the last fortnight of August, three times as many children were fed in the borough under the 1906 legislation empowering local authorities to feed necessitous schoolchildren as had been in the corresponding weeks of 1913. The majority were children of those unemployed because of the war, but 11 per cent were 'military cases', victims of the War Office's dilatoriness in paying dependants' allowances. The furniture and bicycles from some 'better class homes' were, reportedly, being sold to dealers and many other families were pawning, and not redeeming, their household effects. It is a comment on the chronically pitiable condition of the urban poor that their underclothing was not yet going into hock, as it had done during prewar depressions.[2] Much the same story was told of other London working-class boroughs and there was 'general evidence as to non-payment of rent'. The sources suggest that rent was withheld either because working-class tenants sensed that the national emergency relieved them of the moral obligation to pay it or because they had a canny feeling that, in the more indulgent climate of opinion of wartime, magistrates would refuse to evict.[3] Working-class music-halls were badly hit; the London Theatres of Varieties, a chain of twenty working-class halls, lost £10,500 in three weeks after the outbreak of war and this hastened their conversion to cinemas.[4]

By late September, there were, in addition to the many reports of distress in families on 'round about a pound a week', alarming indications of excessive drinking amongst working-class women. It is not easy to distinguish the facts from the prejudice of the evidence, still harder to say why (if it was the case) women were drinking more. But in Fulham, it was a 'universal complaint'; in Islington, it was 'noticeable that women congregate in Public Houses on the days when Separation Allowances are paid'; in Holborn 'the excessive drinking among women continues, and there is said to be a great deal of begging'.[5] So great was

2. Reports of the London Intelligence Committee of the Local Government Board: Bethnal Green district report for the week ending 29 August 1914 (copy in the LSE Library).

3. Ibid., General Report for the week ending 19 Sept. 1914. See also the General Report for the week ending 26 Sept. 1914. Most local reports used the amount of pawnbroking as an index of distress, and most reported an increase in working-class boroughs during September and October 1914. There were exceptions however; e.g. Southwark reported for the week ending 19 Sept. 1914 that 'now that their wives get regular cash allowances the need for pawning is less than in time of peace'.

4. Ibid., Appendix B.2, Section II to the General Report, 29 Aug. 1914.

5. Ibid., reports from Fulham, 19 Sept. 1914, 26 Sept, 1914; from Holborn, 26 Sept. 1914; from Islington, 19 Sept. 1914.

the public alarm at the excessive drinking amongst soldiers' wives that the Metropolitan Police were, in the first months of the war, sent cards from the War Office informing them of all those women in receipt of separation allowances.[6] Policemen were expected to take an active role in the moral supervision of soldiers' wives (although it is clear that they were most reluctant to do so and deliberately adopted a policy of leniency towards those arrested for being drunk and incapable or drunk and in charge of children) and in a small number of cases war allowances were stopped or administered in trust.[7]

By November, the revival of men's employment and the regular payment of servicemen's separation allowances had greatly eased working-class domestic hardship. There were regional variations in the speed with which the booming demand for war *matériel* took up the slack in the labour market; not surprisingly, the metalworking centres responded most rapidly. In Birmingham, the Citizen's Executive Committee noted on 29 October the indications coming from every side of a return to prosperity. The armaments and munitions concerns in the city and the makers of saddlery and accoutrements were finding it difficult to obtain a sufficient supply of trained labour, and were giving employment to an increasing number of workpeople from the depressed trades; cabinet makers, for example, were finding work in the making of wooden trees for cavalry saddles.[8] The adjustment of labour in Birmingham to the industrial requirements of the war was regarded as almost complete by February 1915, 'with the result that, so far as employment and wages are concerned, Birmingham, on the whole is enjoying a time of great prosperity'. Remarkably, even the jewellery trade revived, 'the most unmistakable sign of restored public confidence and of the return of general prosperity'.[9] Henceforth, the metalworking centres of the Midlands experienced chronic labour shortage and, as a consequence, the rapid influx of workers from towns and regions where they had been occupied in non-essential trades. By the end of the war, the jewellery trade had a serious shortage of skilled labour and, in particular, an inadequate supply of lads willing to be apprenticed to the trade.[10]

6. See the evidence of Sir Edward Henry; Chief Commissioner of the Metropolitan Police, to the Women's Committee of the Central (Liquor) Control Board, 17 Nov. 1915, PRO H0185/258.

7. See the letter from E.J. Edwards of the War Office to H.M. Kelly of the Women's Committee giving the figures for the disallowances and numbers administered in trust: Edwards to Kelly, 13 Dec. 1915, H0185/258.

8. Report of the Intelligence Officer to the Birmingham Citizen's Executive Committee, 19 Oct. 1914.

9. Ibid., 6 Feb. 1915.

10. See CAB24/88 G.T. 8107, Report on the Labour Situation for the week ending 3 Sept. 1919.

By February 1915, the demand for men's labour was generalised and unsatisfied: in London, there was not enough casual labour to clear a snowfall in January.[11] Henceforth, the almost universal theme of social comment was to the effect that the working class was enjoying unprecedented prosperity. This is by no means easy to reconcile with the fact that real wages were, on average, declining and much of the comment came from individuals and institutions with the *idée fixe* that the working-class was inherently thriftless. Some of the more persuasive testimony to the decline of want and the improvement in family circumstances from early 1915 onwards comes from the Board of Education's Medical Officers who could assess the condition of the working class from the appearance and nutrition of workers' children. Dr Hamer, reporting on London for 1915, stated that: 'The three indices of straitened home circumstances, viz; the condition of the clothing, of nutrition, and of cleanliness of the children, reflect the improved prosperity brought to certain homes of the poor . . .'.[12] Of London's elementary-school children, 2.6 per cent were classed as having insufficient clothing or footgear in 1915, as compared with 3.9 per cent in 1914, and 6.6 per cent were below normal in nutrition as compared with 9.4 per cent in 1914. In Doncaster, the incidence of subnormal nutrition amongst schoolchildren had fallen from 31 per cent in 1913 to 5 per cent in 1915. From Salford, the classic slum itself, Dr Tatersall wrote that malnutrition was very prevalent soon after the war began but during 1915 nutritional levels had materially improved, 'this being no doubt due to the more liberal allowance made by the Government to the soldiers' dependants, the almost entire absence of unemployment, and the more generous allowance of tissue-building food in the free meal dietary' [i.e. provided under the 1906 Act].[13] The numbers of schoolchildren fed under the 1906 Act provide one of the least ambiguous indices of improved working-class family circumstances. They had been increasing steadily in prewar years as authorities took advantage of this optional measure and in the year ending 31 March 1915 reached a peak of 422,401 with the figure considerably swollen by the short-term but acute distress just after the outbreak of the war. They fell to 117,901 in 1916, 64,613 in 1917 and 52,490 in 1918.[14] Though some part of this fall may have been due to staff shortages, the Board of Education's Chief Medical officer flatly concluded that:

The causes of this decline are obvious. There was a great increase in wages

11. See the 46th Report of the Charity Organisation Society Council for 1914, p. 8.
12. *Annual Report of the Chief Medical Officer of the Board of Education for 1915*, p. 32.
13. Ibid., p. 90.
14. Figures given in the Annual Reports of the CMO.

associated with a rapid progress in employment. In due time this profound social change reflected itself in the homes of the people and in the feeding and clothing of the children. The evidence from school doctors and the Board's medical inspectors in all parts of the country is to the effect that in 1916 the children were, on the whole, better fed and better clothed than at any time since medical inspection was introduced [in 1907].[15]

One reason for the apparent contradiction between the fall in real hourly wages and the extensive evidence for the greater prosperity of the working-class family may be that contemporaries (and until recently historians) underestimated the amount of poverty in prewar society that arose from the irregularity of work. A striking feature of the social comment is the insistence that material improvement was most egregious where, before the war, labour was most prone to casualisation. Thus Bermondsey, by the end of 1915, had

> had a year of unexampled prosperity. A very large number of families, including many which at ordinary times live on casual earnings, have enjoyed a steady and sufficient income from the War Office or Admiralty; . . . male labour had been so scarce that new openings have been made for women, and less able-bodied men have found their market value greatly increased.[16]

Similarly, in Deptford, regular work and regularly paid dependants' allowances were regarded as having placed 'the poor townspeople, especially those ordinarily dependent upon casual employment, in a position of comparative affluence'.[17] In Fulham, the unusual plentifulness of money among the poor, especially the families of casual labourers, was seen as the visible cause of 'an immense waste . . . upon such things as drink, tobacco, cheap jewellery and amusements . . .'.[18] Social workers reported that they no longer heard of the age of forty-five being a fatal bar to those seeking work and in West Ham the struggle of the casual worker to snatch the foreman's ticket was 'a thing of the past'.[19] The material benefits of regular work percolated down to the social residuum who had been shunned by the respectable poor for there was a fall in able-bodied pauperism on a scale previously witnessed only with the introduction of old age pensions and even a decline in vagrancy which 'cannot be attributed in the main to any other cause than that employment has been substituted for vagrancy. It is reassuring . . . because it illustrates the fact that the majority of vagrants

15. *Annual Report of the CMO for 1916*, p. 142.
16. Report of the Bermondsey Charity Organisation Society (COS) District Committee for 1915, p. 3.
17. Report of the Deptford COS District Committee for 1915, p. 4.
18. Report of the Fulham COS District Committee for 1915, p. 8.
19. Report of the South West Ham COS District Committee for 1915.

prefer some kind of work with wages, if it can be got, to the life of the tramp'.[20]

Coupled with the opportunity now open to all for regular work were powerful legal and propagandist pressures leading to more regular behaviour outside work. Following the alarm over excessive women's drinking during the early months of the war, there was a still more bitter outcry in February and March 1915 at the loss of time due to workmen's drinking, particularly in the Scottish and north-eastern shipyards and heavy engineering centres.[21] In due course, this led to the banning, in munitions districts, of 'treating' in pubs, the restriction of licensing hours and the setting up a Central Control Board for the Liquor Traffic with the authority to purchase and manage the traffic in scheduled areas.[22] Heavier beers were eliminated and spirits diluted. Greater sobriety amongst women in pubs and on the streets outside them was both encouraged and enforced by the presence of Women's Foot Patrols, a uniformed body of volunteers, and women police. According to reports received by the Central Control Board, the various restrictive measures had extraordinarily rapid and far-reaching effects on the working-class community. As early as August 1915, the Medical Officer of Health for Liverpool wrote to the Board that since the operation of the liquor control Order the streets were quieter and more orderly and his district staff were especially impressed by the fact that children appeared less neglected. Staff employed in the supervision of common lodging houses reported that there was

> much less rough disorder and rowdyism. . . . The practice of gangs of men congregating in public houses, which used to be a common feature the whole day through, is much less frequent, and this is attributed to the 'Treating Clauses' in the Order . . . these remarks apply more particularly to the Soho Street, Great Hanover Street, and part of Scotland Road districts, all well known drink areas.[23]

The Medical Officer of Health for Newcastle wrote in a similar vein that 'it is perfectly obvious to the most casual observer that there is infinitely less intemperance among the workmen . . . due chiefly to the prohibition of "treating". . . . All my inspectors, including those for Common Lodging Houses, report much less drinking in their districts

20. In the *Poor Law Officer's Journal*, cited in *The Charity Organisation Review*, January 1916.

21. The leading voice was Lloyd George's; see his *War Memoirs*, 2 vols., London, 1938, vol. 1, p. 193.

22. For a recent account of the Board's work, see M.E. Rose, 'The Success of Social Reform? The Central Control Board (Liquor Traffic) 1915–21', in M.R.D. Foot, ed., *War and Society*, London, 1973, pp. 71–84.

23. See the Medical Officer of Health, Liverpool, to Mr Saunders of the Board, 26 Aug. 1915, PRO H0185/260.

and less rowdyism'.[24]

Medical Officers of Health for Newport, Barrow-in-Furness and other areas where the Order applied told of cleaner homes, better-fed and clothed children and less disorderly behaviour on the streets and public transport. Wherever the Order applied, there was a considerable diminution in the number of both the prosecutions and the convictions for drunkenness. In what appears to have been a diversion of purchasing power, and was taken as 'an interesting corroboration of the improvement in general conditions', the general trade of the areas scheduled under the Order was particularly good in articles commonly required by the working classes.[25]

The regularity of work, the greater sobriety and discipline of leisure and a new pattern of spending were social changes which interlocked with each other. They imply a diffusing amongst the lower strata of the working class of a respectable, home-centred style of life which had been more typical of the artisan stratum. This is not to suggest that preoccupations with respectability and domesticity had been uncommon amongst the less skilled or irregularly-employed before the war. Eleanor Rathbone conducted a household survey of Liverpool dockers' families in 1909 and found that even in this most casualised of labour forces: 'The instinct of housepride seems almost never entirely wanting . . . some attempt at ornament is always made, and coloured prints, photographs and dust-collecting knicknacks often abound in houses from which the more pawnable articles of useful furniture have been stripped'.[26] The striking change brought by the war was the ability to sustain respectability and housepride at a quite novel material level. The Liquor Control Board asked its Women's Advisory Committee to enquire into the question of excessive drinking amongst working-class women since the war and it concluded (in February 1916) that there had been none, except possibly amongst women who already drank before the war. It rested its conclusion mainly on the widespread evidence for improvement in the working-class home:

> Evidence comes from all sides. Children are better clothed and fed. The director of a boot factory at Leicester says that the demand for better boots and shoes, both in Leicester and in London, is greater than has ever been known. . . . A pawnbroker in Hoxton reports that his average number of weekly pledges before the war was 1,000 and now is 500. . . . We hear of a great sale in cheap jewellery, in some places of pianos, gramophones, and fur coats in others. . . . The cumulative evidence of children better clothed and fed, and homes improved, received from care committees, school teachers,

24. MoH, Newcastle, to Saunders, 31 Aug. 1915, H0185/260.
25. *First Report of the Central Control Board*, 1915, PP 1914–16, Cd 8117, p. 5.
26. E. Rathbone (for the Liverpool Economic and Statistical Society), *How the Casual Labourer Lives*, Liverpool, 1909, p. xxiii.

health visitors, district nurses, mid-wives, Schools for Mothers, the Salvation Army, S.S.F.A. Visitors, is overwhelming.[27]

The Board refused to publish the report because it was not satisfied with the contention that women were not generally drinking more than they had before the war,[28] but it did not challenge the great body of evidence drawn on by the committee for a new level of domestic consumption. We must treat with some scepticism the numerous reports (which are now a cliché of oral history) of working-class people acquiring pianos for the first time during the war, for the only source of piano mechanisms was Germany and in 1919 the English piano-making industry asked for government assistance to help recover from the disruption of its trade. There can be no doubt, however, that by 1918 the level of consumer demand was much higher than it had been on the outbreak of war. The Board of Trade, when reporting on the state of employment in July 1918, noted:

> Neither retail shops nor wholesale businesses have, taken as a whole, suffered from lack of demand during the war. One of the most striking features in commerce has been the high purchasing power of the community which has remained at an extremely high level during the war, and consequently the demand for labour has been very little reduced. In munition areas, owing to the high rate of wages, combined with increased population, the demand for goods has increased. This is well illustrated by the large growth in the number of persons employed in cooperative and departmental stores. Although there are 30,000 fewer males employed than before the war, the females have increased by nearly 86,000. Dealers in boots and shoes are also employing more people than before the war, since the loss of 8,300 men has been met by an increase of 9,000 women.[29]

The interpretation of working-class consumption is more difficult and controversial than establishing that it happened, as was shown by the debate that took place during the 1960s over the significance of 'affluence' for the class structure. Marwick has claimed that 'the working classes during the war secured a taste of the honey of affluence: their "reference group" altered: henceforth they would demand some of the amenities previously in the jealous preserve of the middle classes'.[30] I would place a different emphasis on the phenomenon, and argue that the demand was largely for amenities which artisans, factory workers

27. Report of the Women's Advisory Committee to the Central Control Board, 18 Feb. 1916, H0185/258.

28. See Louise Creighton to Lord D'Abernon, 8 Apr. 1916, and other correspondence on the Women's Committee Report, in H0185/258.

29. *Confidential Report on the State of Employment in the United Kingdom in July 1918*, prepared by the Industrial (War Enquiries) Branch of the Board of Trade, p. 32 (copy in the LSE Library).

30. A. Marwick, *Britain in the Century of Total War*, Harmondsworth, 1970, p. 98.

in regular employment and other members of the better-paid stratum of the working class were generally securing before the war. To this degree there took place a form of cultural homogenisation within the class and this would seem to be borne out by the greater social sturdiness of the less skilled in the working-class community as they participated more fully in a common way of life. Roberts recalls that: 'Labourers and even the "no class" who only a few years before had "known their place" and kept to it . . . seemed no longer willing to return to the ranks of servility. "Hard-faced" now, in street, pub and club, they began to confront their "superiors", mingling in a way unheard of in pre-1914 England'.[31]

It must be added that this tendency to cultural homogenisation was greatly qualified by the nature of the working-class locale and possibly reversed as the unskilled felt the full force of the postwar slump. A study of the children of the unskilled in Glasgow, Middlesborough and Festiniog by Llewelyn Lewis undertaken in the early 1920s stressed the unskilled's 'lack of sociability' with the other strata of the working class, a form of social exclusion 'largely due to their poverty. They were obliged to inhabit very poor localities and to dwell among people of similar habits'.[32] Lewis found the children of the unskilled to be victims of transmissable cultural deprivation, for there was a 'tendency for [them] to acquire the same habits and customs of living as their parents, to have a very similar outlook on life, and . . . [show] no desire to advance above their social status'.[33] We are entitled to believe, however, that in one crucial respect the groups he studied were either atypical or his methods were faulty: Lewis thought that only about 6 per cent of unskilled families in Middlesbrough had children placed in skilled occupations but, as we have seen (p. 129), Bowley's wider and more systematic postwar survey revealed a far higher proportion than this, and led Ginsberg to conclude that they did not form a stable group.

I have already referred to the considerable losses of the less skilled and the low-paid after 1920. I would, however, suggest that, notwithstanding the disproportionately greater reductions in their wages and their greater susceptibility to unemployment, the 1921–3 depression tended to reinforce the economic and cultural homogenisation of the working class. Why was this so? Firstly, one much-remarked feature of the structural unemployment which afflicted the economy was that it affected better-paid working-class groups, particularly in the export trades, who till then had been relatively secure from the exigencies of

31. R. Roberts, *The Classic Slum*, Harmondsworth, 1973, p. 225.

32. E. Llewelyn Lewis, *The Children of the Unskilled: An Economic and Social Study*, London, 1924, p. 54.

33. Ibid., p. 102.

the labour market. The Cabinet's Relief of Distress Committee warned in October 1921:

> A very large proportion of the unemployed today are not the usual type of unskilled or work-shy men, but are largely people who all their lives have been used to regular work at good wages and many of whom are still making every effort to avoid having to apply to the Poor Law Guardians for relief. A very large proportion of these men fought in the war and they are not prepared to see their families endure misery and want without a serious struggle and even disorder.[34]

The high level of unemployment amongst metal-makers, skilled engineers and shipwrights meant that large numbers who had participated in the artisan way of life found their mode of living collapsing after months of impoverished idleness. Secondly, unemployed labourers and the less skilled were, by the end of 1921, entitled to a level of benefit which came much closer than hitherto to maintaining them and their families at customary standards.

The changes in unemployment insurance between 1916 and 1921 are a complex history which I cannot recapitulate here, but their results were virtually to universalise unemployment insurance amongst manual workers, to raise the level of individual benefit from a supplement to savings to a subsistence income, to link benefit to need by introducing dependants' allowances and to entirely detach insurance from the actuarial principles which had governed the liberal state's first intervention in this field.[35] The huge cost to the Exchequer of benefit payments once the insurance fund was exhausted meant that they were rigorously administered to exclude those deemed not to be genuinely seeking work. For those so excluded, and others who exhausted their entitlements, the Poor Law was the chief form of life support. However, Poor Law relief for the unemployed was itself ceasing to be set at the deterrent level once justified by the presumption that work would always be available at some wage and that unemployment was a symptom of refractory temperament. The relief afforded by Boards of Guardians varied considerably, particularly between boroughs within the London area; but some Boards in poor boroughs adopted a deliberate policy of using outdoor relief not merely to prevent destitution but to maintain and even raise the working-class family's standard of life.[36]

34. Memorandum from the Cabinet's Relief of Distress Committee, 6 Oct. 1921, CAB27/149, C.P. 3371.

35. For a full account of this complex history, see B.B. Gilbert, *British Social Policy 1914–1939*, London, 1970, pp. 54–86.

36. On the local variations in relief measures, see J.J. Astor et al., *The Third Winter of Unemployment*, London, 1923, p. 9. It must be stressed that certain Poor Law areas were still operating the deterrent principle; see also the *New Survey of London Life and Labour*, vol.

Poplar became notorious for giving relief on a scale exceeding the normal earnings of skilled men in other districts and the *cause célèbre* of the Poplar councillors forced the government in 1922 to sanction a scale of relief which, though nominally confined to the Metropolitan area, implied an approval of the same level of relief grants everywhere. This was such as to make the financial public assistance generally available to the unemployed man with a large family equal to unskilled wages and until Chamberlain's reform of Poor Law administration in the later 1920s, some working-class boroughs assisted men at a much higher rate; Stepney offered £3 a week in the mid-1920s to a large family, about one-third more than the lowest basic wage in the borough.[37] Relief was made less stigmatising. The consequence was that the onset of mass unemployment saw the setting up of a welfare safety-net which sustained many of the economic gains made by the less skilled and the low-paid between 1914 and 1920. Working-class living standards tended to be compressed towards one norm because the unemployment of skilled artisans depressed one standard of life and the public assistance for the less-skilled upheld another which had been recently raised.

This, it must be stressed, was a *tendency*, subject to the considerable regional variations in the level of unemployment, the structure of the labour market and the administration of public relief. It was none the less quite marked and was strikingly brought out by the wide-scale inquiry, carried out in the autumn of 1922, and published as *The Third Winter of Unemployment*. The report was based on investigation into a number of provincial centres and its main conclusion was that

> the chief incidence of distress is on a different section of the wage-earning classes from that on which it fell in pre-war depressions . . . ill-paid, irregularly employed workers who were the first to feel the effects of trade depression before the war have gained relatively most from the provision made for unemployment relief, which has ensured at least a regular supply of food. The incidence of distress has changed. While the class that was worse off before the war is now provided for, the better-paid, more skilled and responsible workers are feeling unprecedented strain. . . . The relief available to the poorer class is available for this better paid class also; but it falls short of need. . . . The savings of prosperous years have been exhausted, and it is among the workers most distinguished for their skill, responsibility, foresight and thrift that distress is greatest.[38]

In a later passage, the report stressed that there was little evidence of the actual physical distress which, during prewar trade depressions,

---

1, p. 30, for a discussion of the changes in relief practices for the unemployed in the metropolis.

37. See Gilbert, *British Social Policy*, p. 218.

38. Astor et al., *The Third Winter of Unemployment*, pp. 10–11.

affected 'the great mass of low-paid, unskilled and irregularly employed labourers and their families'. Physical distress had been prevented by insurance allowances, Poor Law relief and the provision of meals for children at school. Medical Officers of Health were convinced that improvements in health won during the war had been maintained unimpaired. Consequently: 'The low-paid and irregularly employed in time of good trade . . . have fallen little in comparison with the general fall'.[39] This could not be said of the skilled, better-paid stratum of the working class for whom the insurance allowance and Poor Law relief represented a much greater fall from accustomed living standards: 'The skilled artisan has suffered a progressive decline in his standard of life. . . . The full effect of unemployment on standards of living is not yet apparent, since the acquisitions of the boom period in the way of clothing, furniture and the like are not yet worn out. But the signs of wear are appearing, and there are no renewals'.[40] Artisans were said to be parting with savings set aside for the education of children (a claim substantiated by the Board of Education sources — see Chapter 8) and withdrawing investments from Cooperative Societies.

One crucial respect in which the war disrupted working-class styles of life and, at least between 1914 and the early 1920s, reinforced the tendency towards cultural homogenisation within the class was by imposing a hiatus on house-building and restricting rent increases. This put an end to the provision of new working-class accommodation by private enterprise and suspended one process by which the artisan stratum was differentiated within the class. True, the provision of working-class housing through the market was already in some disarray before the war. From about 1905, there was a general, steady fall in the amount of new working-class accommodation annually provided. The Chairman of the LCC's Housing Committee warned in late 1914: 'Private enterprise is . . . providing cottages to a steadily decreasing extent, and the new working-class population has to find other means, such as living in old cottages . . . or getting into abandoned middle-class houses or floors, which is an insanitary and undesirable expedient'. Private enterprises had not, it must be stressed, built for the working class as a whole: '. . . hitherto private enterprise in building has met the wants of the artisan class, for the simple reason that they are able to pay such rents as make it quite practicable and profitable to build for them'.[41] The accommodation needs of families on 'round about a pound a week' were met by 'filtering up'; as artisans and clerks moved out of inner-city areas to suburban cottages so the vacated

39. Ibid., pp. 69–70.
40. Ibid., p. 71.
41. B. Holland, 'The Housing Question in Towns', *The Charity Organisation Review*, December 1914.

accommodation was split into sub-lettings amongst families from the poorer strata of the working class. The reasons for the prewar difficulties of the working-class housing market were the rising costs of building materials and labour and, more importantly, the rise in the rate of interest at which builders could obtain capital. Furthermore, increases in local taxation (usually paid by the house owner) were an additional factor to take into account when assessing a profitable rent. In 1914, it appeared that working-class wages were not rising sufficiently to continue building for the working class, although few would have predicted the total collapse of the market.

The war destroyed the provision of new working-class accommodation through the private market for the costs of building labour and the interest charged on capital were such, in the postwar years, as to make it impossible to build for rents which working-class families could afford. The new working-class accommodation of the 1920s was provided by local authorities subsidised by the central state. The Assisted Housing Scheme of 1919 gave a government grant to local authorities wherever the municipal development exceeded the product of a penny rate. This yielded 176,000 houses, but at enormous expense (they cost an average of £1,011 each) and the scheme was curtailed in mid-1922.[42] More important in encouraging the long-term development of low-rent accommodation were the subsidies available under the Wheatley Housing Act of 1924. Over 520,000 new houses were subsidised under this Act, whose terms specified that they would be let to tenants intending to live in them, subletting would be prevented and that in the main the rents would not exceed the usual prewar rents in the district. It was the basis for a vast expansion in municipal house-building.[43]

However, when Bowley undertook his postwar 'five town' survey the remarkable developments in working-class housing of the interwar period lay largely in the future. By the mechanical test of the average number of persons per house or per room there had been singularly little change between 1913 and 1924, and what change had occurred was for the worse. In Stanley, the increase in population had seriously accentuated the deplorable condition of overcrowding revealed in 1913. In Warrington, the proportion of the working-class population reck-

42. On the political background to the Scheme, see: Gilbert, *British Social Policy*, pp. 143–51; K.O. Morgan, *Consensus and Disunity*, London, 1979, pp. 89–98; for its results, see M. Bowley, *Housing and the State, 1919–1944*, London, 1945.

43. See A. Briggs, *The History of Birmingham*, London, 1952, vol. 2, p. 232. Briggs does, however, stress that it was the Addison Housing and Town Planning Act of 1919 which made Birmingham willing to consider large-scale municipal enterprise in a way it would not have done before 1914; ibid., p. 230. Addison did, in this respect, make the critical break with the past. M. Swenarton also notes that: 'It was the First World War that was to create the conditions for a different kind of [public] housing policy . . .', idem, *Homes Fit for Heroes*, London, 1981, p. 47.

oned to be living in overcrowded conditions had more than doubled, from 6 to 13 per cent, and the condition of the houses had deteriorated. In Northampton, the housing position was felt to be very unsatisfactory for, in spite of the postwar building of more than a thousand houses, there was double that number of families on the waiting lists.[44] This deterioration in working-class accommodation, due chiefly to the suspension of house building between 1914 and 1918, was bound to weigh disproportionately on the artisan stratum which had been tolerably provided for by private enterprise in the prewar housing market. Working-class housing standards had been levelled down, although all had benefited from the Rent Restriction Act which had held the general level of rent increases since 1913 at rather less than 50 per cent. Working-class rent was consequently a smaller proportion of the average income than it had been before the war: in Warrington, rent accounted for about 10 per cent of a £3 income in 1924 whereas it had accounted for 14 per cent of the corresponding prewar income.[45]

During the later 1920s, a differentiated pattern in working-class housing was restored. There had been a remarkable change in the accepted notion of what was a fit standard of working-class housing and in this respect the 'Addison Scheme' of 1919 marked what numerous observers considered 'a definite advance in our civilisation'.[46] E.D. Simon, Chairman of the Manchester Corporation Housing Committee during its great spurt of municipal development, claimed that: 'The house which the Corporation is to-day building for the working classes — light, airy, spacious, and equipped with modern amenities — is one in which any family can be brought up as healthily as in a palace'.[47] The hyperbole was not entirely unjustified, for if we compare the photographs he reproduced of a 1922 Corporation housing estate with the industrial barracks of the late-Victorian working class then we can see a new conception of the citizen's environment being realised. But the benefits of this revolution in standards did not go to the poor stratum of the working class:

> The fact seems to be that the new houses have been occupied largely by young married couples, or by others of the clerk and artisan classes who were living in lodgings, or in overcrowded conditions. There must have been a substantial spreading out and a big reduction in overcrowding in the clerk-artisan class, but it has not penetrated to the slum.[48]

The spate of municipal house building during the 1920s also led to

44. A.L. Bowley, M.H. Hogg, *Has Poverty Diminished?*, London, 1925, pp. 5–6.
45. Ibid., p. 7.
46. J.J. Clarke, *Social Administration*, London, 1939 ed., p. 91.
47. E.D. Simon, *How to Abolish the Slums*, London, 1929, p. 24.
48. Ibid., p. 54.

different 'ecologies' of working-class life experience. Within inner city districts, such as Bethnal Green, where a considerable part of the fabric of the late-Victorian slum survived until the 1950s, there persisted a balance of local residence and occupation and of local services and amenities (markets, pubs, shops) which was kept in equilibrium by the strength of extended-family relationships and intergenerational immobility in the area.[49] This ecology was certainly affected by demographic and cultural changes, but these were adaptions in the communal form of life, rather than its supersession by a new one; indeed the ecology adapted to change until swept away by rapid economic growth during the 1950s. On the new estates, by contrast, a privatised mode of living, in which extended-family relationships were greatly attenuated and the separation of residence and occupation much widened, arose.

This difference between 'traditional' and 'new' ecologies was not an effect of the First World War, but a number of changes flowing from the war certainly facilitated its emergence. One was the 1919 housing legislation. Though its contribution, in terms of house completions, to the interwar estates was often small it did compel municipalities to assess their needs and persuade the more enterprising to start building. Another was the dislocation of population after 1914 for this shifted workers to those newer industrial regions (and new occupations) where, typically, 'ecological' change was to be most marked. The huge wartime influxes of workers into munitions centres left a residue of permanent migration that contributed to the rapid growth of certain towns and the depletion of others. Between 1911 and 1921, the male population of Coventry grew by 18 per cent, of Luton by 14 per cent and of Birmingham by 8.5 per cent, as compared with the national growth of the male population of 3.6 per cent.[50] By and large, ex-war workers were retained in these centres by the expansion of light engineering, electrical engineering and vehicle and components manufacture. By contrast Burnley, a town which had lived by the old staple industries of cotton, coal and textile engineering, suffered a net population loss of 3.3 per cent between census dates.[51]

The new estates were as solidly working-class as the 'traditional' working-class community if not more so, since the absence of shops, pubs and small businesses meant they had no *petite bourgeoisie* of small tradesmen and though clerical workers were amongst their first tenants, many appeared to have made the upward movement to home ownership as the cost of house purchase fell.[52] Terence Young wrote of Dagenham that: 'It would have been extremely difficult, if not imposs-

49. See M. Young, P. Willmott, *Family and Kinship in East London*, London, 1957.
50. Astor et al, *The Third Winter of Unemployment*, p. 21.
51. Ibid., p. 126.
52. See R. Jevons, J. Madge, *Housing Estates*, Bristol, 1946, p. 65.

ible to have found another area in England with a population of 100,000 containing such an overwhelming proportion of working-people. More than eight out of every ten men were manual workers'.[53] Furthermore, movement to the estates broke down the differentiations between artisan and labourer and 'rough' and 'respectable' which were characteristic of the traditional working-class community. Economic differences between the Becontree estate families arose principally from family size, with the families of bus drivers and conductors being the most prosperous and stable element of a frequently changing tenantry. When, in the early 1930s, industry moved to Dagenham semi-skilled assembling and machine-minding became an increasingly important source of employment, particularly for the young: '. . . far fewer boys will become skilled workers in the old sense of the word than their fathers; the great majority are factory hands — machine minders, and assemblers and packers'.[54] In her study of the Watling estate, Ruth Durant similarly emphasised its 'undifferentiated social pattern' and the importance of family size in determining its 'simple economic and social stratification'.[55]

In contrast to the undifferentiated social pattern of the estates, there persisted in the traditional working-class community of the inner city considerable differences in the styles of life of the artisan and the labourer. We can appreciate this contrast by drawing on Bakke's study of Greenwich, a typical 'working man's community . . . the home of all classes of workers from the very poorest casual type to the highly skilled artisan'[56] (the specific terms are themselves noteworthy). Greenwich had a greater middle-class presence, in the form of shopkeepers, small employers and clerical workers, than did the new estates but the social differentiation on which Bakke placed most emphasis arose from the earnings and home conditions of artisans and labourers. Skilled workers' rents ranged round about 13s. a week, those of the unskilled about 10s.; artisan families were smaller and labourers often took in lodgers. Hence, about two-thirds of the artisans, but only about one-third of the labourers enjoyed the comfort and convenience of living quarters large enough to average one room for each member of the family.[57] The average wage of a sample of 153 skilled heads of families was 76s. 9d.; the average wage of 185 unskilled heads of families was 56s. 6d. The combination of this wage differential with smaller family size meant that the 'surplus' on which the bulk of the unskilled had to meet all but

53. T. Young, *Becontree and Dagenham: the Story of the Growth of a Housing Estate*, London, 1934, p. 118.
54. Ibid., p. 228.
55. R. Durant, *Watling*, London, 1939, pp. 18, 117.
56. E.W. Bakke, *The Unemployed Man*, London, 1933, p. xvi.
57. Ibid., p. 163.

rudimentary physical needs was between 10s. and 19s., while for the skilled the surplus ranged more often between 30s. and 39s. This differ- ence in family incomes led to a differentiated pattern of advantages and life chances which allows us to speak, in a non-trivial sense, of divergent styles of life: 'The meaning of this surplus in terms of added comforts, wider friendship, better clothes, the possibility of spending "extras" over the amount for rent, food and clothing which is necessary barely to keep a family in existence, the added possibilities of education, cannot be exag- gerated . . .'.[58] Four times as many children of artisans went to secondary schools as children of labourers and, because of the poor prospects of trades blighted by unemployment, artisans were showing a keener interest in preparing their sons for the civil service exams and the police force. Sunday school teachers, club leaders and church deacons were largely recruited in Greenwich from among the skilled workers. Bakke concluded that 'the skilled and unskilled men . . . live in a different world from each other. There is not a world of labour, there are worlds of labour'.[59] This marked differentiation was reinforced by restricted social intercourse between skilled, unskilled and 'blackcoated' workers once they had mar- ried and a 'tendency of each class of worker to live in a neighbourhood largely inhabited by members of his own status'.[60]

The nexus that must, to some extent, have cut across this differentia- tion was kinship. Bakke noted how the strength of extended family relationships was kept intact by the fact that, on reaching adulthood, workers seldom moved far away from their families. These relation- ships often provided the economic means to maintain social honour within the community, for large numbers of families disallowed unem- ployment benefit managed with the help of relatives rather than turning to the Public Assistance authorities. Unless social mobility patterns were wildly different in Greenwich than elsewhere, kin con- tacts must have provided many points where the life experience of the skilled and unskilled overlapped. But movement to the estates led the nuclear family to collapse in on itself. Since there were no local kin to call on, no pubs and (at least in the estates' first years) no indigenous social institutions, 'small families retreat into domestic isolation'.[61] The wireless became the central point of family life.

Despite the persistence of social differentiation within 'traditional' working-class communities and the divergence between ecologies, any summary judgement of the history of the working-class way of life between 1900 and 1930 should emphasise the growing conformity in

58. Ibid., pp. 165–6.
59. Ibid., p. 259.
60. Ibid., p. 195.
61. Durant, *Watling*, p. 89; see also the comments on the isolation of families on the Liverpool estates in The Pilgrim Trust, *Men Without Work*, Cambridge, 1939, p. 92.

material standards and cultural norms. We concluded the last chapter with the evidence Rowntree found of the great relative gains made by the unskilled and semi-skilled in York between the turn of the century and 1935, which meant that many were enjoying the standard of life of the most prosperous stratum. There had been other striking changes in the condition of the working class which are further evidence for its greater social homogenisation, notably a considerable improvement in housing standards, a decline in the number of pubs and of heavy drinking, and the enrichment and diffusion of working-class domesticity.[62] Material and cultural change of this magnitude has no simple causes and no simple explanations. Its total history cannot be written without reference to the secular tendencies in capitalist societies towards higher productivity, smaller numbers of workers on subsistence wages, narrowing differentials and the decline of dependency in the nuclear family; tendencies which have been evident in societies that did not participate in world war. That history lies outside the scope of this study. We are entitled, none the less, to look upon that material and cultural change in a slightly different light than the man who documented it. Writing to a friend just after he had made his second survey Rowntree remarked that: 'Although a devastating war took place between those two years [i.e. 1900 and 1935], the progress nevertheless is startling and encouraging'.[63] Surely one reason for that 'progress' was the devastating war.

## Conclusions

The working class has never been an undifferentiated mass. The classical Marxian conception of proletarianisation has been belied by the structuration of labour by skill, group bargaining power and what Marx himself recognised as powerful historical and moral elements that serve to modify the straightforward determination of wages by the law of supply and demand. Furthermore, workers and their families have dwelt in empirical forms of communal life in which the patterning of social relationships has differed greatly.[64] Any conclusions as to the changing structure of the working class must be abstractions from a material reality of great local variety. That proviso aside, these are

62. B.S. Rowntree, *Poverty and Progress*, London, 1941, pp. 276, 350, 370–1.
63. Quoted in A. Briggs, *Social Thought and Social Action: A Study of the Work of Seebohm Rowntree*, London, 1961, p. 282.
64. See the Pilgrim Trust survey, *Men Without Work*, which drew upon local surveys of the unemployed in Deptford, Leicester, the Rhondda, Crook (Co. Durham), Liverpool and Blackburn, provides interesting indications of the differences in the social patterns of working-class communities. See, in particular, the contrast drawn between Crook (a mining village) where 'there is apparently only one class in society', and Blackburn, where the distinction between the employed and unemployed was a 'class distinction', pp. 323–4.

warranted: firstly, the working class conformed more closely to the Marxian conception as a result of the war in the sense that labour was less socially differentiated. The propensity for skilled artisans to form into a distinct stratum with its identifiable way of life was greatly modified, above all in those 'export' or 'unsheltered' trades which before 1914 had been the strongholds of the artisanate. At the same time, the social residuum of the destitute was reduced in size and there were changes in the industrial and occupational structures which allowed casual workers, and those in low-paid work on the peripheries of organised industry (outworkers, garret-workers), to move to better-paid fields of employment. There have been few periods when the economic differences between workers have been as small as in 1916 to 1920 and, for reasons I have outlined, not all the economic homogenisation that resulted from the inflationary spiral was dissipated by the postwar slump. Secondly, new historical and moral elements entered the determination of wages during the war which accentuated the narrowing of economic differences and emphasised the solidary characteristics of the working class. The inflationary spiral certainly had class-divisive consequences (and they are discussed in the next chapter) but the comparison of earnings with the cost of living and the profits of capital, and the introduction of industry-wide flat-rate wage awards, strengthened solidary tendencies in the class at the expense of the sectional and particular. Thirdly, the war was an important phase in the incorporation of the working class in the capitalist social structure by political means (principally the amplification of social security rights and benefits) which have themselves emphasised the homogeneous character of the class. The granting of the out-of-work donation to the demobilised soldiers and war workers severed the insurance principle and drew the state away from its obligations to paupers and towards income maintenance of workers. We have seen that one result of the postwar slump was to compress the standards of life within the working class and this was to continue to be a characteristic outcome of the major social problem of the interwar period and the state's response to it. Between 1920 and 1931 the real value of unemployment benefits for a man with a dependent wife and two children rose by 240 per cent. The Pilgrim Trust found that it was a commonplace that '"unemployment is a great leveller" — while it reduces severely the livelihood of those who are accustomed to some degree of comfort, and to the spending of money on other things as well as rent and food, yet there are others, whose value in the labour market is low, for whom unemployment assistance, by providing a steady income at a rate well above that of the lowest wages, definitely raises the standards'.[65]

65. Ibid., p. 101.

# 6

## Class Awareness, Class Consciousness and the War on the Home Front: Industrial Workers

Most would accept that the differentiation of society that arises from capitalist market relationships leads to a persistent patterning of social consciousness into class mentalities. It is useful to distinguish between what, following Giddens, I call 'class awareness' — that is, the attitudes, beliefs and values more or less common to a class — and 'class consciousness' which involves the recognition of other classes.[1] The class awareness of manual workers arises from similar conditions of life which are conducive to similar modes of thinking and acting. This awareness tends to a social solidarism of manual labour and to conceptions of the world which, though disjointed and unsystematic, embody a 'common knowledge' or popular lore. Frank Parkin argues that, in relation to the dominant values of the middle and upper classes, this popular lore represents a subordinate system of values and meanings 'of purely parochial significance . . . a design for living based upon localised social knowledge and face-to-face relationships'.[2] His characterisation draws on studies of working-class culture in the recent past — notably Richard Hoggart's *The Uses of Literacy* — but it can be aptly applied to the values and attitudes recorded by Edwardian commentators such as Mrs Loane, Stephen Reynolds and Lady Bell.[3]

Within the subordinate, accommodative subculture of the working class, class differentiation is usually acknowledged in terms of 'them' and 'us' and the dichotomy stresses the relative powerlessness of 'us' to affect events. This dichotomy was certainly sharpened in the early twentieth century by workers' sense of the greater symbolic com-

---

1. A. Giddens, *The Class Structure of the Advanced Societies*, London, 1973, p. 111. It is an illustration of the lack of uniformity in the terminology employed by social scientists and social historians that Marwick uses 'class awareness' 'to signify the definite sense of belonging . . . to a distinctive class . . .', in idem, *Class: Images and Reality*, London, 1980, p. 19. His usage is, of course, unobjectionable but I follow Giddens in taking a possible form of 'class awareness' to be the denial of the existence of social classes, which is incompatible with Marwick's terms.

2. F. Parkin, *Class Inequality and Political Order*, St Albans, 1972, p. 90.

3. See, amongst others, M. Loane, *Neighbours and Friends*, London, 1910; S. Reynolds et al., *Seems So! A Working-class View of Politics*, London, 1911; Lady F. Bell, *At the Works*, London, 1907.

petence of the middle and upper classes and the feelings of inferiority this induced.[4] There are levels of consciousness above the acknowledgement of other classes: where the perception of class unity is linked to a recognition of opposition of interest with another classes or class we can speak of a 'conflict level'; where class conflict is seen as the means for overthrowing the socio-economic order we have a 'revolutionary level' of class consciousness. The them/us dichotomy does not customarily express a sense of class conflict for, I would argue, it is normally used within a context of popular lore and aphorisms with which the inequalities of class society are shrugged off or deflected ('its the rich as gets the gravy . . .'). However, the dichotomy can certainly be raised to the conflict level in specific historical circumstances, particularly (as I will attempt to establish) when 'they' are held responsible for affronts to the moral ideas embedded in class awareness. Whereas 'conflict' consciousness can be distilled from class awareness, this is not true for 'revolutionary' consciousness, which draws on conceptions of the world antithetical to a parochial community-orientated meaning system.

Industrial sociologists have taken a considerable interest in trying to specify the conditions which lead to conflict consciousness and there is evidence that employment in large-scale factory plant under the close supervision of managerial staff which allows little autonomy for workers tends to induce a sense of class antagonism.[5] From the point of view of this study, the historical fluctuations in wider market relationships, associated, as a rule, with antagonistic class consciousness, are more pertinent. Class antagonism thrives on rapid inflation, for the obvious reasons that workers come into conflict with employers when seeking wage rises to keep abreast with prices and that the tempo of wage-bargaining during rapid inflation brings a wider understanding of the reward structure.[6] There is the further reason that, in the past at least, prices have had a certain customary or moral element and, in affronting a popular 'moral economy', inflation has focused hostility on middlemen, profiteers and other 'social parasites'. It must certainly be

4. Lady Bell noted that: 'Many among [working-class families] have a quite insurmountable aversion towards embarking upon anything which would necessitate coming into contact with officials, filling up forms, etc . . . ', *At the Works*, p. 120.

5. See Giddens, *The Class Structure of the Advanced Societies*, p. 203, and the references given there. For a comparative historical study covering the period 1890 to 1914, see P.N. Stearns, *Lives of Labour*, London, 1975, pp. 167–72. Stearns points out that some factory workers found advantages in big business; thus the association between plant size and 'conflict' consciousness may have been much weaker when the conditions of labour in sweat shops and the garret trades were appalling.

6. There is surprisingly little analysis of the social consequences of inflation in historical perspective; for a preliminary study, see C.S. Maier, 'The Politics of Inflation on the Twentieth Century', in F. Hirsch, J.H. Goldthorpe, eds., *The Political Economy of Inflation*, London, 1978, pp. 37–71.

added that there are contradictory consequences for class awareness during rapid inflation since the solidarities of manual labour can be undermined by competition in the wage market and the erosion of differentials.

The importance of drawing the distinction between class awareness and class consciousness is quite simply that many of the attitudes and values common to the working class have frequently been inimical to developed levels of class consciousness. This is most obviously true of patriotism, nationalism and working-class chauvinism, which have deep historical roots in English popular culture. Geoffrey Best, when reviewing the now classic study of the formative period of working-class consciousness, pointed out the neglect of the 'flag-saluting, foreign-hating, peer-respecting side of the plebeian mind'.[7] These mentalities were widely represented in late-nineteenth-century mass entertainment and the press; 'popular' national consciousness became more deeply ingrained with the integration of a national political community during the period of High Imperialism. National consciousness was not necessarily antithetical to class consciousness and there are good reasons for thinking of the integration of the national political community and its division along lines of social class as complementary rather than contradictory. The fact that much of the politically articulate support for the war from amongst the working class came from those who saw it as a struggle against 'Prussianism' and wished to defend and extend working-class liberties at home is, in a way, evidence for this complementarity. It shows that, politically, national and class interests could be combined. Furthermore, the industrial behaviour of many workers during the war revealed a mutual inflection of class and national attitudes; there were, for example, groups of workers who resisted the suspension of their trade practices and dilution and were antagonistically class conscious at work, but were also strongly opposed to the moves for a negotiated peace that were initiated by the socialist movement. Workers' patriotism was often an adapted version of the values expounded by the dominant classes. It was fluid through time, but for most it remained throughout the war a limiting context for their class consciousness.

The argument that certain features of the war economy and the postwar inflation led to a more acute sense of conflict consciousness amongst industrial workers and expanded the restricted, community-orientated awareness characteristics of, in particular, the lower strata of the working class before 1914 commands widespread assent. The unsatisfied demand for labour, the harsher authority structure of

7. Quoted in the 'Postscript' to the 1968 paperback edition of E.P. Thompson's *The Making of the English Working Class*, Harmondsworth, 1968, p. 916.

industry, the disturbance of the working-class family economy by price inflation and shortages, and hatred of profiteering would, too, be generally accepted as amongst the dynamic features responsible for this change. In addition to documenting workers' responses to them, we need a wide-ranging explanatory hypothesis which will encompass both the class cohesive *and* class divisive consequences of war industrialism. Such a one is to be found in the work of W.G. Runciman who, in setting attitudes to poverty in the early 1960s within their historical context, has argued that the domestic impact of the war disrupted for good the prewar pattern of reference groups by which the working class established a sense of economic and social grievance.[8] The war and the postwar boom, he argued, brought a more intense feeling of working-class relative deprivation as part of a syndrome generally associated with periods of real advance in prosperity. The movement of workers to different districts and different work led to new standards of comparison with those outside the working class (although the most important continued to be with fellow workers). Government propaganda, assisted by Labour patriotism and the Reconstruction movement, raised expectations of a better postwar world which could not in their entirety be fulfilled. There is much that needs to be refined in Runciman's brief survey; one might note, for example, how much militancy had its roots in apprehension as to the economic future as well as rising standards of expectation.[9] None the less, the historical sources bear out so forcibly the contention that the changing consciousness of deprivation can be systematically related to the altering of common frames of reference as to affirm the explanatory utility of reference group theory. Thus, the Labour Report to the Cabinet in December 1919 argued:

> . . . the constant raising of money-wages, so far from producing contentment in the ranks of labour, gives rise to increasing dissatisfaction and unrest. The causes of this are in the main two. So long as the rise in the cost of living continues, no award of increased wages can be regarded as final. The rise in prices automatically dislocates every industrial settlement. Further, during the war the normal relations between different grades and classes of workers, as expressed in wages, have been seriously dislocated, and as a result whole classes of workers feel intense dissatisfaction, not only absolutely, i.e. dissat-

8. W.G. Runciman, *Relative Deprivation and Social Justice*, Harmondsworth, 1972, pp. 65–8.

9. 'As the prospects of victory brighten, freer expression is given to industrial grievances. The prospect of peace is the prospect of labour losing its monopoly value, and there is clearly an inclination in many quarters to consolidate and extend the gains which it is now possible to secure. . . . The fear of unemployment after the war is a chief factor in producing the demands for shorter hours and the restriction of dilution. The desire to strengthen labour in collective bargaining is responsible for the campaign against non unionists. . .', Ministry of Munitions, Intelligence and Record Section, Weekly Labour Notes, 6 Sept. 1918, PRO MUN5/55 300/47.

isfaction with regard to the status and remuneration of labour as such, but also relatively, i.e. dissatisfaction with their own particular level of wages in comparison with some other class or grade whose wages appear to have been raised disproportionately. . . .[10]

This passage underlines the complexity of the war's effects on workers' consciousness; there were many issues which brought them together, crucially the sense that the conduct of the war on the Home Front should conform to their notion of a 'moral economy'. The war also had deeply divisive social consequences for workers: within the industrial enterprise there was a clash of interests between skilled craftsmen and less skilled dilutees; outside the workplace there was growing hostility between men eligible for conscription, working-class soldiers on leave or convalescing, and men in protected occupations. Furthermore, the wage inflation of 1918 to 1920 brought an intra-class market competitiveness which placed important limitations on the threat posed to the social structure of capitalism by industrial conflict.

Although I have not attempted to analyse systematically the consequences of the military experience for class awareness and class consciousness, I would stress the historical importance of those areas where the civilian and military experience intersected. Families were in contact with relatives in the army and there is powerful evidence (cited below, pp. 230–1) that it was conditions on the Home Front as they

10. Report on the Labour situation for the week ending 10 Dec. 1919, PRO CAB24/94 C.P. 285. These weekly reports are the most important single source on which I have drawn for this chapter and it is worth noting when and how they came into being. The decision to institute systematic surveillance of the working class was taken at a conference of representatives of the Home Office, the War Office, the Ministry of Munitions, the Ministry of Labour, the Admiralty Shipyard Labour Department and the National Service Department, 15 April 1917. It was decided that the Ministry of Labour would furnish Arthur Henderson with a statement as to stoppages, disputes and settlements, and labour propaganda brought to its notice during the week, together with a general appreciation of the labour situation. Arrangements were made for the Board of Trade to furnish information on purely civil industries. Scotland Yard, the Military Intelligence Unit at the War Office and GHQ Home Forces were to furnish the Ministry of Labour with all reports bearing on labour questions which might be received from their agents, and with information on the same topics coming to them through the censorship. See 'Labour Intelligence', 15 April 1917, CAB24/13 G.T. 733. These reports have the obvious defect of being coloured by ruling-class perceptions of working-class attitudes; they do have the minor virtue of having been written (or at least signed) by men who had spent a lifetime in the labour movement: David Shackleton, first permanent secretary of the Ministry of Labour, and G.H. Roberts, who replaced John Hodge as Minister of Labour in August 1917. Both were trade union MPs who had served on the Executive Committee of the Labour Party. They have the more considerable virtue of being a *continuous* (and synoptic) record of working-class attitudes which enable us to reconstruct change through time. Henceforth, they will be referred to simply as 'Labour situation, week ending. . .'. On the creation of the Ministry of Labour itself, see R. Lowe, 'The Demand for a Ministry of Labour: its establishment and initial role 1916–1924', University of London, unpubl. PhD. thesis, 1975.

touched working-class wives and children which most affected the temper of the men at the Front. Many soldiers were returned to civilian life before the end of the war, sometimes under military discipline (as was the case with 'Class W' men) while certain units (such as Dock Labour Battalions) worked alongside civilian colleagues. The points of contact between the civilian and military experience were often the sources of change in social consciousness. Soldiers who returned from the Front to industrial work before the end of the war brought disenchantment as to the nature of the fighting and many showed a more truculent awareness of the defects of the industrial system they reentered. Furthermore, the history of the attitudes and values encompassed in my terms 'class awareness' and 'class consciousness' has a chronology closely tied to that of the bloody attrition. There was a brutal division in the military experience of the war with the death of idealism and voluntarism on the Somme. The changes in the character of the civilian war were not marked so starkly, but the gradual application of the dilution and disciplinary clauses of the Munitions of War Act and the introduction of conscription in two stages in 1916 together effected a division in the civilian experience of the war, for they established a coercive apparatus of munitions and military tribunals which dispelled the voluntary character of participation and of the industrial truce. These measures mark the transition from a liberal state at war to the modern warfare state. The spontaneous patriotism of August 1914 was not exhausted by this transition, for the threat of military defeat in March 1918 led to its extraordinary revival, but between these two events lay an intricate set of processes by which class awareness was 'heightened' to class consciousness.

## Working-class Patriotism and the Industrial Truce

The outbreak of European war in August 1914 brought an abrupt end to a phase of acute industrial conflict. The summer of that year was a time when: 'Everywhere the ear of the social reformer seemed to detect those subterranean rumblings which are the precursors of revolt'.[11] There was a bitter and protracted lock-out in progress in the building trades and either actual or threatened conflict in the mines, on the railways and in engineering. The gravity of the industrial situation was publicly admitted by Lloyd George in a speech to city financiers and merchants in July. Speaking in the knowledge that the Triple Industrial Alliance was preparing for joint action in support of the railwaymen's claim against the companies, and fearing this would coincide with a

11. J.H. Harley, 'Labour and the War', *Contemporary Review*, January 1915.

military–political crisis in Ireland, he warned of a situation which would be 'the gravest with which any government had had to deal for centuries'.[12] Concerted action by the Triple Alliance would have paralysed industry and been tantamount to a general strike; had one occurred it would have been the climax to a four-year period of labour unrest which was the most serious since the establishment of early industrial capitalism during the 1830s and 1840s.

The seriousness of this actual and threatened industrial crisis poses a considerable problem of interpretation for the historian of war and social change. Was it the case that the war 'headed off' a major challenge to the fundamental institutions of state and society? Or was the government and the capitalist class confronted only by a particularly serious problem of managing or negotiating the industrial conflict which is endemic in an economic and social system which recognises the right to collective bargaining? An affirmative answer to the first question is obviously favoured by those who consider syndicalist doctrine and influence to have been a major cause of industrial conflict.[13] An affirmative answer to the second is favoured by those who stress the apolitical character of the unrest, the growing sophistication of the machinery of industrial negotiation and the greater willingness of the government to intervene in and actively promote, collective bargaining.[14] For — to develop the second line of argument (with which I concur) — the recognition of the legitimacy of economic conflict, and the actual propensity to strike for a greater share of the profits of industry, strengthen rather than weaken the fundamental institutions of capitalist society. They maintain that 'orientation to economism' in the Labour movement which 'allows for the persistence of the prevailing system of industrial authority, and more generally for the continuing separation of the economy and the polity which [is] a distinctive feature of capitalist society'.[15] Those historians, such as Halévy and Phelps Brown, who have discounted the revolutionary potential of the mounting industrial unrest before 1914 generally do so because they

12. Quoted in E. Halévy, *A History of the English People in the Nineteenth Century: the Rule of Democracy, 1905–14*, London, 1934, vol. 2, p. 486.

13. G. Dangerfield, *The Strange Death of Liberal England*, London, 1935, 2nd ed. 1966, is the classic popular account: see esp. pp. 190–2; Bob Holton, *British Syndicalism 1900–1914*, London, 1976, is a better-researched and more cogent argument for the significance of syndicalist doctrine, although he tends to equate the spread of industrial militancy with the expansion of syndicalist influence, esp. pp. 133–8; J. Hinton, *Labour and Socialism*, Brighton, 1983, pp. 90–3 gives a judicious summary of the strengths and weaknesses of syndicalism during the 'Labour unrest'.

14. See H. Pelling, 'The Labour Unrest, 1911–14', in *Popular Politics and Society in Late Victorian Britain*, London, 1968, pp. 147–64; E.H. Phelps Brown, *The Growth of British Industrial Relations*, London, 1959; C. Wrigley, 'The Government and Industrial Relations', in idem, ed., *A History of British Industrial Relations 1875–1914*, Brighton, 1982.

15. Giddens, *The Class Structure of the Advanced Societies*, p. 268.

regard the prewar years as a particularly constructive phase in industrial relations and industrial politics.[16]

If we are to regard the prewar unrest as a challenge to the fundamental institutions of state and society, then this makes even more remarkable the submergence, in the autumn of 1914, of working-class industrial
militancy in the will to victory. The *History of the Ministry of Munitions*
was later to describe the 'first six months of the war' as 'a time of peace
in the labour world such as had never existed before and has not
existed since'.[17] From 72,000 men involved in various disputes in
mid-July, the number fell to practically nil by the following February.[18]
This passivity of industrial labour expressed that uncritical acceptance
of the legitimacy of the war by the vast majority of the population
which the government secured by disingenuously portraying it as a
defensive crusade on behalf of Belgium. Passivity went deeper than the
industrial truce proclaimed by the Labour movement for it included a
paralysis of trade union activity which did not involve strikes or the
threat of strike; distributive workers, for example, gave up their campaign against 'living-in'. There were technical reasons for this, such as
the enlistment of trade union officials and the financial difficulties of
unions brought about by the collapse of credit and the machinery of
exchange, but *The Shop Assistant* singled out as the basic cause that
'spurious patriotism' which regarded any 'militant attitude [from]
which friction would arise between employer and employee' as disloyalty to the country.[19]

It is true that the evidence as to working-class attitudes to the war
during its early days suggests a more complicated set of feelings than
the conventional picture of mass enthusiasm. The government had
been under no popular pressure to declare war and, in the first days of
August, local working-class organisations — especially the trades and
labour councils — actively promoted demonstrations to 'stop the war'.
On the 9 August, a representative conference of the London Labour
movement condemned it by a large majority as 'a war of rulers and not
of the people' in a resolution eloquently expressing international working-
class solidarity.[20] This opposition was extremely short-lived: before the

16. Halévy, *The Rule of Democracy*, pp. 476–7; Phelps Brown, *The Growth of British
Industrial Relations*, pp. 322ff.

17. *The History of the Ministry of Munitions*, 1920–4, vol. 1, pt. 2, p. 31.

18. W.A. Orton, *Labour in Transition*, London, 1921, p. 18.

19. See *The Shop Assistant*, 12 Dec. 1914; also the General Secretary's Report to the
1915 Annual Conference of the National Amalgamated Union of Shop Assistants,
Warehousemen and Clerks, ibid., 17 April 1915.

20. See London Trades Council, minutes of the Delegate Meeting, 13 Aug. 1914; for
similar 'stop the war' activity in Birmingham, see Birmingham Trades and Labour
Council, minutes of the special meeting of the Executive Committee of the Labour
Representation Section, 3 Aug. 1914.

end of August, the executive of the TUC identified the war with 'the preservation and maintenance of free and unfettered democratic government' and the Labour Party wholeheartedly supported the parliamentary recruiting campaign.[21]

It would be rash to presume, however, that such public declarations either signalled or caused an all-embracing patriotic fervour. After weighing a good deal of evidence, C.E. Playne — a close student of public opinion — concluded that it was 'some time before the mass of British workers became thoroughly inflamed by enthusiasm for the war'.[22] Anti-German 'atrocity' stories and the sinking of the *Lusitania* were highly influential in whipping-up this feeling. None the less, it was still not one with which all identified, for — apart from the principled opposition of pacifists and antiwar socialists — there appears to have been some persistent indifference amongst an impoverished minority whose view of the war reflected their alienation from authority. The London correspondent of *The Times* remarked in his diary during August 1915 on 'those members of the poorer and more discontented working class who ask why they should fight? What has the country done for them?', although it must be added that he considered them only an 'insignificant section of the community . . . temperamentally out of step with the vast majority of their fellows with regard to the war'.[23] Such a minority is bound to leave few traces in the historical record, but about the same time a voice at a working-women's club meeting was recorded as saying: 'She did not see what difference it would make if the Germans did come and rule England. She had always been poor, and didn't suppose she would be worse off with them than without them'.[24]

The conventional picture of the autumn of 1914 rests, of course, on some indisputable facts: weekly enlistments rose from just under 44,000 in the second week of August to a staggering 175,000 in the first week of September, with scenes of unprecedented social mingling at recruiting stations and public meetings 'where men shoved and fought to get attestation papers and where with incredible difficulty they . . . succeeded in becoming members of the herd of men inhabiting the various training camps'.[25] Working-class men and lads obviously participated in this movement, and specific occupational groups — such as the Doncaster miners — were singled out for their patriotic spirit.[26] The patriotism of the

21. Orton, *Labour in Transition*, p. 19.
22. C.E. Playne, *Society at War 1914–1916*, London, 1931, p. 87.
23. M. MacDonagh, *In London During the Great War*, London, 1935, p. 91.
24. H. Anstey, 'The Home Side of War Time', *Contemporary Review*, Oct. 1915.
25. The weekly enlistment figures are given in 'Notes on Recruiting in England showing the transition from the "voluntary" to the "modified compulsory" system', Major Storr, 13 Apr. 1918, PRO CAB21/107; two quotations from R.H. Mottram, *Sixty-Four, Ninety-Four*, cited in Playne, *Society at War*, p. 58.
26. See Halifax to Kitchener, 5 Oct. 1914, PRO Kitchener Papers, 30/57/73.

worker who could not be persuaded that his work was indispensable was the prime cause of the indiscriminate recruiting which in the first months of the war seriously interfered with the supply of munitions.[27] But volunteers came predominantly from the country's young bachelors: nearly half the men aged 19–25 (83 per cent of whom were single) enlisted before the introduction of conscription, and in December 1915 bachelors outnumbered married men in the army by more than two to one.[28] Since working-class men married, on average, younger than middle-class, it would seem highly probable that it was marital status (rather than class differences in attitudes to the war) which accounted for the fact that the occupations of banking, finance and commerce were proportionately the largest source of volunteers.[29] Moreover, a very high proportion (about 40 per cent) of those volunteering in the opening months of the war were rejected on health grounds.[30] This tended to discriminate against working-class men whose physique was generally inferior to that of middle-class men. Later in the war recruiting boards drastically lowered their standards and conscripted men formerly rejected for voluntary service. Since ardour for military service had cooled in the meantime the authorities' relaxed standards were a source of understandable bitterness.

The voluntary service system had the effect of rapidly 'creaming off' the most patriotically committed amongst the young and untied of all classes. Weekly enlistments in October 1914 averaged only 17,325 and though the numbers coming forward thereafter fluctuated in response to particular events and appeals it was clear by the late summer of 1915 that they were insufficient for a war of attrition. Enlistment did not exhaust the reserves of popular patriotism, however, since many industrial workers were keenly loyal to the country even if restrained by family and other ties from making the ultimate sacrifice. Their patriotism was reflected in the working of the badging system for civilian war service, introduced to protect pivotal men in industry from the over-zealous recruiting officer. War-service badges were prized by workers as evidence that they were engaged on work of national importance and strikes were actually threatened with the object of getting badges.[31] Badges marked out wearers

27. *The History of the Ministry of Munitions*, vol. 1, pt. 2, p. 12.

28. See 'Results of National Registration Figures', memorandum of W. Langton to W. Beveridge, 28 Sept. 1915, PRO MUN 5/65 322/131; 'Memorandum on Recruiting', 23 Dec. 1915, WO 162/28.

29. See the First (Interim) Report on the Sub-committee on the Demobilization of the Army, Appendix II, Table 1, PRO RECO 1/832. I owe this reference to J.M. Winter, 'Some Aspects of the Demographic Consequences of the First World War in Britain', *Population Studies*, 30, 3, p. 549.

30. The percentage given by A. Chamberlain to the Prime Minister, 30 Dec. 1915, memorandum of the committee appointed to examine Lord Derby's figures, WO 162/28.

31. Report of the Ministry of Munitions, Labour Department. signed H. Llewellyn Smith, PRO MUN 5/49 300/15.

as participants and were used to attract women to war work. They brought social honour and certain privileges, such as precedence in the rush for a crowded tramcar.[32] Working-class loyalty to the country was again demonstrated by the preference which workers quickly showed for working for what they took to be the state rather than a private employer. The Defence of the Realm Act introduced a system of controlled establishments and the Ministry of Munitions later found ample evidence that the effect of declaring a factory controlled had very beneficial consequences for labour relations; many employers asked to be controlled in order to settle labour difficulties. Even the running up of the Union Jack outside a factory was known to have a salutary effect on morale.[33]

Reinforcing the patriotism of industrial workers were powerful social pressures to conform to the national consensus. By no means all originated outside the working class and, for organised workers, those articulated through trade union journals and the working-class press may have been more powerful because they linked solidarity with the fighting men with the solidarity of labour. Union members at home were kept posted of their brothers with the colours and the mood of the ranks channelled back to the workshops through letters and the reports of trade union officials touring military bases and the Front. Often implicit in this mood was the notion that industrial truculence was disloyalty to the class no less than to the country. Typical of this pressure was the letter from the local official of the Associated Iron and Steel Workers of Great Britain serving as a sergeant which ran: 'One thing I do hope, I should hate to think that our fellows, who are left to do their bit in the mills and forges, will put any obstacle in the way of supplying plenty of war ammunition to those who, in the fields of France and Belgium, are enduring to the end'.[34]

Within the factory or workshop community, workers' patriotism could be a rather brutal force when directed against fellow workmen who did not, either from conviction or indifference, wholly identify with the national cause. When the Derby scheme was introduced in October 1915 munition workers presenting themselves for service but who were not immediately required went back to their factories with a khaki armlet. There they sometimes came into open conflict with men who had refused to attest. From the West Midlands, several incidents were reported of a minority being compelled to attest under the duress of their workmates, with one instance of non-attested men being deprived of their shoes and stockings, placed in wheelbarrows and driven in mock military procession to the Recruiting Officer's table. So powerful was the resentment of non-attestors in the region, that a general

32. Memorandum of the Labour Supply Department, 23 March 1917, MUN5/53 300/102.
33. Llewellyn Smith's Report, MUN5/49 300/15.
34. *The Iron Workers' Journal*, May 1915.

movement of refusal to work with them was threatened.[35] This was the treatment often given to non-unionists and for men to make a principled stand against such patriotic 'moral suasion' required some courage. The unscrupulous who wanted to avoid military service preferred to do so by venal means, for under the Derby Scheme a black market developed in the official cards which identified a man as not accepted for military service, while after the passage of the Military Service Acts in 1916 many thousands avoided conscription by bribing civilian clerks to remove their white files from recruiting offices.[36]

Incidents such as have just been described, and the evidence for widespread venality, suggest that patriotism was the hegemonic ideology but not an all-binding social cement; it could be a divisive force on the shop-floor and coexisted with many other sentiments, of which the common man's sense of self-preservation was not the least important. Up to 1916, these tensions in popular feelings were scarcely registered in local and national organisations of industrial workers, whose proceedings were clearly dominated by patriotism. At the September 1915 TUC only seven out of the 607 delegates could be found to oppose the resolution justifying the war and expressing a determination to give every assistance to the government. Amongst 100 resolutions only twelve were even remotely connected with the tremendous issues which the war was producing in conditions of labour and in relations of workers and employers.[37] Again, this collective refusal even to discuss the war was evident at the November 1915 conference of the London Labour Party, where the Chairman refused to allow the following mild resolution to be placed on the Agenda: 'That the Government has no right to demand sacrifices of the people without explaining the object to them, and calls upon the Government to say what are the terms of peace which it would accept'.[38]

The Labour patriotism expressed in the abnegation of the 1915 TUC remained a powerful and persistent force in spite of the political setbacks the Labour movement experienced with the introduction of conscription. In July 1916 it was sufficiently strong to secure a majority in the London Trades Council for a resolution portraying the war as a defensive crusade against Prussian militarism and to defeat an amendment expressing international working-class solidarity, which before

35. See the Report of the Ministry of Munitions Divisional Officer in the West Midlands Division, undated [late 1915]. Copy in the Lloyd George Papers, House of Lords Record Office, D/27/1/5. See also the *ASE Monthly Journal and Record*, January 1916, Divisional Report No. 9.

36. See J. Rae, *Conscience and Politics*, London, 1970, pp. 18, 65.

37. See Playne, *Society at War*, p. 89; also J.O. Stubbs, 'Lord Milner and Patriotic Labour, 1914–18', *English Historical Review*, October 1972, vol. 87, p. 722.

38. Playne, *Society at War*, p. 87.

August 1914 would have been thought innocuous.[39] After the spring of 1917, those 'patriots' on the Trades Council committed to complete victory over the Central Powers were outnumbered by those in favour of some form of negotiated peace. The calling of the Leeds Conference in June 1917 brought this division, which was replicated in the wider Labour movement, into the open. But the prospect of victory in 1918 reversed the balance on the Council for in June of that year resolutions in favour of peace negotiations were defeated and substantial majorities found for prowar amendments. In October, when the imminence of the war's end meant that local Labour bodies were operating in the context of a revival of working-class chauvinism, a motion supporting the German government's offer to negotiate on the basis of the Fourteen Points was defeated in favour of a more belligerent resolution calling for the Central Powers' acceptance of the peace terms of the Allied Labour Parties.[40]

Patriotism tended to be part of the class awareness of the trade union official (and, we must presume, many of the men he represented) whose political attitudes included a suspicion of socialism as the 'fad' of middle-class intellectuals and whose conception of the Labour movement was limited to the defence of trade union interests. The ideological division between this type and the socialists who were increasingly antiwar (or at least pro a negotiated peace) which in London remained within the Trades Council led in Birmingham to an open split. The unity of the local Labour movement was more fragile in the Midlands because it was, at the beginning of the war, a very recent achievement; only in March 1914 did the Trades Council and the Labour Representation Council agree to unification.[41] Furthermore, Birmingham trade unionists had political attitudes closely attuned to the often intimate relationships between masters and men that characterised local industry; local unionists were prominent in both the National Alliance of Employers and Employed and in the British Workers' League.[42] At the beginning of the war, the Labour Representation Section of the Trades Council had been the focus of the local agitation to stop the war. The division between it and the Labour patriots in the industrial section was first revealed by the issue of conscription for, though a majority in the Council opposed the introduction and extension of compulsory service, a large minority (fifty-five to seventy-two) supported an

39. London Trades Council (LTC), Minutes of Delegate Meeting, 13 July 1916.
40. LTC, Minutes of Delegate meetings, 27 June 1918, 10 Oct. 1918.
41. See the circular letter from the Trades and Labour Council Secretary of 18 March 1914 announcing the unification; copy in the Birmingham Trades and Labour Council (BTLC) Minute Book.
42. See the circular letter of the BTLC, 5 Aug. 1918, condemning the participants in a rival industrial council as 'members of the British Workers' League'.

amending resolution affirming 'the duty of every Trade Unionist and Socialist who believes in Political Action to support the State which claims him in this great crisis, to work or fight to bring about the success of the allies, which our comrades are doing in France'.[43]

The councillors divided in almost equal numbers on the question as to whether delegates should be sent to the Leeds conference and the withdrawal of the Industrial Section from the Trades and Labour Council was foreshadowed by the 'highly contentious' decision of the majority to be represented at a conference called to set up Workmen's and Soldiers' Councils.[44] In April 1918, when 'the Pacifists' were claiming a majority on the Council, its patriotic secretary, Mr Kesterton, resigned and several union branch organisations disaffiliated.[45] The 'acute division of opinion in the Council on Political matters' was contained within the organisation until the summer of 1918 when local Labour patriots established a rival Trade Union Industrial Council.[46] Their circular letter clearly expressed the limited objectives of Labourism:

> ... we believe that the trade unions of Birmingham and district should be linked together ... in an Industrial Council, on entirely non-political lines, for the specific purpose of safeguarding and promoting Trade Union interests. ... Too long have we in Birmingham seen what should be a Congress of Trade Unionism in existence for Trade Union purposes used as a hunting ground of political activity. Wage movements and industrial problems of all kinds have been made secondary to political action.[47]

Remarkably, these divisions within the grass-roots organisations of Labour did not stop them taking on a new and very important role in the working-class movement, as will be evident in my discussion on the politics of consumption and distribution.[48] Here, I want to suggest that

43. BTLC, minutes of the Council Meeting, 6 May 1916.

44. BTLC, minutes of the Council Meeting, 2 June 1917 (seventy-seven councillors were in favour of sending delegates to Leeds and fifty-seven against. The minutes are terse, but it is apparent that the issue was contested at length); see also the minutes of the Adjournment Meeting, 28 July 1917.

45. See the minutes of the Council Meeting, 27 April 1918.

46. See the minutes of the Executive Committee, 24 April 1918.

47. Circular letter from the Birmingham and District Trade Union Industrial Council. At the September 1918 Trades Union Congress, W.J. Davis of the Birmingham Brassworkers moved a resolution in favour of a distinct Labour Party for the Trade Union movement. He was clearly a leading spirit behind the short-lived Trade Union Industrial Council in Birmingham and claimed that 100,000 unionists were affiliated to it. This was probably a gross exaggeration. See the clippings collection at the front of the Industrial Council's Minute book.

48. See A. Clinton, *The Trade Union Rank and File*, Manchester, 1977, chap. 4, for a survey of the work of Trades Councils during the First World War; also J. Foster, 'British Imperialism and the Labour Aristocracy' in J. Skelley, ed., *The General Strike*, London, 1976, pp. 27ff.

the phenomenon of patriotic and popular Labourism has suffered a dual neglect: in the history of elite politics it has been discounted as the manipulated tool of a social-imperialist clique in league with a handful of corrupt trade union bosses;[49] from the perspective of the left it has been seen as an irrelevance in the course of Labour's development as the chief party of the working class. Both obscure the accord between Labour patriotism and popular sentiment and tend to preclude enquiry into the sources and nature of working-class loyalty to the country. Popular sentiment was, of course, protean and diverse; it included, at various stages of the war, the hooligan chauvinism manifested in the pillage of German bakers and the break-up of pacifist meetings, and the deep war-weariness of the bereaved. But identification with the country was *the* socio-psychological relationship which, at crucial moments of the war, gave popular sentiment community and structure. One such moment — the military crisis of the spring of 1918 — is referred to in more detail later. Another was the approach of victory. In October 1918 even shop stewards were echoing the demand that: 'We must give the German b———s socks now we have got them on the run', and were caught up in the enthusiasm for a draconian peace and the anti-German hysteria which was the basis of the Coalition victory.[50] The Labour patriots — such as John Hodge, G.H. Roberts and George Wardle — who ignored the instructions of their party and remained with the Coalition fared extremely well in the December election; their ideology of apolitical trade unionism and national loyalty provided the ideal political bridge between the class awareness of their constituents and anti-German passions of the moment.

## Industrial Attitudes and Behaviour in Wartime

The division of authority within the industrial enterprise has consistently given rise to conflict consciousness in the labour force of capitalist society and it was that consciousness, and the industrial attitudes and behaviour linked to it, which undermined the industrial truce and seriously impeded the management of the huge productivity drives of the wartime economy. Classical Marxism tied conflict consciousness at the workplace to an understanding of wider, political class interest; the actual history of industrial and political attitudes since the later nineteenth century has, largely, belied any necessary connection between the two. Furthermore, classical Marxism somewhat exaggerated the

49. See, for example, R.J. Scally, *The Origins of the Lloyd George Coalition: the Politics of Social-Imperialism, 1900–1918*, Princeton, NJ, 1975, pp. 262–5.

50. Fortnightly Report on Pacifism and Revolutionary Organisations in the United Kingdom and Morale in France and Italy, 21 Oct. 1918, PRO CAB24/87 G.T. 8059.

tendency of factory work to homogenise the workforce. The type of conflict consciousness which takes the form of craft conservatism or the defence of the privileged position won by the more skilled section of the labour force was not an anticipated feature of industrial relations in advanced capitalist society, although it in fact remains a common type of labour militancy.

The industrial and political attitudes of workers in wartime were often marked by acute contradictions between the conflict consciousness that arose at the workplace and their support for the war. One example reveals these contradictions with startling clarity: at the Elswick munitions centre it was actually suggested, in late 1915, that before the dilution of production be permitted representatives of the men should be allowed to go to the Front and ascertain whether all the guns alleged to be required were really needed.[51] Yet in August 1917, when there was considerable controversy within the Labour movement as to whether its political leaders should participate in the Stockholm conference, the Elswick branch of the Amalgamated Society of Engineers passed a resolution to the effect that it would not tolerate any peace meeting which did not include in its proposals Germany's full submission to the Allied terms and that these terms should include annexations and indemnities.[52] Although the high rate of labour turnover in the munitions industries makes it possible that different individuals were involved in these incidents, it is more likely that they expressed the ability of basically the same body of men to distinguish sharply between the world of work and the world at war.

### Conflicts within the labour force

The contradictions or tensions between industrial and political attitudes were themselves complicated by the different fortunes of different types of labour in the wartime market. Labourers and the semi-skilled who gained relatively more from the wartime labour shortage than skilled craftsmen were less exposed to the tension between conflict arising from the work-place and endorsement of the war. Many key skilled workers in the engineering industry (about whom we know the most) tacitly withdrew from the industrial truce of late 1914 to early 1915, because they saw in the war's industrial impact a threat to their special status within the labour force. The labour shortage evident by the spring of 1915 was felt most acutely as an unfulfilled demand for skilled engineering workers. By June 1915, practically any workman with any pretensions to skill at all in the engineering industry had so

51. Llewellyn Smith report, MUN5/49 300/15.
52. Labour situation, week ending 22 Aug. 1917, CAB24/24 G.T. 1822.

little difficulty finding work the moment he wanted, that he had little economic motive left for remaining with his employer if he was in any way dissatisfied.[53] The measures taken to counter this were firstly to spread skilled labour more thinly — to 'dilute' it — and so permit the use of semi-skilled and rapidly trained labour on machines and processes hitherto reserved for skilled men and, secondly, to introduce the Leaving Certificate in the first Munitions of War Act as an impediment to labour mobility. The first of these measures suggested that the war would swiftly bring about the culmination of long-term industrial trends which were breaking up the hierarchy of the labour force and that this would be done at the expense of the apprenticed craftsman. At the Treasury Conference, the Chairman of the ASE argued that 'the introduction of unskilled and semi-skilled labour in this industry is a long-standing menace to the skilled. We have no desire to prevent anyone rising in the social scale, but we don't think we are called upon to allow him to rise in the social scale to the detriment of the skilled worker'.[54]

The skilled men's attitude to their craft had connotations reminiscent of the 'mystery' of the medieval guild. Lloyd George was asked by one of their spokesmen at the Treasury Conference whether after the war he could 'devise ways and means of eliminating the skilled knowledge which the semi-skilled men will have acquired'.[55] At important stages in the history of industrial relations in the war this fear that the collective property of their craft knowledge was under attack was reiterated with great vehemence by the skilled men's spokesmen. During the protracted and difficult negotiations with the unions concerning the withdrawal of the Trade Card Scheme in April 1917, Mr Brownlie, general secretary of the ASE argued:

> The unskilled unions stand to gain by the system of dilution whereas we . . . have allowed people to come into our trade who have no legitimate right to be in our trade to assist the nation in its hour of need . . . the unskilled unions . . . have no trade right such as the skilled craftsman's right. [They are] acquiring a knowledge of our trade which may be used to the detriment of skilled craftsmen at the end of the war.[56]

It has been argued that the real impact of dilution on industrial labour was more limited than the subjective reactions to it would

53. Memorandum on Labour for Armaments, signed Llewellyn Smith, 9 June 1915, MUN5/57 320/21.

54. *The History of the Ministry of Munitions*, vol. 5, pt. 1, p. 20.

55. Ibid., p. 21.

56. Verbatim Report of the Conference with the ASE with regard to the Trade Card Scheme, 23 April 1917, MUN5/62 322/17.

suggest.[57] This impact was certainly uneven: in October 1917, of the 2.228m. males and 878,000 females in the metal and chemical trades, 41 per cent of the males (924,000) and 45 per cent of the females (397,000) were officially reckoned as dilutees; i.e. people drawn into the trades by wartime circumstances who would not normally expected to have have entered them. They were heavily concentrated in the manufacture of military stores for war purposes: almost 60 per cent of the men and 54 per cent of the women engaged on making destructive munitions were 'dilutees'. Outside the munitions-making sector only one-third of the men, and fewer than one-fifth of the women were 'dilutees' in the sense just given (this in spite of the fact that 90 per cent of the total labour force in the metal and chemical trades was reckoned as engaged on government work).[58] Whether these proportions — which varied considerably, with major trades (such as shipbuilding) experiencing very little dilution — justify the view that its impact was generally limited is a moot point. Amongst the craftsmen and their union leaders, the male dilutees aroused more hostility than the female, partly because they released young skilled men for conscription and partly because they were seen as a permanent threat to craft status (which women were not).[59] It could well be argued that the average ratio of one male dilutee to two non-dilutees was quite sufficient to account objectively for the anxieties and resentment dilution unquestionably aroused. That is to say, these were not 'unreal' or irrational fears, given the frequency of complete 'strangers' even outside the munitions-making sector. Furthermore this strict definition of 'dilutee' does not give us the full measure of labour substitution which often involved the transfer of men and women already industrially employed to new occupations and processes.

In addition to the threat to industrial status and the fear of the loss of a monopoly of knowledge, there was the more practical concern with the role of dilutees and specially-trained newcomers in the industrial disputes which many saw would follow the war. In prewar years, large numbers of handymen and improvers working in non-unionised shops, particularly in the Midlands, had represented a threat to the district rate. Understandably, wartime improvements in the training of workers on the bench and the demonstrable capacity of dilutees to perform

57. See A. Reid, 'Dilution, trade unionism and the state in Britain during the First World War', in S. Tolliday and J. Zeitlin, eds., *Shop Floor Bargaining and the State*, Cambridge, 1985, pp. 46–74.

58. These figures come from 'Memorandum on the probable State of Employment in the Metal and Chemical Trades at the end of the War', dated 26 Apr. 1918, PRO MUN4/5035 (pt. ii).

59. The women drawn into industry by the war were generally expected to leave at the end of it.

complex tasks on foolproof machinery led to 'the fundamental apprehension of the skilled man . . . that a body of unskilled men and
women will have learnt sufficient of his craft during the war to be
competitors for employment after the war, necessarily at lower rates of
wages. . . . Dilutees are potential post-war "blacklegs"'.[60]

Long experience of rate-cutting and a natural unreadiness amongst
the skilled unions to recognise variations in the wages of their members
based on the actual variations in their individual skill, made the skilled
men insist that the rate went with the machine. Hereby arose the
wartime anomaly of dilutees and up-graded workers earning more on
repetition piece-work than the craftsmen paid by time to make the jigs
and gauges and perform the setting-up which made piece-work possible. Dilutees and the up-graded came to monopolise the 'fat' parts of
jobs, provoking discontent, not only amongst the skilled men but also
'in the other grades of ordinary unskilled labour, where the earnings of
the workers have been but slightly increased . . .'.[61]

The government's attempt to redress the anomaly by the award of a
special 12.5 per cent bonus to skilled time-workers in the industry in
October 1917 merely sharpened the jealousy and competition between
workers that derived from the inflationary spiral. It proved impossible
to isolate the men deserving of the award by a single sweeping measure
and led to the demand for similar treatment from semi-skilled and
unskilled men on time. The general discontent was rendered even more
acute by a widespread rumour that the masters were placing men on
piece-work in order to evade payment of the new award.[62] The resentment of the skilled time-worker was not allayed and led to a spate of
strikes in the last months of 1917, as well as proving one of the factors
behind the last of the major wartime industrial conflicts in Coventry in
June 1918. The very words with which this resentment was articulated
are worth citing since they illustrate so nicely the craft mentality
behind the craft grievance:

> The skilled man, especially in Coventry, has been debarred from securing
> the advantages which his skill naturally should have given him . . . [W]hen
> the skill of the skilled man is required, the skill of hands, the training which
> he has had, his brains and knowledge and the methods of doing jobs are
> brought to bear on making jigs and tools with which the production can be
> obtained [then] the skilled man feels that he is not only doing the physical
> work but he is doing the mental work too, and is simply being paid a matter
> of £4.10s a week, whereas any Tom, Dick and Harry can come in and use the

60. Memorandum on the Administration of Wages in the Munitions Industries,
signed Gordon Campbell, 3 Oct. 1918, MUN5/62 322/17.
61. Report of the Commission of Enquiry into Industrial Unrest. No. 3 Division,
Yorkshire and Midlands Area, PP 1917, Cd 8664, pp. 3–4.
62. Labour situation, week ending 7 Nov. 1917, CAB24/31 G.T. 2542.

tools he has made foolproof and secure a very much larger amount than that. . . .[63]

Schism between the skilled and the less skilled, manifested organisationally as inter-union conflicts and quarrels between union leaders, but also in the form of disputes amongst the rank and file, is a swelling theme in wartime industrial relations. It underlines the point that we must not think of the war as simply tending towards a wider class consciousness in Marxist terms. The fact that craft privileges were under attack sharpened the craft consciousness of the skilled worker. The necessity for the government to deal separately with the ASE because of its dominant position in the engineering industry reinforced the pretensions of the engineers to special treatment (particularly with regards to conscription) but also excited an enormous hostility amongst the general unions which were growing in size and influence. The granting (initially to the ASE but later to more than twenty skilled engineering unions) of the right to process their members for military conscription under the Trade Card Scheme inaugurated in November 1916 caused anger and dismay throughout the Labour movement and particularly amongst representatives of the less skilled. Whereas the leaders of the skilled saw the erosion of craft privilege as a threat to wartime unity, the unskilled spokesmen saw the special treatment accorded to the ASE in exactly the same terms. J.R. Clynes, speaking for the general unions during the negotiations on the withdrawal of the Trade Card Scheme, said that 'we saw it was going to break up the feeling of harmony that prevailed in the Trade Union ranks of Britain with respect to the successful prosecution of the war'. He spoke of 'the feeling of enmity' between worker and worker which the scheme induced and argued that 'we ought to put an end to the distinction that has grown up recently in these matters of consulting trade unions. . . . Why should we [i.e. representatives of the non-trade card unions] be brought together separately from the aristocracy of labour with whom for the moment we are not permitted to meet?'[64]

Admittedly, we must be cautious in making too ready a translation of the views of union officials into the sentiments and consciousness of the men they represented. Union leaders such as Clynes were particularly concerned by the opportunities for membership 'poaching' which the scheme afforded (government ministers were themselves convinced that the card had been used as inducement to attract men to the skilled

63. Minutes of Evidence given before Mr Justice McCardie's Commission of Enquiry into the Embargo Dispute, 14 Aug. 1918, evidence of Mr Givens, MUN5/57.

64. Verbatim Report of the Conference with the non-trade card unions on the Trade Card Scheme, 4 April 1917, MUN5/62 322/16.

unions)[65] while Brownlie for the ASE and others righteously argued that the lower subscriptions of the general unions and the greater social influence of their MPs such as Charles Duncan had attracted men who ought properly to be in the craft societies.[66] It is not easy to see where men on the shop-floor stood in relation to the welter of claims and counter-claims. When, however it came to the issue of shop-floor representation the schism between skilled and less skilled was clearly a barrier to the full implementation of the demand for 'all-grades' representation being put forward by the theorists of the Shop Stewards' Movement. Of the wartime Workers' Committees affiliated to the Movement, only that in Sheffield was truly representative of all grades and occupations in the factories and even there shop-floor unity was fragile and brief-lived. The engineering unions' attempt to negotiate with the employers a national agreement which would constitutionalise the steward's role (and keep the unofficial movement in check) brought out:

> The difficulty which has always been foreseen [in] that the unions will be unable to agree amongst themselves as to a basis of representation on any central body that may be established and on their relations to each other in particular works. The craft unions are adverse to their members being represented by Shop Stewards who belong to an un-skilled union and vice versa. These difficulties represent feelings of rivalry and jealousy which are strong in the executives of the various unions, but which also exist to a large extent among the rank and file.[67]

As the end of the war approached, the schism between skilled and unskilled organisations was seen by employers as a serious weakness in the campaign for 'Labour preparedness', but not fully appreciated by the Labour movement itself.[68] On the shop-floor, the requirements of further 'comb-outs' under the Manpower Act and as a result of the military crisis in the spring of 1918 exacerbated the tension between skilled and less skilled. The problem was most acute in Lancashire since it was here that the skilled engineers felt threatened by the possibility of the extension of dilution to non-war work, particularly to the extensive textile machinery trade. In late March 1918, in spite of the spontaneous patriotism which gripped the working class generally, the ASE in Preston instructed its members not to supervise or grind or

65. For the defects of the scheme see Memorandum on the History of the Trade Card Scheme (undated), MUN5/62 322/33.

66. Conference with the ASE with regard to the Trade Card Scheme, 23 April 1917, MUN5/62 322/17.

67. Labour situation, week ending 19 Dec. 1917, CAB24/36 G.T. 3062.

68. Ministry of Munitions Intelligence and Records Section, Weekly Labour Notes, 13 Sept. 1918, MUN5/55 300/47.

set up the tools of any man of military age and medical classification Grade I as a protest against the right of dilutees to remain in industry while young engineers were called to the colours. As a consequence, semi-skilled machine-minders had to be put on labouring work. During the negotiations arranged to settle the dispute in May, local officials of the union carried their separatism so far as to refuse to meet representatives of other unions concerned although they were prepared to confer with government officials and employers. The general unions riposted by threatening to refuse to do any work set up by skilled men of military age and classified Grade I.[69]

Capping the skilled man's grievances, and reinforcing his craft defensiveness was a deep suspicion of government intentions concerning the trade practices which had been suspended under the Treasury Agreements and the trade union executives who had agreed to their suspension. Since the success of the munitions programme seemed to demonstrate just how much of an impediment to industrial efficiency these practices were, it was mooted at the highest level that some *quid pro quo* should be reached with the unions by which the government's promise to restore prewar practices on the outbreak of peace could be given up for 'some provision for affording stability of employment and industrial security in its widest sense'.[70] Furthermore, whether intentionally or not, many employers were slack in recording the numerous departures from workshop practice as they were required to under the Munitions Acts, and trade union officials did little to correct this.[71] The danger, then, that the hard reality of protective custom built up by the craftsmen and maintained by their local vigilance would be traded in for some vague measure of paternalist 'welfare' or eroded by the negligence of employers and union officials was a real one. The anxiety that the government would find some way round its promises to the skilled unions (recorded in most industrial districts as a source of unrest in mid-1917)[72] became intermingled with a larger, customary distrust of the state. The Commissioners of Enquiry into the North

69. Weekly Labour Notes, 7 June 1918, MUN5/55 300/47.

70. In a confidential memorandum, dated 4 Oct. 1918, entitled 'Industrial Unrest', and forwarded by Stephenson Kent to Churchill, MUN5/51 300/61.

71. The Minutes of the Minister of Munitions Trade Union Advisory Committee (not verbatim) for 27 March 1918 states that 'the Department were doing their utmost to secure records of all departures [from workshop practice] . . . but very little assistance had been rendered in the securing of these records by the Trade Unions and Local Labour Advisory Boards. . . . It was safe to assume that there were still many changes unrecorded', MUN5/52 300/76. The Labour Research Department set up a special unit to undertake this work.

72. Commission of Enquiry into Industrial Unrest, No. 1 Division, North Eastern Area, Cd 8662, p. 7; No. 2 Division, North Western Area, Cd 8663, p. 13. The summary by G.N. Barnes ranked this apprehension third, below food prices and the restriction of personal freedom, in the list of working-class grievances.

Western Area, charged with investigating industrial discontent in the wake of the May 1917 strikes, lamented:

> It was painful to hear the common use of the phrase 'a scrap of paper' so constantly used by working men in describing what they felt about government promises . . . working people have a vague and uneasy feeling that the authorities are not really working in their interest, and if they permit various things to be done which are new to them they will after the war find that their conditions have altered for the worse.[73]

### Reactions to the strengthened authority-structure of wartime

Conflict consciousness at the workplace was greatly sharpened by workers confronting, after the passing of the Munitions of War Act in July 1915, an authority structure in industry which gave employers and managers new disciplinary powers over the labour force. The Munitions Tribunals set up under the Act were not intended to resemble courts of law, but their informal procedure and the presence of a labour representative on the tribunal could not disguise the fact that employers now had statutory powers to impose time discipline, stamp out drinking, card playing and idling at work, and control workers' movement and behaviour on the shop-floor; men could be fined, for example, for using 'more than peaceful persuasion' in trying to persuade workmates to join a trade union.[74] One danger soon perceived in the tribunals system was that it would 'supersede or set aside largely, in the matter of domestic offences and trade disputes, the [trade-union] machinery of local and Central Conferences. [Although] the novelty of the business, however, is in the fines imposed for lost time, disobeying orders, quarrelling, and a general want of decorum — all essentials, as it seems, in the acceleration of output'.[75]

There was a widespread sense that the 'servile state' had materialised in the tribunal and Leaving Certificate systems and what the ASE's journal described as 'a growing and justifiable dissatisfaction . . . against the action of employers using the Act to impose working conditions upon men which in other times would be strongly resented'.[76] The Munitions Act was condemned for undermining the consensus in wartime industry during the early months of the war and for 'the opportunities it affords to tribunals to oppress by coercion

73. Ibid., pp. 19–20.
74. See the discussion of cases dealt with by the North East Coast Munitions Tribunal, Newcastle, in the ASE *Monthly Journal and Record*, November 1917.
75. ASE, *Monthly Journal and Record*, September 1915, Divisional Report from Newcastle.
76. ASE, *Monthly Journal and Record*, November 1915, Divisional Report from Hammersmith; also J.H. Harley, 'The Conscription of Industry', *Contemporary Review*, May 1916.

rather than win confidence by cooperation with the Trade Union movement'.[77] According to a report from the North Eastern engineering district of the ASE in mid-1916: '[What] some firms regard as the whole art of management is being prominent [sic] in munitions courts'.[78] Furthermore, workers could have had little doubt that employers' organisations saw in the disciplinary power that came with the wartime emergency legislation the possibility of permanent changes in time-keeping, sobriety and working habits, and improvements in man-productivity which would enable them to meet foreign competition[79]. It must be added that employers themselves could be summoned before tribunals — most commonly for refusing Leaving Certificates without due cause — and the tribunals' judgements proved favourable to time-served apprentices, for it became an offence to refuse a Leaving Certificate to a young engineer who, on completing his apprenticeship, was not offered the full district rate of pay.[80] Generally, however, men felt that the principle of equity governing the tribunals did little to mitigate the disparity of power between the individual worker and his employer; delays in making awards were, for example, of no account to businesses, but a serious matter to the compulsorily unemployed man who had been wrongly refused a Leaving Certificate.

After the introduction of conscription, the military tribunals became a critical intersection between industrial employment and the Army. Indirectly, they further strengthened the power of employers over workers for there was a widespread belief (and the practice probably occurred in some cases) that employers furtively colluded with the Ministry of Munitions to represent truculent workers as industrially dispensable before the tribunals.[81] The workings of these tribunals were a source of bitter resentment, particularly amongst skilled workers who in the early months of the war had been persuaded to stay at

77. ASE, *Monthly Journal and Record*, December 1915, Divisional Report from Middlesex.

78. ASE, *Monthly Journal and Record*, June 1916, Divisional Report from Newcastle.

79. A particularly explicit statement of the employers' desire to see a major 'moral' reform result from the war is to be found in the Memorandum of the Steel Castings and Manufacturers' Association to the Board of Trade Departmental Committee on the Iron and Steel Industries after the War: 'There is great lack of discipline [amongst the men] both towards their own Labour leaders in cases of trade disputes, and also in their daily work. We hope to see a very marked improvement in this as one of the results of the present War.' The memorandum advocated the continuation of decreased facilities for drinking. Similar demands were pressed by other manufacturers' associations who were circularised by the Committee. See the papers deposited by the Iron and Steel Trades Confederation at the Modern Records Centre, MSS 36, Box 18.

80. See ASE, *Monthly Journal and Record*, July 1916, Divisional Report No. 6.

81. See 'The Sequel to the Engineers' Strike: An Historical Memorandum', 1 Oct. 1917, drawn up by the Ministry of Munitions Intelligence and Records Section, copy in PRO LAB2/254. The memorandum records this belief and, somewhat ambiguously, refers to collusion as an 'actuality'.

the bench or who had been withdrawn from the armed forces in 1915 because of the labour shortage and were then called up under compulsory service. There was 'a time when it was easier for a camel to pass through the eye of a needle than for the most pugnacious engineer to enter into any of the combatant branches of the services of the Crown'.[82] The Army's demand for physically fit men after the huge losses of the Somme and later campaigns radically altered that situation and the tribunals (and the 'man-hunting' yellow press) treated with arrogance and ignorance the claim of the patriotic industrial worker, backed by his trade union representative, that his skill was of greater value to the country than his fighting prowess. J.L. Hammond, after visiting men in military camps in England in the spring of 1917, wrote of

> the great bitterness of the men in the army . . . directed in part against their treatment in the Army and in part against their treatment before they entered the Army. There are rankling memories of Military Tribunals, bullying methods, gross inequalities. . . . [He suggested that] recruits who have entered the Army since the Military Service Act was passed are older and more serious than the earlier volunteers [and added that] the resentment with which men in the Army reflect on the working of the Military Tribunals and the general circumstances under which they have been put into khaki tends, I am told, to embrace the general conditions of their lives before the War.[83]

We must treat with some scepticism any hypothesis that military service is, *tout court*, a politically radicalising experience; for every piece of evidence which points to that we can find another which suggests that the comradeship of the trenches, military discipline and the exemplary leadership of junior officers encouraged the ranks to endorse the dominant political and social values. There does seem good reason to suggest, however, that, from 1916, the two-way passage between the industrial and fighting fronts was particularly important in undermining patriotic zeal. Official reports in May 1917 spoke of industrial workers as brought to a 'much more vivid realisation of the actual horrors of war due to the large numbers who [had] returned home with the experience of it fresh upon them'.[84] In October 1916, the Garton Foundation's Memorandum on the Industrial Situation after the war noted that:

> Many of the men who return from the trenches to the great munition and

82. Ibid.

83. Report by J.L. Hammond on visits to camps and YMCA centres at home, 17 April 1917 and 1 May 1917, dated 20 June 1917, PRO RECO1/45 Docket 89.

84. Labour situation, week ending 23 May 1917, CAB24/14 G.T. 832.

shipbuilding centres are, within a few weeks of their return among those who exhibit most actively their discontent with present conditions. Among those who have fought in Flanders or who have been employed in making shells at home, there are many who look forward to a great social upheaval following the war . . . They regard the present struggle [against Prussianism] as closely connected with the campaign against capitalist and class-domination at home. . . .[85]

### Rank-and-file organisation and industrial militancy

Wartime industrial relations proved very propitious for the growth of rank-and-file organisations, not just in the engineering industry (where they have been the subject of a fine monograph by James Hinton),[86] but also on the railways, in the mines and even in the service and distributive trades. Moreover, the fact that dilution had in practice to be negotiated by employers and government officials with shop-floor representatives gave a considerable stimulus to the spread of syndical-ist and Guild Socialist ideas of workers' or joint control. Doubtless, proponents of workers' control — notably G.D.H. Cole — exaggerated the inroads made into prerogatives of capitalist management under the duress of war and the extent to which the Labour movement had, by 1919, become committed to industrial democracy.[87] There is evidence, however, that the war created a popular receptivity to this ideal in a way prewar syndicalism had not. At the McCardie enquiry into the 'Embargo' disputes of July 1918, Mr Hutchinson, an ASE national official, spoke of 'the very large agitation on foot for at any rate a greater voice by the workman in the conditions under which he is going to be employed than he has had in the past . . .'. The comments of members of the committee of enquiry and witnesses show that the pamphlets of J.T. Murphy, and other working-class theorists, were reaching a much larger audience than the sects of the far Left.[88] Workers participating in this 'agitation' were voicing their sense of the dispensability of employers and management. It was reported to the Ministry of Munitions on April 1918 that:

85. The Garton Foundation, *Memorandum on the Industrial Situation after the War*, Lon-don, October 1916, p. 8.

86. J. Hinton, *The First Shop Stewards' Movement*, London, 1973.

87. See G.D.H. Cole, 'The State and the Engineers', ASE, *Monthly Journal and Record*, April 1915; idem, 'Introduction', *The World of Labour*, London, 1919, p. xiii; idem, 'Recent Developments in the British Labour Movement', *American Economic Review*, September 1918; see also B. Pribicevic, *The Shop Stewards' Movement and the Demand for Workers' Control*, Oxford, 1959.

88. See the Minutes of Evidence given before Mr Justice McCardie's Committee of Enquiry, evidence taken on 21 August 1918 and 22 August, MUN5/57. Murphy claimed that his pamphlet *The Workers' Committee* sold 150,000 copies; J.T. Murphy, *New Horizons*, London, 1942, p. 64.

Throughout this movement [i.e. industrial unrest in Coventry] the workers are certain that they are going to have entire control of the Firms. At their bidding Managers, Works Managers and all the hated class are to be turned out, their places to be filled by elected Shop Stewards and Trade Union members. A Works Manager told me the other day that he was stopped in the street by a Shop Steward who said: 'You have not much longer to run, and we are going to turn you all out. We have the men ready to take your places'.[89]

A principal reason for the growth of rank-and-file organisations was the disruption of the normal influence and power which trade union leaders exercised over their constituents. Those executives who agreed to the suspension of workshop practices in the engineering trades had before the war been much criticised as out of touch with the rank and file, but the war brought a number of factors which made the rupture between central authority and local membership that much more pronounced. The established authority of the executives was weakened by wartime legislation which made strike pay illegal — on a number of occasions the skilled unions were forced to withhold recognition from wartime strikes when they thought them deserving of recognition[90] — and consequently an important element in the normal control exercised over the rank and file was missing. But at the same time the executives were called upon to exercise an abnormal degree of restraint over their constituents. The Fabian view regarded the war as having accorded the trade union leadership fully accredited status as the diplomatic representative of the working class; but to the men on the bench the leadership often appeared to act as the intermediary of the government departments which in wartime occupied the position of predominant or universal employer. With these employing interests the executives were by the end of the war suspected of being more and more entangled. Mr Robinson, a spokesman for the Coventry Aircraft Committee (a rank-and-file organisation) at the McCardie enquiry complained '. . . we cannot get our Executives to move along the lines that we think ought to be moved owing to the fact that we consider they have sold themselves to the Government . . .'. Asked if that was a view held by many men, he replied:

That is the general view . . . up to the present we have had nothing throughout the history of this war that would allow us to say for one moment that the Executives were acting in a just and proper manner. They have let us down on numerous occasions in our estimation, and they have never come forward to explain the position when we have been in dispute. . . .[91]

89. Weekly Labour Notes, 12 April 1918, MUN5/55 300/47.
90. This was forcefully stated by Hutchinson in his evidence to the McCardie Committee.
91. Evidence of Mr Robinson, 20 August 1918.

His colleague, Mr Higgins, said of the trade union officials who had accepted government positions: '. . . these men have used the workers in the various unions as stepping-stones and kicked them down when they have got so far'. Directly addressing the trade union members who sat on the committee of enquiry he told them it was '. . . your business as paid officials of the workers, to have put the workers wise to what was going on . . . you had the knowledge and have not used the knowledge in the way you have been paid for using the knowledge'.[92]

While the rupture between trade union executives and the men at the bench was one reason for the growing strength of rank-and-file organisations, another was the great stimulus the war gave to work-shop collective bargaining. The introduction of dilution between 1915 and 1917 and the determined efforts made by government and employers in the later stages of the war to extend payment by results transformed the functions and powers of engineering shop stewards. From being a minor functionary charged with collecting dues and checking trade union cards, the steward became the elected intermediary between the workmen and the management, often settling questions of work practice which had once been directly negotiated by the individual craftsman and the foreman. Since dilution came as a long series of piecemeal changes '. . . the shop stewards were always kept busy'.

> As soon as they had settled the case of the substitution of half a dozen semi-skilled workers for skilled tradesmen on as many capstan or turret lathes in one part of the shop, their attention would be engaged by a proposal to employ women on a grinding or milling, or boring machine, . . . Questions as to the price to be paid, under war-time guarantees safeguarding piece-work rates on diluted processes, arose all day and every day. All this made the individual worker far more dependent on his shop steward than under the normal, and comparatively unvarying conditions of workshop practice, and called, on the steward's side, for unceasing vigilance and readiness to deal with any cause of friction.[93]

Once workshop collective bargaining had become accepted practice with the introduction of dilution, it became impossible to resist its extension to negotiation of piece-work prices and premium bonus payments, matters which before the war were generally settled by 'mutuality', or individual bargaining between the workman and the foreman or rate-fixer. There was a specific form of mutual antagonism intrinsic to piece-work price fixing: when the price was being settled, management sought the shortest possible time in which the job could be done, while the men tried to ensure that they took long enough to guarantee that on future occasions the job would always allow the

92. Evidence of Mr Higgins, 20 August 1918.
93. G.D.H. Cole, *Workshop Organisation*, Oxford, 1923, p. 53.

worker a good piece-work balance. Workers were suspicious of highly-paid jobs, fearing that management would in the future find some way of 'cutting' the price or of balancing the account by fixing the prices for other operations at a correspondingly low level. 'Speeding up' and 'ca' canny' were the constant results of this intrinsic friction.[94] The collective bargaining of piece-work prices and premium bonus payments by stewards and workers' committees generalised the antagonism.

During the war, the shop steward entered the demonology of the patriotic press, but the negotiations he undertook often smoothed rather than impeded the way to changes in workshop practice and did not necessarily strain relations with management and the government bureaucracy. Cole was to assert that the great mass of the shop stewards never became revolutionaries or even socialists in any theoretical sense and he stressed the 'essentially unrevolutionary character' of the work they did throughout the war period.[95] The attachment of the stewards and the evolving structure of workshop organisation in certain heavy engineering districts to a revolutionary movement led by syndicalists and industrial unionists took place because of the disintegration of the normal authority of trade unionism and the impact of dilution on craftsmen who, in 1914, still displayed 'the psychology of the producer' aspiring to 'direct responsibility for production'.[96] The Shop Stewards' Movement could draw on one element of class consciousness at the point of production amongst heavy engineering craftsmen which not even their patriotism and their knowledge of their importance to the war effort could eradicate: '. . . the workmen, though engaged on armament work, still feel themselves to be working essentially for private employers, with whom they have only a "cash nexus"'.[97] Because of the strength of the craft mentality, this element of class consciousness was never successfully developed to embrace the wider, revolutionary objectives of the Shop Stewards' Movement: the demand for workers' control remained for the majority the control of dilution; the anti-war campaign that developed during the winter of 1917/18 was a plea for the immunity of young engineers from conscription; generally the grass roots of the Movement 'did not . . . show itself keenly interested in far-reaching industrial and political programmes and was not willing to act unless for quite definite and immediate aims'.[98] That dilution was the critical factor in determining local

94. Ibid., pp. 57–9.
95. Ibid., pp. 54–5.
96. Gramsci, commenting on soviets in Italy, quoted in Hinton, *The First Shop Stewards' Movement*, p. 334.
97. Memorandum on Labour for Armaments, signed Llewellyn Smith, 9 June 1915, MUN5/57 320/1; see also *The History of the Ministry of Munitions*, vol. 1, p. 98.
98. Historical Memorandum on the Shop Stewards' Movement drawn up by the

support is confirmed by the case of Coventry, where prewar changes in technology and industrial organisation had already effected the dilution of craft labour and the revolutionary Shop Stewards' and Workers' Committee movement was confined to a small number of factories. In Coventry, the popular agitation for control was contained within a system of militant but non-revolutionary Joint Engineering Committees that were for certain purposes recognised by the unions. Relations between these JEC's and the revolutionary shop stewards were, apparently, very hostile.[99]

The largest outbreak of industrial unrest that took place during the war, and the most impressive demonstration of the power of the 'unofficial' rank-and-file movement in engineering, were the strikes of April and May 1917. These revealed the tensions between patriotism and industrial militancy, and between the different sections of the labour force. The Ministry of Labour's account of the strikes asserted that they had:

> Obviously . . . not arisen out of any desire to stop the war. . . . On the one hand [the men] were reluctant to hold up the war to the detriment of their relatives in the trenches. On the other hand, it seemed important to them, in their own interests, to keep their trade privileges intact. One has an impression in short, of unrest paralysed by patriotism — or, it may be, of patriotism paralysed by unrest.[100]

As an illustration of the engineers' attitude towards the war, the account cited the resolution of the men at Crayford Works in London that those engaged on producing anti-submarine devices should not down tools with the others. The strikes had two basic and interrelated causes: the withdrawal of the trade card which the government had been forced to concede to the skilled unions after an unofficial strike in Sheffield in November 1916 and the intention (written into a Bill amending the Munitions of War Act) to extend dilution to production for non-war purposes. Although the craftsmen struck over immediate grievances, they also felt they were defending their long-term future in the industry. George Peet, Secretary of the Manchester Joint Engineering Shop Stewards' Committee, declared: 'If we are beat on these two matters, then the shutters may as well be put up so far as the working-class movement is concerned'.[101] The fear that the exigencies

---

Intelligence Division of the Ministry of Labour, February 1920, p. 12, copy in MUN5/53 300/99.

99. See the evidence of Mr Charles Davis, a spokesman for the Coventry JEC, to the McCardie Enquiry, 13 August 1918.

100. 'History of the ASE strike, May 1917', dated 29 August 1917, LAB 2/254.

101. Quoted in a memorandum by Mr Chorley on the engineers' strike, 9 Nov. 1917, LAB2/254.

of wartime production would lead to a permanent breach of the protective wall of trade union custom and practices took the form of a rumour that dilution was to remain in force for seven years after the war. Moreover, the craftsmen were acutely conscious that their trade was being sectionalised by the specialisation of labour and the subdivision of functions and they were striking to preserve its integrity. The men, according to the Ministry of Labour's account, resented the accusation that their action was dictated by an aversion to serving in their trenches and claimed to be doing no more than imitating the professional egoism of the Law Society and the Medical Association, both of which had refused to suspend corporate rules and allow the 'dilution' of professional work.[102]

These two basic causes of the strikes were not uniformly operative in all engineering districts. In Coventry, neither the extension of dilution nor the abolition of the trade card provoked much discontent and the men struck over the (then) local grievance of the maldistribution and shortage of food. There, many of the less skilled workers organised in the Workers' Union joined the strike. In the north-east, the shipyard and marine engineering workers were not seriously threatened by the extension of dilution and worked normally throughout the strike. Remarkably, 'Red' Clydeside did not participate, apparently because of the 'jealousy and suspicion of the English districts which had refused to come out in sympathy when they themselves were out'.[103] Generally, the grievances were too sectional to unite the different sectors of the engineering labour force and Coventry was exceptional in witnessing extensive support for the strike amongst the less skilled. In London, when the local officials of the ASE asked the Workers' Union shop stewards for support the response was very hostile. A mass meeting of the Union resolved unanimously not to come out in sympathy and the principal speaker was reported as saying he hoped the Government would not concede a point to the ASE.[104] In Sheffield, the less skilled workers, egged on by wounded soldiers, barracked the strike meetings of the craftsmen.[105] Government censorship of the press and its control of the media of communications successfully isolated the strikes from the mass of the industrial working class. The streets in the affected districts were, as a rule, deserted and there was little public indication that a big stoppage was in progress. The largest measure of popular sympathy for the strikers came from the electricians, a group who were

---

102. See 'The Sequel to the Engineers' Strike: An Historical Memorandum', 1 Oct. 1917, LAB2/254; see also *The Labour Leader*, 3 May 1917: 'The doctors have prescribed by example for the workers' ills . . .'.
103. Chorley memorandum, LAB2/254.
104. Ibid.
105. See Hinton, *The First Shop Stewards' Movement*, p. 210.

themselves beginning to adopt a policy of craft militancy. Despite their isolation, the engineering rank and file showed considerable tenacity. Since they had been earning wages in excess of their spending power they had little economic difficulty in holding out, but their resolve was still remarkable given the absence of any firm national leadership or coordination. Strikers were not immediately cowed by the arrest of eight men prominent in the Shop Stewards' Movement, and the great measure of success of the strike (for the amending Bill was withdrawn) strengthened their attachment to the 'unofficial' Workers' Committees: the Ministry of Labour recorded that '. . . it is certain that the action of these Committees has been forceful and efficient in its treatment of the claims and grievances of the workmen, and the latter are not likely to relinquish an organisation which has proved its usefulness'.[106]

Works and shop committees were feared, by government ministers and trade union executive alike, as 'the thin end of the wedge [which] will ultimately become the substitute for the work of the existing Trade Union organisation'.[107] But, somewhat paradoxically, one of the more important long-term consequences of an agitation led by revolutionary syndicalists and industrial unionists was the adaptation and strengthening of the local and national structure of 'reformist' trade unionism. Admittedly, one strand of the agitation had sought the amalgamation of the craft societies and their transformation into revolutionary instruments, and the Shop Stewards' Movement had rejected the strategy of 'dual unionism' (wisely, to judge by its disastrous results when attempted by the Communist Party in the later 1920s). The consequence was, therefore, less contradictory than it appears at first sight. The shop steward attained a permanently enhanced role in the engineering industry and its trade union structure as a result of the wartime experience, a role codified in the National Shop Stewards' Agreement of 1919 and in the wider definition of his powers in the constitution of the Amalgamated Engineering union of 1920.[108] Stewards were recognised as having a direct right to assist in policy-making by their representation on the District Committees of the Union and through the Shop Stewards' Quarterly Meetings to be held in each district. The amalgamation itself owed a considerable amount to the rank-and-file pressure which had built up in the Joint Engineering Committees of the Midlands (in Coventry, twenty-one different unions had been represented on the JEC and in Birmingham thirteen) although the Union retained much of the craft character of the ASE.[109] Of the centres of

106. 'Historical memorandum on the Engineers' Strike', LAB2/254.
107. Churchill, then Minister of Munitions, speaking to his trade union advisory committee, 28 Aug. 1917, verbatim minutes, MUN5/52 300/76.
108. See J.B. Jefferys, *The Story of the Engineers 1800–1945*, London, 1946, pp. 189–94.
109. Ibid., p. 208.

wartime industrial unrest, it was Coventry, rather than Sheffield or the Clyde, which proved the 'model' of future working-class militancy: during the latter stages of the war, local officials of different unions acted jointly in the single-minded pursuit of maximum rewards for their members from the wartime labour shortage. Technological change in the city's industries tended towards a more socially cohesive labour force but also militated against the 'producer's psychology' of the craftsman. It was clearly to the 'model' of industrial conflict that had developed in the Midlands to which the Ministry of Labour referred when it concluded in February 1920:

> [Now] disputes will have to be dealt with more regionally or locally and by direct negotiation with delegates elected from the works, rather than by centralised officialdom . . . [there is] an increasing tendency for the trade unionists of one shop, works or small district, to act together, irrespective of their division into crafts or occupations. What is called 'class consciousness' is obliterating the distinctions between those who follow different occupations in the same works. It is sometimes said that the new machinery has destroyed the old distinction between the skilled and unskilled; and this is said by many who conclude from it that trade unionism will therefore be weaker. But this very assimilation creates a stronger bond between all workers, and an organisation based upon that bond may be much stronger than any group of craftsmen.[110]

Although it was only in the engineering industry that the war's impact on industrial relations led to a revolutionary rank-and-file organisation, the stresses placed on the normal authority of trade union executives and on customary work practices led to analogous developments in workshop organisation, and analogous pressures for trade union amalgamation, in other industries. Amongst railwaymen, wartime rank-and-file radicalism was manifested in early 1916 by the appearance of Railway Vigilance Committees; it is evident from the report of the General Secretary of the NUR to the Union's Annual Conference that by late March they were already a thorn in the flesh of the Executive.[111] These committees had brought rank-and-file pressure on union officials to resist the tendency for the wartime truce with the companies to result in the less-than-vigorous negotiation of wage and war bonus awards. The Liverpool Vigilance Committee quickly proved amongst the more militant and in June its members were fined 10s. apiece for issuing an unauthorised circular unduly critical of the Executive.[112] As with the shop stewards' committees in the engineering

110. Ministry of Labour memorandum on the Shop Stewards' Movement, Feb. 1920, MUN5/53 300/99.
111. See the General Secretary's Report in the record of the Annual Conference of the NUR, *Railway Review*, 23 March 1916.
112. Ibid., 30 June 1916.

industry, much of the work of Vigilance Committees was of a routine
character (such as securing time and a quarter for special duty) and
devolved on rank-and-file organisations because wartime circumstances left union bureaucracies short-staffed. The movement became
politicised in two directions: one was towards demanding a greater
measure of organised working-class control over the distribution of
food; the other towards militating for a negotiated peace. The first
national conference of the railwaymen's rank-and-file movement in
August 1917 registered a combination of industrial and political objectives: amongst the principal resolutions adopted were those calling for
the termination of the industrial truce, increases in wages, a reduction
in hours and the conversion of the war bonus to a war wage, the more
equitable distribution of food under democratic control; and the conference threatened militant action in the event of the Government refusing
passports to the Labour delegates to Stockholm.[113] In the winter of
1917/18, the Vigilance Committee movement became one of the industrial forces behind the 'stop the war' agitation.[114]

The NUR was the most rigidly centralised of the great unions and
the railway industry was conducted under a highly formalised code of
discipline; consequently, the scope for local negotiation between direct
representatives of the labour force and managers was much more
limited than in engineering where workshop organisation developed on
a localised tradition of craft militancy. For this reason, militants in the
Vigilance Committee movement were as much preoccupied with problems of distribution as with purely industrial questions. In October
1916, rank-and-file NUR leaders in London helped establish the Workers' Food Prices Committee, an organisation that foreshadowed the
London Food Vigilance Committee.[115] Local bodies such as these were
important in bringing about the closer relationship between the Labour and co-operative movements which occurred during the war.[116]
Food distribution was one of the issues which brought co-operators and
trade unionists into close alliance: the co-ops felt they were unfairly
treated with regard to the government's distribution of supplies to
wholesalers; trade unionists who resented profiteering in food saw the
non-profit-making co-ops as the natural source for working-class supplies. Railway workers active on Food Vigilance Committees (such as

113. See the account of the conference of District Councils and Vigilance Committees,
ibid., 24 August 1917.

114. Ministry of Labour memorandum on the Shop Stewards' Movement, Feb. 1920,
MUN5/53 300/99, p. 27.

115. See *Railway Reveiw*, 3 Nov. and 10 Nov. 1916.

116. On the impact of the war on the Co-operative Movement and the remarkable
strengthening of its links with the trade unions, see Sidney Pollard, 'The Foundation of
the Co-operative Party', in A. Briggs, J. Saville, eds., *Essays in Labour History*, vol. 2,
London, 1971, pp. 185–210.

W.T.A. Foot, secretary of the London District Council of the NUR) saw in the Labour–co-operative alliance the kernel of 'alternative' administration during nation-wide industrial disputes.[117]

Militants in the three unions that organised labour in the industry, the NUR, ASLEF and the Railway Clerks' Association, pressed the case for industrial unionism in the Railway Workers' One Union movement. This organised meetings enthusiastically attended by members of the three unions in late 1917 and 1918.[118] Amongst the Railway Clerks, Mr Chadwick of Leeds was particularly forceful in advancing the industrial unionist case; for him, syndicalist conviction had been strengthened by the experience of wartime industrial relations. As he told the RCA Annual Conference in June 1917, when moving a proposal for fusion with the NUR: 'During the War Bonus negotiations, the RCA had been attached to the tail of the NUR . . . and most of the concessions the RCA had got had been in the nature of a pat on the back'.[119] The Conference produced a large majority for fusion and negotiations between the NUR and RCA executives were entered into as a result of the rank-and-file agitation. They did not have the results the industrial unionists desired (for reasons discussed more fully in the context of the war's impact on white-collar unionism, pp. 249–63) although closer working arrangements and the refusal of the clerical grades to undertake uniformed men's work during strikes did follow. None the less, the strength of the rank-and-file amalgamation movement amongst railway workers in the latter stages of the war is an indication of a shop-floor pressure which had many parallels elsewhere.

Wartime industrial relations undoubtedly brought a wider tendency to union amalgamation, closer working arrangements and the federation of trade unions. The beginning of 1918 saw the birth of seven important federations.[120] In 1917, a new organisation, BISAKTA, was created for the iron and steel industry into which existing unions were slowly incorporated, while amalgamations took place amongst general

117. See Labour situation, week ending 8 Oct. 1918, CAB24/89 G.T. 8290, and the Report on Revolutionary organisations in the UK for the week ending 25 March 1920, CAB24/101, for Foot's proposals for trade union and co-operative unity during national strikes.

118. For the first conference of the Railway Workers' One Union Movement on 29 Sept. 1917, organised under the auspices of the Leeds and Yorkshire District Council, see *Railway Review*, 5 Oct. 1917. P.S. Bagwell's otherwise excellent history of the NUR dates its formation to 'early in 1918', see idem, *The Railwaymen*, London, 1963, p. 384.

119. From his speech moving the 'fusion' motion at the RCA 1917 Annual Conference; the full report is in *Railway Clerk*, 15 June 1917.

120. The National Federation of General Workers, the Iron and Steel Trades Confederation, the National Federation of the Foundry Trades, the Federation of Post Office Unions, the National Association of (woollen) Textile Trade Unions, the National Federation of Building Trade Operatives and the National Council of Societies representing Colliery Workers (other than miners).

workers and in the shipbuilding and wood-working trades. The scale of
the activity went far beyond the rationalisation characteristic of the
peacetime development of trade unionism. Obviously it owed much to
the change in trade union law in 1917 which made it easier for trade
union officials to fulfil the legal requirements for amalgamation, but it
also owed something to rank-and-file pressure and the specific circumstances of collective bargaining in wartime.

Workers in the cotton trade responded to the impact of the war on
their industry and their wages by analogous efforts to strengthen
shop-floor representation and reform trade union practice. The war
brought a steady erosion of real earnings to adult workers, particularly
the predominantly male spinners, although juveniles were in such short
supply that they found they could obtain a 'big' piecer's wage on
leaving school. In 1917 and 1918, the war also brought a cotton famine
and extensive short-time working imposed by the Cotton Control
Board. The appearance of the Operative Cotton Spinners' Shop Stewards was first noted in mid-October 1917, when they issued a circular
charging the Executive Council of the Spinners' Amalgamation with
accepting only one-half of the amount demanded in wage negotiations,
with making agreements to deal with bad spinning after the Brook-
lands Agreement had been broken and with shelving certain questions
of factory welfare under the industrial truce. At the same time an
extensive strike broke out in the Oldham Spinning District as a direct
result of the reduction of spindlage imposed by the Cotton Control
Board. Young operatives were threatened by wage reductions of about
£1 a week and agitators went from the Broadway Mill bringing out the
hands in neighbouring factories until over seventy mills were idle.[121]
The exact role of the Shop Stewards' Movement in the spontaneous
protest is unclear, although its anti-union character may have stemmed
from the movement's campaign against the Executive. Propaganda
meetings on behalf of the Cotton Spinners Shop Stewards' Movement
took place in December 1917 and with greater regularity after June
1918.[122] The tactical objective of the activists was the development of
the 'shop club' in the spinning-room as an instrument for making the
union more responsive to the rank and file and the linking-up of shop
clubs in an unofficial organisation parallel to the Amalgamation. Shop
clubs' members were levied at 1d. a month for organisation and propaganda. The stated aims of the movement stressed its constitutionality

121. For the Spinners' Shop Stewards' movement and the Oldham strike, see *Cotton
Factory Times*, 12 Oct. 1917.
122. See *Cotton Factory Times*, 21 Dec. 1917 and the correspondence columns for 9 Aug.
1918, for reactions (usually hostile) to the 'power which has arisen during recent
months . . .'. The latter issue of the paper gives an account of the stewards' meeting at
Oldham on 4 Aug. 1918.

and moderation, but also the failure of official trade unionism to substantially affect working conditions for a generation of operatives:

> It is not our intention to attempt to smash up either our Amalgamation or any section of it, but so to organise the general body of members as will speedily result in the attainment, in a constitutional manner, of some of the reforms which we contend are so long overdue. . . . [P]owers have been allowed to drift into the hands of the officials. . . . We have only gained one hour reduction in the hours of labour since 1875. From 1869 to 1914 . . . we have only received 8.91% advance in wages, whilst since 1914 our wages have not risen in proportion to the rising prices of the necessities of life. . . . The best working conditions obtain at those mills with solid shop organisation and vice versa, the worse conditions where there is no shop organisation. . . .[123]

It is difficult to say how extensive the influence of the movement was and how real its achievements. It may have had some bearing on the setting up of mill committees during the period of demobilisation to ease the return of men to their former jobs and its spokesman claimed an important role in the framing of a new constitution for the Amalgamation of February 1918.[124] Cole remarked that the unofficial movement in the cotton industry appeared to have possessed little stability, although he added that the shop stewards system had, seemingly, become permanently established in certain provinces of the Operative Spinners' Amalgamation.[125] The scope of workshop organisation was greatly restricted by the uniformity of production in the industry and the historical traditions of wage-bargaining based upon the negotiation by paid officials of an extraordinarily complex piece-list system.

It was in the weaving side of the cotton industry that a system of 'co-exploitation' of (largely) female labour by employers and working-class chargehands had most profoundly divided the work-force. Whatever the substance of the innumerable complaints of the spinner 'lording it' over his subordinate workers, the opportunities for the abuse of delegated industrial authority were as nothing compared with the 'driving' and intimidation of weavers by overseers whose wages were directly dependent on the output of their charges. In spinning, 'co-exploitation' was largely formal; in weaving it was genuine. There is evidence that the antagonism between overseers and their charges was much softened during the war, quite possibly because of the new opportunities for girls to work outside the weaving sheds, although contemporary comment ascribed the change to the growing influence

---

123. See *Cotton Factory Times*, 6 Sept. 1918 (for the quoted aims) and 25 Oct. 1918.
124. W.B. Whitbread, letter to the editor of *Cotton Factory Times*, 25 Oct. 1918, in defence of the stewards' movement.
125. Cole, *Workshop Organisation*, p. 106.

of the Northern Counties Trades Federation, which federated weavers'
and overlookers' unions, and to a greater sense of social solidarity:

> Complaints of driving, bullying and bad language are now very rare com-
> pared with pre-Federation days. . . . Overlookers themselves have arrived at
> the decision that they will not, if they can help it, have their earnings
> dominated by the labour of others. Their claim for a minimum or fall-back
> wages has been recognised. . . . The spirit of comradeship between all the
> sections is now greater than at any other time. . . . 'Caste' is disappearing
> (we mean the spirit that appeared to say one section was of greater import-
> ance than another), and there is a general recognition that they are of equal
> importance as workers.[126]

### The legacy of wartime industrial relations

The wartime economy and its industrial relations left a complex and
ambiguous legacy for working-class organisations, and had equally
complex influences on the attitudes and values of workers who, in
increasing numbers up till the end of 1920, joined them. (An unprecedented density of unionisation was reached at the end of that year.)[127]
A devolution of social authority to labour representatives took place
during the war, though often at the expense of harmonious relations
between them and the men they represented. In some instances, this
devolution extended beyond the Labour elite to give the men themselves a say in, literally, matters of life or death. It was found necessary,
for example, to obtain the consent of dockers in the administration of
the Military Service Acts and, in 1916, Joint Committees of employers
and workpeople known as Port Labour Committees were set up by the
Board of Trade in thirty-two of the largest ports. These committees
advised the government as regards the release of men for military
service and the issue of exemption certificates, and they also dealt with
questions of registration, the issue of tallies and the concentration of
calling-on stands.[128] Similarly, the problem of absenteeism in the pits
led to the formation, from 1916, of Pit Committees with the powers to
discipline both men and company officials. Many miners hoped to turn
these into instruments for encroaching control, but the attitude of the
owners largely circumscribed their functions and their chief importance lay in the stimulus they gave to rank-and-file 'Reform' movements. Furthermore, the wartime truce had led to the initiative in

126. *Cotton Factory Times*, 25 Oct. 1918.
127. The density of trade union membership was 37.6 per cent of the total labour force
in 1921 (as compared with 17.9 per cent in 1911). It fell rapidly with the onset of
structural unemployment and did not regain 1921 proportions until the Second World
War; see G.S. Bain, *The Growth of White-collar Unionism*, Oxford, 1970, Table 3.1, p. 22.
128. See Board of Trade, [Balfour] Committee on Industry and Trade, *Survey of
Industrial Relations*, London, 1926, pp. 168–9.

wage-bargaining devolving to the shop-floor and such breaches of the truce as had occurred

> had the general effect of leading the workpeople in the great pivotal indus-
> tries at any rate to place a high estimate on their economic bargaining
> strength. While their leaders generally realise that this strength was largely
> due to the exceptional labour shortage of the war period, the rank and file
> have gained a confidence in themselves that remains when conditions have
> changed.[129]

Within the field of industrial relations then, two dimensions of Marwick's analytical framework were clearly operative: the stress placed by war on existing working-class institutions and their conse-quent adaptation, and the participation of hitherto excluded groups within decision-making processes leading to their greater social pres-tige and material rewards. The extent to which the participation dimension operated was heavily dependent on the social influence already exerted by the group in question. There is no more telling illustration of this than the exclusion of women's labour representatives from the trade union advisory committee to the Ministry of Munitions. Both the Minister and the men's leaders were united in keeping out women's organisations.[130]

While the notions of 'testing' and 'participation' are useful and help explain the strengthening of working-class organisations and the greater self-confidence of their rank and file, they do not take us far in unravelling the complexities of the social impact of inflation. I have called the legacy of wartime industrial relations 'ambiguous' because its consequences for industrial workers were both 'solidaristic' (in that they strengthened workshop organisation and other forms of collective action) and 'fissiparous', for they unleashed antagonistic competition in the wage market. Official labour policy contributed palpably to the inflationary spiral by introducing wage agreements of extremely lim-ited duration. Before the war, wage agreements usually provided that the rate established should run for at least a year, and frequently for longer periods. In February 1917, agreements were made in important groups of trades (chiefly engineering) for a four-monthly review of wages by the Committee on Production and their increase on a cost-of-living basis. The regulation of wage increases by this procedure was, from the winter of 1917/18, steadily undermined by the militancy with

---

129. On pit committees, see G.D.H. Cole, *Labour in the Coal-mining Industry 1914–1921*, Oxford, 1923, p. 69; idem, *Workshop Organization*, pp. 109–111; quoted remarks are from the Labour situation report, week ending 19 Feb. 1919, CAB24/75 G.T. 6845.

130. The shorthand notes of the proceedings of the Trade Union Advisory Committee for 28 Aug. 1917 are a remarkable verbatim record of ministerial and working-class male chauvinism, MUN5/52 300/76.

which local groups of workers pressed their market advantages and the willingness with which employers conceded wage increases in order to secure lucrative munitions contracts. Armaments firms bidded unscrupulously for skilled labour against their competitors, thus forcing up its price and educating munitions workers in the laws of the market. (In an unsuccessful attempt to control wage drift and labour mobility, a number of the best-paying firms in the Midlands were, in mid-1918, forbidden to recruit fresh labour except under licence.) By October 1918, labour administrators were confronted by a 'revolution in all the factors hitherto determining the various industrial wage systems'.[131]

The outbreak of peace extended market competitiveness by releasing trade unions from the obligation to resort to arbitration and removing the (tattered) notion that their industrial policies should conform to the national interest. Under the Wages (Temporary Regulations) Act, the Interim Court of Arbitration took over some of the wage-regulatory functions of the Committee on Production, as part of the government's strategy to avoid the socially perilous consequences of savage deflation. In trades not covered by such agreements, a feature of 1919 was a constant series of claims and counter-claims in connection with wage increases. Wages did not advance proportionally within trades, since advances on a 'cost-of-living basis' favoured the lower-paid, nor uniformly between trades. The erosion of differentials, which had begun with wartime labour policy, continued during the postwar inflationary spiral. This led to

> the dislocation of established [working-class] relations. . . . No more certain cause of industrial unrest could be devised. Industrial peace depends on maintaining these relations, which, however lacking in moral or economic justification they may be, have the authority of prescription and are regarded as just. Once they are dislocated, comparisons are instituted; every worker almost can point to someone else who has done better relatively than himself, and is correspondingly disgruntled.[132]

Wage competition was sustained by three standards of reference: the first, comparison with the inexorably rising cost of living, heightened class consciousness for the rise in prices was widely attributed to profiteering. The second was the customary, local standard of comparison with men of a similar industrial status in the district. Sir Robert Horne, then Minister of Labour, brought to the Cabinet's attention a microcosm of the wage spiral from Liverpool which illustrated the continuing importance of district rates in setting working-class economic standards; in the city, the ship-repairing industry dominated

---

131. Memorandum on the administration of wages, 3 Oct. 1918, MUN5/51 300/61.
132. Labour situation, week ending 3 Sept. 1919, CAB24/88 G.T. 8107.

employment for skilled tradesmen and the need to refit, as quickly as possible during the postwar boom, ships which had been used by the Government for war purposes made shipowners consider that the prices paid for repair were comparatively immaterial. This resulted in an increased base rate for the operative in the yards. The rates paid to carpenters on ship-repairing led to the concession of a demand for 2s. an hour for tradesmen in the building trade, which in turn led to a claim for a rate of 2s. for nearly all classes of tradesmen in the district. In the meantime, the original increase having been secured with comparative ease, those who obtained it were now (March 1920) asking for 2s. 6d.[133] The third frame of reference was derived from the system of national wage awards which the war had done so much to establish. Basil Thomson, the police official charged with reporting to the Cabinet on 'revolutionary' unrest and organisations, claimed that comparisons arising from this third frame of reference were the source of immense dissatisfaction:

> Jealousy between workers in the different industries is immeasurable. The railwaymen consider they are worth as much as the dockers, and unskilled trades claim that the dockers are unskilled; in any case they are inclined to regard the suggested dockers' rates [i.e. those claimed by the Transport Workers' Federation before the Shaw Inquiry] as a minimum. The Law Clerks' Federation and the National Union of Docks, Wharves and Shipping Staff are taking action on this basis, and Lancashire miners are looking covetously at the spinner's wages. Even the police are reported to be weighing their new scale of wages against the recent advances in the scales of manual labourers.[134]

Thomson's reports were frequently absurd and possibly only fed to the Cabinet in order to cajole its reactionary members into agreeing to social and labour policies they found distasteful, but this diagnosis of a source of social grievance carries conviction. (It is referred to in the more trustworthy reports from the Ministry of Labour and the outburst of white-collar and public service industrial militancy, to which Thomson alluded, can be interpreted as a collective response to the erosion of differentials between manual labour and salaried employment.) Doubtless, the profoundest cause of resentment was the persistence of inflation, since it made real advances in living standards elusive (though they did take place) and created a disparity between unprecedented money wages and the actual achievement of greater economic wellbeing.

133. 'The Present Tendency of Wages', memorandum by Sir Robert Horne, 5 March 1920, CAB24/100 C.P. 806.

134. Report on Revolutionary organisations in the UK, 15 April 1920, CAB24/103 C.P. 1086.

The final part of the complex legacy of wartime industrial relations I wish to mention was a closer connection between workers' attitudes to the seemingly more 'visible' inequalities of society and their industrial behaviour. 1919 was a year of extraordinarily high profits and witnessed what even *The Economist* considered an 'orgy of extravagance' on the part of the well-to-do.[135] Apart from the stimulus these gave to wage-claims, they led to a widespread refusal to increase productivity, in spite of the reduction of hours that took place in nearly all major industries at the beginning of the year. It was reported in October 1920 that: 'All who have followed the reception of exhortation to the manual workers to produce without stint have noticed in the working-class psychology of the time not merely an apathy in production but a deadweight of resistance to any suggestion that output should be increased'.[136]

A so-called 'widespread sourness of mind' amongst the rank and file of labour was attributed partly to a disappointment of aspirations raised during the war and a reaction from the idealist rhetoric which had motivated the Home Front: 'The very nobility of the purpose for which men laboured in the war militates against their acceptance of meaner or vaguer purposes for their labour now. They ask — What for?' It was suggested that while very few consciously 'slacked' as a protest against the maldistribution of wealth many were at least indirectly influenced by the real indignation this aroused in Labour leaders: 'Thus, while the ordinary working man may not imbibe a doctrine, his general discontent is canalised into resentment against any suggestion that output should be increased. . .'. Moreover, with reference to the techniques of public persuasion which had been refined during the war and played such an important part in the government's handling of postwar industrial unrest, the same report warned that '"labour" cannot be treated as mere congeries of individuals, each free to respond to the incitements of a poster. Labour is now an organised class and the mass-psychology of the organisation must be moved before any change in the policy [of the Labour movement] is effected'.[137]

The government and its advisors did not believe that the 'temper' or consciousness of this class was revolutionary (even Thomson regularly insisted that the working class was basically 'sound', patriotic and obsessed with sport) and there is very little evidence that they feared a junction between the still-fragmented Marxist revolutionary movement

135. *The Economist*, 21 Feb. 1920, quoted in Runciman, *Relative Deprivation and Social Justice*, p. 66.
136. Labour situation, week ending 22 Oct. 1920. CAB24/90 G.T. 8228.
137. Ibid.

and the Labour rank and file.[138] They did, however, specify three 'ideas now [October 1919] dominating the mass' which were the elements of an at least proto-revolutionary popular consciousness: they were the ideas that 'the more the working class produce, the more the "idle rich" will waste'; that a 'a man cannot work his best in a system run for private profit'; and 'that the landowners and capitalists should loose their stranglehold on land and money before they begin to lecture labour on restricting production'.[139] To counter these ideas, it was suggested that expenditure on luxuries should be restricted and more forceful action be taken by the 'Profiteering' Tribunals set up to investigate excess profit-making. We cannot, of course, be sure how accurately civil servants monitored phenomena as elusive as workers' attitudes and values but there are reasons for believing that the popular ideology discerned by officialdom was not a figment of its imagination. The most compelling are the remarkable successes achieved by the Labour Party in the November municipal elections when its candidates campaigned with a new vitality, in close alliance with trade union organisations, and often articulated these 'ideas' said to be dominating the rank and file.[140]

### Consumption, Profiteering and the 'Them/Us' Dichotomy

Marxism accords analytic priority to the relations of production, and takes the point of production to be the locus for critical changes in social consciousness. Marx presumed that radical opposition to the political order of capitalist society would develop from the conflict between capital and labour in industry. Though Lenin ceased to believe that this conflict would generate mass revolutionary consciousness, he would certainly have endorsed the view that changes in consciousness which arise from the relations of consumption and social distribution are secondary or epiphenomenal. Somewhat heretically, I would suggest that the Marxian emphasis on production relations as the locus of change, and the Leninist view of the 'economistic' limits to 'spontaneous' working-class consciousness leave unexplained a fundamental shift in popular ideology that took place during the war.

As we have seen (Chapter 2) the very word 'profiteering' entered the language of class in the latter stages of the war. When, in late August 1919, the Ministry of Labour warned of 'the growing resentment of profiteering', it pointed out that 'the wage earner is . . . also a pur-

---

138. See R.H. Desmarais, 'The British Government's Strike-breaking Organization and Black Friday', *Journal of Contemporary History*, 6, 2, 1971, pp. 112–27.

139. Labour situation, week ending 22 Oct. 1919.

140. See K.O. Morgan, *Consensus and Disunity*, London, 1979, pp. 46–7, p. 167.

chaser, and in him are combined resentment against being cheated as a purchaser, and disinclination to do his best as producer in an industrial system which tolerates the "profiteer"'.[141] Its report accepted as an accurate assessment of the shift in popular thought, the analysis of the guild socialist journal, *The New Age*:

> The popular adoption of the word '*Profiteering*' and the application of it to particular abuses of profit-making, has . . . contributed to bring profit into wider disrepute. There has been a marked change during the war in the public attitude towards the profit maker. The Socialist case has in conse-quence been much strengthened, and the view that the individualist system of industry is iniquitous and intolerable has spread and intensified among working men. . . . [P]rofit . . . finds itself confronted with this new element, the spirit which denounces its former pretensions as immoral.[142]

This 'new element' in working-class consciousness did not arise pri-marily at the point of production and from the conflict between labour and capital in industry. It arose instead from an indignation with the immorality of capitalist profit-making at the expense of the national community and the least complicated and most widespread source of resentment was the exploitation of the working-class consumer whether by wholesalers, traders or 'hoarders'. Issues such as excess profits, high food prices and inequalities of distribution were affronts to the 'moral economy' of the English working class, and particularly explicit af-fronts given the lip-service paid to the ideals of self-sacrifice and communal effort in war. Furthermore, resentment of profit-making, of the high price of food and its shortage of supply disrupted a sense of the reciprocity of class relationships which was, I believe, part of the subordinate value system. Implicit in the working-class 'design for living' (as Parkin has called it) was a contractural notion that the dominance of 'them' over 'us' carried certain obligations to respect 'our' interests. Workers expected the regime of economic inequality to be regulated by 'fairness'. 'A fair day's work for a fair day's pay' was the commonest expression in popular lore of this sentiment and, according to Stephen Reynolds, 'fair play is [the working man's] chief standard of judgement'.[143]

The transition from a liberal to a warfare state both involved measures which the working-class citizen and consumer deemed to be 'unfair' and demands that the organisation of society for war should be more closely attuned to his conception of 'fairness' (as with the call for the conscription of wealth and the proposal for a capital levy to pay off

141. Labour situation, week ending 27 Aug. 1919, CAB24/87 G.T. 8037.
142. Quoted in ibid.
143. Reynolds et al., *Seems So!*, p. 147.

war debt).[144] The taxation of manual wages was felt to be 'unfair' because it fell principally on overtime earnings which (with a standard working week of fifty-three hours) were bought dear in terms of loss of health and scant leisure. The demand that, on these grounds, overtime payments should be tax-exempted was made in the summer and autumn of 1917 as part of the quite extensive resistance to income tax.[145] But the inflation of food and other basic commodity prices (especially coal) was the cause of a much more intense and widespread feeling of working-class 'unfairness'. It is, of course, true that many professional families on static incomes felt the pinch but there were good reasons why food supply and price inflation were seen as griev-ances of a class, for the war economy tended to accentuate the disad-vantages of the working-class consumer in comparison with the middle-class housewife. Longer hours and work for wives cut down the opportunities to 'shop around' while lack of means and space (for bulky necessities such as coal) stopped many from economising by bulk-buying. Moreover, wartime labour regulations did not deal equitably between manual workers and professional employees: the working-class breadwinner employed in the munitions industries was restricted by the Leaving Certificate regulation, and other measures of industrial direction, from taking advantage of the law of supply and demand while it operated in his favour, but felt the inexorable pressure of that law on the necessities of life.[146] The evidence submitted by the Iron and Steel Trade Confederation to the Commission of Inquiry into Indus-trial Unrest made the 'class' resentment generated by the rising cost of living particularly explicit:

> In the matter of supply [the workmen] attribute their inability to obtain fuel and food not so much to the actual shortage as to the entire failure on the part of the Government to obtain control and to establish machinery for more equitable distribution. They point to the fact that the 'potato queue', 'sugar queue', etc. are practically confined to working class people, and working class districts, and even so the foods they need are not obtainable,

144. See J.S. Stamp, 'The Capital Levy: Theoretical and Academic Aspects', undated [late 1918], PRO IR74/48. Royden Harrison has drawn attention to the important part the demand for a capital levy played in the crystallisation of Labour Party ideology. As he emphasises, it was seen in terms of 'fair play' and 'equality of sacrifices' between classes: see 'The War Emergency Workers' National Committee 1914–20', in A. Briggs, J. Saville, eds., *Essays in Labour History*, vol. 2, esp. pp. 254–7.

145. See the (Final) *Report of the Committee on Labour Embargoes* (December 1918), p. 8. Copy in MUN5/57. For workers' opposition to income taxation, see Labour situation, weeks ending 8 Aug. 1917, 15 Aug. 1917, CAB24/22 G.T. 1660, G.T. 1748, and week ending 22 Aug. 1917, CAB24/24 G.T. 1822.

146. The Leaving Certificate was abolished in August 1917 but labour mobility was restricted by the obligation placed on large categories of men to join the War Munitions Volunteers scheme and the embargo restraining certain firms from recruiting skilled labour.

while stories of ample supplies and even waste so far as the well-to-do are concerned, are prevalent.[147]

To the discontent caused by shortages in working-class districts was added, by early 1917, 'the deep-seated conviction in the minds of the working classes that the prices of food have risen not only through scarcity, but as a result of the manipulation of prices by unscrupulous producers and traders'.[148]

Price inflation, and an awareness of its accompanying social contrasts, can be coupled with excessive hours of monotonous work, restricted leisure and atrophied family life as subterranean reasons for the debilitation of working-class patriotic zeal. But their cumulatively subversive effects did not in themselves seriously undermine the prosecution of the war before the late autumn of 1917. The Government's Commissioners of Enquiry into Industrial Unrest in the North Western Area (where the May strikes had originated) were at pains

> to emphasise the fact that on all occasions the witnesses before us prefaced their evidence with an expression of their determination to assist the Government of the country and their fellow citizens at the front to the best of their endeavour in prosecuting the war to a satisfactory conclusion. Throughout the area the patriotic spirit of men and employers was manifest and clearly expressed.[149]

Food prices had led directly to neither industrial nor civil disturbances up to June 1917 (although actual shortages were to do both in succeeding months); they had, however, been the chief cause of a generalised discontent which amounted to a heightened 'them/us' view of the world. By creating new categories of 'them' — particularly profiteers, hoarders, disciplinary tribunals in the munitions industry — and by giving legal sanction to the social authority of employers, the war sharpened the customary sense of social dichotomy. In popular usage there were the new classes of those who were bleeding for the country and those who were bleeding the country. Increased geographic and occupational mobility brought many workers face to face with ostentatious wealth and again heightened the sense of 'them/us'. In the labour magnet of Coventry in November 1917 a contributory factor in the strike over the recognition of shop stewards was considered to be 'the attempt which is being made with some success to accentuate the

147. Notes of evidence submitted to the Commission of Enquiry into Industrial Unrest by Arthur Pugh for the Iron and Steel Trades Confederation, University of Warwick, Modern Records Centre. MSS.36, Box 4.
148. Commission of Enquiry into Industrial Unrest, No. 1 Division, North Eastern Area, p. 2.
149. Idem, No. 2 Division, North Western Area, p. 12.

existing class feelings by wide advertisement of the facility with which the rich obtain luxuries, the cost of which precludes the working class from their enjoyment'.[150]

The experience of food shortages in the winter of 1917 and 1918 did most to sharpen the sense of dichotomy. Even papers not particularly sympathetic to the working-class movement laid great stress on the inequality of sacrifice in the matter of food. Strong contrasts were depicted between the wife of the working man who was compelled to stand for hours in a queue in the hope of obtaining a meagre supply of inferior margarine and the propertied lady who could sit at home and await delivery of her butter. The Labour report for 2 January 1918 warned that: 'Recent experiences of food shortage have unfortunately fortified the arguments of those whose aim it is to wage class-warfare'.[151] In Birmingham, one of the cities most affected by the shortage of supplies, Saturday morning shopping queues became so serious a problem in the autumn of 1917 that the municipal authorities inaugurated a ration scheme to minimise queuing and 'to introduce a more equitable method of distributing the available food supplies in the city'[152] (an acknowledgement that until then inequality of supply had been a material fact). This had no immediate effect. In mid-January 1918, queues were reported as beginning before dawn and by midday they had assumed such lengths in working-class districts that the services of the police were required to marshall and control them. Shortages were most evident in those shops, such as pork butchers, which had a predominantly working-class custom and the prices in the central market were such that the most moderate expression of resentment they aroused was: 'It's daylight robbery of the working classes'.[153] In late January munitions workers coming off the night shift were beginning to form queues when they left work, despite notices that shops would not be open until 10 or 10.30 a.m. A month after the introduction of the city's rationing scheme, there still remained 'a belief amongst the working classes that the distribution of food is not carried out in an equitable basis'.[154]

Working-class perceptions of inequality and the visible differences in life experience did not result merely in a greater alienation between classes. They had political consequences, for food queuing and food shortage did more to disturb the working-class will to victory and to undermine the morale of troops than the more overtly subversive

150. Labour situation, week ending 28 Nov. 1917, CAB24/33 G.T. 2799.
151. Labour situation, week ending 2 Jan. 1918, CAB24/37 G.T. 3196.
152. See *Birmingham Daily Post*, 12 Dec. 1917, for the introduction of the city's rationing scheme.
153. Ibid., 5 Jan. 1918, 14 Jan. 1918.
154. Ibid., 30 Jan. 1918.

challenges raised in the wake of the March revolution and the call for a negotiated peace. In the late summer of 1917, the government was in no doubt that there was negligible enthusiasm for military service, that the insensitivity of the conscripting authorities gave rise to a great deal of resentment amongst men more keenly appreciative of the rights of citizenship, and that many felt that the 'ideals that were in men's hearts in the first months of the war had been forgotten by the governing classes'.[155] It could take some satisfaction, however, from the relative isolation of the demand for a negotiated peace from the popular masses. Much of the impetus given to the peace movement by the Leeds Convention of June 1917 (called to 'Hail' the Russian Revolution) was misspent in its disastrous attempt to set up Workers' and Soldiers' Councils. The trades and labour councils had little enthusiasm for what could have been rival bodies, but popular chauvinism — whipped up by the demagogue press — was a more serious obstacle. Initiatory meetings of Workers' and Soldiers' Councils in late July excited violent and hostile demonstrations on the part of workers and soldiers on leave.[156] The proposal to attend a conference of the Socialist International at Stockholm in August, where labour representatives would have consorted with German and Austrian socialists, was supported by a large majority at a special Labour Party conference. However, the government received many indications that rank-and-file workers were opposed to the Stockholm *démarche* — the miners, in particular, were noted for their hostility — and this may have strengthened its hand in refusing passports to the Labour delegates.[157]

In mid-September, the government was given strong reason for believing that morale at home was being sustained by the letters which soldiers were sending back from France. In order to ascertain the extent of war-weariness amongst troops, the Directorate of Secret Intelligence ordered the examination of a large sample (4,552) of letters in green envelopes (i.e. those which had not already been censored either at the Front or at bases in France). Of these only twenty-eight or 0.61 per cent contained any expression of complaint or war-weariness and seven of these contained specific complaints that were not related to war-weariness. The examiners reported that the

155. The quotation is from the Labour situation report, week ending 15 Aug. 1917, CAB24/22 G.T. 1748; see also, 'The Theory and practice of Recruiting', memorandum by Brig.-Gen. Geddes, 23 July 1917, CAB24/20 G.T. 1481.

156. See *Labour Leader*, 2 Aug. 1917; Labour situation, week ending 1 Aug. 1917, CAB24/21 G.T. 1593. The council movement was struck a further blow when a riot prevented it from holding a conference at Southgate Road Brotherhood Church on 7 Oct.; Report on Labour in Great Britain, October 1917 (dated 12 Nov. 1917), MUN5/56 300/108

157. See Labour situation, weeks ending 22 Aug. 1917, 29 Aug. 1917, 5 Sept. 1917, CAB24/24 G.T. 1822, G.T. 1891, CAB24/25 G.T. 1962.

general impression gained was that British troops in France were very cheerful and determined, and that the love of fighting had eradicated the peacetime habit of grumbling.[158] (The examiners were pathetically deluded. Front-line officers knew that soldiers' letters home were a demotic literary genre whose conventions ensured a decent solicitude for the feelings of the recipient and a complete disguise of those of the sender.[159] But the incident is relevant because, apparently, there was a change in the tone of soldiers' correspondence when conditions worsened on the Home Front.)

The first queues appeared in the spring of 1917 but did not become a source of bitter and persistent social grievance before October. Prior to this, however, the issue of food control had become extremely important to the Labour movement. This was chiefly because such Food Control Committees as had been formed under the aegis of the first Food Controller, Lord Devonport, were unduly representative of local traders and pressure groups regarded as inimical to working-class interests. In London much of their personnel was derived from local War Savings Committees which themselves had been a fief of charity organisers and promoters of patriotic thrift.[160] We can trace the growing importance of food control to the working-class movement through the rise of parallel Food Vigilance Committees representing a combination of local activists — usually local Labour Parties, trades councils and cooperators.[161] In London such a committee was formed in June 1917 with the objectives of obtaining definite representation on Food Control Committees, including the Grosvenor House Committee, the formation of local Food Control Committees through local authorities, with an adequate proportion of Labour representatives, the extension of powers to municipal authorities, the registration of the distributors in each locality and the utilisation of the Co-operative Societies as machinery for equitable distribution.[162] The Committee advertised its grievances and objectives at a well-supported ('huge' in its own estimation) demonstration in Hyde Park on 29 July. Two days later representatives of the Committee, led by Duncan Carmichael, argued their case before Lord Rhondda, Devonport's successor. Carmichael claimed that it was an insult to Labour at a time when the government

158. Note on the Morale of British troops in France as disclosed by the Censorship, Directorate of Secret Intelligence, 13 Sept. 1917, CAB24/26 G.T. 2052.

159. For a brilliant insight into the conventional character of soldiers' letter-writing, see Paul Fussell, *The Great War and Modern Memory*, London, 1975, pp. 181–3.

160. See the 12th Annual Report of the Thrift and Savings Sub-committee of the (London) Charity Organisation Society, p. 17.

161. For the rise of Food Vigilance Committees, see the Ministry of Munitions Intelligence and Record Section, Quarterly Report on the Industrial Situation as viewed by Labour for May, June, July 1917 (dated 4 Aug. 1917), MUN5/56 300/108.

162. Minutes of the London Trades Council Executive Meeting, 26 June 1917.

was urging the Germans to democratise themselves for Rhondda to offer one seat in twelve on proposed municipally-controlled Food Committees to the workers who were nine-tenths of the population. Carmichael urged that it was only the desire not in any way to injure the men in the trenches that was keeping the people quiet; the attitude of the women at meetings held in the poorer districts like Battersea and Poplar and the earnestness of the men and women who carried the banners from East Ham and other districts to Hyde Park proved that unless something was done trouble of a serious nature would occur. Rhondda conceded nearly all of Labour's case; he admitted that when he took over his job the producers and wholesalers were overrepresented, while the Co-operative Societies and retailers were not considered and he was certain that a revolution was near if prices were not lowered. The trades councils were encouraged to bring local pressure in order to get better representation and he expressed his disappointment with the small penalties magistrates were inflicting on traders convicted of selling at higher than the fixed prices.[163]

Class inequality in distribution was exacerbated by the Food Ministry's first measures of compulsory rationing, for its own civil servants conceded that the principle of allotting supplies of sugar, butter and bacon to districts on the basis of consumption in previous years had 'the cardinal defect that it favours rich against poor districts'.[164] But rather than a knowledge of these defects being a spur to more egalitarian methods, it was pressure from industrial workers, the example set by go-ahead municipalities such as Birmingham and the fear that food queues were stamping grounds for pacifist and revolutionary agitators which drove the government to a larger measure of collectivism. There may have been some association between dissatisfaction with the food situation and bigger and more sympathetic audiences for Herald League meetings in London and the Women's Peace Crusade in Lancashire in October, and there is evidence that privation made the idea of a negotiated peace more widely attractive.[165] In November, the importance of the food question as a contributory cause to industrial

163. There is a detailed account of the meeting in *The Shop Assistant*, 11 Aug. 1917.
164. Memorandum on 'The prevention of Queues', signed S.G. Tallents, 19 Dec. 1917, PRO MAF (Ministry of Food Records) 60/243.
165. Labour situation, weeks ending 3 Oct. 1917 and 10 Oct. 1917, CAB24/27 G.T. 2199, CAB24/28 G.T. 2266. Similarly, there was reported, in early December, considerable support amongst the Birmingham working class for Lord Lansdowne's letter to *The Daily Telegraph* (29 Nov.) advocating a negotiated peace, see Labour situation, week ending 12 Dec. 1917, CAB24/35 G.T. 2592. A police raid organised by Thomson (5 Dec. 1917) on the leading pro-peace organisations found evidence of wider working-class support for the Peace Negotiations Committee in the large number of small subscriptions — 2s. 6d to 5s. — especially from the North of England, see Pacificism: Report of Basil Thomson after police raid on books and papers of principal pacifist societies, CAB24/35 G.T. 2980.

unrest in the Midlands was stressed in the Cabinet's labour report.[166] At Coventry, on 17 November 1917, there occurred one of the first instances of a Saturday protest strike against food prices and food queues.[167] The December conference of the Shop Stewards' Movement found it 'still looking for some large question on which [it could] unite all the workers in the shops with the view to producing another major strike which would demonstrate [its] powers'. A speech by Arthur MacManus, president of the Movement, at Barrow suggested it had found a suitable grievance in the food question.[168]

By January 1918, the conjunction of the food question with the unrest created amongst engineers and miners by Auckland Geddes's manpower proposals presented the government with a general crisis of defeatism. In a circular letter to all Chairmen of Food Control Committees, J.R. Clynes later recalled that: 'There was a danger in the opening months of this year that the conduct of the war itself might be imperilled unless an end could be put to food queues in the towns and food shortages in the rural districts'.[169] The example set by Coventry munitions workers of short protest strikes was taken up throughout the country. At Manchester on 16 January men and women in eight of the largest munition factories in the Openshaw and Gorton districts ceased work for three hours and marched down to Albert Square to protest against the queues and to demand a national system of rationing with equal distribution of food amongst all classes. In the evening, the Trades Council adopted a recommendation from the Joint Committee of the Council, the Gorton Trades Council and the Manchester and Salford Labour Party, in favour of all trades participating with the ASE in a general stoppage of work at 9 a.m. on 26 January in order to protest against the unequal distribution of food.[170] At Erith on Saturday 19 January all of the engineers employed at Vickers took the morning off to do their family shopping. At Woolwich a meeting at Plumstead Baths demanded the handing over of food supplies to the Co-operative Societies and the elimination of profit in their marketing. It is important to stress that, unlike the engineers' opposition to the manpower proposals which divided the ASE from other unions, the food question united the Labour movement and generated dissent amongst unskilled organisations as no other did. All societies in the Woolwich district were represented at the Plumstead meeting — including the ASE, the NUR, the Transport Workers, the Electrical Trades Union, the Licensed Vehicle Workers and the labourers' union —

166. Labour situation, week ending 28 Nov. 1917, CAB24/33 G.T. 2799.
167. *The History of the Ministry of Munitions*, vol. 6, pt. 1, p. 26.
168. Labour situation, week ending 19 Dec. 1917, CAB24/36 G.T. 3062.
169. Circular letter dated 3 Oct. 1918, MAF60/236.
170. *Manchester Guardian*, 17 Jan. 1918.

and they were coordinating a campaign through the local Food Vigilance Committee which, it was feared, would lead to a general stoppage.[171] The London District Vigilance Committee of ASE was working with the Triple Alliance towards a 'down tools' policy on the food question while the general unions in Coventry and Birmingham regarded unequal food distribution and profiteering as so important as to bring them to support the engineers' opposition to conscription.[172] On 29 January practically the whole of the munitions workers in Bedford (about 10,000) held a demonstration against the local Food Committee and a similar affair took place at Luton. More serious stoppages were only narrowly averted. In the first week of February it was reported that: 'The number of workers involved in short strikes which are occurring all over the country as protests against the food situation is becoming a matter of serious national importance'.[173] With the strikes and the threat of strikes went indications of social break-down such as outbreaks of lawlessness in Birmingham, where butchers' shops were raided by munitions workers, and the intimations of land-ladies in Barrow that lodgers would be turned into the streets unless more supplies were forthcoming.[174]

Even more disturbing for the government was the repercussion of working-class discontent with the food situation on the temper of the country's soldiers. The extent to which anxieties and irritations amongst the civilian population affected the fighting men is powerful confirmation of the magnitude of the crisis. In February 1918 the Head Censor at Calais reported to GHQ:

It is immediately obvious that the effect on men in France is very serious and that their morale has suffered considerably in consequence. It is clear that the question is very universally discussed. Men hear from their relations at home and see accounts in the papers, but the greatest effect appears to be produced by men returning from leave. A large proportion of the extracts [from censored mail] are either remarks made by such men or comments based on accounts given by them. The result is that the question at present looms larger in the minds of the mass of men than any other; questions as to their own food are, for the time being, in the background, and men suggest, not uncommonly, that rations in the B.E.F. should be reduced in order to increase the amount at home. A few men are found to treat the matter lightly, but these men are an almost negligible minority.[175]

171. Labour situation, week ending 23 Jan. 1918, CAB24/40. G.T. 3442.

172. Labour situation, weeks ending 9 Jan. 1918 and 16 Jan. 1918, CAB24/38 G.T. 3293, CAB24/39 G.T. 3369.

173. Labour situation, week ending 6 Feb. 1918, CAB24/41 G.T. 3545.

174. Labour situation, weeks ending 23 Jan. and 6 Feb.

175. This extract and what follows are taken from the lengthy memorandum: 'The Effect of Food Queues at Home on Men at the Front' drawn up by Sydney Walton for Lord Rhondda, 16 April 1918, MAF60/243.

The authorities had reason to believe that the danger to morale was even more extensive than the evidence. They were aware of the central place of the food queue in hundreds of thousands of letters from home — queueing was often the only incident of note in the housewife's drab day — and believed this was giving an exaggerated and depressing picture of conditions in England. The Head Censor found that, typically, men were replying to their wives and relatives in these terms:

> It is a load off my mind to know that you are lucky enough to get sufficient food. I think the Government will have to do something if it lasts much longer. We out here won't have our wives and children starving, War or no War, those at home have got to see our dependents [sic] get sufficient food.

> Yes dear, I do think you have had a hard battle to get food. All the men's wives seem to tell their husbands about the trouble they have to get the foodstuffs. You would think they would come to some terms when they see the country in that state. Suppose they don't feel it else they would.

> I am sorry to hear that things are getting so bad at home, for by what I can read in the papers and a few things from the lads that return on leave we get a very good insight of what you have to put up with at home, and I do hope things will soon improve. It makes one think that it is time this was brought to an end.

It would be unwise to treat these extracts as an unvarnished expression of sentiment, for letter-writing home remained a highly conventionalised mode, but assuming (as I think we reasonably can) that the Censor did take a fairly representative sample, then they point to a heightened 'them/us' view of the social order and a sense that the reciprocity implicit in this dichotomy had been ruptured.

## The Revival of Patriotism and the Triumph of Conservatism

There are a number of reasons why the social crisis of early 1918 did not become more serious for the authorities. Firstly, the ASE isolated itself from other organisations by pursuing a rigid opposition to the Manpower proposals which derived from the aristocratic pretensions of the craftsmen to a privileged status *vis-à-vis* conscription. The ASE committed a serious tactical error by demanding a special and separate conference with the Minister of National Service and 'everywhere weakened its power by its attitude of superiority to and aloofness from workers belonging to other unions'.[176] Secondly, the government defused the food crisis by reversing the rise in the price of food in early

---

176. Labour situation, week ending 23 Jan. 1918.

1918, extending rationing and co-opting Labour representatives onto Food Control Committees. Thirdly, by late February the progress of negotiations at Brest-Litovsk led to the beginnings of a revival of anti-German feeling and 'King and country' patriotism[177] which the onslaught on the Western Front from 21 March completed. Lastly, the government had to hand a formidable armoury of public persuasion which it used to restore optimism and influence working-class opinion.

The crisis of defeatism of early 1918 was followed by a revival of working-class patriotism highly reminiscent of the early months of the war. The government had, some weeks before the German offensive, already weathered the worst of the militant opposition amongst young engineers to its Manpower proposals, but it was certainly expecting trouble. However, as the news of the German advances reached the workers, first the ASE executive and then the Strike Arrangements Committee of the Shop Stewards' Movement repudiated strike action, while the rank-and-file reaction against any suggestion of a stoppage was overwhelming.[178] Cole and Hutchinson, both ASE officials, wrote in *The Herald*: 'There must be no strike during the present crisis. Only one thing could justify a strike today: a reasoned determination on the part of the majority of the people to end the war at any cost. That determination, we know well, does not exist'.[179]

There was a precipitous fall in the amount of strike activity. In November 1917, more than half a million days were lost in the munitions industry as the result of strikes, and in the months of December and January 1918 about a quarter of a million days apiece. In April 1918, only 15,000 days were lost.[180] In the mining industry,

177. Labour situation, week ending 22 Feb. 1918, CAB24/43 G.T. 3769. According to the same report, Bolshevik policy in the Ukraine alienated many who had been attracted to the policy of revolutionary defeatism.
178. W.S. Churchill, Report on the Labour position in the munitions industries, 23 March 1918, CAB24/46 G.T. 4074.
179. Quoted in ibid.
180. Statistics of strikes in the munitions industries:

|  | No. of days lost (000s) | % of possible working days | 1 day lost in |
|---|---|---|---|
| **1917** Nov. | 511 | 0.76 | 132 |
| Dec. | 238 | 0.38 | 262 |
| **1918** Jan. | 250 | 0.36 | 281 |
| Feb. | 98 | 0.16 | 636 |
| Mar. | 112 | 0.17 | 605 |
| Apr. | 15 | 0.02 | 4,387 |
| May | 59 | 0.08 | 1,112 |
| June | 122 | 0.17 | 526 days |

*Source*: Cabinet reports on the labour position in the munitions industries

the urgency of national necessity converted the Miners' Federation to assisting the government in the comb-out while a considerable number of miners enlisted in the army without waiting for their call-up notices. In Nottinghamshire, the number of miners required under the comb-out was obtained entirely by voluntary means. The response to the Government's appeal to munitions workers to work over the Easter holidays proved almost embarrassing.[181]

This intense patriotism waned during the summer months, partly because workers relaxed their productive efforts in response to the greatly improved military situation, but also because they were opposed to new methods of labour direction which smacked of industrial conscription. However, the prospect of victory in October 1918 brought a sharp recrudescence of the meaner forms of working-class chauvinism which powerfully affected the tone of the post-Armistice election. It would seem likely that the Coalition government's electoral rhetoric in the run up to the polls was greatly influenced by the reports it received of the strength of popular revanchism. Several weeks before Lloyd George first spoke publicly of making Germany pay for the war, it was reported in October that in working-class circles even former advocates of a round-table conference with the enemy powers were not only determined to beat the Germans, but to make them pay the cost of the war 'even if it takes a 1,000 years to do it'. [182] It was claimed that the workers were aware that, in 1871, the Germans had imposed a massive indemnity on France after a briefer and less costly war and considered that similar treatment of the vanquished was morally justifiable since, as the victors were giving the Germans democracy, they should be made to pay for it. (Five weeks after this was reported to the Cabinet, Lloyd George first made the comparison with the indemnity of 1871 a major theme of a speech at Newcastle.)[183] House-to-house visiting by the Women's Peace Crusade in Liverpool brought abuse on the heads of the crusaders. In Jarrow, the ship-workers lodged a collective protest against John Hill, General Secretary of the Boilermakers, framing a Peace Resolution to be adopted by his execu-

181. Labour situation, weeks ending 10 April 1918, 1 May 1918, CAB24/47 G.T. 4197, CAB24/50 G.T. 4407; Report on the Labour position in the Munitions Industries, 8 May 1918, CAB24/51 G.T. 4503.

182. Fortnightly report [No. 24] on pacificism and revolutionary organisations in the UK and morale in France and Italy, 24 Oct. 1918, CAB24/67 G.T. 6079. See also report No. 25, 5 Nov. 1918, CAB24/69 G.T. 6201.

183. See A.J. Mayer, *Politics and Diplomacy of Peacemaking*, London, 1968, p. 156: '. . . it was not until November 29 that Lloyd George . . . explicitly took up the indemnity issue. Speaking as lawyer, historian and peacemaker he argued that in court the loser invariably assumed the cost of litigation; that in 1871 the Germans had made the French pay; and that now, too, Germany would have "to pay the costs of the war", though only "up to the limit of her capacity"'.

tive committee.[184] These reports of working-class revanchism in advance of elite opinion were filed by Thomson and, despite the reservation we must have about his testimony, on this occasion he gauged the tenor of popular sentiment with some accuracy. MPs who had opposed the war were defeated massively at the polls in December, victims (to borrow Best's phrase) of 'the foreign-hating side of the plebeian mind'.[185]

The election was, as Trevor Wilson has shown, a triumph for Conservatism not the Coupon.[186] This immediate political outcome of the war clearly throws into doubt all the claims made so far as to the relationship between the domestic impact of the war and the greater 'visibility' of the class structure, for the first electoral results of full democracy returned to power a party whose identification with the capitalist class and whose antipathy to working-class organisations had never been more publicly adverted. We are tempted to conclude that either greater class consciousness is an imaginary construct of the historian or that it was largely irrelevant to political choice, in which case the phenomenon was rather trivial. The personally embarrassing part of this conclusion can be mitigated if we recall how the war clarified the 'visibility' of the nation and the earlier claim that throughout the war 'national' consciousness was a limiting context for class consciousness. Both by their traditions and by reason of political circumstances, the Conservatives were in a position to arrogate the nationalist and military 'virtues': they had been out of office when the war began, but they had been the fiercest proponents of total victory and the means (such as conscription) to secure it.

Furthermore, Conservatism's electoral base was strengthened by the English propensity to defer to the theatrical show of society. In clarifying the 'visibility' of the nation, the war made the monarchical symbols of unity a powerful focus for popular loyalty and it left a residue of forms of public life (e.g. Remembrance Sunday) in which class differentiation was sublimated. The social image of the Crown was transformed during the war by the rationing applied to the Royal Family, the

---

184. Fortnightly report on pacificism, 24 Oct. 1918.

185. For the rabid tone of the election in constituencies represented by antiwar MPs, see D. Marquand, *Ramsay MacDonald*, London 1977, pp. 234–7. This was a curious election; contemporary liberal opinion was shocked by the debasement of political argument, yet considered the election 'apathetic' (the description is Christopher Addison's, in idem, *Four and A Half Years*, London, 1934, p. 597. There are many similar comments). The average turnout was very low, but this was partly because of a large number of uncontested seats and working-class abstentionism will not explain the crushing defeats of the leading Labour antiwar figures — notably Snowden and MacDonald — who defended constituencies where the turnout was considerably above average.

186. T. Wilson, *The Downfall of the Liberal Party 1914–1935*, London, 1968, pp. 194–5. In Manchester, where the Coupon was not used, the Conservative candidates were still sweepingly successful.

anglicisation of its name and by the publicity given to the simplicity, even austerity, of its family life. Here were the origins of the modern monarchy. Its popularity in postwar years was, so far as we can judge, remarkable. Visits by the Prince of Wales and the King and Queen to industrial centres such as Sheffield, Leicester and Birmingham in the spring and summer of 1919 drew such enthusiastic crowds that Thomson thought it worthwhile stressing the counter-revolutionary value of working-class royalism in his reports to the Cabinet.[187] In a survey of revolutionary feeling during 1919 he placed at the head of a list of 'steadying influences' on the working class the 'popularity of the Royal Family' and 'sport'.[188] Doubtless it was naively put, but there was something so obviously true in that claim that it is surprising that historians have been loath to examine working-class monarchism more closely and assess its relationship with political Conservatism.

## Conclusions

The electoral triumph of Conservatism and the strength of popular deference to historic conservative institutions is less incompatible with the argument that the war strengthened class consciousness if we accept that the latter is a differentiated phenomenon and only at its 'revolutionary' level is it exclusive of other mentalities. Becoming class conscious can be likened to learning a language and, if there are 'levels' of consciousness then, to extend the analogy, there are certain 'dialects' of class consciousness. From their wartime experiences and from the publicity given to wartime profit making, working-class consumers learned a dialect specific to one level of class consciousness. It was a dialect whose key terms were 'equality of sacrifice', 'fair shares' and 'profiteering'. The popular usage of the last term enables us to argue that, for many, the war made more transparent the roots of inequality in capitalist market society.

The combination of the rapid advances in money wages during 1918–20 with the price inflation furthered this process of clarification because working-class consumers developed a new sensitivity to profit-making in certain consumer goods they were coming to regard as prerequisites of a decent way of life. This sensitivity was particularly evident when, in mid-1919, as part of the measures to restore business confidence, the government simultaneously decontrolled a large number of consumer goods industries (such as wool and cotton) and halved

187. Reports on Revolutionary organisations in the UK for 7 April 1919, 28 May 1919, 12 June 1919: CAB24/77 G.T. 7091, CAB24/80 G.T. 7367, CAB24/81 G.T. 7463.
188. 'A Survey of Revolutionary Feeling during the year 1919', CAB24/96 C.P. 462.

the rate of excess profits tax. Profits and prices soared, notoriously in wool where the prices rose by 30 per cent to 50 per cent within a brief time after decontrol, and there were similar rapid rises in the price of boots, furniture and most household utensils. It was reported that

> . . . neither inflation nor the rise in labour costs due to increased wages and shorter hours will satisfactorily account in most cases for the prices now being charged. The effect of this on the minds of the working classes may easily be conceived. Every man and every woman is hit by high prices of domestic articles, which they know are largely due to excessive profits . . . [189]

In early August 1919, resolutions protesting the rise in prices and excess profit-making were being forwarded every day to trade councils, local Labour Parties and trade unions.[190] A Hyde Park demonstration on 21 September, organised jointly by trade unionists and co-operators, was credited with attracting over half a million people who heard the government violently denounced from a number of platforms for sheltering profiteers.[191] The institution of profiteering tribunals to investigate allegations of excess profit-making left many keenly disappointed with the small numbers successfully prosecuted and the trifling fines imposed. In December 1919, Thomson warned: 'Little can be added to the stress repeatedly laid in these reports on the grave nature of the unrest caused by profiteering'. It was a major theme of the December TUC and the indignation of the delegates 'was a reflex of the feeling not only amongst [organised] Labour but amongst the general public'.[192] Official and unofficial investigation added to the stock of public knowledge of the capitalist system. The Joint Committee on the Cost of Living, set up by the TUC, argued that the operation of the Profiteering Acts was important, not because of any real check the Acts exercised on soaring profits, but because they were 'a recognition by the Government of a widespread phenomenon which had inflamed and exasperated the general public'. It further maintained that the obstacles which certain traders had put in the way of the investigative Committees set up under the Acts were as 'illuminating' as the abuses being investigated.[193]

The word 'illuminating' reminds us that in a commonplace metaphor, the war was a 'star shell' which had lit up social and industrial conditions and furthered the cause of reform. The metaphor can be

---

189. Labour situation, week ending 9 July 1919, CAB24/82 G.T. 7672.

190. Labour situation, week ending 6 August 1919, CAB24/86 G.T. 7912.

191. 'Report on Revolutionary organisations in the UK', 25 Sept. 1919, CAB24/89 G.T. 8228.

192. Ibid.

193. Parliamentary Committee of the TUC, Joint Committee on the Cost of Living, *Final Report*, 1921, pp. 43, 47.

extended to the public enlightenment of the economic system. Workers acquired greater knowledge of the returns of capital and a more acute sense that they were 'unfair'. This 'enlightenment' interlaced with a strengthening of the solidarism in working-class awareness by processes at work on the Home Front. Despite the conflicts of interest between different grades of worker, the ties of a common subculture became stronger as workers accustomed themselves to the homogenising influences of the war on labour. It was a change in attitudes and values evident in the two primary sites of working-class experience: the work place and the local community. The raising of the wages of the unskilled and the less skilled relative to the skilled and the stimulus given to general labourers' unions broke down much of the exclusivity and subordination which had characterised relations between the different strata of the working class. We can perceive the echoes of this in the working-class press:

> One might have expected that the 'classes' among workers had died out in the past few years; but I heard a conversation a few days ago wherein an 'unskilled' union man was roundly denouncing the 'so-called aristocracy of Labour' for their 'selfishness and craft-pride'. He went on to say the 'unskilled' were 'now running the blooming show', etc. He boasted of the big wages he was getting and generally put the 'old fossilised unions' in their place. One of his complaints was that the craftsmen had built up benefit funds for themselves 'instead of organising the poor labourer'.[194]

That there was greater solidarism of labour was a major conclusion of the best-informed of the contemporary historians of the Labour movement and industrial relations:

> The skilled worker can no longer think of the less skilled workers quite as he was apt to think of them before the War, and the less skilled worker will no longer be conscious of the same subordination to the skilled worker. The less skilled classes of labour have secured a greater measure of recognition, and are more disposed to make considerable claims on their own behalf than they were before the War. . . . the fundamental effect is to draw the two groups more closely together . . .[195]

With respect to relationships within the working-class community, Robert Roberts has described how: 'Socially, the barriers of caste that had previously existed between the skilled workers and his family and the lower industrial grades were permanently lowered; the artisan felt less superiority, the labourer and semi-skilled man more self-assurance'.[196]

194. *Cotton Factory Times*, 20 June 1919 ('Wayside Gleanings').
195. G.D.H. Cole, *Trade Unionism and Munitions*, Oxford, 1923, p. 4.
196. R. Roberts, *The Classic Slum*, Harmondsworth, 1973, p. 200.

There was a further change so obvious that we take it for granted. The war introduced into working-class awareness a specific, historical element which persisted in popular memory as long as the generation which had lived and worked through the war survived. This event had so broken the normal flow of time and so dislocated the worker's sense of his own place in society that it had a special place in the remembered past. A Hackney shoemaker whose recollections form part of the 'People's Autobiography' of the borough explains:

> It is a paradox of war that whatever the position of a man or woman, whatever may be the attitude of 'others' toward him in times of peace, he suddenly seems to be elevated and mysteriously becomes a better person in times of war. What I am trying to say is that a hard, relentless, uncompromising employer suddenly finds the man he has treated like dirt is not such a bad person after all. In these periods [i.e. war-time], people who have not been able to hold down a job or perhaps have become unemployable, suddenly find they are not so useless after all. They suddenly have a job, and money, and prospects.[197]

Testimony such as this presents its own problems of interpretation for there is a danger of taking firmly-held beliefs (or, in a non-pejorative sense 'myths') as factual representations of the history they describe. My point is simply that such myths were themselves social facts of some consequence in the working-class meaning-system.

When we turn from working-class awareness to workers' class consciousness then the fundamental change effected by the war was a raising of expectations whose attempted fulfilment brought them into conflict with employers. This was well-described by a contemporary analyst of industrial relations who considered that, as an influence of post-war negotiation, the 'change in the temper, and certain changes in the methods and organisation of wage-earners' were more important even than the instability of prices:

> The war and post-war boom raised their expectations . . . the new experience of indispensability during the war, the deference of Governments, the promise of politicians, the spectacle of unprecedented profits easily won and lightly spent, the expansion of State activity, the general dislocation of pre-existing social arrangements, all conduced to the same result.[198]

Linked to this was the breakdown of the customary framework of comparison by which the fairness of wage differences were judged. Before the war, the habit of comparison with allied and neighbouring groups of workers acted as a restraining influence on wage bargaining,

197. Arthur Newton, *Years of Change*, London, 1974, p. 48.
198. H. Clay, *The Problem of Industrial Relations*, London, 1929, p. 92.

preventing a group from exploiting to the full any temporary market advantage it possessed. With the wartime changes in the labour market and the regulations of wages, the habit of comparison operated in the opposite direction, stimulating further demands which pressed on what the market could bear. Furthermore, the range of comparison was extended by national wage awards, the mobility of labour, the struggle to keep abreast with the rise in the cost of living, greater access to the consumer goods market and a temporary narrowing of economic differences between the working class and white-collar employees. It is fundamentally misleading to think of a class as a social actor and we should, therefore, when discussing class consciousness avoid terms drawn from the psychology of individuals. Occasionally, however, they can scarcely be avoided: the dominating impression in the contemporary studies of the mentalities of the prewar working class is of an 'introverted' social and cultural formation in which events were accepted as they came, with a kind of fatalism, and social comparisons were constrained by the magnitude of differences within the class. By altering relations within the class, the war made this formation more 'extraverted'.

# 7

## The Class Awareness and Class Consciousness of 'Servile' and Black-coated Workers

This brief chapter analyses the social consciousness of workers in the 'buffer zone', particularly with respect to changing attitudes to trade unionism and collective bargaining. Such an emphasis, it could be argued, merely adds to the condescension which posterity and theory have showered on them, for the trade union ethic was normally incongruent with the social consciousness of salaried employees. Their class awareness has, typically, emphasised individualism. A belief in promotion on personal worth in the course of a life-long career, the perception of society as a whole as a meritocracy and the focusing of aspirations for one's children on the educational system have been widely identified as fundamentals of the normative framework of the salaried employee, and as distinguishing him from the manual worker.[1] For clerks, in particular, these attitudes have been concomitant with a work situation which has isolated them from other clerks and manual workers.[2] But 'individualism' scarcely exhausts the normative framework of salaried employees and there is evidence that individualism at the workplace was combined with a high degree of participation in voluntary associations outside it.[3] Men who could not be persuaded to combine as employees were, paradoxically, great 'joiners', and a sympathetic appraisal of their values would, ideally, examine the associational aspects of suburban life, as well as the individualist resistance to trade unionism. It is useful to remind ourselves that the window on black-coated consciousness provided by trade union sources (the chief ones used here) magnifies the egoism of salaried workers and obscures their social solidarism.

As we have already noted in the discussion of the language and imagery of class, the Suburban mentality was remarkable for a strong moral commitment to the symbols and institutions of the existing social

1. See, for example, the characterisation of the 'petty bourgeois ideological subensemble' in N. Poulantzas, *Classes in Contemporary Capitalism*, London, 1978, p. 292.
2. See D. Lockwood, *The Blackcoated Worker*, London, 1958, p. 81.
3. See Masterman's comments on the Suburbans' participation in voluntary associations in idem, *The Condition of England*, London, 1911, p. 76; also H. McLeod, *Class and Religion in the Late Victorian City*, London, 1974, pp. 134–5.

order (such as the Crown and Court) and for a perception of that order as a detailed and legitimate hierarchy (p. 40). In short, Suburbans were — or were thought to be — deferentials. The reputation of low-paid clerks, employees in the 'respectable' distributive trades and similarly placed workers for obsequiousness was such that they were often lumped together as a 'servile class'. These deferential attitudes are concordant with a resistance to trade unionism but are by no means easy to reconcile with the meritocratic aspects of the salaried employee's consciousness and it would be unwise to attribute them indiscriminately to the 'buffer zone'. Modern studies of deference suggest strongly that the concept should be considered not as an ideological disposition of individual employees, but as typifying certain relationships they enter into their work,[4] and here I will attempt to relate deference to specific features of shop life and clerical work. However, before turning to these details, it is worth recalling that there is much contemporary comment recording a change in the tone of English social relationships from about mid-1916 which was often referred to as a 'decline of the caste spirit'. This strongly suggests an erosion of certain forms of deferential and servile behaviour at *all* levels of society. Gleason, in the first of several books written for an American audience, sought to show the passing of 'the caste system' of old England and believed that 'in its places has arisen a far more formidable, far more democratic state . . .'.[5] In a later work, he recorded:

An old Oxford friend said sadly to me: "Ten years ago, when I came into a crowded bus, a working man would rise and touch his cap and give me his seat. I am sorry to see that spirit dying out." The workers are beginning to use a manner of jaunty equality in dealing with those passengers who travel through life on a first-class ticket. . . . The workers believe that they have been 'had'. The porter, waiter, miner, machinist have penetrated the secret of the significant class, and have found it is not fixed in the eternal scheme of things that the worker should ensure the harmonious leisure of a superior caste . . . the class idea falls away in England. . . . Reverence for the gentry, for the privileged, for the idle, has withered . . . the change in spirit, beginning to show itself in 1910 [has been] hastened by the war.[6]

Generalised reference, such as this, to an erosion of deferential or servile behaviour is difficult to substantiate in terms of reliably recorded social habits and their changing patterns. We can certainly adduce some reasons for the war having undermined an acceptance of the legitimacy of certain forms of hierarchy and subordination: notably, the demand for and mobility of labour, the extension of political

---

4. See H. Newby, *The Deferential Worker*, London, 1977, esp. pp. 415–17.
5. A. Gleason, *Inside the British Isles 1917*, London, 1917, pp. 296, 350.
6. Idem, *What the Workers Want*, London, 1920, p. 250.

rights, the official designation of the state as a 'democracy' in the definition of war aims, the exposure of the incompetence of the traditional governing elites to public gaze, the recognition of the desirability of employee organisation in the Whitley Report and so on. What is more difficult is to connect satisfactorily these developments to the desuetude of deferential attitudes and behaviour. This is partly because deferential behaviour is both a cluster of intersubjective, 'lived' meanings that is common to a culture (and which can change as the rules of social etiquette and 'language games' of that culture change) and is also a characteristic of specific social relationships.

Rather than attempting to explain a general cultural phenomenon, I will relate the decline of servile and deferential forms of behaviour to social groups who specifically identified them as aspects of their employment. The most obvious example, although strictly speaking outside the parameters of this study, were female domestic servants for whom 'loss of caste' had long been a fundamental objection to service. The unwillingness of former munitions girls to return to domestic service, laundry work and other forms of demeaning employment during the period of demobilisation was notorious, although they were driven back by restrictions on the out-of-work donation, the influx of demobilised men into peacetime occupations and by employers' shedding female labour after the granting of a women's wage award in engineering in early 1919. They were, as well, tempted back by the well-advertised notion that the more servile and onerous aspects of their work were to be made less obvious in the postwar period.[7] This refusal to return to service was noted in Luton and Manchester in December 1918, then in January 1919 inquiries in Bradford, Coventry, Derby, Leeds, Newcastle, Nottingham, Rochdale and Sheffield showed that the vast majority of discharged women workers refused to go into domestic service, preferring to live on the unemployment donation. In April, the refusal to go into laundry work was noted.[8] Regional differences in the availability of alternative employment for working women conditioned, to some degree, the willingness to return to the prewar service role. In Lincoln, the absence of established industries made the reemployment of displaced female munitions labour particularly difficult and most of the younger women had little choice but to acquiesce in a return to domestic service and shop work, while married women

7. The 'servant problem' was one of the stock issues of postwar journalism and by general consent one part of its solution was greater personal consideration on the part of mistresses for their domestics. See, for example, the series in the *Daily Chronicle* for the last fortnight of February 1919; cuttings are filed in the Gertrude Tuckwell papers in the TUC Library, together with other miscellanea on domestic service.

8. Ministry of Munitions, Demobilisation and Resettlement Department (Intelligence and Record Branch), Daily Notes, 19 Dec. 1918, 4 Jan. 1919, 7 Jan. 1919, 24 April 1919, MUN4/5337; Munitions Council Daily Report, 9 Dec. 1918, MUN4/3412.

returned to their homes.[9]

Domestic service was objectionable because of its long hours and low pay, but what is most relevant in this context are the objections voiced to the self-abnegating conditions of service that arose from residing in the employer's home. A meeting of five hundred servant and ex-servant girls in Bristol in February 1919 gave collective expression to resentment of the social forms required of servants (they were asked from the platform 'What is it about domestic service that you don't like? — is it the caps and aprons?' and this brought an alarmingly aggressive 'Yes' in reply) and led to the demand for the eight-hour day, no caps and aprons and increased pay. In that same month, there was reported a general 'tendency among girls who are going back to domestic service to undertake daily work only . . . for a day's work from eight to six, £1 a week plus plain food is considered a fair wage'.[10]

The contemporary explanation for former servants resisting the reimposition on them of servile forms of behaviour was quite straightforward: many had had an opportunity of doing another kind of work during the war which was better paid, brought more companionship and where definite hours of employment meant greater freedom outside them. 'They had also felt that every bit of their work was tremendously worthwhile doing and helped in the war. They did not want to give up their freedom and companionship, or the better status they had enjoyed.'[11] The explanation was, perhaps, simplistic, but it cannot be pursued further here.

Amongst male workers in prewar society, servility and an affirmative acceptance of a hierarchical social order were integral to the job and market situation of shop assistants and wholesale distributive workers, particularly in trades such as drapery which were considered 'respectable'. Before 1914, male shop assistants and distributive employees were almost as numerous as male clerks and many shared that social awareness characteristic of the clerical stratum which envisaged society as a social scale up which the individual could advance. This conception was fortified by the generally acknowledged gradations of respectability of shop life. 'The butchers, fishmongers and greengrocers came at the bottom of the scale; then the grocers; the drapers and outfitters ranked a little higher; above them came the chemists.'[12] Furthermore, shop work was still associated with the prospect of advancement to the

---

9. Munitions Council Daily Report, 19 Dec. 1918.

10. See the *Bristol Times and Mirror*, 7 Feb. 1919, and the Demobilisation and Resettlement Department, Daily Notes, 7 Feb. 1919 and 12 Feb. 1919, MUN4/5336.

11. A Miss Baron, speaking at a meeting of Bristol servant girls, as reported in the *Bristol Evening News*, 19 Feb. 1919. (Had they really felt this, working a 70-hour week in a shell-filling factory?)

12. W.B. Whitaker, *Victorian and Edwardian Shopworkers*, Newton Abbot, 1973, p. 174.

status of self-employed businessman. The union which attempted to organise distributive workers (the National Amalgamated Union of Shop Assistants, Warehousemen and Clerks) maintained that: 'The long cherished hope that in the sweet bye-and-bye the shop assistant would have a shop of his own is passing into an illusion, the day of the small trader in most towns is gone by, except in side streets or the poorest localities where it is a struggle and a constant worry to eke a living'.

It attributed the shattering of this illusion to the rise of large-scale retailing and 'trustification in the distributive trades'.[13] This exaggerated the extent and effects of the retail revolution before 1914, although it is true that concentration in retailing was most affecting the more prestigious types of shop-keeping, such as pharmaceutical retailing. Shop assistants and distributive workers were, like the clerks, difficult to organise and the conventional explanation for this was 'their sham gentility', as well as 'a half-conscious feeling that one day they would become employers themselves'.[14] A union organiser, reporting in 1913 on a district claim for 27s. a week for drapers' assistants complained of 'this very respectability which had hitherto been one of the greatest stumbling-blocks in the way of better pay and conditions. We have been too respectable to use the successful weapon of combination'.[15] To the 'cloak of gentility' which hung over shop life were attributed a number of sins: on the one hand, an acquiescence in 'bad health, too many hours of work and very low wages; and on the other hand, caste snobbishness and priggishness'.[16]

As Lockwood and others have argued, 'snobbishness' will not adequately explain the difficulties of white-collar unionisation, which have had more to do with the relatively low density of employment in white-collar jobs and the refusal of employers to recognise organisations representing white-collar staff.[17] 'Snobbishness' may have been a protective strategy on the part of men whose salaries were often no better than the wages of semi-skilled labour but whose work required them to adopt some of the social style of the middle class. There was a particular need for a protective strategy in those (highly respectable) parts of the drapery and wholesale textile trades where living-in was virtually a condition of employment. The NAUSAWC saw the consequences of living-in as 'the loss of individuality, the denial of the rights

13. *The Shop Assistant*, 8 Feb. 1913.
14. Fabian Tract No. 90, 'Shop Life and its Reform', quoted in Whitaker, *Victorian and Edwardian Shopworkers*.
15. *The Shop Assistant*, 7 June 1913.
16. Ibid., 18 Oct. 1913.
17. Lockwood, *The Blackcoated Worker*, pp. 150–1; also G.S. Bain, *The Growth of White-collar Unionism*, Oxford, 1970, pp. 48–50, 183–8.

and responsibilities of citizenship, the enforced celibacy with all its attendant dangers, and its depressing influence on wages', although it regretted that these were 'often . . . unrealised by those chiefly concerned'.[18] As a result of the Union's vigorous campaign against living-in, many high-class provincial drapers abandoned the system after 1907 but, amongst the minority who retained it, there remained strong opposition to its abolition until the outbreak of war.[19] A milder tie of dependence — the practice of taking dinner and tea on the employer's premises — was more common.[20] Fines were frequently imposed for trivial misdemeanours at work and the assistant's economic liberty restricted by the obligation to sign 'radius agreements' not to seek similar employment within a certain distance on leaving a post.

The initial impact of the war on workers in service industries was deleterious, especially for assistants in the drapery, jewellery and fancy trades where employers dismissed staff, reduced wages without reducing hours and in some instances asked remaining employees to work unpaid overtime.[21] Moreover, the rapid growth of trade unionism amongst distributive workers, which had followed the introduction of National Insurance, was brought to a halt, as were the district negotiations to establish minimum wages. In so far as this initial impact of war halted the campaign against the living-in system, it emphasised the servile status of the most 'respectable' distributive employers. Because their labour was so dispensable, shop workers found themselves exposed to a particularly iniquitous form of economic conscription in the early months of the war as employers, out of self-interest and for patriotic motives, shook off labour.[22]

Unlike most labour organisations, the distributive workers' union found its membership falling, not simply in the opening phase of the war, but up to mid-1917. Furthermore, during the war the union had a bigger proportion of its membership in uniform than any other organisation and found local branches atrophying in the absence of key officials and militants. The autumn of 1917 brought a rally to the union's fortunes partly because it successfully linked vigorous 'trade movements' with a campaign for an advanced policy on educational reform and a demand for the application of the Trade Boards Act to the

18. See the President's Address to the 1913 Annual Delegate Meeting of the NAUSAWC, *The Shop Assistant*, 5 April 1913. Resident service workers were ineligible for the franchise.

19. See the report of the union deputation to the Home Secretary, Reginald McKenna, asking for legislative action on "living-in", *The Shop Assistant*, 14 Feb. 1914.

20. See the *Report of the Committee into the operation of the Truck Acts*, PP 1908, Cd 4442, p. 68.

21. *The Shop Assistant*, 24 Oct. 1914.

22. See the General Secretary's Report to the 1915 Annual Conference of the NAUSAWC, *The Shop Assistant*, 17 April 1915.

distributive trades, but principally because the chronic labour shortage was affecting even this type of work. According to the union these factors produced 'a silent revolution . . . inside shop life' in late 1917 and early 1918 and 'encouraging signs of a general awakening amongst the members to a realisation of the power which organisation gives them to alter their conditions'.[23] Where distributive workers were congregated in sufficiently large numbers — as in London's wholesale pharmaceutical trade — they imitated the rank-and-file organisation and collective bargaining practices which had developed amongst industrial workers. In August 1918, it was reported that: 'The shop stewards' movement [in the London wholesale pharmaceutical trade] is coming in for general recognition, most firms now recognising rightly-elected persons to speak on behalf of the staff, some firms having actually placed rooms at their disposal, and in at least one instance having granted clerical assistance'.[24]

Similarly, a movement amongst workers in the City wholesale textile houses led to a mass meeting in October 1918 of workers from twelve firms and the election of a representative committee whose members functioned as 'quasi-shop stewards'.[25] The social impact of the war in its latter stages assisted one aspect of the union's attack on the shopworker's servile status by effectively killing off the living-in system. The shortage of supplies in 1917 meant that the minority of employers who were maintaining the system found it expedient to commute the board they provided to a living-out allowance and such living-in arrangements as survived the war bore little resemblance to the prewar state of things.[26]

With the important exception of co-operative employees, most shop workers remained isolated by their market situation, and such factors as the size of the groups they worked with, from organised labour. The lingering notion of the 'respectability' of shop life made more tolerable the servile aspects of their work and cut them off from 'the sense of movement' which is woven into the social history of the war and postwar period. Yet whether willingly or not, shop workers found their

23. See the extract from the NAUSAWC Annual Report in *The Shop Assistant*, 6 April 1918; the Special Report of the London Conference — Minimum Wage Committee Report, *The Shop Assistant*, 13 April 1918; also the résumé by John Turner of the effects of the war on the organisation, *The Shop Assistant*, 30 Nov. 1918.

24. Ibid., 3 Aug. 1918.

25. Ibid., 26 Oct. 1918. This issue quotes the *Drapers' Record* on the Shop Assistants' 'very vigorous campaign among employees in each section of the [London] drapery trade, wholesale, retail and workrooms', and thus confirms from a hostile source the impression of considerable unrest amongst this group of workers.

26. See H. Llewellyn Smith, ed., *New Survey of London Life and Labour*, vol. 5, *London Industries*, Pt. II, London, 1933, pp. 151–2; and P.C. Hoffman, *They Also Serve*, London, 1949, p. 64.

working lives increasingly governed by the actions and achievements of organisation and, to an extent inconceivable in the prewar decade, they undertook concerted action. The favourable position of labour organisations in the wartime economy enabled the shop assistants' union to begin, in 1916, a series of negotiations with the great multiple firms, such as Home & Colonial and Lipton's, which aimed at establishing uniform conditions in the grocery trade and culminated in the National Agreement of 1919. Joint application by employers' associations and the union brought the trade within the orbit of the Trade Board Acts in 1920 and the establishment of an assistant's rate, at the age of twenty-five, of 58s. in rural areas, 70s. in London and 68s. elsewhere for a 48-hour week.[27] (These rates were reduced, in September 1921, after the fall in the cost of living. Moreover, flagrant violation of the Trade Board's fixed rates in the drapery trade by South Coast firms had led to only petty fines for employers. The experience of raised economic status for shop assistants was brief and probably more patchy than the signing of national agreements between employers' associations and unions suggests.)

Militant action was undertaken by the 'genteel' employees of the big departmental stores, particularly in London. The labour shortage and the state's advocacy of trade union recognition broke down employers' objections to trade union branch formation while the achievements of organised manual labour eroded the prejudices of workers who had considered themselves a 'class apart'. In December 1918 the shop assistants' branches of two of the biggest London stores, the Army and Navy and the Civil Service, affiliated to the London Trades Council.[28] These firms were far bigger employers than the average London factory and, briefly, their labour force showed an awareness of the bargaining strength which group size gave them. Months of negotiations over wages and conditions culminated in the strike by 4,000 employees at the Army and Navy in December 1919, the largest in the history of the retail trade. Unrest was widespread amongst departmental stores workers, and according to the Ministry of Labour 'had [it] not culminated in the 48-hour strike at the Army and Navy Stores, it might have found expression in a similar way in any of a dozen large establishments in the West End'.[29] The award of the Industrial Court to which the parties applied to settle the dispute was quickly accepted by the leading West End employers and the successful outcome of the dispute brought the shop assistants' union large accessions of numbers. Seven thousand shop workers attended the Albert Hall meeting on the

---

27. Hoffman, *They Also Serve*, pp. 97–100.
28. London Trades Council, Executive Minutes, 30 Dec. 1918.
29. Labour situation, week ending 7 Jan. 1920, CAB24/96 C.P. 422.

3 January at which a Mr Turner, the union's secretary, announced the award.[30] Employees of the Civil Service Supply Association rapidly followed the example of the Army and Navy Stores and put forward similar demands for improved working conditions and recognition of the shop assistants' union.[31] Such successes were achieved at the height of the postwar boom when wage increases could be passed on to the consumer, and at a time when public support for Whitleyism was pushing outwards the frontiers of trade unionism. Later action was less successful. A six-week strike at John Lewis's was defeated, in spite of financial support from workers in other London firms. A sixteen-week strike at Beatties in Wolverhampton ended in defeat and proved the last strike by drapery shop workers for many years.[32]

Perhaps the least expected example of the sloughing off of servility and the most unlikely of the rank-and-file organisations which flourished briefly in the postwar period was the London hairdressers' Shop Steward's Movement which was responsible for conducting a protracted hairdressers' strike in January and February 1919. Shop-floor representation was a key issue in the dispute for as well as the correction of economic grievances, the strikers demanded 'the right to organise, regulate conditions, and the maintenance of Shop Stewards'.[33] The six-week strike could not have been maintained without the talent for spontaneous action which workers had developed during the war. Between them the hairdressers raised £1,500 to open a club called the Hairdressers' Rendezvous in Archer Street, off Piccadilly Circus in London, which provided a reading room and billiard saloon but above all a meeting-place for workers whose normal work situation was so inimical to collective action.[34]

This upsurge of distributive and service workers' militancy lends some empirical support to the view that servile forms of behaviour, individualism and 'caste' affectation were integral to their normally highly dependent relationships with employers rather than deeply internalised attitudes and values. That is to say, the notion, so frequently put forward in the contemporary sources, that shop life was conducive to a servile 'personality' or a consistent ideological framework with which to interpret society is, apparently, belied by the readiness with which shop assistants organised and militated when the terms of the market for their labour, and governmental attitudes, were briefly in their favour. It may also be the case that shop assistants and

30. Hoffman, *They Also Serve*, p. 178.
31. Labour situation, week ending 17 Dec. 1918, CAB24/95 C.P. 317.
32. Hoffman, *They Also Serve*, pp. 193–4.
33. *The Shop Assistant*, 1 Feb. 1919. The report on the strike is by P.C. Hoffman, at this time the union's London district organiser.
34. Hoffman, *They Also Serve*, p. 110.

service workers were especially sensitive to those changes in the rules of social etiquette which were, by all accounts, making England a less deferential society. The longer-term influences of the war on service workers' awareness are rather more difficult to assess: the dominating factors appear to have been the change in the balance of the labour force towards women's employment (although in the late 1920s the numbers of male and female shop assistants in London were still approximately equal) which brought the status of the work even closer to domestic service, and a further decline in prospects of self-advancement.[35]

From the point of view of the analysis of the 'images of society' and the forms of awareness typical of the 'new middle class', the most interesting phenomenon of the war and its immediate aftermath were the steps taken to organise clerical, supervisory and administrative staff, and lower professional workers such as draughtsmen and technical engineers. How much we can infer about changes in attitudes and values from the development of collective organisations is debatable (since exogenous factors, such as Whitleyism, were clearly important causes), but it seems reasonable to claim these steps could not have been taken without *some* shift in the cognitive perspectives of the white-collar employees who were being organised. In Marxist writing, the unionisation of low-paid white-collar workers has often been seen as part of the process of proletarianisation which is (or will) detach them from their allegiance to the dominant classes, and it is frequently linked to the degradation of white-collar work by office mechanisation and dilution by female labour.[36] This is a very imperfect explanation of historical white-collar unionisation (though it may have some validity for the very recent past) even with respect to those organisations which affiliated with the Labour movement and followed militant industrial policies. Admittedly, there were politically radical, class-conscious activists within clerical unions who advocated a 'proletarian' strategy, but the principal rationale for organisation was to defend those advantages of white-collar employment over manual labour which were deemed a legitimate reward for certain skills and responsibilities. (This 'egoism' was not incompatible with a general sympathy for the Labour movement.)

The organisation of professional workers presents even more serious problems for a dichotomous theory of class society since it can be shown, at least in the historical context I am discussing, that one aim of that organisation was to assert the separate interest of professional

35. *New Survey of London Life and Labour*, vol. 5, pp. 139, 149.
36. The classic analysis on these lines in British Marxist writing is by F.D. Klingender, *The Condition of Clerical Labour in Britain*, London, 1935; also H. Braverman, *Labor and Monopoly Capital*, New York, 1974.

employees from that of the capitalist class *and* organised labour. The new, professional organisations of the period immediately after the war expressed a specific form of the middle-class consciousness which, as has already been noted, the war did much to encourage.

The changes in attitudes and values which we can infer from these developments in collective organisation (and I would stress the hazardous nature of the inference) were, amongst low-paid clerical labour, a greater sense of the industrial and social solidarity of clerical employees and a further erosion of certain 'deferential' attitudes towards corporate employers, such as railway companies, the Civil Service and local authorities. The historian of the National Association of Local Government Officers has seen evidence for the decline of these deferential attitudes in the new temper of the clerks who returned from the forces: they were 'different beings from the straw hatted clerks who had flocked in 1914 to join Kitchener's army . . . witnesses of the strength of united action, they were in no mood to return to the respectful, cap-in-hand approach to employers of the past'.[37] The shift in the consciousness of the 'new' professional workers is a matter for more detailed research, but two changes are apparent from the sources: a more militant sense of the economic struggle for a professional style of life induced by inflation and the desire to establish greater control over, and autonomy for, their professional organisations.

There are two reasons why I shall turn to the clerical employees of the railway industry to give some empirical substance to the claims I have made with respect to low-paid white-collar workers: firstly, they were their own sociologists who explicitly debated in their union journal and at their conferences the social rationale for white-collar unionism; secondly, the railways clerks should, all things considered, have conformed to the proletarianisation thesis. They were the best organised body of clerical workers before 1914 (and amongst the lowest paid) and achieved a remarkable density of organisation by the end of the war. They worked in close proximity to well-organised manual workers and the Railway Clerk's Association enjoyed a more amicable relationship with the country's largest industrial union, the NUR, than did the latter's blue-collar rivals, ASLEF and the ASE. (The NUR competed with the ASE in the organisation of railway workshop engineers.) Railway clerical work was 'diluted' by an influx of female clerks during the war and there was at least a widespread apprehension that the career structure of clerical employment was being undermined by bureaucratic change within the companies. In late 1918 and early 1919, the RCA adopted an increasingly militant attitude towards the Railway Executive Committee and the companies

37. A. Spoor, *White Collar Union: Sixty Years of NALGO*, London, 1967, p. 72.

over the issue of union recognition, and in February went to the brink of nation-wide strike action with (according to reliable testimony) solid rank-and-file support. But what should have been highly favourable conditions for 'proletarianisation' did not produce the normative changes implied in that term nor, more specifically, did they lead to an industrial policy on the part of the RCA which would have accorded with it.

In his presidential Address to the RCA's 1914 conference (which was circulated as a separate pamphlet amongst railway clerks), Mr Romeril explained how the need for their organisation was made more manifest year by year in the experience of other black-coated workers in analogous occupations. State schooling had produced a superabundant supply of clerical labour and the economic position of 'clerks as a class' had been steadily encroached upon. There was, he said, really no choice in the matter:

> Our status will be destroyed, and our rates of pay reduced to the lowest subsistence level, unless we clerical workers as a class organise so strongly that we ourselves will be able to control the supply of our labour and to fix and maintain the rates at which it can be engaged, just the same as the lawyers and doctors through their trade unions fix their fees and maintain their social and economic positions.[38]

The Association had reason to be pleased with its own growth for, between 1906 and 1914, membership rose from about 4,000 to 29,000, and to a density of unionisation of about 38 per cent (considerably higher than the national average density of union membership).[39] None the less, it regarded that progress and its effectiveness as a negotiating body as vitiated by the social attitudes characteristic of the white-collar worker. The conditions of railway clerical service, the Association admitted, had until recent years compared favourably both with other white-collar employment and those of the manual grades, especially with respect to security of tenure and opportunities for promotion. These opportunities were cited by the companies both to legitimate low starting salaries and to encourage 'individualism' amongst its staff. Companies often refused to treat salary claims *en bloc*, but insisted on considering clerks' demands individually. Consequently, the railway clerical worker was

> just as dissatisfied with his own position and anxious to improve it as is any other average worker; but this dissatisfaction is usually restricted to his own

38. *Progress, Combination and Agreement amongst Clerks*, publ. by the Railway Clerks Association, 1914.

39. The figures are given in the Annual Conference Reports published in *The Railway Clerk*. The average density of union membership in 1911 was 17.9 per cent; see Bain, *The Growth of White-collar Unionism*, Table 3.1.

position. For example, if conditions in his office are bad he tries to get a move out of the office rather than join in an attempt to improve the conditions. His efforts towards improvement are self-centred; he is not concerned about uplifting his class. This spirit, which happily is disappearing, is fostered by the officials, who hold out the hope of individual advancement and encourage their men to learn of Samuel Smiles rather than Sidney Webb . . . in the prospect of promotion there has been and is a possible way of escape from the general level of railway clerical conditions and the men have sought and still seek that way, and have been and still are indifferent to trade unionism as a means of improving their individual positions by raising the general conditions.[40]

Promotion prospects had diminished with the completion of the railway network and amalgamations between companies, working agreements and pooling arrangements. They had also been curtailed by the introduction of managerial cadetships for public school and university-educated entrants into the railway service.[41] To the railway clerical worker's growing dissatisfaction with declining promotion prospects, there had, by 1914, been added increasing worry as to his security of tenure. Railway managers had warned the Departmental Committee on Railway Agreements and Amalgamations of 1912 that the rationalisation of the industry could involve staff redundancies.[42] Moreover, the companies' reaction to the unionisation of their clerical staff had been predictably hostile and their organ, *The Railway News*, warned that 'if clerks change their whole attitude to their employers [by joining the RCA] they can hardly object to being treated on a commercial basis, and if their services are not required they must look elsewhere, as in every other business'.[43]

With the outbreak of war, the RCA, in conjunction with other white-collar unions, formed a War Emergency Clerical and Administrative Workers' Committee to ensure 'that clerks as a class should not suffer unduly in consequence of the War'.[44] The significance of this step has been overlooked by historians of the Labour movement for it clearly showed that the clerical organisations did not feel that their members' interests would be secured by the (now well-documented) War Emergency Workers' National Committee. Mr Romeril hoped to make the

40. *The Railway Clerk*, August 1913.
41. See the Presidential Address to the RCA Annual Conference, 1910, in *The Railway Clerk*, June 1910. On the growth of the cadet system for public school and university entrants (mostly in the north-western and north-eastern companies), see *The Railway Clerk*, April 1914.
42. Ibid., April 1912, where some of the evidence to this committee is cited.
43. *The Railway News*, 11 May 1912, quoted in *The Railway Clerk*, June 1912.
44. See the Presidential Address to the 1915 Annual Conference of the RCA, *The Railway Clerk*, July 1915. The work of this committee is also referred to in *The Shop Assistant*, 24 Oct. 1914.

clerical workers' emergency committee the basis for a future Federation of Clerks but this suggestion was opposed by syndicalist members of his own Association who believed that the best line of union development lay in a federation or amalgamation with other railway trade unions. Romeril, defending the formation of the Clerical Workers' Committee, argued that: 'Surely it will not be denied that the conditions of railway clerical workers are analogous to and determined by the conditions of postal and mercantile clerks rather than by the conditions of members of the uniform grades of our railways?'[45]

The war exposed some of the differences in conditions of the clerical and uniformed grades on the railways: the families of enlisted married salaried employees were allowed four-fifths of the man's salary while he was on military service, but the companies refused on principle in the first year of the war to pay clerical workers for the many hours of overtime they worked. Furthermore, negotiations for war-bonus awards to meet the rising cost of living showed that the major railway unions had gone much further to achieving effective recognition from the companies than the RCA; in the north-west, the companies refused to meet the Association's representatives.[46] Finally, from the spring of 1916 the dilution of clerical work by women's labour became a source of increasing dissatisfaction amongst the railway salariat. (The number of women clerks rose from just over a thousand in August 1914 to 14,000 by November 1916.)

Wartime circumstances were very propitious for the RCA's expansion but they exposed it to a dilemma which arose from the desire to organise the stationmasters and supervisory grades and the contradictory demand of a militant faction within the Association for amalgamation with the NUR. The effects of inflation made the stationmasters and supervisory grades ripe for recruitment by the Association and an editorial in its journal put the case for their joining in familiar terms:

> You [stationmasters] are an important body of public servants, but your incomes are quite inadequate to enable you to maintain your social status and to meet the many calls made upon your pockets, some of which calls, as you know, are incidental to and consequent upon the very position you occupy. You cannot live in the same style as the men who hold similar public or private positions to yourself; nor can you give your children the same education and opportunities of advancement as these men give their children. . . .[47]

The RCA's claim to organise the supervisory grades was the principal

45. Presidential Address to the 1915 Annual Conference.
46. See the Commission of Enquiry into Industrial Unrest, No.2 Division, North Western Area, Cd 8663, p. 27.
47. *The Railway Clerk*, Dec. 1916.

stumbling block to its recognition by the companies and the Railway Executive Committee, who feared the division of the loyalty of these grades, and a break-down of the rigid authority structure regarded as essential to the industry's discipline. Moreover, the claim to represent the supervisory grades raised serious difficulties for those within the Association pressing for fusion with the NUR, for the latter was unlikely to treat sympathetically, when formulating its industrial policies, the special relationship of the higher grades with the companies that arose from superannuation schemes and the other advantages of their salaried employment.

These dilemmas became acute when the June 1917 Conference of the RCA voted in favour of a motion, put forward by the syndicalists of its Leeds branch and other militants from the Railway Workers' One Union Movement, for fusion.[48] This was clearly against the wishes of its executive and in subsequent months came under considerable criticism from the Association's rank and file. A letter in the RCA journal, signed 'Status', dismissed the notion that opposition to fusion arose from 'snobbishness'. The salariat, the writer argued, differed from the proletariat by reason of a different psychology of time:

> A man employed for a day at a time is a casual labourer; a man employed for a week at a time . . . is a workman; a man . . . who is employed by the month is in the first grade of the salariat. . . . The recognition of the different status of the clerk as set forth in the foregoing and evidenced on the railways by better holidays, payment during sickness, superannuation, etc., is not snobbishness but profound wisdom, and it would be a disaster if in the desire for amalgamation that status were lowered.[49]

Cole and Page Arnot, in their study of railway trades unionism published in 1917, were alive to the opposition to fusion amongst railway clerks and feared it would prove a set-back to the remarkable growth of solidarity amongst the clerical staff. Rank-and-file opposition to fusion arose because 'it is argued that the operative grades do not understand the peculiar grievances and, still more, the peculiar needs of the clerical staff. . . . Fusion with the operative grades . . . would mean levelling down'.[50] The accuracy of their analysis was borne out by the RCA's special conference of February 1918, called by the executive to respond to the Labour Party's invitation to submit names of additional prospective Parliamentary candidates, to consider the

48. See the Report of the 1917 Annual Conference of the RCA in *The Railway Clerk*, June 1917.

49. Ibid., July 1917. There was a considerable correspondence in the journal during subsequent months on the subject of fusion and class consciousness; see, in particular, ibid., Oct. 1917.

50. G.D.H. Cole, R. Page Arnot, *Trade Unionism on the Railways*, London, 1917, p. 96.

growing demand for full recognition by the railway companies (and, in effect, the government) and to authorise the executive to break off the fusion negotiations with the NUR which it had entered on the instructions of the 1917 annual conference. All three issues indicate that this was a critical moment in the history of the Labour movement and of white-collar unionism and its relationship with government and organised manual labour. However, fusion undoubtedly aroused the greatest interest. The Leeds delegate moved an amendment attacking the executive for its handling of fusion negotiations in the wake of the 1917 conference, but the amendment was defeated by a large majority. During the debate on this issue, Mr Moss of Manchester said the possibility of fusion was having a deterrent effect upon the work of organising men in the higher grades. Romeril (no longer President but a delegate from the Railway Clearing House) agreed: his own feeling was

> that for some years to come the clerical and administrative workers would have to do essential work upon their own lines, strengthening their position, and maintaining all they had got, including some of the things the other grades did not posses, and had not even asked for; such things as continuity of pay, whether working, sick or on holiday, and a progressive scale of advances through life, also the improvement of the position of men who were required to carry out responsible supervisory duties on unsatisfactory terms. The youngest and the most poorly-paid clerks could all rally round the RCA standard in support of these claims because they were all on the same road and were themselves entitled to reach supervisory positions.[51]

The second of the issues debated at the conference, full recognition by the companies, showed that the white-collar worker's rational determination to defend the market advantages of his symbolic skills was (now) coexisting with a willingness to achieve this by militant, collective action. The RCA was hugely indignant that a government which had 'eulogised the Trade Unions generally and, through the Whitley Report, given its benediction to something that was apparently intended to go far beyond the ordinary recognition of the past' should tolerate the withholding of official recognition by one of its own agencies, the Railway Executive Committee.[52] One customary reason for non-recognition, failure to represent a majority of the staff, now had no validity since the Association organised over 60 per cent of the 100,000 clerical employees in the railway industry. As the executive explained to Conference, the RCA would have been accorded recognition some time earlier had it agreed to waive principles 'essential to the solidarity of organisation amongst clerical and administrative workers', namely the claim to organise supervisory staff. The executive

---

51. The report of the special February Conference is in *The Railway Clerk*, March 1918.
52. Ibid. for the General Secretary's report to the special conference.

asked for a strike mandate on the issue of recognition, and none endorsed this more forcefully than Romeril. In a rousing speech, he appealed for solidarity with their enlisted colleagues who were looking to the RCA to defend their livelihood with the same courage with which they were defending the country. The time for the 'old policy of persuasion' was past. His call for the executive to threaten the companies with a strike was carried by unanimous acclaim.

Cole and Page Arnot had considered in 1917 that the RCA was not ripe for a strike, for they had assumed that a general railway stoppage would arise from the militancy of the uniformed grades in the NUR and equated the propensity to strike with the class consciousness of manual workers. In fact, the white-collar workers preceded the blue-collar grades in the industrial offensive on the railways that followed the armistice. Faced by the continued opposition by the companies and the Board of Trade to its claim to represent the supervisory grades and stationmasters, the RCA called for a national strike in February 1919. Initially, Sir Albert Stanley, President of the Board of Trade, was disposed to back the Railway Executive Committee and the companies, but he was overruled by a majority in the Cabinet who admitted the need to extend white-collar unionism amongst the supervisory grades lest press and public opinion turn against the government.[53] After the government's retreat, the RCA withdrew its strike call. The significance of the Association's strike threat had not been lost on other organisations of white-collar workers: 'It would be a new experience', *The Shop Assistant* noted, '— a very salutary one — for the country to be confronted with a big strike movement by a large and moderate body of "workers by brain" such as the members of the RCA. Such a strike would be a significant manifestation of the "New Labour"'.[54] Railway clerks themselves felt that the strike threat had ruptured the personal ties of loyalty and deference to the companies which had been assiduously cultivated in the traditions of railway service. One member wrote in the Association's journal that, not so many years previously:

> If someone had told many of [our members] they would in 1919 be willing to participate in a strike he would have been considered a fit subject for a lunatic asylum . . . it is almost impossible for anyone outside the railway service to adequately realise what a revulsion of feeling and change of view have taken place. Ever since we joined the service, the idea of unswerving and unquestioning loyalty to the company we were employed by, had been so dinned into our ears that at last it had become almost an article of faith. . . . As late as only a few years ago railway clerks had a childlike belief in the good intentions of the companies. Today a change has come over the

53. See notes of a conference held at the Board of Trade with the RCA, CAB24/74 G.T. 6739; also K.O. Morgan, *Consensus and Disunity*, London, 1979, p. 48.
54. *The Shop Assistant*, 8 Feb. 1919.

scene, and this state of confidence has given way to an attitude of deep distrust and in many instances of grave suspicion. To the vast majority the very thought of a strike meant, not very long ago, a sense of personal degradation, and an agony of spirit, yet the determination to come out was, at the very last, absolutely unanimous.[55]

The transformation of the attitudes towards collective organisation and militant wage-bargaining which took place amongst lower-grade civil servants during the war and its aftermath was even more remarkable than that which occurred amongst the railway salariat. In 1914 civil servants were densely, but ineffectively organised in a large number of departmental associations with little formal structure, no access to Head of Departments or the Treasury and whose activities were largely confined to organising round robin petitions, and occasionally getting a question asked in Parliament about civil service matters. By 1920 the civil service unions had forced the government to set up and admit them to an elaborate system of conciliation, they were seriously considering a strike policy, some had affiliated to the Labour Party and they were in process of the amalgamation which would lead to the forming of the Civil Service Clerical Association as an interdepartmental organisation of most civil service clerical staff. The lower clerical staff were evincing a political radicalism which had no precedent in the prewar world.

The causes of this transformation have been fully discussed by Humphreys and others and will be only briefly reiterated here.[56] First in order of time (and probably of importance) was the very adverse position in which the traditions of Civil Service wage-bargaining, and the direct relationship with governments charged with the control of inflation, placed civil servants *vis-à-vis* the rise in the cost of living. During the first year of the war, there were no changes in civil service salaries at all and some had been virtually static for ten to forty years.[57] Mounting discontent with real hardship, and the influx of temporary employees and temporary bureaucrats with 'market' conceptions alien to Service traditions, broke down the system of departmental petitioning for salary awards. The establishment, in November 1916, of a Conciliation and Arbitration tribunal in which the unions were recognised as negotiating bodies in individual departments acted as an immediate stimulus to organisation. Arbitration rights 'created an aura of respectability around unionism'.[58]

Secondly, the wartime expansion of the Civil service hastened changes

55. *The Railway Clerk*, 15 March 1919.
56. B.V. Humphreys, *Clerical Unions in the Civil Service*, Oxford, 1958, pp. 78–128; also V.L. Allen, *Trade Unions and the Government*, London, 1960, pp. 71–89.
57. Humphreys, *Clerical Unions in the Civil Service*, p. 82.
58. Ibid., p. 97.

in its bureaucratic structure which were formally endorsed by the Reorganisation Committee of 1920. These tended to greater uniformity amongst the clerical employees of different departments. Several departmental classes were absorbed into general classes common to the Service whose structure (to this day largely unchanged) was prescribed by the 1920 committee.[59] One effect of bureaucratic reorganisation was to alter patterns of promotion and sharpen the divide between clerical and executive grades. Prior to this bureaucratic change grievances had arisen largely within different departments at different times; after it, they tended to arise simultaneously amongst general service classes.

Thirdly, the government which endorsed the recommendations of the Whitley Committee Report found it difficult to resist their extension to its own employees (although it had a good try). Faced by mounting unrest amongst clerical officers in the spring of 1919, the government agreed to a Whitley Council for the Civil Service which had the function of negotiating general conditions of service including wages and working conditions.[60] The institution of the Whitley system propelled the civil servants to the amalgamation of their own organisations, for they were too many to negotiate effectively on the Joint Council.

Fourthly, changes in the political consciousness of enlisted and wartime civil servants had taken place independently of material and bureaucratic change. Demobilised ex-servicemen clerks formed a special and radical interest group within the postwar Civil Service and they are a group with whom we can clearly identify a relationship between military service, a raising of expectations and new-found support for left-wing politics. In 1916, the Assistant Clerks Association held a referendum which gave majority approval to affiliation to the Labour Party. At the time, the significance of this was debatable since so many members were in the army, but the links between the clerical Civil Service unions and Labour grew stronger with the return of demobilised men and it was to the Labour Party that the unions first turned when seeking political allies in its conflict with the Treasury over the starting-pay controversy.[61]

Affiliation to the Labour Party provides one issue where the 'proletarianisation' thesis has, *prima facie*, a limited validity, especially in view of the fact that affiliation to the Party divided the organisations of clerical employees from the new associations of genuinely professional workers. The normative change was not the revolution in conscious-

59. See the *Report of the Royal Commission on the Civil Service*, PP 1930–31, Cmd 3909, pp. 5–8.
60. Humphreys, *Clerical Unions in the Civil Service*, pp. 110–28.
61. Ibid., pp. 98–105; also Allen, *Trade Unions and the Government*, pp. 77–8. The 'starting-pay' controversy arose over the terms on which temporary clerks were to be absorbed into the established Civil Service in the postwar period.

ness implied by that cumbersome term, but it can scarcely be denied that participation in the Labour movement indicated some considerable shift in the attitudes and values of Civil Service clerical workers. (There are obvious difficulties in assessing rank-and-file sentiments from the political policies of the clerical organisations but these apparently reflected the feelings of large numbers.)[62] However, this shift in attitudes and values cannot, I believe, be assessed in isolation from the change in the character of the Labour Party itself. When the Party was reconstructed in 1918, Sidney Webb and fellow *étatiste* socialists placed great emphasis on the cross-class character of the new party ('of workers by hand and brain') in implied contrast with the prewar party of, almost exclusively, organised manual workers. The development of organisation amongst white-collar workers, particularly national and local government officers, was a social fact which accorded particularly happily with the 'classless' bureaucratic socialism Webb and others were trying to make the ideology of the party. Additionally, as the successor to the Liberal party, Labour was obliged to appeal to a coalition of social forces similar to the prewar Liberal constituency. Clerical workers were affiliating to a Labour Party which was less 'proletarian' but more 'socialistic'. As Hobsbawm has argued, the character of the socialism adopted by the party had a structural relationship with the *nouvelle couche sociale* of administrators, professional employees, teachers and upwardly-mobile white-collar workers which had made a comparatively belated appearance in late-nineteenth-century English society.[63] This was a stratum with an assured place in either the Webbian socialist commonwealth or advanced capitalism. Though the adoption of socialist values by clerical workers in government employment during and after the First World War is a profoundly interesting indication of war's impact on political consciousness, we must recall that these values included an abjuration of political change through the class struggle and were, in a sense, homologous with the awareness characteristic of public employees.

White-collar unionism in the private, manufacturing and commercial sectors had a quite different pattern of development between 1914 and 1921 as compared with the civil service or the railway industry. The explanation for much of this difference must surely lie in the more favourable conditions for organisation provided by larger, more bu-

---

62. Humphreys, *Clerical Unions in the Civil Service*, p. 105. The author provides extensive evidence for the political radicalisation of Civil Service clerical staff between 1918 and 1920. Affiliation to the Labour Party was outlawed by the 1927 Trade Disputes and Trade Union Act, passed after the General Strike (for which the Civil Service Clerical Association had voiced its sympathy although civil servants continued to work).

63. Hobsbawm, 'The Fabians Re-considered', in idem, *Labouring Men*, London, 1964, pp. 250–71.

reaucratised units of administration and the greater susceptibility of public service employment to political influences. (The railways remained, of course, privately-owned, although administered by a public body. It is worth noting that the railway clerks could reasonably believe that wartime state control had brought nationalisation — which they had long advocated — much closer.) The only organisation specifically for clerks in industry was the National Union of Clerks, although some were able to join the clerical sections of manual workers' unions and there did exist staff associations patronised and funded by employers. NUC membership grew very rapidly during the war (from under 11,000 members in 1915 to over 43,000 in 1919, of whom about one-quarter were in engineering) but these figures are quite illusory indications of the real strength of white-collar unionism in the private sector. The chief reason for the accession of new members was the work the Union undertook on their behalf before the wartime arbitration tribunals in order to secure war bonuses. The union's strategy which, as its historian noted, 'must often have seemed to the well-established unions to be unorthodox and even undignified, was necessarily conditioned, not only by the "contract status" of most of the members and by the "middle-class" traditions of many of them, but also by the financial weakness of the Union as an organisation'.[64]

Clerks flocked to the NUC in great numbers, but lapsed in batches as soon as their immediate claims were satisfied. In the first quarter of 1917 there were 5,000 new entrants, some of whom had lapsed by the end of the year, but nearly all requiring claims to be lodged for war bonuses or other concessions. This was a costly business for the union, which found it necessary to impose a qualifying period of membership as a condition of taking up claims for increased pay.[65] The problem of 'short-distance passengers' was even more acute during 1919 and 1920 when the rapid inflation temporarily drove clerks militating for salary increases into the Union's ranks.

The break in the inflationary spiral and the onset of unemployment brought a swift reversal in the Union's fortunes: numbers fell to 14,000 in 1921 and 7,000 in 1924. The Union was forced to reduce and then suspend benefit payments and came within measurable distance of liquidation.[66] Clerical unemployment has been seen as the chief reason for the collapse of white-collar unionism in the private sector (which ironically occurred at the point when the Engineering Employers' Federation agreed to recognise the NUC as a national negotiating body for white-collar engineering workers). While it was obviously one

64. F. Hughes, *By Hand and Brain*, London, 1953, p. 46.
65. Ibid., p. 50.
66. Ibid., p. 71.

reason, it seems insufficient explanation of the near-extinction of the NUC when compared with the far greater stability of the draughts-men's organisation whose members were concentrated in the industries most affected by unemployment. It would seem highly likely that the rapid fall in the cost of living and the relative improvement of the market advantages of salaried, clerical work over manual labour that occurred with the onset of depression were just as important as unem-ployment in the decline of clerical unionism. Inflation, the narrowing of differentials and wartime arbitration were manifestly conditions for the NUC's growth and the rapid turnover of membership demonstrates the instrumental, frankly egoistic attitudes of clerks to unionisation. It is probable, too, that the great mobility of clerical labour during the war period was a further condition for growth since this disrupted familiar relationships with known employers who would promote clerks and award increments on personal merit. Clerical workers recruited to the vastly expanded munitions establishments were exposed to the anony-mity of the wage market and adopted working-class bargaining prac-tices in default of their customary 'individualist' form of negotiation. With the onset of the depression these conditions no longer held. Some employers attempted to restore familiar relationships with their clerical employees by the encouragement of sports clubs, staff associations and by cultivating corporate loyalty.[67]

The unstable organisation of clerks in the private sector contrasts strongly with certain quasi-professional bodies, such as the Association of Engineering and Shipbuilding Draughtsmen, which evolved ex-tremely rapidly during the war but sustained most of their gains with the onset of the depression. The draughtsmen are particularly interest-ing because they became a politically militant body with the ambition to control the supply of their own labour; they were not 'proletarian-ised' as the classical Marxist concept would suggest, but formed an élite, technical vanguard resembling 'the new working class' as that term was understood by neo-Marxist theorists of the late 1960s.[68] The Association dated only from 1913 and at the beginning of the war organised only about four hundred draughtsmen in the shipbuilding and engineering trades; by 1920, it had enrolled 14,750 members or 90 per cent of eligible workers.

Commenting on the growth of organisation amongst the supervisory,

---

67. Klingender, *The Condition of Clerical Labour in Britain*, p. 81.
68. See A. Giddens, *The Class Structure of the Advanced Societies*, London, 1973, pp. 195–7, for the theory of the 'new working class'. The theory postulated that engineers, scientists and technicians would constitute a vanguard of the working class because they would come to experience in an acute form a 'contradiction' between the need for autonomous control over their work (the production of knowledge) and the bureaucratic exigencies of the organisation to which they were subject.

managerial and technical grades, the Ministry of Labour noted that the 'peculiar conditions created by the war would appear to have had a strong effect in breaking down obstacles to organisation'. Organised manual workers had kept pace with the rise in the cost of living: 'This was . . . not only an example of the advantage of organisation, but a very great inducement to common action of a drastic nature, since the supervisory, technical and clerical grades found themselves being left behind by manual workers who were their inferiors in training and education as well as in conventional standards of living . . .'. It added that the new organisations had 'entered the field just at the time when the question of industrial control is more prominent than ever before . . .'.[69] These grades were in a key position with respect to conflicts over control and their organisations were assiduously cultivated by the National Guilds League and by Cole and the Labour Research Department.

The draughtsmen evinced a political class consciousness which makes invocation of the concept of 'the new working class' by no means fanciful. They voted against application of the Whitley Report to their industry, and registered a decision to withdraw all connection with the Employment Exchanges and to control their own labour supply, as the first step to control of industrial conditions by the workers.[70] The hostility of engineering and shipbuilding employers to the organisation of their professional workers was undoubtedly a spur to this militancy. Employers were unwilling to allow the draughtsmen a 'separate identity' from themselves and subsequent events suggest that this was chiefly because the draughtsman's career would, not unusually, lead to supervisory, administrative and planning functions (for when limited recognition was eventually conceded in 1924 it excluded men exercising those functions). In 1917, the federated employers had refused to meet the Association in order to discuss a war bonus and in 1918 again refused to confer for discussion on a national wage policy for draughtsmen. In the meantime, the Association had affiliated with the TUC and early in 1919 it called its first strike.[71]

The draughtsmen's Association is only one example of the immense stimulus the war gave to the organisations of the professional salariat: a conference convened by the Labour Research Department in February 1919 for the purpose of setting up a National Federation of Professional, Technical, Administrative and Managerial Associations was attended by representatives of the Society of Technical Engineers, the Shipbuilding, Engineering and Iron and Steel Commercial Staffs Association, the Electrical Power Engineers' Association, the Association

69. Labour situation, week ending 7 May 1919, CAB24/78 G.T. 7186.
70. Ibid.
71. See Bain, *The Growth of White-collar Unionism*, pp. 151–2; also J.E. Mortimer, *A History of the Association of Engineering and Ship-building Draughtsmen*, London, 1960.

of Supervisory Electricians, as well as organisations of bank officials, law clerks and the staff employees of architects, accountants and surveyors.[72] All had evolved extremely rapidly since 1915. This conference revealed, however, that the draughtsmen were somewhat isolated from the other technical and professional societies by their industrial and political militancy. The majority of these societies were suspicious that, despite the disclaimers of the Labour Research Department, the new federation would seek to ally itself with organised labour (a move the draughtsmen had already made). The Society of Technical Engineers proposed, as an alternative to the suggested federation, an organisation of professional associations, independent of employers' organisations on the one hand and manual workers' unions on the other, 'and free to negotiate with both in the interests of the professional worker'. The Ministry of Labour commented: 'The societies which are promoting this scheme believe that the interests of the professional classes are not safe in the hand of labour, because manual workers cannot be trusted to value adequately the contribution made by the salaried officials. They therefore advocate the formation of a third party in industry representative of management and technical ability'.[73] In the climate of opinion created by the Whitley Report, the outlook for this 'third party' or professional institute policy was not sanguine; the basic assumption of the Report was that there were only two parties in industry and the efforts made by organisations of managerial and technical staff to obtain separate representation as third parties on Joint Industrial Councils met with little encouragement in 1919 and 1920. However, the longer-term results of Whitleyism outside the public sector were very modest and this may have favoured organisations adopting a 'third party' policy.[74]

When we recall what was said in an earlier chapter of the Middle Classes Union and the eruption of protest against high taxation, government spending and expensive social policies and reconsider the empirical material just discussed, then it is clear the war led to two generic types of middle-class militancy. It is tempting to identify them with the 'old' and the 'new' middle class respectively, although much more needs to be known about the connections between local Chambers of Commerce (and other organisations of the 'old' middle class) and the 'anti-waste' movement before this can be done with confidence. Office employees probably formed a high proportion of those attracted

72. See the Labour situation report, dated 28 Jan. 1920, for the preparation of this conference, CAB24/97 C.P. 521.
73. Labour situation report, 29 Jan. 1920, CAB24/97 C.P. 523.
74. For an interesting contemporary survey of lower professional organisations in manufacturing industries, see G.W. Thomson, 'Professional Workers and Organisations', *Sociological Review*, vol. XIX, July 1927.

to the Middle Classes Union and that organisation was certainly regarded as competing with the National Federation of Professional, Technical, Administrative and Supervisory Workers.[75] Even allowing for an overlapping affiliation, they remain generically different forms of militancy. The new white-collar unions and the professional associations were collectivities of workers, sharing a common market capacity and drawn together by the desire to regain and defend a place in the reward structure. The Middle Classes Union, by contrast, was an aggregate of consumers and taxpayers; its rhetoric suggests the classical ideal of a civil society composed of unattached individuals, free from the constraints of organised labour, federated capital and interventionist government. The upsurge of white-collar unionism that resulted from the war demonstrates that neither an aversion to collective organisation nor an anti-socialist political outlook were necessary features of the awareness of the black-coated worker. Black-coated industrial militancy sprang from a dislocation of normal market relations but, particularly in public service and analogous employment, it could become allied with social democracy in the search for a fair reward for skills and services.

75. This competition was noted in the Labour situation report, 18 Feb. 1920, CAB24/98 C.P. 960. The NFPTASW appears to have been the 'third party' organisation that the Society of Technical Engineers had proposed in February 1920.

# 8

## Secondary Education and Social Class

It is a characteristic of social classes that they are 'open' and the extent
and type of mobility between them has a crucial bearing on the form
the class structure will take in an historical context and people's
awareness of and responses to their class situation. In England, during
the first half of the twentieth century, differential access to selective
secondary education was of considerable importance in both stabilising
the class structure over time and facilitating such mobility as occurred
between social classes. This double relationship between educational
chances, social openness and social closure was one of the main findings
of the 1949 social mobility enquiry undertaken by the London School of
Economics. The type of secondary school a boy attended affected the
degree of association between parental and filial occupational status
and the survey showed that from this point of view it was the grammar
school (or its equivalent) which stood out sharply.[1] (Before 1944, only
those who attended grammar schools regarded themselves, and were
generally accepted as having had, a secondary education at all.) Given
a grammar school background, there was a high parental–filial association for subjects whose fathers were in the upper status categories and
a low association for subjects whose fathers were in the low status
categories. For the latter group of subjects, a grammar school education increased the distance ascended in the status scale; for the
former group, it reduced the distance descended. Furthermore, the
critical connections between education and social class were made at
the secondary stage; further education had only a reinforcing effect.
However, the type of education attained was highly dependent on
parental occupation in the first instance; boys born into the upper
strata of the occupational hierarchy in the last decade of the nineteenth
century had nearly ten times the chances of receiving a secondary
education as did the sons of skilled manual and routine clerical workers
and about seventeen times the chances of those born into the less-skilled
working class. For those of secondary school age in the 1930s differential

1. J.R. Hall, D.V. Glass, 'Education and Social Mobility', in D.V. Glass, ed., *Social
Mobility in Britain*, London, 1954, pp. 291–307, esp. p. 306. They found that of subjects
who attended grammar school or its equivalent, 33.7 per cent achieved status categories
1 or 2 (the professional, administrative and managerial strata of the middle class) while
only 3.2 per cent of those whose schooling was senior elementary achieved that status.

chances had narrowed to about four times and five times respectively.[2]

During the First World War there was both a growth in the total numbers of pupils at secondary schools and a modification of class differences in access to them. The onset of economic recession and the restriction of public expenditure by the Geddes Committee curtailed expansion, although in many localities it continued at a slower rate. The returns of the numbers of pupils at secondary schools eligible for grant in England are set out in Table 8.1 and it will be seen that numbers increased from about 150,000 in prewar years to about 330,000 by 1921–2. The significance of this period of growth in a longer-term context is illustrated by the graph of secondary-school expansion in south-west Hertfordshire (Watford) and Middlesbrough between 1904 and 1944 (Figure 8.1). In suburban Watford and its environs the post-1916 acceleration was much more marked than in working-class Middlesbrough, but in neither place can it be accounted for by an extrapolation of prewar trends.

The greater availability of secondary school education was, all things being equal, bound to improve the absolute chances of the working-class child receiving more than the minimum elementary education demanded by the law. There were more than twice as many working-class children at secondary schools in 1921 as there had been in 1913. There was, moreover, some improvement in his or her relative chances. In 1909, 18 per cent of boys and 18.6 per cent of girls on the grant list in England and Wales were the children of skilled and unskilled workers. In 1921, 22.5 per cent of boys and 23.7 per cent of girls at the secondary schools were workmen's children (see Table 8.2, p. 269 below).

This wartime expansion of secondary education was widely attributed to working-class prosperity. The Board of Education's account of 'The Recent Development of Secondary Schools' argued that: 'The sudden outburst of demand [for secondary-school places] as contrasted with the foregoing slow growth was certainly to a considerable extent due to "War" wages, which made the payment of fees at that time a comparatively easy matter . . . '.[3] Confirmation of this would seem to rest in the fact that it was the fee-payers coming from the public elementary schools who contributed most to the expansion. When the economy went into recession in 1921, the proportion of fee-payers from the public elementary schools declined sharply:[4] they were 38.5 per

2. See J. Floud, 'The Educational Experience of the Adult Population of England and Wales as at July 1949', in ibid., pp. 98–134.

3. Board of Education, *Annual Report 1923–24*, PP 1924–5, Cd 2443, p. 23.

4. The percentages are given in a table of ages on date of admission of full-time secondary school pupils, PRO ED12/328/04987. The effects of the post-1921 depression on the educational aspirations of artisan families is amply documented in ED12/328 5.654/13.

**Fig. 8.1.** Provision of grammar-school places for boys in SW Hertfordshire, and Middlesbrough, 1904–44

Total number of places

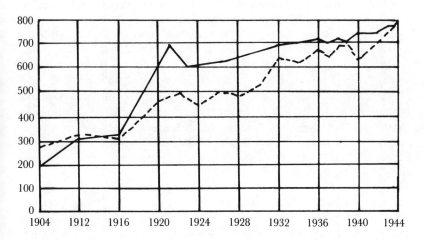

SW Hertfordshire ———  Middlesbrough-----

Reproduced from Jean Floud et al., *Social Class and Educational Opportunity*, London, 1957, p. 11.

cent of new entrants in 1919–20, but only 32 per cent in 1921–2.

Secondary schooling for the working-class child did not, of course, guarantee social mobility, but it made it much more likely. The secondary schools drew their pupils largely from professional, commercial and clerical milieux, but they despatched them in even greater numbers to these milieux. This is evident from Table 8.3 (see p. 270 below) which tends to exaggerate the flow from the secondary schools to manual employment, since many secondary-school educated boys whose first occupation was manual and industrial moved on to supervisory and managerial work. This was particularly true of boys from secondary schools who went into apprenticeships. In fact, the newer 'engineering' (as opposed to 'trade') apprenticeships of the interwar period were normally confined to ex-secondary-school boys and usually led to supervisory or managerial positions.[5]

5. See Ministry of Labour, *Report of an Enquiry into Apprenticeship and Training for the skilled occupations in Great Britain and Northern Ireland*, 1927–8, General Report, p. 88.

**Table 8.1.** Number of pupils at secondary schools eligible for grants in England, 1908–1925

| | Boys | Girls | (1) No. of schools | (2) LEA controlled schools | (1) Free placers | (2) as % of total | No. of pupils per 1,000 population England & Wales |
|---|---|---|---|---|---|---|---|
| 1908–09 | 135,766 | | 804 | — | 47,200[b] | 31.2[b] | — |
| 1909–10 | 73,273 | 62,401 | 841 | — | 50,146[b] | 31.8[b] | 4.4 |
| 1910–11 | 76,699 | 64,450 | 862 | — | — | — | — |
| 1911–12 | 79,321 | 66,288 | 885 | — | — | — | — |
| 1912–13 | 81,383 | 69,222 | 898 | — | 52,583 | 34.9 | — |
| 1913–14 | 91,347[a] | 78,889 | 910 | — | — | — | 5.5 |
| 1914–15 | 96,039 | 84,468 | 929 | — | 65,799[b] | 33.1[b] | — |
| 1915–16 | 99,205 | 90,282 | 931 | — | — | — | — |
| 1916–17 | 103,819 | 94,940 | 931 | 440 | — | — | — |
| 1917–18 | 113,460 | 103,519 | 943 | 444 | — | — | — |
| 1918–19 | 128,454 | 117,539 | 961 | 455 | 72,386 | 29.4 | — |
| 1919–20 | 147,268 | 134,840 | 1,022 | 524 | 82,632 | 29.3 | 8.1 |
| 1920–21 | 160,779 | 150,979 | 1,076 | — | 95,107 | 30.5 | — |
| 1921–22 | 170,088 | 160,384 | 1,115 | — | 107,301 | 32.5 | — |
| 1922–23 | 171,393 | 160,427 | 1,129 | 590 | 113,405 | 34.2 | — |
| 1923–24 | 170,850 | 156,751 | 1,137 | 600 | 112,332 | 34.3 | — |
| 1924–25 | 327,281 | | 1,145 | — | 130,188[b] | 36.2[b] | 9.5 |

a.: Change in date of enumeration   b. Figures for England and Wales

**Table 8.2.** Secondary schools on the grant list, England and Wales; pupils classified according to occupation of father

| | Totals | | Percentages | | |
| --- | --- | --- | --- | --- | --- |
| | 31 Jan. 1913 | 31 March 1921 | 31 Jan. 1909 | 31 Jan. 1913 | 31 March 1921 |
| **1. Number of boys** | | | | | |
| Total | 92,923 | 171,774 | 100.00 | 100.00 | 100.00 |
| *Occupation of father* | | | | | |
| Ministers of religion | 1,815 | 2,404 | 2.3 | 2.0 | 1.4 |
| Teachers | 3,649 | 5,383 | 3.7 | 3.9 | 3.1 |
| Members of other professions | 11,990 | 20,827 | 12.6 | 12.9 | 12.1 |
| Farmers | 5,147 | 9,215 | 5.7 | 5.5 | 5.4 |
| Wholesale traders (proprietors and managers) | 9,323 | 15,443 | 11.0 | 10.0 | 9.0 |
| Retail traders (proprietors and managers) | 17,809 | 30,625 | 19.5 | 19.2 | 17.8 |
| Traders assistants | 894 | 1,401 | 0.9 | 1.0 | 0.8 |
| Contractors | 2,119 | 3,804 | 2.6 | 2.3 | 2.2 |
| Minor officials | 4,547 | 8,312 | 4.5 | 4.9 | 4.8 |
| Clerks, commercial travellers, agents | 12,915 | 13,016 | 13.2 | 13.9 | 14.0 |
| Postmen, policemen, seamen, soldiers | 2,034 | 6,526 | 1.9 | 2.2 | 3.8 |
| Domestic and other servants | 1,788 | 3,020 | 1.8 | 1.9 | 1.8 |
| Skilled workmen | 15,112 | 33,815 | 15.8 | 16.3 | 19.7 |
| Unskilled workmen | 2,254 | 4,795 | 2.2 | 2.4 | 2.8 |
| No occupation given | 1,527 | 2,178 | 2.3 | 1.6 | 1.3 |
| **2. Number of girls** | | | | | |
| Total | 81,500 | 165,062 | 100.00 | 100.00 | 100.00 |
| *Occupation of father* | | | | | |
| Ministers of religion | 1,650 | 2,513 | 2.2 | 2.0 | 1.5 |
| Teachers | 3,381 | 5,569 | 4.0 | 4.2 | 3.4 |
| Members of other professions | 10,625 | 19,707 | 12.6 | 13.0 | 11.9 |
| Farmers | 4,107 | 9,013 | 4.8 | 5.0 | 5.5 |
| Wholesale traders (proprietors and managers) | 7,850 | 14,049 | 10.5 | 9.6 | 8.5 |
| Retail traders (proprietors and managers) | 15,271 | 27,837 | 18.6 | 18.7 | 16.9 |
| Traders' assistants | 842 | 1,321 | 1.1 | 1.0 | 0.8 |
| Contractors | 1,856 | 3,773 | 2.5 | 2.3 | 2.3 |
| Minor officials | 3,815 | 7,867 | 4.4 | 4.7 | 4.8 |
| Clerks, commercial travellers, agents | 10,772 | 21,672 | 12.4 | 13.2 | 13.1 |
| Postmen, policemen, seamen, soldiers | 1,845 | 6,451 | 2.1 | 2.3 | 3.9 |

**Table 8.2** *continued*

|  | Totals | | | Percentages | |
|---|---|---|---|---|---|
|  | 31 Jan. 1913 | 31 March 1921 | 31 Jan. 1909 | 31 Jan. 1913 | 31 March 1921 |
| Domestic and other servants | 1,589 | 3,172 | 2.1 | 2.0 | 1.9 |
| Skilled workmen | 13,850 | 33,853 | 16.9 | 17.0 | 20.5 |
| Unskilled workmen | 2,100 | 5,228 | 2.7 | 2.6 | 3.2 |
| No occupation given | 1,947 | 3,037 | 3.1 | 2.4 | 1.8 |

*Source*: Statistics of Public Education

**Table 8.3.** Secondary schools on the grant list, England and Wales, 1925/6

| Occupation | Occupations of fathers of all pupils in the schools | | | Occupations (as known) taken up by pupils who left school during or at the end of the school year | | |
|---|---|---|---|---|---|---|
|  | Boys | Girls | Total | Boys | Girls | Total |
| Teaching profession | 3.5 | 3.8 | 3.6 | 5.7 | 29.0 | 14.2 |
| Other professional, commercial and clerical | 60.5 | 59.8 | 60.2 | 65.8 | 63.9 | 65.1 |
| Industrial and manual | 31.4 | 31.7 | 31.5 | 22.5 | 5.8 | 16.4 |
| Agricultural and rural | 4.6 | 4.7 | 4.7 | 6.0 | 1.3 | 4.3 |

*Source*: Ministry of Labour, *Report of the Committee on Education & Industry, Second Part*, 1928, Appendix IV, p. 76

# 9

## Summary and Conclusions

In a study often preoccupied with local detail, the wider context of the international conflict has frequently disappeared from view. This is unfortunate because in many respects the war's consequences for English society were secondary to, and flowed from, its consequences for the world system of competing sovereign states and international capitalist trade and finance. It is obvious enough, but will bear repeating, that to a considerable degree the structure of English society before 1914 was determined externally by Britain's position in the international system of political power and the global division of labour and economic resources. Admittedly, 'to a considerable degree' is one of those weasel phrases which covers up an inability to specify the degree! However lamely expressed, the gist of the claim can be established by reference to the steady extraversion of Britain's economy that proceeded apace with industrialisation (and was, in turn, the principal motor of imperial expansion) and to her pivotal position in the prewar international monetary and trading system. The interdependence between Britain and the rest of the world reached its peak in the 1870–1914 era, as a result of the concentration of her resources on a limited range of industries exporting high proportions of total outputs, the scale of Britain's investment overseas, and the City of London's dominance of international financing. These factors made Britain the hub of a multilateral trading system.[1] Their influence on social structure was manifested in the shrunken size of the agricultural labour force, the concentration of manual workers in export industries and in the part played by overseas investment in sustaining the wealth of the upper class.

It was the simultaneity of the war's politically revolutionary aftermath with its impact on international economic arrangements which made it such a great axis of modern history. The war accomplished the destruction of the autocratic monarchies of Central and Eastern Europe, undermined the multilateral capitalist world economy, shifted economic and political power away from Western Europe to America and Japan (whose industrialisation it rapidly accelerated) and within Western Europe weakened the liberal parties and interest groups who had

1. I have drawn on the discussion in D.H. Aldcroft and H.W. Richardson, *The British Economy 1870–1939*, London, 1969, pp. 62–5.

presided over the expansion of industrial capitalism. Since the war ushered in a division between capitalist and socialist states (and, subsequently, democratic and fascist regimes), it brought an epochal change in the international context in which the advanced societies developed. Major, long-term societal consequences stemmed from this distruption of the world economic and political order. For example, the split between reformist Labour movements, now included within the political system of their respective countries, and revolutionary socialist parties affiliated to the Communist International, though it originated in prewar schisms in social democracy, was everywhere deepened and hardened by the experience and results of the war.

These societal consequences stemming from the new international order overlaid adjustments in the social and political structures of the combatant states determined by the level of military technique required to wage it. The social relations of warfare were shaped by the level of development of the forces of destruction in a way that vindicates the claim of Marx that the 'human slaughter industry brilliantly confirmed' his theory of historical materialism.[2]

Generally speaking, warfare and the control of military power were never clearly related to the core principles of Marx's historical thought, and the possibility of wars once begun having an autonomous force in history was not envisaged.[3] The longer-term results of the First World War, especially with regard to the international balance of power, highlight the defects and absences of a theory too exclusively concerned with the social. Nevertheless the conduct of the war suggests (in the sketch I offer) the preponderance of military technique over other factors in determining the social organisation of the belligerents.

The conduct of the war was dominated by the heavy gun and constrained by the superiority of the defensive. Developments in armaments technology since the later nineteenth century had enormously increased the weight of firepower which could be brought to battle without any commensurate increase in its mobility once armies had left their railheads. In consequence, infantry offensives ground to a halt both for want of covering bombardments when they outstripped the range of their own artillery and to let the guns catch up. This relative immobility of firepower rendered decisive military breakthroughs elusive and imposed a static character on the war. Those changes in military practice which enhanced the advantages of the defensive were

2. Marx to Engels, 7 July 1860: 'Is there anywhere where our theory that the organisation of labour is determined by the means of production more brilliantly confirmed than in the human slaughter industry?', *Marx and Engels: Selected Correspondence*, London, 1936, p. 209.

3. See W.B. Gallie, *Philosophers of Peace and War*, Cambridge, 1978, for an appreciative but critical analysis of Marx's and Engels' view on war's role in history, esp. p. 75.

the use of barbed wire, the digging of increasingly secure trenches to protect infantry, and the deployment of machine-guns in ever greater numbers. It was these technical possibilities and constraints which determined that for most of its duration this was a war of attrition on its major fronts: between October 1914 and March 1918 no attack or series of attacks was able to move the line of the Western Front as much as ten miles in either direction.[4] The failure of Eastern outflanking movements on the part of the Allies confirmed the dominant belief that victory would be won where the greatest concentration of enemy power lay: in France and Flanders. Offensive strategy came to consist of assembling huge concentrations of artillery to pour preliminary bombardments on sectors of the enemy front in the hope that the physical and moral devastation would permit the infantry to occupy his lines and engage in open warfare: 1.75 million shells were fired off by the British in the preliminary bombardment to the Somme; over 4 million in that preceding Passchendaele.[5] This strategy expended life and *matériel* in prodigious fashion and placed great stresses on the populations and industrial resources of the combatants. It was a strategy which demanded the total mobilisation of the economy and manpower in a way which (to offer an illuminating contrast) the *Blitzkrieg* methods of Germany during the opening years of the Second World War did not. The elusiveness of a resolution to the war on the battlefield meant that the Home Fronts acquired ever greater significance as the stalemate was prolonged.

Military technique and strategy determined that the combatants experienced similar crises of munitions supply after the opening months of the war; they made comparable efforts to augment and rationalise production; and instituted similar measures to resolve the conflict between industry and the military in the competition for manpower. War collectivism took different forms, but common elements were collaboration between organised capital and the state, and the accommodation of patriotic, organised labour (even Russia experienced something like the latter with the election of labour delegates to her War Industries Committees). Furthermore, the mobilisation of the combatants' economies set up a common range of pressures which included population movements to industrial centres, price and wage inflation, shortfalls of labour and industrial skills, shortages of food, fuel and accommodation, labour militancy, profiteering and its accompanying popular discontent. The rhythms and social patterns of everyday life, and its customary social sanctions, were in every state profoundly disturbed.[6]

4. J.F.C. Fuller, *The Conduct of War 1789–1961*, London, 1972, p. 160.
5. Ibid., p. 171.
6. A point made by Barrington Moore, Jr., with respect to Imperial Germany, but

It may be that the uprooted quality of wartime daily life encouraged a closer sense of identity between the working classes and the nation, for the disruption of accustomed norms and the chronic anxiety of wartime made (if this supposition is correct) common nationality a source of values, consolation (for the bereaved) and psychological security. This was the greatest of all wars of nationality, and once the initial patriotic fervour had subsided nationalist ideologies legitimised the war and defined its objectives.[7] A demotic nationalism — different in tone and style from the patriotism of the *union sacrée*, the *Burgfrieden* and the voluntary British enlistment of August 1914 — was in most states a legacy of war. *John Bull* was its English voice. Its political expressions were the Conservative-dominated coalition government of postwar Britain, the *Bloc National* in France, the broadening base of the 'new' radical right in Italy and Germany, and the determination of the majority SPD to preserve national unity in coalition with deeply reactionary forces. Political nationalism was far from being a straight-forwardly integrative force, but it could now draw upon a more inclusive and deeply sedimented sense of national identity in societies which had conscripted millions of young men and directed large proportions of their civilian labour force to national war work.

Despite greater national cohesiveness, the pressures generated by the mobilisation of the combatants' economies greatly accentuated the force of social divisions. Inflation, caused by the expansion of govern-ment credit, the greater volume of 'inconvertible' paper money and the high price the state was forced to pay for goods and services, was acutely divisive because it had such disparate effects on different social groups. High prices, inequalities in distribution and the official re-straints placed on labour undermined the moral community of patriot-ism and created a pent-up discontent which broke out into widespread industrial conflict in the aftermath of war: the '40-hour' strikes and the stoppages in the mines, in engineering and on the railways in Britain, the General Strike in France, the strike wave in postwar America, all followed a similar pattern of class conflict erupting in a political context dominated by the nationalist right.

In the foregoing I have tried to indicate the importance of economic and political change at an international level, due to the war, for social development and to sketch out the general relationship between mili-tary technique and wartime social organisation. My remarks are much too brief to do justice to these themes which should, properly, form the subject of a full-length, comparative study. Their presence is justified

---

clearly applicable to Britain, France and Russia; see idem, *Injustice: the Social Bases of Obedience and Revolt*, London, 1979, p. 276.

7. J. Roberts, *A General History of Europe 1880–1945*, London, 1967, p. 265.

here, I believe, as a corrective to a social history too preoccupied with popular mentalities and experience. Tacit agreement has — largely — left the history of class, social conflict and popular consciousness to radical historians while politics, states and the international state system have been reserved for their more conservative colleagues. The result for social history has been a certain blindness to the way societies and structures of social power in the modern world depend on the integrity of the state for their persistence.[8] There has been, too, an unwillingness to acknowledge that solidity of the modern state which comes from its being a popularly accepted, legitimate focus for national identity in a language community. The fact that the state is implicated in the class inequalities of capitalist society — its disparities of property and power — has made its focal role seem unreal or illusory. In fact, the national unity embodied in the state has, for many, been the most real aspect of its existence. The sacrifices made on behalf of the working-class movement and of socialism in Britain have been as nothing compared with those her citizens have made, more or less willingly, for the nation-state. The state — we are told — is character-ised by its monopoly of legitimate violence in a continuously bounded territory; what this formula overlooks is the state's ability to *elicit* violence and military obedience from men whose lives and habits of thought are, in the vast majority, peaceful.

This is to digress from the main themes of a book which has attempted to trace the relationship between the first total war and some aspects of a complex process of social differentiation we call, mislead-ingly, the class structure. The first point to stress by way of conclusion is the incompleteness of the enquiry. There are several crucial issues which need detailed investigation before the question with which I began can be said to be answered: far more needs to be known about the structuration of the upper class after 1914 and the recruitment to and relationships between the financial, industrial and administrative elites; the longer-term changes in the styles of life of middle-class professionals and black-coated workers demand detailed and sym-pathetic examination. But no individual historian could exhaustively answer the question: 'How did the first total war affect the class structure of English society?' The most one can achieve is an empirical examination, tolerably consistent with a body of social theory, of a number of problems subsumed by it.

Before summarising the conclusions of that examination, a second and more formidable difficulty must be raised and faced. All advanced industrialised societies have experienced rapid change as a matter of

8. T. Skocpol goes some way to correcting this narrowness of vision in her *States and Revolutions*, Cambridge, 1979.

course: change in their technological infrastructure, the size of capital units, the productivity of labour, the distribution of the work force between industrial sectors, in rates of social mobility and in levels of educational provision. How, we must ask, is it possible to isolate the effects of the war from the inherently dynamic character of the society we are studying? Henry Pelling, in his study of the Second World War, points out that it was assumed too frequently in the postwar period that changes which had occurred since 1939 were the direct outcome of the war, but as historians were able to get a clearer picture of long-term trends, then what was ascribed to the impact of the war could be seen as having more deep-seated causes: 'All too often the observer . . . had failed to avoid the commonest of historical pitfalls, the fallacy of *post hoc, ergo propter hoc*'.[9] That pitfall would appear to be still more of a hazard with respect to an earlier war which was shorter, involved less state intervention in the economy and labour market and was followed by a speedier and more complete return to economic 'normalcy'.

Furthermore, if we need to maintain a healthy scepticism about the causal relationship between war and social change, we also need to keep in perspective the dimensions of change within English society. One way of doing this is by international comparison. As Alan Milward suggests: 'Were we to ask a citizen of Japan, Russia or Germany whether he perceived an extraordinary degree of change in our society over the period from 1914, and were he to use his own society as a yardstick, he might well reply that he did not'.[10] Milward questions whether the effects of the world wars on the international economy were not more serious for the British domestic economy than their effects on the purely domestic scene; a query I have reiterated in a slightly different vein. Neither Pelling nor Milward are concerned directly with the problem of the relationship between total war and class structure but their comments would lead us to doubt whether historical change in the class structure between 1914 and 1924 was either the result of the war or (even if that has been satisfactorily demonstrated) very considerable. Comparison with Germany, where capital holdings have twice almost been wiped out in the aftermath of war, underlines the fact that in one of its important aspects the English class structure has enjoyed a high degree of continuity in spite of the wars.

Would the class structure of English society have been much different in 1924 had the Archduke's driver not taken the wrong turning in 1914 and the European powers avoided continental war for another decade? Certain contemporaries believed that England was about to

9. H. Pelling, *Britain and the Second World War*, London, 1970, p. 297.
10. A.S. Milward, *The Economic Effects of the Two World Wars on Britain*, London, 1970, p. 24.

experience unprecedented class conflict when the war broke out. 'I always recognised' wrote Masterman 'that the race was between the vertical and horizontal divisions. The vertical just won — and I think by a few years.'[11] Bevin argued before the Transport Workers' Enquiry that in 1914 the country was on the eve of 'one of the greatest industrial revolts the world has ever seen . . .'.[12] It does, indeed, seem probable that the prewar strike wave would have continued into 1915. If we exclude the miners from the statistics of working days lost through strikes (their national strike in 1912 greatly inflates the figure for that year) there is no sign of a declining trend in industrial disputes. New upheavals were expected in mining, on the railways and in engineering while organisation was proceeding rapidly amongst less skilled groups. The underlying causes of the strike wave — inflation and full employment — remained. There seems no reason to believe that the acerbity of industrial conflicts which had led to the use of troops against strikes and the imposition in some instances of martial law would have been any less bitter. There are, however, reasons for thinking that a prolongation of the strike wave would have been contained within the sphere of industrial conflict and not spilt over into a general political confrontation with the state. One is the conservatism of the great majority of trade union leaders, many of whom were drawn into strikes not of their own choosing during 'the Great Unrest'; another the rapid spread, under official auspices, of organised collective bargaining which gave the unions a recognised status within capitalist society and limited trade unionism's revolutionary potential.

It is difficult to discern the likely impact of continued international peace and prolonged industrial conflict on the configuration of politics. Their main trends (or putative trends) are in any case a contentious matter amongst historians. Some have argued that Liberalism had successfully made an adjustment to the shift from 'cultural politics' to 'class-based' politics that took place in early-twentieth-century Britain.[13] It had, so the argument runs, secured an electoral base amongst the urban working class with a social reform programme derived from the 'New Liberalism'. Labour had not broken from the electoral confines to which Liberal toleration (and the Gladstone– MacDonald entente) confined it during the two 1910 General Elections, and showed little sign of doing so in the by-elections which preceded the outbreak of war. There are indications that Labour was strengthening its organisation and, despite major internal dissensions over National Insurance, Women's Suffrage and other issues, growing in self-confidence, but it was far more likely to suffer from a rupture of

11. C.F.G. Masterman, *England After the War*, London, 1922, p. xii.
12. PP 1920, Cmd.936, p. 495.
13. Most notably P.F. Clarke, *Lancashire and the New Liberalism*, Cambridge, 1971.

the entente with the Liberals than the Liberals themselves. Cole, writing in 1913, was convinced that: 'If a General Election came tomorrow, there is not the least doubt that Labour would lose many seats, and that those it retained would belong to it by Liberal favour and sufferance'.[14] Labour's electoral subordination to Liberalism was complemented by its indistinct political identity: it studiously refused to call itself a socialist party and only seven of its thirty-nine MPs in the 1914 Parliament were socialists, the rest Liberals, 'often' — as Cole put it — 'of the mildest type'. As has been pointed out, there were significant regional variations in the pattern of relations between Liberalism and Labour,[15] but there is no conclusive evidence that Labour was poised to replace Liberalism as the main anti-Unionist party. The notion that it was 'bound by the some inexorable sociological law [to do so], would have seemed absurd, not only to most Liberals, but to most Labour men as well'.[16]

When we turn from Labour to the far left of the political spectrum then there seems still less reason to believe that the industrial class conflict of the prewar years was, in itself, abetting revolutionary and socialist politics. Membership of the British Socialist Party was declining in the two years before the war and its remaining adherents were demoralised and inactive. The Independent Labour Party was troubled by internal dissentions which culminated in the resignation of its best-known figures from its NAC. Neither party found an adequate response to the labour unrest, which partly accounts for the attractiveness of syndicalism to rank-and-file militants in the South Wales coalfield and elsewhere, although syndicalism's limited support and inchoate doctrines indicate that it was scarcely a serious alternative to socialist politics.

It is, in the end, idle to speculate about what would have happened to the configuration of politics had the war not broken out. Class, and other structural factors, set limits to politics but do not determine them in any precise sense. The fortunes of political parties are contingent in the short and even the medium term on quite local decisions and issues (such as, to give an early-twentieth-century example, Chamberlain's Tariff Reform campaign). We can, nevertheless, make the assumption that the general arrangements of the capitalist economy and polity would have been maintained intact and then ask whether certain features of the empirical class system of the early 1920s would have

---

14. G.D.H. Cole, *The World of Labour*, London, 1913, p. 395.
15. A.W. Purdue, 'The Liberal and Labour Parties in North-East Politics 1900–14: the Struggle for Supremacy', *International Review of Social History*, vol. XXVI, 1981, pt. 1. Compare with K. Laybourn, J. Reynolds, *Liberalism and the Rise of Labour 1890–1918*, London, 1984, esp. p. 178: this latter study is based on West Yorkshire.
16. D. Marquand, *Ramsay MacDonald*, London, 1977, p. 151.

been evident had the war not broken out. There are techniques for making such a thought experiment an invaluable tool of historical enquiry with respect to quantifiable problems in economic and demographic history and they could be usefully addressed to several questions relevant to the empirical form of the class structure. It is the case, for example, that in 1924 profits were taking a lesser share and salaries a greatly increased share of the national income, the share of rent had fallen considerably, average productivity per hour worked had increased and wage distribution was less dispersed. By a highly complex form of extrapolation it should be possible to construct a model of economic development which would tell us whether these changes would have occurred on the same scale had there not been a war. The difficulties in making such a calculation are profound (and the skills required beyond the competence of this author) but until it is made many of the assumptions about war and socio-economic change are unproven in the sense that the quantifiable difference between the postwar society and the notional society untouched by war has not been measured.

At the present, it is unrealistic to demand this degree of proof from social historians of the First World War and, in arguing that the war did indeed bring change, their yardstick of comparison is the society of 1914. The argument of this study can be summarised as the contention that there took place between 1914 and 1924 a concatenation of changes in English society which altered the specific form of the class structure but did not fundamentally disturb those processes of social differentiation which are generic to a capitalist market society. In brief, these changes were an elimination of much of the poverty of prewar England, a redistribution of national income in favour of the salariat and manual workers, a narrowing of working-class wage differentials and middle-class salary differentials, a reduction of some of the large incomes derived from wealth and some redistribution of that wealth, an expansion of the educational opportunities that led to white-collar employment and a strengthening of civic integration by the steps taken to include the working class and the Labour movement within a community of citizenship. It is, as yet, impossible to measure the contribution of the war towards effecting these changes by the method I have indicated but induction leads me to believe that the war was instrumental in bringing them as a linked series and compressing them within a brief span of time. The specific form of the class structure of the postwar period differed from that of Edwardian England principally in the greater economic and cultural homogeneity of the working class, although tendencies to homogenisation were also evident in the middle and upper classes. Connected with the changes I have itemised were alterations in social consciousness. The most important are to be explained chiefly by the disruption of customary, working-class frameworks of comparison and the antipathy between a popular 'moral economy' and the capitalist profit motive.

# ——————— Bibliography ———————

This bibliography lists those unpublished sources, official published papers and secondary works used in the preparation and writing of this book. It is arranged thus:

**1.** Unpublished primary sources
**2.** Published official primary sources
**3.** Newspapers, periodicals and reviews
**4.** Other contemporary sources
**5.** Diaries, memoirs, autobiography
**6.** Selected secondary works
**7.** Articles from learned journals
**8.** Unpublished theses and dissertations

## 1. Unpublished primary sources

(i) *At the Public Record Office*
CAB 23, CAB 24, CAB 27, CAB 37 — Cabinet papers and
memoranda
ED 10, ED 11, ED 12, ED 24 — Board of Education papers
HO 185 — (Home Office) Papers of the
Central Control Board
(Liquor Traffic)
INF 1/4 — Ministry of Information
papers
IR 64, IR 74, IR 75 — Inland Revenue papers
LAB 2, LAB 17, LAB 34 — Ministry of Labour papers
MAF 60 — Ministry of Food papers
MUN 3, MUN 4, MUN 5 — Ministry of Munitions papers
RECO 1 — Ministry of Reconstruction
papers
T 170, T 172 — Treasury papers

(ii) *At the Greater London Record Office*
London Charity Organisation Society: Annual Reports of the Council
and of the London District Committees, 1912–1920
EO/PS/3 — Chief Education Officer's papers

(iii) *At the London School of Economics and Political Science Library*
The London Intelligence Reports of the Local Government Board

Beveridge Collection on Munitions

(iv) *At the University of Warwick Modern Record Centre*
MSS 36 — Boxes of documents pertaining to the history of the Iron and
Steel Trades Confederation

(v) *At the House of Lords Record Office*
David Lloyd George papers

(vi) *At the Trades Union Congress Library*
Minute Book and Annual Reports of the London Trades Council
The Gertrude Tuckwell collection

(vii) *At the Birmingham Central Reference Library*
Birmingham Trades and Labour Council Minute Book and Annual
Reports

(viii) *At the National Library of Scotland*
Viscount Haldane papers

(ix) *At the University of London Library Depository*
Caroline Playne collection

## 2. Published official primary sources

(i) *Parliamentary Papers*

Annual General Reports of the Board of Education, 1908/9–1924/5
Annual Reports of the Commissioners of Inland Revenue, 1917–21
PP 1908, lix, Cd 4442, *Report of the Committee to inquire into the operation of
the Truck Acts*
PP 1908, cvii, Cd 3864, *Report of an Enquiry by the Board of Trade into
Working Class Rents, Housing and Retail Prices*

Earnings and Hours of Labour of the Workpeople of the United Kingdom:
PP 1909, lxxx, Cd 4545      — The Textile Trades
Cd 4844      — The Clothing Trades
PP 1910, lxxxiv, Cd 5806     — The Building and Woodworking Trades
PP 1911, lxxxviii, Cd 5814    — The Metal, Engineering and Shipbuild-
ing Trades
PP 1912–13, cviii, Cd 6053 — The Railway Service

PP 1910, xxxviii, Cd 5314   — *Report on Back-to-back houses*
PP 1914, xvi, Cd 7340       — Appendices to the Fourth Report of the
Royal Commission on the Civil Service
PP 1914–16, xxxi, *Report on the Administration of the National Relief Fund*

up to the 31st March, 1915

PP 1914–16, xxviii, *Report of the Departmental Committee appointed to inquire into the Conditions prevailing in the Coal Mining Industry due to the War*

PP 1914–16, xxv, *First report of the Central Control Board (Liquor Traffic)*

PP 1914–16, xxxix, *Report of the Earl of Derby on Recruiting*

PP 1916, xiv, Cd 8286, *Report on the Administration of the National Relief Fund up to the 31st March 1916*

PP 1917–18, xi, Cd 8512, *Final Report of the Departmental Committee on Juvenile Education in relation to employment after the war*

PP 1917–18, xi, Cd 8577, Summary of evidence and appendices to above

PP 1917–18, xv, Cd 8558, *Third Report of the Central Control Board (Liquor Traffic)*

PP 1917–18, xviii, Cd 8606, *Report of the Sub-Committee of the Ministry of Reconstruction on the Relations of Employers and Employed*

PP 1917–18, xviii, Cd 8516, *First Annual Report of the National War Savings Committee*

*Reports of the Commission of Enquiry into Industrial Unrest*:

PP 1917–18, xv, Cd 8662, North Eastern Area

Cd 8663, North Western Area

Cd 8664, Yorkshire and Midlands Area

Cd 8665, West Midlands Area

Cd 8666, London and South Eastern Area

Cd 8667, South Western Area

Cd 8668, Wales and Monmouthshire

Cd 8696, Summary by G.N. Barnes

PP 1917–18, xvii, *Report of the War Pensions Statutory Committee for 1916.*

PP 1918, xii, Cd 9230, *Report of the Machinery of Government Committee*

PP 1918, vii, Cd 8980, *Report of the Working Classes Cost of Living Committee*

PP 1918, ix, Cd 9107, *Interim Report of the Adult Education Committee of the Ministry of Reconstruction on Industrial and Social Conditions in relation to adult education*

PP 1918, xiii, Cd 9071, *Report of the Departmental Committee appointed by the Board of Trade to consider the position of the Iron and Steel Trades after the war*

PP 1918, xii, Cd 9073, *Report . . . on the position of the engineering trades after the war*

PP 1918, xii, Cd 9092, *Report . . . on the position of the shipping and shipbuilding industries after the war*

PP 1919, xiii, Cd 9236, *Ministry of Reconstruction: Report of the Committee on Trusts*

PP 1919, xxviii, Cmd 321, *Final Report of the Adult Education Committee of the Ministry of Reconstruction*

PP 1919, xxvi, Cmd 504, *Report of the physical examination of men of military age by National Service Medical Boards from Nov 1st 1917 to Oct 31st 1918*

PP 1919, xxiv, Cmd 501, *Memorandum on the causes of Labour unrest submitted to the National Industrial Conference*

PP 1919, xxiii, Cmd 288–1, Minutes of evidence and appendices to the Royal Commission on the Income Tax

PP 1920, xviii, Cmd 615, *Report of the Royal Commission on the Income Tax*

PP 1920, xxvii, Cmd 594, *Suggested taxation of wartime increases of wealth: Memorandum submitted by the Board of Inland Revenue to the Select Committee of the House of Commons*

PP 1920, xxiv, Cmd 936, *Report by a Court of Inquiry concerning Transport Workers—Wages and Conditions of Employment of Dock Labour*

PP 1920, xv, Cmd 968, *Report of the Departmental Committee on Scholarships and Free Places*

PP 1927, xi, Cmd 2800, *Report of the Committee on National Debt and Taxation*

PP 1927, xxiv, Cmd 2849, *Seventeenth Statistical Abstract for the United Kingdom for each of the fifteen years 1911–1925*

PP 1928–9, vii, Cmd 3282, *Final Report of the Committee on Industry and Trade*

PP 1930–1, x, Cmd 3909, *Report of the Royal Commission on the Civil Service*

(ii)  *Non-parliamentary papers*

**Board of Education**

*Annual Reports of the Chief Medical Officer, 1914–1919*

*Report of the Consultative Committee on Psychological Tests of Educable Capacity* (1924)

*Report of the Consultative Committee on the Education of the Adolescent* (1926)

*Report of the Departmental Committee on Private Schools* (1932)

*Report of the Consultative Committee on Secondary Education* (1938)

*Report of the Committee on Public Schools: the Public Schools and the General Education System* (1944)

**Board of Trade**

Industrial (War Inquiries) Branch: *Confidential Reports on the State of Employment in all occupations in the United Kingdom*

*Industrial Survey of the Lancashire Area (excluding Merseyside)* (1932)

*Industrial Survey of the North-East Coast Area* (1932)

**Committee on Industry and Trade**

*Factors in Industrial and Commercial Efficiency: Being part 1 of a Survey of Industries* (1927)

*Further Factors in Industrial and Commercial Efficiency: Being Part 2 of a Survey of Industries* (1928)

*A Survey of Metal Industries* (1928)

*A Survey of the Textile Industries* (1928)

Committee on National Debt and Taxation: *Minutes of Evidence and Appendices* (1927)

## Ministry of Labour

*Report on an Inquiry into the Conditions of Boy Labour on the Docks at Liverpool* (1920)

*Report of the Committee appointed to enquire into the present conditions as to the supply of female domestic servants* (1923)

*Report of an Investigation into the personal circumstances and industrial history of 10,000 claimants to unemployment benefit* (1924)

*Report of the Committee on Education and Industry: England and Wales:* Part 1 (1926); Part 2 (1928)

*Annual Report for 1929 of the Employment Committee of the Incorporated Association of Head Masters of Public Secondary Schools* (in cooperation with the Ministry of Labour)

*Report of the Port Labour Inquiry* (1931)

*Ministry of Labour Gazette*, 1926 through 1927 — returns of an enquiry into the Earnings and Hours of Labour of Workpeople in Great Britain and Northern Ireland in 1924

*Report of an Enquiry into Apprenticeship and Training for the skilled occupations in Great Britain and Northern Ireland* (1927–8)

## Ministry of Munitions

*Dilution of Labour Bulletin*, 1916–18
*Reports on Labour in Controlled Establishments*
*History of the Ministry of Munitions*, 12 vols. (1920–4)

## Ministry of Reconstruction

*Juvenile Employment during the War and After* (1918)

## 3. Newspapers, periodicals and reviews

**(i) Newspapers** (mostly consulted only occasionally)
*Birmingham Daily Post*
*Bristol Evening News*
*Bristol Times and Mirror*
*Cotton Factory Times* (read throughout 1912–20)
*Daily Chronicle*
*The Herald*
*Labour Leader*
*Manchester Guardian*
*The Times*
*West London Observer*
*Yorkshire Factory Times*

## (ii) Trade union newspapers and journals

Amalgamated Society of Engineers' *Monthly Journal and Record*

British Steel Smelters' and Tinplate Workers' *Monthly Report*
*The Clerk* (National Union of Clerks)
*The Ironworkers' Journal* (Associated Iron and Steel Workers)
*The Railway Clerk* (Railway Clerks' Association)
*The Railway Review* (National Union of Railwaymen)
*The Record* (Transport and General Workers' Union)
*The Shop Assistant* (National Amalgamated Union of Shop Assistants
    Warehousemen and Clerks)

## (iii) Reviews, periodicals, etc.
*Athenaeum*
*Cassell's Saturday Journal*
*Charity Organization Review*
*Contemporary Review*
*The Economist*
*Fortnightly Review*
*Hibbert Journal*
*The Highway*
*Journal of the Royal Statistical Society*
*The Nation*
*Nineteenth Century and After*
*Plebs*
*The Sociological Review*
*The Times Educational Supplement*

## 4. Other contemporary sources

(place of publication is London, unless otherwise stated)

Two exhaustive bibliographies of contemporary sources are:

M.E. Bulkley, *A Bibliographical Survey of Contemporary Sources for the Economic and Social History of the War*, Oxford, 1920

W. Chamberlin, *Industrial Relations in Wartime, Great Britain 1914–1918: An Annotated Bibliography*, 1940

J.E. Allen, 'Some Changes in the Distribution of the National Income during the War', *Journal of the Royal Statistical Society*, LXXXIII, 1920

I.O. Andrews, *The Economic Effects of the War upon Women and Children in Great Britain*, Washington, 1918

W.J. Ashley, Reports of the Intelligence Officer to the Birmingham Citizens' Executive Committee, 1914–1915, Birmingham

G.R. Askwith, *Industrial Problems and Disputes*, 1921

J.J. Astor et al., *The Third Winter of Unemployment*, 1923

E.W. Bakke, *The Unemployed Man*, 1933

Lady F.M. Bell, *At the Works*, 1907

E.L. Bogart, *Direct and Indirect Costs of the Great World War*, New York, 1920
*Charles Booth's London*, Harmondsworth, 1969, ed. A. Fried and R. Elman (selections from *Life and Labour of the People of London*)
A.L. Bowley, *The Change in the Distribution of the National Income 1880–1913*, Oxford, 1920
——, *The Nature and Purpose of the Measurement of Social Phenomena*, 1915, 1923
——, *Prices and Earnings in Time of War*, 1915
——, *Prices and Wages in the United Kingdom 1914–1920*, Oxford, 1921
——, *The War and Employment*, 1915
——, A.R. Burnett-Hurst, *Livelihood and Poverty*, 1915
——, M.H. Hogg, *Has Poverty Diminished?*, 1925
——, J.C. Stamp, *The National Income — 1924*, Oxford, 1927
V. Branford, P. Geddes, *The Coming Polity*, 1917
R.H. Brazier, E. Sandford, *Birmingham and the Great War*, Birmingham, 1921
British Association for the Advancement of Science, *Report on the Amount and Distribution of Income below the Income Tax Exemption Limit* (E. Cannan, A.L. Bowley et al.), 1910
C.V. Butler, *Social Conditions in Oxford*, 1912
——, ed., *Domestic Service*, 1916
G.G. Butler, *The Tory Tradition*, 1914
A. Carr-Saunders, *The Professions*, Oxford, 1927
——, D. Caradog Jones, *A Survey of the Social Structure of England and Wales*, 1927
S.J. Chapman, ed., *Labour and Capital after the War*, 1918
L. Chiozza Money, *Riches and Poverty: 1910*, 1913
H. Clay, 'The Distribution of Capital in England and Wales', *Trans. of the Manchester Statistical Society*, 1924–5
——, *The Problem of Industrial Relations*, 1929
G.D.H. Cole, *Labour in the Coal Mining Industry 1914–1921*, Oxford, 1923
——, *Labour in War-time*, 1915
——, *The Payment of Wages*, Fabian Res. Dept., 1918
——, *Trade Unionism and Munitions*, Oxford, 1923
——, *The World of Labour*, 1913, 1919
——, *Workshop Organization*, Oxford, 1923
——, 'Recent Developments in the British Labor Movement', *American Economic Review*, Sept. 1918
——, R. Page Arnot, *Trade Unionism on the Railways*, Fabian Res. Dept., 1917
D.H.S. Cranage, ed., *The War and Unity*, Cambridge, 1918
H. Dalton, *Some Aspects of the Inequality of Incomes in Modern Communities*, 1920
M.F. Davies, *Life in an English Village*, 1909
N.B. Dearle, *A Dictionary of Official War-time Organisations*, 1928
——, *An Economic Chronicle of the Great War for Great Britain and Northern Ireland, 1914–1919*, 1929
——, *Industrial Training*, 1914
P. Descamps, *La Formation sociale de l'anglais moderne*, Paris, 1914
P. Devinat, *Scientific Management in Europe*, 1927
S.P. Dobbs, *The Clothing Workers of Great Britain*, 1928

H.A.L. Fisher, *Educational Reform*, Oxford, 1918

P. Fitzgerald, *Industrial Combination in England*, 1927

Garton Foundation, *Memorandum on the Industrial Situation after the War*, 1916

——, *The Industrial Council for the Building Industry*, 1919

M. Ginsberg, 'Interchange between Social Classes', *The Economic Journal*, Dec. 1929, repr. in *Essays in Sociology*, 1931

A. Gleason, *Inside the British Isles, 1917*, 1917

——, *What the Workers Want*, 1920

E. Halévy, 'La politique de la paix sociale en l'Angleterre', n.p., 1919, repr. in *L'Ere des tyrannies*, Paris, 1933

J. Hallsworth, R.J. Davies, *The Working Life of Shop Assistants*, Manchester, 1910

M.B. Hammond, *British Labour Conditions and Legislation during the War*, New York, 1919

C.B. Hawkins, *Norwich: A Social Study*, 1910

L.T. Hobhouse, *The Rational Good: A Study in the Logic of Practice*, 1921

J.A. Hobson, *Democracy after the War*, 1917

F.J. Keeling, *Child Labour in the United Kingdom*, 1914

P. Kellogg, A. Gleason, *British Labor and the War*, New York, 1919

R. Kenney, *Men and Rails*, 1913

A.W. Kirkaldy, ed., *Labour, Finance and the War*, 1916

*The Land and the Nation: the Rural Report of the Liberal Land Committee, 1923–1925*, 1925

F. Lavington, *The English Capital Market*, 1921

W.T. Layton, *The Relations of Capital and Labour*, 1914

E. Llewelyn Lewis, *The Children of the Unskilled: An Economic and Social Study*, 1924

K. Lindsay, *Social Progress and Educational Waste: Being a Study of the 'Free Place' and Scholarship Systems*, 1926

M. Loane, *Neighbours and Friends*, 1910

C.S. Loch, *Charity and Social Life*, 1910

*London and Cambridge Economic Service: Occupational Change in Great Britain, 1911–1921*, Special Memo 17 by A.L. Bowley, 1926

——, *Numbers occupied in the industries of England and Wales, 1911–1921*, Special Memo 17A by A.L. Bowley (1926)

——, The British Motor Industry, Special Memo 18 by G.C. Allen (1926)

——, *The Economic Position of Great Britain*, Special Memo 23 by A.C. Pigou (1927)

London County Council, *The Education Act 1918: Scheme of the Local Education Authority*, 1920

W. McDougall, *Social Psychology*, 1908

J.M. MacTavish, *What Labour Wants from Education*, 1916

——, *Education in Relation to Labour and Industry*, 1919

A. Mansbridge, *An Adventure in Working Class Education*, 1920

C.F.G. Masterman, *The Condition of England*, 1909, 1911

——, *England After the War*, 1922

J. Morgan Rees, *Trusts in British Industry 1914–1921*, 1922

J.T. Murphy, *Compromise and Independence: An Examination of the Whitley Report*,

Sheffield Workers' Committee, 1917

——, *The Workers' Committee*, Sheffield, 1917

*New Survey of London Life and Labour*, ed. H. Llewellyn Smith, 9 vols., 1930–5

C. Norwood, *The English Tradition of Education*, 1929

W.A. Orton, *Labour in Transition*, 1921

C.S. Peel, *How We Lived Then*, 1929

M. Phillips, *The Young Industrial Worker*, Oxford, 1922

The Pilgrim Trust, *Men Without Work*, Cambridge, 1939

M.A. Pollock, ed., *Working Days*, 1926

H. Quelch, B. Belfort Bax, *A New Catechism of Socialism*, 1909

E. Rathbone, *How the Casual Labourer Lives*, Liverpool, 1909

Mrs P. Reeves, *Round About a Pound a Week*, 1914

S. Reynolds, *A Poor Man's House*, 1908

—— et al., *Seems So! A Working-class View of Politics*, 1911

D.H. Robertson, *The Control of Industry*, 1923

P. de Rousiers, *The Labour Question in Britain*, 1896

J.W.F. Rowe, *Wages in Practice and Theory*, 1928

B.S. Rowntree, *Poverty: A Study of Town Life*, 1899, 1902

——, *The Human Needs of Labour*, 1918

——, *Poverty and Progress*, 1941

——, M. Kendall, *How the Labourer Lives*, 1913

B. Russell, *The Principles of Social Reconstruction*, 1916

G. von Schulze-Gaevernitz, *The Cotton Trade in England and on the Continent*, 1895

J.W. Robertson Scott, *England's Green and Pleasant Land*, 1925; Harmondsworth, 1949

A. Siegfried, *Post-war Britain*, 1924

E.D. Simon, *How to Abolish the Slums*, 1929

D.H. Smith, *The Industries of Greater London*, 1933

J.C. Stamp, *British Incomes and Property*, 1916, 1922

L. Stoddard, *Social Classes in Post-war Europe*, New York, 1925

G. Sturt (pseud. Bourne), *Change in the Village*, 1912

R.H. Tawney, *The Sickness of an Acquisitive Society*, 1921

——, ed., *Secondary Education for All*, 1922

H. Tout, *The Standard of Living in Bristol*, 1938

Trades Union Congress: Parliamentary Committee of the TUC, Joint Committee on the Cost of Living, *Final Report*, 1922

——, *Education for Children Over Eleven*, 1926

W. Trotter, *Instincts of the Herd in Peace and War 1916–19*, 1953 ed.

H.M. Vernon, *Industrial Fatigue and Efficiency*, 1921

G. Wallas, *Human Nature in Politics*, 1910

J. Wedgwood, *The Economics of Inheritance*, 1929

E. Welbourne, *The Miners' Unions of Northumberland and Durham*, Cambridge, 1923

E. Wertheimer, *Portrait of the Labour Party*, 1929

*What Happened at Leeds*, Council of Workers' and Soldiers' Delegates, 1917

W.C.D. Whetham, *The War and the Nation*, 1917

——, C.D. Whetman, *Heredity and Society*, 1912
A. Williams, *Life in a Railway Factory*, 1915
Workers' Educational Association, *Educational Reconstruction*, 1916
——, *Tradition, Policy and Economy in English Education*, 1915
——, *What is Democratic Education?*, 1920
W.B. Worsfold, *The War and Social Reform*, 1919


## 5. Diaries, memoirs, autobiography

C. Addison, *Four and a Half Years*, 1934
——, *Politics from Within 1911–1918*, 1924
G.N. Barnes, *From Workshop to War Cabinet*, 1923
H.M. Burton, *There was a Young Man*, 1958
C. Carrington, *Soldier from the Wars Returning*, 1965
H.A.L. Fisher, *An Unfinished Autobiography*, 1940
A.M. Hale, *The Ordeal of Alfred M. Hale*, ed. P. Fussell, 1975
J. Hodge, *From Workman's Cottage to Windsor Castle*, 1931
A.S. Jasper, *A Hoxton Childhood*, 1969
D. Lloyd George, *War Memoirs*, 2 vol. ed., 1938
M. MacDonagh, *In London during the Great War*, 1935
L. Masterman, *C.F.G. Masterman*, 1939
S. Mays, *Reuben's Corner*, 1969
J.T. Murphy, *New Horizons*, 1942
A. Newton, *Years of Change*, 1974
E. Percy, *Some Memories*, 1958
C.C. Repington, *The First World War 1914–1918*, 2 vols., 1920
C.P. Scott, *The Political Diaries of C.P. Scott*, ed. T. Wilson, Ithaca, NY, 1970
R.H. Tawney, *The Attack and Other Papers*, 1953
*R.H. Tawney's Commonplace Book*, ed. J.M. Winter and D.M. Joslin, Cambridge, 1972
*Beatrice Webb's Diaries 1912–1924*, ed. M.I. Cole, 1952


## 6. Selected secondary works

P. Abrams, *The Origins of British Sociology*, Chicago, 1968
D.H. Aldcroft, H.W. Richardson, *The British Economy 1870–1939*, 1969
V.L. Allen, *Trade Unions and the Government*, 1960
——, *The Sociology of Industrial Relations*, 1971
S. Andreski, *Military Organisation and Society*, 1954, 1963
L. Andrews, *The Education Act, 1918*, 1976
R. Aron, *Main Currents in Sociological Thought*, vol. II, New York, 1970
P.S. Bagwell, *The Railwaymen*, 1963
G.S. Bain, *The Growth of White-collar Unionism*, Oxford, 1970
O. Banks, *Parity and Prestige in English Secondary Education*, 1955

R. Barker, *Education and Politics: A Study of the Labour Party*, 1972

R. Bendix, *Nation-Building and Citizenship*, New York, 1964

H. Benyon, *Working for Fords*, Harmondsworth, 1973

N. Blewett, *The Peers, the Parties and the People; the General Elections of 1910*, 1972

T. Bottomore, R. Nesbit, eds., *A History of Sociological Analysis*, 1978

A.L. Bowley, *Some Economic Consequences of the Great War*, 1930

——, *Wages and Incomes since 1860*, Cambridge, 1937

M. Bowley, *Housing and the State 1919–1944*, 1945

H. Braverman, *Labor and Monopoly Capital*, New York, 1974

G. Braybon, *Women Workers in the First World War*, Beckenham, 1981

E.J.T. Brennan, ed., *Education for National Efficiency: the Contribution of Sidney and Beatrice Webb*, 1975

A. Briggs, *A History of Birmingham*, vol. II, 1952

——, *Social Thought and Social Action: A Study of the Work of Seebohm Rowntree*, 1961

——, J. Saville, eds., *Essays in Labour History*, 1960

——, *Essays in Labour History*, vol. II, 1971

A. Bullock, *The Life and Times of Ernest Bevin*, vol. II, 1960

M. Bulmer, ed., *Working-class Images of Society*, 1975

K. Burk, ed., *War and the State: the Transformation of British Government*, 1982

J. Bush, *Behind the Lines: East London Labour 1914–1919*, 1984

H. Campion, *Public and Private Property in Great Britain*, 1939

S.D. Chapman, ed., *The History of Working-class Housing: A Symposium*, Newton Abbot, 1970

R. Charles, *The Development of Industrial Relations in Britain*, 1973

C. Clark, *National Income and Outlay*, 1937

J. J. Clarke, *Social Administration*, 1939

H.A. Clegg, A. Fox, A.F. Thompson, *A History of British Trade Unions since 1889*, vol. I, *1889–1910*, Oxford, 1964

H.A. Clegg, ibid., vol. II, *1910–1939*, Oxford, 1985

A. Clinton, *The Trade Union Rank and File*, Manchester, 1977

G.D.H. Cole, *Studies in Class Structure*, 1955

——, R. Postgate, *The Common People*, 1938, 1961

P. Connerton, ed., *Critical Sociology*, Harmondsworth, 1976

J. Cronin, *Labour and Society in Britain 1918–1979*, 1984

R. Dahrendorf, *Class and Class Conflict in an Industrial Society*, 1959

G. Dangerfield, *The Strange Death of Liberal England*, 1966

N.F. Dreisziger, ed., *Mobilization for Total War: the Canadian, American and British Experience, 1914–18, 1939–45*, Ontario, 1981

R. Durant, *Watling*, 1939

F. Fairer Smith, *War Finance and Its Consequences*, 1936

C.H. Feinstein, *National Income, Expenditure and Output of the United Kingdom, 1865–1965*, Cambridge, 1972

J. Floud, ed., with A.H. Halsey, F.M. Martin, *Social Class and Educational Opportunity*, 1957

M.R.D. Foot, ed., *War and Society*, 1972

J. Foster, 'British Imperialism and the Labour Aristocracy', in *The General*

*Strike 1926*, ed. J. Skelley, 1976

A.L. Friedman, *Industry and Labour*, 1977

P. Fussell, *The Great War and Modern Memory*, 1975

H.J. Fyrth, H. Collins, *The Foundry Workers*, Manchester, 1959

H.H. Gerth, C.W. Mills, eds., *From Max Weber*, 1948

A. Giddens, *The Class Structure of the Advanced Societies*, 1973

——, P. Stanworth, eds., *Elites and Power in British Society*, Cambridge, 1974

B.B. Gilbert, *British Social Policy 1914–1939*, 1970

D.V. Glass, 'Education and Social Change in Modern England', in *Education, Economy and Society*, ed. A.H. Halsey et al., 1961

——, ed., *Social Mobility in Britain*, 1954

S. Glynn, J. Oxburrow, *Inter-war Britain: a Social and Economic History*, 1976

J. Goldthorpe et al., *Social Mobility and Class Structure in Modern Britain*, Oxford, 1980

——, D. Lockwood, F. Bechhofer, J. Platt, *The Affluent Worker in the Class Structure*, Cambridge 1969

J.L. Gray, P. Moshinsky, 'Ability and Opportunity in English Education', in *Political Arithmetic*, ed. L. Hogben, 1938

R.Q. Gray, *The Aristocracy of Labour in Nineteenth-Century Britain 1850–1914*, 1981

R. Gregory, *The Miners and British Politics 1906–1914*, 1968

W.L. Guttsman, *The British Political Elite*, 1963

——, ed., *The English Ruling Class*, 1969

G. Haines, *Essays on the German Influence upon English Education and Science*, Hampdem, Conn., 1969

E. Halévy, *A History of the English People in the Nineteenth Century: the Rule of Democracy 1905–1914*, 2 vols., 1934

A.H. Halsey, ed., *Trends in British Society since 1900*, 1972

—— et al., eds., *Education, Economy and Society*, 1961

——, A.F. Heath and J.M. Ridge, *Origins and Destinations: Family, Class and Education in Modern Britain*, Oxford, 1980

L. Hannah, J.A. Kay, *Concentration in Modern Industry*, 1977

R. Harrison, 'The War Emergency: Workers' National Committee', in *Essays in Labour History*, vol. II, ed. A. Briggs, J. Saville, 1971

H.D. Henderson, *The Inter-war Years and other Papers*, Oxford, 1955

U. Hicks, *The Finance of British Governments 1920–1936*, Oxford, 1938

J. Hilton et al., *Are Trade Unions Obstructive? An Industrial Inquiry*, 1935

J. Hinton, *The First Shop Stewards' Movement*, 1973

——, *Labour and Socialism*, Brighton, 1983

E.J. Hobsbawm, *Labouring Men*, 1964

——, *Revolutionaries*, 1977

P.C. Hoffman, *They also Serve*, 1949

L. Hogben, ed., *Political Arithmetic*, 1938

R. Hoggart, *The Uses of Literacy*, 1957

R.J. Holton, *British Syndicalism 1900–1914*, 1976

P. Horn, *Rural Life in England in the First World War*, New York, 1984

F. Hughes, *By Hand and Brain*, 1953

B.V. Humphries, *Clerical Unions in the Civil Service*, Oxford, 1958
A. Hutt, *The Post-war History of the British Working Class*, 1937
R. Hyman, *The Workers' Union*, Oxford, 1971
B. Jackson, D. Marsden, *Education and the Working Class*, 1962
J.B. Jefferys, *Retail Trading in Britain 1850–1950*, Cambridge, 1954
——, *The Story of the Engineers 1800–1945*, 1946
R. Jevons, J. Madge, *Housing Estates*, Bristol, 1946
P.B. Johnson, *Land Fit for Heroes*, Chicago, 1968
J. Keegan, *The Face of Battle*, 1976
J.M. Keynes, *How to Pay for the War*, 1940
M. Kinnear, *The British Voter: An Atlas and Survey since 1885*, 1968
J. Klein, *Samples from English Culture*, 2 vols., 1965
F.D. Klingender, *The Condition of Clerical Labour in Britain*, 1935
D.S. Landes, *The Unbound Prometheus*, Cambridge, 1969
K. Laybourn, J. Reynolds, *Liberalism and the Rise of Labour 1890–1918*, Beckenham, 1984
S.M. Lipset, *Political Man*, 1969
D. Lockwood, *The Blackcoated Worker*, 1958
G.A.N. Lowndes, *The Silent Social Revolution*, 1937, 1969
G. Lukács, *History and Class Consciousness*, 1971
R. McKibbin, *The Evolution of the Labour Party 1910–1924*, 1974
I. McLean, *The Legend of Red Clydeside*, Edinburgh, 1983
B. Mallet, C.O. George, *British Budget. Second series 1913/14–1920/21*, 1929
J. Marchal, B. Ducros, eds., *The Distribution of National Income*, 1968
D. Marquand, *Ramsay MacDonald*, 1977
T.H. Marshall, *Citizenship and Social Class*, Cambridge, 1950
——, *Social Policy*, 1970
R.M. Martin, *TUC: The Growth of a Pressure Group*, Oxford, 1980
A. Marwick, *Britain in the Century of Total War*, 1968
——, *Class: Images and Reality in Britain, France and the USA since 1930*, 1980
——, *The Deluge: British Society and the First World War*, 1965
——, *War and Social Change in the Twentieth Century*, 1974
*Karl Marx: Selected Writings in Sociology and Social Philosophy*, ed. T. Bottomore and M. Rubel, 1956
A.J. Mayer, *Politics and Diplomacy of Peacemaking*, 1968
S. Meacham, *A Life Apart: the English Working Class 1890–1914*, 1977
K. Middlemas, *Politics in an Industrial Society*, 1979
N. Middleton, S. Weitzman, *A Place for Everyone*, 1976
R. Miliband, *Parliamentary Socialism*, 1973
——, *The State in Capitalist Society*, 1973
A.S. Milward, *The Economic Effects of the Two World Wars on Britain*, 1970
R. Moore, *Pitmen, Preachers and Politics*, Cambridge 1974
K.O. Morgan, *Consensus and Disunity: the Lloyd George Coalition Government 1918–1922*, 1979
J.T. Murphy, *Preparing for Power*, 1934
J.U. Nef, *War and Human Progress*, 1950

G. Orwell, *Inside the Whale and Other Essays*, Harmondsworth, 1962

S. Ossowski, *Class Structure in the Social Consciousness*, 1963

F. Parkin, *Class Inequality and Political Order*, St Albans, 1972

G. Peele, C. Cook, eds., *The Politics of Reappraisal*, 1975

H. Pelling, *Popular Politics and Society in Late Victorian Britain*, 1968

——, *The Social Geography of British Elections 1885–1910*, 1967

H. Perkin, *The Origins of Modern English Society*, 1969

E.H. Phelps Brown, *The Growth of British Industrial Relations*, 1959

C.E. Playne, *Society at War 1914–1916*, 1931

——, *Britain Holds On*, 1933

G. Poggi, *The Development of the Modern State: A Sociological Introduction*, 1978

S. Pollard, *A History of Labour in Sheffield*, Liverpool, 1959

——, 'The Foundation of the Cooperative Party', in *Essays in Labour History*, ed. A. Briggs, J. Saville, vol. II

N. Poulantzas, *Classes in Contemporary Capitalism*, 1974

K. Prandy, R.M. Stewart, R.M. Blackburn, *White-Collar Unionism*, 1983

B. Pribicevic, *The Shop Stewards' Movement and the Demand for Workers' Control*, Oxford, 1959

R. Price, *An Imperial War and the British Working Class*, 1972

M. Pugh, *Electoral Reform in War and Peace 1906–1918*, 1978

J. Rae, *Conscience and Politics*, 1970

A. Reid, 'Dilution, trade unionism and the state in Britain during the First World War', in S. Tolliday, J. Zeitlin, eds., *Shop Floor Bargaining and the State*, Cambridge, 1985

B.C. Roberts, *The Trades Union Congress*, 1958

R. Roberts, *The Classic Slum*, Harmondsworth, 1973

M.E. Rose, 'The Success of Social Reform? The Central Control Board (Liquor Traffic) 1915–1921', in *War and Society*, ed. M.R.D. Foot, 1972

G. Routh, *Occupation and Pay in Great Britain 1906–1960*, Cambridge, 1965

P. Rowland, *The Last Liberal Government: Unfinished Business 1911–1914*, 1971

W.D. Rubinstein, *Men of Property*, 1981

W.G. Runciman, *Relative Deprivation and Social Justice*, Harmondsworth, 1972

R.J. Scally, *The Origins of the Lloyd George Coalition: the Politics of Social Imperialism 1900–1918*, Princeton, NJ, 1975

G.R. Searle, *Eugenics and Politics in Britain 1900–1914*, Leiden, 1976

——, *The Quest for National Efficiency*, Oxford, 1971

B. Semmel, *Imperialism and Social Reform*, 1960

G. Sherrington, *English Education, Social Change and War, 1911–1920*, Manchester, 1981

B. Simon, *The Politics of Educational Reform 1920–1940*, 1974

M.A. Simpson, T.H. Lloyd, eds., *Middle Class Housing in Britain*, Newton Abbot, 1977

J. Skelly, ed., *The General Strike 1926*, 1976

A. Spoor, *White Collar Union: Sixty Years of NALGO*, 1967

N.A.H. Stacey, *English Accountancy 1800–1954*, 1954

J.C. Stamp, *Taxation during the War*, 1932

P.N. Stearns, *Lives of Labour*, Beckenham, 1975

J. Stubbs, 'The Impact of the Great War on the Conservative Party', in G. Peele, C. Cook, eds., *The Politics of Reappraisal*, 1975

R.H. Tawney, *Inequality*, 1931, 1964

——, *The Radical Tradition*, Harmondsworth, 1966

A.J.P. Taylor, *English History 1914–1945*, 1965

E.P. Thompson, *The Making of the English Working Class*, Harmondsworth, 1968

F.M.L. Thompson, *English Landed Society in the Nineteenth Century*, 1963

P. Thompson, *The Edwardians*, 1975

R.M. Titmuss, *Essays on 'The Welfare State'*, 1962

S. Tolliday, J. Zeitlin, eds., *Shop Floor Bargaining and the State*, Cambridge, 1985

U. Urwick, E.F.L. Brech, *The Making of Scientific Management*, 1945

M. Weber, *The Theory of Social and Economic Organization*, ed., T. Parsons, New York, 1947

J. Westergaard, H. Resler, *Class in a Capitalist Society*, Harmondsworth, 1976

W.B. Whitaker, *Victorian and Edwardian Shopworkers*, Newton Abbot, 1973

T. Wilson, *The Downfall of the Liberal Party, 1914–1935*, 1968

M.J. Winstanley, *The Shopkeeper's World 1830–1914*, Manchester, 1984

J.M. Winter, *Socialism and the Challenge of War*, 1974

——, *The Great War and the British People*, Cambridge, 1986.

——, ed., *War and Economic Development*, Cambridge, 1976

C.J. Wrigley, *David Lloyd George and the British Labour Movement*, Brighton, 1976

M. Young, P. Willmot, *Family and Kinship in East London*, 1957

T. Young, *Becontree and Dagenham: the Story of the Growth of a Housing Estate*, 1934

F. Zweig, *The British Worker*, Harmondsworth, 1952

## 7. Articles

P. Abrams, 'The Failure of Social Reform 1918–1920, *Past and Present*, 24, April 1963

R. Barker, 'Ramsay MacDonald, Myth and the Making of the Labour Party', *History*, 61, October 1976

D.H. Close, 'The Collapse of Resistance to Democracy: Conservatives, Adult Suffrage and Second Chamber Reform 1911–1928', *Historical Journal*, 20, 4, 1977

D.W. Dean, 'H.A.L. Fisher, Reconstruction and the 1918 Education Act', *British Journal of Educational Studies*, October 1970

R.H. Desmarais, 'The British Government's Strike-Breaking Organization and Black Friday', *Journal of Contemporary History*, 6, 2, 1971

P. Dewey, 'Military recruiting and the British labour force during the First World War', *Historical Journal*, 27, 1, Mar. 1984

——, 'British farming profits and government policy during the First World War', *Economic History Review*, 37, 3, Aug. 1984

J. Floud, 'Educational Opportunity and Social Mobility', *The Year Book of Education*, 1950

L. Hannah, 'Managerial Innovation and the Rise of the Large-scale Company in Inter-war Britain', *Economic History Review*, 2nd ser., XXVII, 2, 1974

N. Hans, 'The Independent Schools and Liberal Professions', *The Year Book of Education*, 1950

R.J. Holton, 'Daily Herald v. Daily Citizen, 1912–1915: the Struggle for a Labour Daily in Relation to the Labour Unrest', *International Review of Social History*, XIX, 3, 1974

R. Lowe, 'The Ministry of Labour: Fact and Fiction', *Bulletin of the Society for the Study of Labour History*, Autumn 1980

——, 'The Failure of Consensus in Britain: the National Industrial Conference, 1919–1921', *Historical Journal*, 21, 3, 1978

A. Marwick, 'The Impact of the First World War on Britain', *Journal of Contemporary History*, 3, 1, 1968

H.C.G. Matthew, R. McKibbin, J.A. Kay, 'The Franchise Factor in the Rise of the Labour Party', *English Historical Review*, vol. XCI, no. 361, October 1976

H.F. Moorhouse, 'The Marxist Theory of the Labour Aristocracy', *Social History*, 3, 1, 1978

W.D. Rubinstein, 'Wealth, Elites and the Class Structure of Modern Britain', *Past and Present*, 76, April 1977

J. Sheail, 'Land Improvement and Reclamation: the Experience of the First World War in England and Wales', *Agricultural History Review*, 24, 2, 1976

S. White, 'Soviets in Britain: the Leeds Convention of 1917', *International Review of Social History*, XIX, 2, 1974

J.M. Winter, 'The Impact of the First World War on Civilian Health in Britain', *Economic History Review*, 2nd ser., XXX, 3, 1977

——, 'Some Aspects of the Demographic Consequences of the First World War in Britain', *Population Studies*, 30, 1976

## 8. Unpublished theses and dissertations

W. Craig Heron, 'The Commission of Enquiry into Industrial Unrest', University of Warwick MA diss., 1976

M. Kozak, 'Women Munition Workers during the First World War with Special Reference to Engineering', University of Hull PhD, 1977

R. Lowe, 'The Demand for a Ministry of Labour: its Establishment and Initial Role, 1916–1924', University of London PhD, 1975

# Index